Democracy Betrayed

Democracy

Edited by David S. Cecelski and Timothy B. Tyson

Foreword by John Hope Franklin

The
Wilmington
Race Riot
of 1898
and Its
Legacy

Betrayed

The
University
of North
Carolina
Press

Chapel Hill
and London

© 1998 The University of North Carolina Press
All rights reserved
Designed by April Leidig-Higgins
Set in Electra by Keystone Typesetting, Inc.
Manufactured in the United States of America

The paper in this book meets the guidelines for
permanence and durability of the Committee on
Production Guidelines for Book Longevity of the
Council on Library Resources.

Library of Congress Cataloging-in-Publication Data
Democracy betrayed : the Wilmington race riot of
1898 and its legacy / edited by David S. Cecelski and
Timothy B. Tyson. / p. cm. Includes bibliographical
references (p.   ) and index.
ISBN 0-8078-2451-8 (cloth: alk. paper)
ISBN 0-8078-4755-0 (pbk.: alk. paper)
1. Wilmington (N.C.)—Race relations.   2. Afro-
Americans—North Carolina—Wilmington—
History—19th century.   3. Riots—North Carolina—
Wilmington—History—19th century.   I. Cecelski,
David S.   II. Tyson, Timothy B.
F264.W7D46   1998   98-3467
975.6'27041—dc21   CIP

02 01 00 99 98   5 4 3 2 1

To Vera and Guy, Hope and Sam

Contents

In the history of the United States, and especially the history of the South, the past seems not to have receded significantly, even today. In some very fundamental ways, change has come slowly, sometimes almost imperceptibly. Thus, while our past is interwoven with our present, some of our past stands out in stark relief, as if it were some relic held over from an earlier time. Despite the increased population density in places long settled, the spirit of the raw frontier persists among those who reject new "rules of the road." Such persons retreat to places where they insist on making their own rules or abiding by the old ones, frontier style. Consequently, the mountain men at Ruby Ridge and the Branch Davidians at Waco insisted that at some point history had taken the wrong turn, and they refused to follow that course. Instead, they would follow the old rules that would lead them down the *right road*.

This disinclination to follow the "rules of the road" is not confined to the likes of Idaho's mountain men or the part religious cult, part paramilitary group at Waco. It is also characteristic of others who prefer to focus on past ways rather than countenance current trends. They would see history—their sacred, misunderstood past—as their security and would retreat to it rather than venture from an uncomfortable present into an uncertain future.

Those who resist change are reminiscent of the ex-Confederates who, in the years following the Civil War, preferred to dream of a South that never was and never could be rather than accept one that was within the reach of all, if they would join together and make it so. But many whites in the post–Civil War South saw change—any change—as unsettling and dangerous, and they wanted no part of it. Surely they wanted no part of an uncivilized, uncultured South in which their former slaves would enjoy the vote and equal rights in all aspects of educational, social, and economic life. To move in such a direction would be catastrophic as well as tragic. Retreating to a safer, more secure past was infinitely more attractive and desirable than proceeding into a reckless future that seemed to offer the revulsive prospect of "social equality."

The history of the South in the 1880s and 1890s is essentially the history of a search for a past so attractive that many regarded it as a nirvana. If other parts of the country did not share in this search, at least they would not interfere with it, especially as they came to regard the new dispensation as beneficial in many ways. The collusion was complete as Northern financiers and industrialists reaped enormous benefits from economic developments in the South. And, if these Northerners sinned as accessories in stimulating sharecropping, peonage, and convict labor, they did penance by offering pittances to educate the former slaves in ways that would not be offensive to Southern mores and predispositions.

As the new South emerged and as it exported huge quantities of material goods to the North and even tried its hand at manufacturing many things, from cotton textiles to electric power, the North-South partnership was consolidated further. White families, North and South, began to intermarry; Southern homes in New York were matched by Northern homes in Florida. Blacks began the Northern trek that would reach a high point during World War I. Thus, the Southernization of the North and the Northernization of the South began in earnest.

All of this was accelerated by the determination of Southern whites to replicate the slave period in everything but name. Their attack on the Civil Rights Act of 1875 found success in the 1883 decision of the United States Supreme Court that declared the act unconstitutional. In 1890, Mississippi found a way in its new constitution to disfranchise blacks effectively, and by the end of the century a trend had set in that led

South Carolina and Louisiana to follow in creative and ingenious ways. The temptation to segregate blacks and whites was encouraged further by the 1896 Supreme Court decision of *Plessy v. Ferguson*.

The only thing left was to make certain that blacks who claimed any equal rights under the Constitution were blocked in whatever attempts they might make to realize their claims. If blacks thought that the "rules of the road" had changed since the Civil War, they must be made to understand that the rules had not changed. If they entertained the vague notion that they could exercise their right to vote according to the provisions of the Fifteenth Amendment, they must be persuaded otherwise. As Alfred Waddell, the Wilmington firebrand, told his listeners the night before the election in 1898, "If you find the Negro out voting, tell him to leave the polls, and if he refuses, kill him, shoot him down in his tracks. We shall win tomorrow if we have to do it with guns" (*Outlook*, 19 November 1898).

This was the clear, unequivocal position of the people in a part of the South where the slave code had been "humanized" and duly elected freedmen had occupied seats in the Congress as well as positions in local government. These very achievements were enough, however, to persuade Waddell and his cohorts that the course of history must be changed, even reversed, if racial peace was to be achieved in Wilmington and elsewhere in the state. This was the spirit that prevailed in North Carolina's statewide white supremacy campaign in 1898 in which Wilmington served as a metaphor for violent change.

The spirit that led Wilmington to its lawless escapade in 1898 persisted long after Alex Manly and his fellow travelers had fled from the wrath of the self-appointed keepers of the white South's purity and integrity. It would rear its head from time to time, but seldom so crudely as in 1995, when a duly elected district attorney in Wilmington sought to drive out of a place of public accommodations another customer whose only offense was that he was an orderly, well-mannered African American athlete with a national reputation. This time, however, the public official could not change the rules, and he discovered that his drunken condition was no defense for having attempted to do so. In 1995, there was no Alfred Waddell and no groundswell of supporters for his would-be successor. Almost a century after the Wilmington riot, an important lesson had been learned.

Just as there are lessons to be learned from the recent past, there are lessons to be learned from the events of a century ago. This volume will inform some and remind others that our past can help us understand the challenges that this nation confronts as it undertakes to deal with the problem of race in the twenty-first century. As we stand on the threshold of a new century, we can look at our past and learn much from it. We can better understand the promise of real equality, made by the Founding Fathers more than two centuries ago, a promise neither they nor their successors kept. This promise was given new urgency by the poet Langston Hughes, who said, "Let America be America again . . . the land that never has been yet." We can better understand this if we learn well the lesson that there is something unethical and immoral about changing the rules merely to suit those who no longer enjoy special advantages that they never really earned or deserved.

John Hope Franklin

Foreword

This collection of essays commemorates the centennial of the Wilmington, North Carolina, race riot of 1898. It is intended to draw public
attention to the tragedy, to honor its victims, and to bring a clear and
timely historical voice into the lively debate over its legacy. We have
gathered what we consider the best emerging scholarship about the race
riot, but we have also sought to avoid the temptations of narrow scholarly
debate. We want to address a more general audience, one that may
never have heard of the race riot or the white supremacy movement of
which it was the most tragic episode. We believe this history furnishes
insights that will help all of us navigate the labyrinth of racial anguish
that marks public life in what James Baldwin called "these yet-to-be
United States."

The contributors to this volume approach the Wilmington race riot of
1898 as scholars, but not only as scholars. Though several of us teach at
universities as far away as the West Coast and New England, most—
including both editors—have deep roots in North Carolina. Tim Tyson

lived in Wilmington in the early 1970s, when his father served as minister of a church there. At that time, harrowing racial conflicts forced the city's residents to contemplate the enduring legacy of the race riot on a daily basis. Michael Honey cut his teeth as a social activist in the political trials of the "Wilmington Ten," a group of black activists, including the Reverend Benjamin Chavis, who were tried and convicted for—but eventually exonerated of—burning a local grocery store during race riots in 1971. Richard Yarborough of UCLA had a great-grandfather who was a barber in Wilmington at the time of the race riot and a great-aunt from Wilmington who became the first African American woman to star in a previously all-white U.S. opera company. Glenda Gilmore, currently a professor at Yale, is a seventh-generation North Carolinian on both sides of her family.

We will not belabor these personal ties to Wilmington and its past, or those held by other contributors, but we think it is only fair to let readers know from the start that we see *Democracy Betrayed* as more than a scholarly project. The ties that bind us to home have made this book a labor of love. Despite its painful contradictions, we believe that there is no better place than the South to look for answers to the many-sided agonies of the color line. "If, in moving through your life, you find yourself lost," singer and scholar Bernice Johnson Reagan of the Smithsonian Institution instructs, "go back to the last place where you knew who you were, and what you were doing, and start from there." A hundred years ago, a historic experiment in interracial democracy blossomed in North Carolina. Most people have never heard of that experiment or of the Wilmington race riot that helped to destroy it. But the fact that thousands of black Americans have been returning to the South in a stunning reverse migration might encourage all of us to look south for a moment, toward the roots of many of our families and many of our predicaments.

A unique set of circumstances sparked the race riot in Wilmington, but the riot was only one small piece of a white supremacy crusade that swept the American South in the 1890s and the early part of the twentieth century. And, in fact, during these years a wider tide of racist violence reached beyond the Mason-Dixon Line and targeted other groups in addition to African Americans. It was felt in the ethnic ghettos of the Midwest, the Mexican barrios of Texas, and the Chinatowns of California and Washington state. It even found expression in American foreign policy, where national political leaders used white supremacist ideology to justify violence during the colonial occupation of the Philippines and Cuba. Though the Wilmington race riot stands out for both its brutality and the cool deliberation behind it, Wilmington was not fundamentally more prone to racial enmity or mob violence than the next town, county, or state. The racial conflicts that scarred Wilmington in 1898 had deep roots in the American soil, and, in the pages that follow, most readers, like the contributors, should be able to glimpse some part of their own past, their own hometowns.

As Americans search the past for insights into our racial dilemmas today, Wilmington itself is one place to look for guidance and hope. For a hundred years, Wilmington's leaders denied the facts of the race riot. Today Wilmington is a booming Sun Belt city with a historic downtown of antebellum manors, tourist attractions, and gift shops. You cannot help but feel the romance of the Old South when you stroll its broad avenues shaded by live oaks and crape myrtles. Thalian Hall is one of the most beautiful antebellum theaters in America, and the architectural majesty of the Bellamy Mansion seems right out of *Gone with the Wind*. Yet, despite the city's proud celebration of dozens of historic sites, the most important event in Wilmington's history remains unmarked. As of this writing, not a single monument or museum commemorates the African Americans who were killed or exiled by the race riot of 1898. City leaders did more than deny the tragedy of 1898: school children learned to view the white crusade's leaders as heroes, and civic boosters honored the white vigilantes by naming public parks, buildings, and streets after them. This official repudiation of the past left whites defensive and blacks bitter, creating an explosive racial climate marked by fear, guilt, and misunderstanding. No aspect of Wilmington society that required interracial cooperation was able to prosper: not the schools, not the sense of public safety or community, not downtown businesses. But, of course, this situation was not unique to Wilmington, and we would suggest that, in experiencing the withering effects of racism, Wilmington was, in short, a typical American city.

The centennial of the race riot of 1898 has begun to change Wilmington. Whites and blacks are engaged in a communitywide commemoration of the riot impossible to imagine only a few years ago. Wilmington is marking the centennial with candlelit vigils, a scholarly conference, race relations workshops, the dedication of memorials to the black victims, a new theatrical work about the riot, a remarkable number of interracial study groups, and a host of other church, school, and civic events. Led by a biracial coalition of local groups called the Wilmington Centennial Foundation, the commemoration points toward a racial reconciliation grounded in a clear historical understanding of an afflicted past. At least as important, and more difficult, these local citizens seek to build community support for overcoming the enduring legacies of racism, from the persistent poverty of inner-city neighborhoods to the official neglect of public schools. The contributors to this volume are honored to have been invited to play a small part in these events and hope that Wilmington will provide an example for other communities—North, South, and West—to confront the history of American racism and its hold on the present. It is a struggle fraught with pitfalls, and community activists in Wilmington recognize, as we do, that history is not likely to offer tidy lessons or easy answers. And yet we all remain committed to what Charles W. Chesnutt called "the shining thread of hope," nurtured even through a hard and bitter history, that permitted him to close his account of the Wilmington race riot by declaring: "There's time enough, but none to spare."

David S. Cecelski and Timothy B. Tyson
4 February 1998

Democracy Betrayed

We have fought for tariff and against tariff; we have
fought for internal improvements and against them; for
a tax on liquor and against it. We have fought for this
issue and against that policy, but everywhere and all the
time we have fought for white supremacy.
–Charles Aycock, governor of North Carolina, 1901–1905

**Timothy B.
Tyson and
David S.
Cecelski**

Introduction

In February 1971, Wilmington, North Carolina, trembled on the edge of race war. Buildings burned every night. White vigilantes roared through the city, spraying bullets at black citizens. Black snipers fired at police officers from rooftops downtown. Six hundred frightened National Guard troops patrolled the streets. Racial violence in the hallways of newly integrated public schools threatened to bring public education to a halt. In the midst of the upheaval, a white Methodist minister called a meeting of black and white parents to see whether something could be done to bring peace and find a pathway toward racial reconciliation.

At the meeting the preacher heard African American parents make bitter references to "what happened" and "what caused all this"—as if the causes of Wilmington's racial troubles were obvious. Yet the quizzical expressions and vacant nods of white parents made the minister suspect that the white parents were oblivious to something that every black parent understood. "When you say, 'what caused all this,' what are you talking about?" he finally asked the black parents. At first, the black parents refused to believe that he did not know what they meant. Finally, one black mother paused to point in the direction of the Cape Fear River. Flashing her mind's eye seventy years into the past, to 10 November 1898, she told him, "They say that river was full of black bodies."[1]

Though largely forgotten beyond the banks of the Cape Fear River, the Wilmington race riot of 1898 signaled a turning point in American history. On a chilly autumn day one hundred years ago, armed columns of white business leaders and working men seized the majority-black city of Wilmington by force. For almost a year, the Democratic Party—the self-avowed "party of white supremacy"—had conducted a statewide campaign of racist appeals and political violence aimed at shattering the coalition of black Republicans and white Populists that had been in office since 1894. Advocating freer elections, popular control of local government, and regulation to contain the excesses of monopoly capitalism, this interracial "Fusion" coalition had captured the governorship, the General Assembly, and countless local offices, threatening the power of both the remnants of the old planter class and the emerging industrial leaders of the New South. For the first time since Radical Reconstruction in 1868–70, black North Carolinians and a sizable number of whites had come together in a common cause. White Democrats found this unbearable. "We will not live under these intolerable conditions," Colonel Alfred Moore Waddell told a crowd of cheering Democrats. "We will never surrender to a ragged raffle of negroes, even if we have to choke the current of the Cape Fear with carcasses."[2]

On 8 November, two days before the massacre, Democrats captured Wilmington's elections by fraud and the threat of violence. Waddell, a Confederate veteran and former U.S. congressman, shouted to a mass meeting of white citizens the night before the election: "Go to the polls tomorrow, and if you find the negro out voting, tell him to leave the polls, and if he refuses, kill him."[3]

Victory at the polls did not satisfy the Democrats, however, since municipal offices up for election in the off years remained in Fusionist hands. Two days later, conservative leaders put into action a plan intended to make certain that African Americans would never again be a force in North Carolina politics. Led by Waddell, white vigilantes first burned the printing press of Alexander Manly, publisher of what was said to be the only black-owned daily newspaper in the United States. Next they marched into the neighborhood called Brooklyn, where they left a trail of dead and dying African Americans. Armed with repeating rifles and rapid-fire guns, they outgunned the black men who sought to defend their homes with antique revolvers and shotguns. That night and the next day, hundreds of black women and children huddled in the swamps outside Wilmington. The white insurgents forced the city's officials who had not been up for election two days earlier to resign and took power for themselves. Colonel Waddell assumed the mayor's office. Conservatives drove their political opponents, black and white, into exile and banished the city's most prominent black professionals at gunpoint. Fourteen hundred African Americans fled the city in the next thirty days. "We have taken a city," the Reverend Peyton H. Hoge boasted from the pulpit of First Presbyterian Church. "To God be the praise."[4]

Nobody knows how many African Americans died in Wilmington one hundred years ago. The most conservative estimate is seven; the most readily confirmed is fourteen; the leader of the white mob said "about twenty."[5] Hugh MacRae, the textile mill owner and pioneering industrialist who also helped lead the mobs, boasted of ninety dead. Echoing the stories of their great-grandparents, many Wilmington blacks believe that the death toll exceeded 300. Yet not even the highest estimates of the dead aroused white outrage. Approval, not condemnation, thundered down on the city's vigilantes from white pulpits, editorial pages, and political podiums across the United States. White dissent would have been vocal even in North Carolina during much of the 1890s, but not by the fall of 1898. Democrats had turned white solidarity into a litmus test of manhood and honor that white men dared not fail. Indeed, Democratic activists had intimidated white "race traitors"— Fusionists—at least as much as African Americans.

This intimidation of both blacks and whites may have been harshest in Wilmington, but it reached into every corner of North Carolina during the electoral campaign of 1898. Few communities escaped racial terrorism—if only one city became an enduring reminder of the dangers of democratic politics and interracial cooperation.[6] And, as historian Joel Williamson has written, "Once the riot had actually occurred in Wilmington, there was no need for it to happen elsewhere."[7] No one, black or white, could deny that the racial massacre signaled a sea change in how white Americans would regard civil rights for African Americans. White people in Wilmington had violently seized their government, and no one had acted to stop them.

What happened in Wilmington in 1898 so thoroughly defies the conventional ways Americans talk about their history that it is difficult to find the right words to fit these events. For a century, historians have obscured the turmoil in Wilmington by referring to it as a riot—even though it was certainly not the spontaneous outbreak of violence that "riot" implies. Far from it: what happened in Wilmington was part of an orchestrated campaign to end interracial cooperation, restore white supremacy, and in the process assure the rule of the state's planter and industrial leaders. In recent years, scholars have begun to lean away from "race riot" and tested other descriptive terms: "coup d'état," "massacre," "revolt," "pogrom," "revolution." Each conveys a part of the truth, yet none captures the full scope of these events. In choosing a subtitle for this book, the editors reluctantly settled on the traditional term "race riot" to ensure that we would be understood. Having paid homage to conventional usage, however, we and the other contributors will use various other words and phrases to describe the combination of racial massacre and political revolt that occurred in Wilmington a century ago. In its overall effect, however, the event was nothing less than a revolution against interracial democracy: its aftermath brought the birth of the Jim Crow social order, the end of black voting rights, and the rise of a one-party political system in the South that strangled the aspirations of generations of blacks and whites.

Timothy B.
Tyson and
David S.
Cecelski

This book is not the first effort to explore the history of what happened in Wilmington.[8] In 1984, H. Leon Prather Sr. published *We Have Taken a City: Wilmington Racial Massacre and Coup of 1898*, the first book-length study of these events. Building on the fine work of an earlier African American scholar, Helen G. Edmonds, Prather blazed a path for other historians to follow. His contribution to this volume, "We Have Taken a City: A Centennial Essay," is a distillation of his book and unfolds the specific events that took place in Wilmington that autumn a century ago. Prather closely examines both the violence and its victims in a detailed narrative that captures the basic facts and tragic drama of the story. Prather's account is an essential starting point for understanding the racial killings and the social order to which they gave birth.

The racial violence in Wilmington was fundamentally a white response to African American political strength and the threat that the interracial Fusion coalition posed to the state's elite. White conservatives first turned to violence and intimidation to win the elections that autumn because they could not defeat the interracial coalition in a fair election. David S. Cecelski's essay "Abraham H. Galloway: Wilmington's Lost Prophet and the Rise of Black Radicalism in the American

South," demonstrates that a radically democratic political tradition had risen to challenge white supremacy and elite rule in the late nineteenth century. Galloway was a slave who ran away from Wilmington in 1857 and returned to North Carolina during the Civil War as a Union spy and abolitionist leader. Exploring Galloway's life, we begin to realize how much was at stake in Wilmington, for it was his brand of black manhood, political egalitarianism, and interracial cooperation that the violence of 1898 sought to suppress.

In her essay, "Captives of Wilmington: The Riot and Historical Memories of Political Conflict, 1865–1898," Laura F. Edwards examines other forms of black self-assertion that, in her words, "centered on issues never articulated by any political party, that never reached the pages of any newspaper, that unfolded in obscure places, and that [were] spearheaded by people whose names have long since been forgotten." If we remember only the "race riot" and not the black and white working-class assertions of citizenship, both Cecelski and Edwards show, we close off "promising alternatives for understanding the past and the present."

If white supremacy provided the fuel for the conflagration of 1898, Democrats used the rough side of sexual politics to strike the match. LeeAnn Whites, in her essay on Rebecca Latimer Felton, shows how complex and combustible race and sex could be in the South at the turn of the century. Felton, a leading woman's rights activist and political reformer in Georgia, had given a racist speech that portrayed black men as sexual predators and faulted white men for failing to protect white womanhood. An editorial in response to the speech by Alexander Manly, a black newspaper publisher in Wilmington, was seized upon by North Carolina Democrats as their most potent appeal to white voters. Glenda E. Gilmore's contribution, "Murder, Memory, and the Flight of the Incubus," examines how white Democrats manufactured tales of "Negro outrages" against white womanhood in order to manipulate white men to commit mass murder. For Gilmore, the compelling truth of the terror in Wilmington may be found in the way that white leaders killed to preserve their status, their manhood, and their whiteness. "Sometimes," she adds, "murder does its best work in memory, after the fact. Terror lives on, continuing to serve its purpose long after the violence that gave rise to it ends."

In his essay, "The Two Faces of Domination in North Carolina, 1800–1898," Stephen Kantrowitz explains that the "murderous threat" of violence and the "paternalistic concern" that followed it represented the double-edged sword of the Southern master class. The exercise of violence and paternalism, Kantrowitz demonstrates, had its roots in the political traditions of slavery. When Alfred Waddell and Hugh MacRae led white mobs into Wilmington's black neighborhoods, they sought to end decades of striving by blacks for dignity and respect that had been steadily wearing away both the political and psychological hold established by whites during generations of slavery. The white revolutionaries could not let that happen. The purposes of the violence, Michael Honey argues in his essay, "Class, Race, and Power in the New South: Racial Violence and the Delusions of White Supremacy," included the continuing domination of poor and working-class whites by the state's elite. The one-party South that the white supremacy revolution created "provided the vehicle for the nearly undisputed power of an oligarchy of landlords, commercial leaders, and industrialists."

Implicit in many of the essays is the theme made explicit in Kantrowitz's—the paradoxical history of North Carolina in which paternalism and violence are intimately intertwined. "There are three ways in which we may rule," Charles B. Aycock told supporters prior to his gubernatorial victory in 1900. "We have ruled by force, we can rule by fraud, but we want to rule by law."[9] The racial paternalism Aycock embodied served to consolidate a social order carved out by violence but preserved by civility. The tragic events were scarcely over in Wilmington before conservative leaders moved briskly to "protect" the black community and become the guardians of social stability and political legitimacy. The new social order combined a commitment to white domination with measured but unequal support for black education, a posture of "moderate" white supremacy, and a constraining civility in race relations. Democratic leaders knew that one "Wilmington" was enough. Another would call their legitimacy into question. Newspapers that had brayed against black advancement and stoked the fires of racism felt that they could finally afford to set aside the "bloody shirt." Thus, *Raleigh News and Observer* editor Josephus Daniels celebrated the new order as "permanent good government by the party of the White Man."[10]

The paternalist ethos that emerged in the wake of the Wilmington violence preserved white supremacy at least as effectively as bloody repression would have. The "spirit of Aycock," as V. O. Key called North Carolina's much-vaunted racial moderation, confined racial politics within an etiquette of civility that perpetuated white domination even as it offered cramped opportunities for black advancement.[11] Powerful whites, congratulating themselves on their generosity, would support limited black education and social welfare programs, but only so long as African Americans remained powerless, deferential, and segregated.

Timothy B.
Tyson and
David S.
Cecelski

U.S. senator Lee Overman, one of a generation of white politicians who came to power because of their roles in the white supremacy campaign, claimed that this arrangement brought "satisfaction which only comes of permanent peace after deadly warfare."[12]

The social order that 1898 built was a world in which the notion of white supremacy, originally concocted as a justification for slavery, permeated daily life so deeply that most white people thought about it no more than a fish contemplates the wetness of water. The racial etiquette that emerged was at once absurd, arbitrary, and nearly inviolable, inscribed in what W. E. B. Du Bois called "the cake of custom."[13] A white man who would never shake hands with a black man might refuse to permit anyone but a black man to shave his face, cut his hair, or give him a shampoo. A black woman could share a white man's bed but never his table. Most whites regarded African Americans as inherently lazy and shiftless, but when a white man said that he had "worked like a nigger," he meant that he had engaged in dirty, backbreaking toil to the point of collapse. Raymond Gavins explores the segregated world that Wilmington created—and the black survival strategies that emerged within it—in his essay, "Fear, Hope, and Struggle: Recasting Black North Carolina in the Age of Jim Crow." The racial caste system nailed into place at the turn of the century would take many years and cost many lives to overturn.

In the age of Jim Crow, black leaders worked to establish community institutions that could build a black future. In his essay, "Race, Rhetoric, and Revolution," John Haley explains that "the black men who stepped forward at this critical period were not conservatives" but rather "conservators of what little remained of their people's rights and dignities." African Americans in North Carolina, Haley points out, "understood only too well that any unraveling of this political settlement could bring 'another Wilmington.'" Not that all African Americans were silent: as Richard Yarborough's essay, "Violence, Manhood, and Black Heroism: The Wilmington Riot in Two Turn-of-the-Century African American Novels," shows, black writers produced their own accounts of what happened in 1898 that affirmed black humanity despite the triumph of white supremacy.

The racial etiquette that 1898 produced featured "patterns of paternalism and accommodation that had to be broken before change could occur," William H. Chafe wrote in his landmark study of the Greensboro sit-ins.[14] As Timothy B. Tyson shows in his essay, "Wars for Democracy: African American Militancy and Interracial Violence in North Carolina during World War II," the war against fascism brought African

Americans their first viable opportunities to break the confines of that civility and challenge what one black North Carolinian called "our Hitlers here in America."[15] When they did so, white Southerners were quick both to conjure up the ghosts of Wilmington and to turn to violence once again. In response to "radical agitators" for racial equality, North Carolina governor J. Melville Broughton reminded a Wilmington crowd of what could happen if black demands persisted: "Forty-five years ago . . . blood flowed freely in the streets of this city," he warned them.[16] Acts of violence often greeted efforts to undermine racial oppression. "Beneath the green ivy of civility," Tyson writes, "stood a stone wall of coercion." Though the wartime struggle did not end segregation, World War II marked a watershed moment: African Americans broke away from the decades of patient institution building that began in 1898 and launched the decades of political activism that would win back their full citizenship during the 1960s.

Timothy B. Tyson and David S. Cecelski

It is no wonder, then, that the furious conflict that marked the black freedom movement in Wilmington in 1971 brought back memories of bodies drifting in the waters of the Cape Fear. Wilmington's African Americans realized that the legacy of the racial massacre still haunts the city. And this is no less true today than it was in 1971. Far beyond North Carolina and 1898, the tragic events that transpired in Wilmington force us to contemplate the meaning of America's racial past and its hold on the living. From our vantage point a century later, we can see that the white supremacy campaigns of the 1890s and early 1900s injected a vicious racial ideology into the heart of American political culture in a way that we have yet to transcend fully. These upheavals ushered in a specific kind of racially divided society—known as Jim Crow—that for all our earnest striving we have not completely overcome. We can see too that the generations of one-party control over Southern politics caused the very meaning of "democracy" to wither, as voter turnout declined steadily throughout the twentieth century and ordinary citizens of all races failed to gain the kinds of experience in pluralistic political activism so essential to a democratic society. We can see, finally, that the victory of the white supremacists has made us forget that we may have much to learn from the losers of 1898, that black and white people have long before us tried to hammer out a more meaningful vision of grassroots democracy and racial justice in America.

The fact that few people have heard of the Wilmington "race riot" of 1898 or the historic experiment in interracial politics that it helped to destroy has left all of us inadequately prepared to address the racial crisis that is now so abundantly evident in American life. We all make history, to be sure, but we do not make it out of whole cloth. We must weave the future from the fabric of the past, from the patterns of aspiration and belonging that have made us. We look to Wilmington in 1898, as to all this nation's racial history, then, not to wring our hands in a fruitless nostalgia of pain, but to redeem a democratic promise rooted in the living ingredients of American life.

Notes

1. Interview with Rev. Vernon Tyson, by David S. Cecelski, 15 July 1997, Southern Historical Collection, University of North Carolina at Chapel Hill.

2. *Wilmington Morning Post*, 25 October 1898.

3. Frank Weldon, "North Carolina Race Conflict," *Outlook* 60 (19 November 1898): 707–9.

4. *Raleigh News and Observer*, 13 November 1898.

5. Alfred M. Waddell, *Some Memories of My Life* (Raleigh: Edwards & Broughton, 1908), 243.

6. There were compelling reasons why the racial massacre occurred in Wilmington: the political power of its majority-black population, its status as the state's largest city, and a legacy of black militancy that had long rankled white conservatives, among them. Yet in reading the state newspapers, personal papers, and public records from 1898, one can readily conclude that the massacre could have occurred in almost any corner of North Carolina. Scholars have never written about the white supremacy campaign of 1898 in Elizabeth City, for example, but it seems as if events in the small port could easily have ended in a tragedy like Wilmington's. Local business leaders closed their stores on election day and monitored the polls to cajole their employees into casting ballots for Democrats. Most carried guns. "In being armed," the Democratic editor of the town's leading newspaper said, "they were not law-abiding, but an old classic proverb says that laws are silent amid arms." Elizabeth City Democrats warned white Republicans and Populists that they would "pay the first blood" if the Fusionists voted in force, and only the success of Democratic intimidation in keeping the Fusionists from voting "saved [the city] from scenes that would have made humanity shudder." The town's only black newspaper closed its doors prior to the election. See the *Economist* (Elizabeth City, N.C.), 30 September 1898 and 11 November 1898. For secondary sources on racial violence and intimidation outside of Wilmington just prior to and during the elections of 1898, see especially Jeffrey C. Crow and Robert F. Durden, *Maverick Republican in the Old North State: A Political Biography of Daniel L. Russell* (Baton Rouge: Louisiana State University Press, 1977), 120, 133–34, and Janette Thomas Greenwood, *Bittersweet Legacy: The Black and White "Better Classes" in Charlotte, 1850–1910* (Chapel Hill: University of North Carolina Press, 1994), 190–91, 195–96.

7. Joel Williamson, *The Crucible of Race: Black-White Relations in the American South since Emancipation* (New York: Oxford University Press, 1984), 195–96.

8. Readers interested in learning more about the Wilmington race riot of 1898 can find a variety of scholarly accounts. For excellent overviews of the racial violence

and the political culture of the late nineteenth century, see especially Glenda Elizabeth Gilmore, *Gender and Jim Crow: Women and the Politics of White Supremacy in North Carolina, 1896–1920* (Chapel Hill: University of North Carolina Press, 1996); H. Leon Prather, *We Have Taken a City: Wilmington Racial Massacre and Coup of 1898* (Cranbury, N.J.: Associated University Presses, 1984); Crow and Durden, *Maverick Republican*; Helen G. Edmonds, *The Negro and Fusion Politics in North Carolina, 1894–1901* (Chapel Hill: University of North Carolina Press, 1951); Herbert Shapiro, *White Violence and Black Response, from Reconstruction to Montgomery* (Amherst: University of Massachusetts Press, 1988), 65–75; and Williamson, *The Crucible of Race*, 195–201. Jerome A. McDuffie's "Politics in Wilmington and New Hanover County, North Carolina, 1865–1900: The Genesis of a Race Riot" (Ph.D. diss., Kent State University, 1979), remains the standard work on the complex local political struggles that foreshadowed the racial massacre. While recent scholarship has very appropriately begun to clarify the long-neglected perspectives of African Americans in Wilmington, we have been disappointed that so little research has examined critically the white supremacists and their ideology, and particularly the lives of political leaders such as Charles B. Aycock, Josephus Daniels, and Furnifold Simmons, who organized the white supremacy campaign. While scholarship for seventy years after the "race riot" tended to characterize the white supremacist leaders as heroes who saved the state from "Negro rule," more recent scholarship may have gone too far the other way, caricaturizing the white vigilantes in such a way that we cannot see them as human enough for their actions to cast light on the more general roots of racial violence or see their racism as conceivably related to racism in society today. Two splendid books that begin to examine the complex wellsprings of white racist thought behind the Wilmington riot are Eric Anderson, *Race and Politics in North Carolina, 1872–1901: The Black Second* (Baton Rouge: Louisiana State University Press, 1981), and Paul D. Escott, *Many Excellent People: Power and Privilege in North Carolina, 1850–1900* (Chapel Hill: University of North Carolina Press, 1985). We also hope that scholars will increasingly investigate what happened in other parts of North Carolina during the white supremacy campaign of 1898. Without looking closely at the rest of the state, one might imagine that what happened in Wilmington was an isolated incident that grew from predominately local political events and thus grasp little of the top-down character of the white supremacy campaign or its far-reaching consequences. A good example of what can be learned from such case studies is found in Greenwood, *Bittersweet Legacy*, 147–237.

9. Quoted in Crow and Durden, *Maverick Republican*, 149.

10. Quoted in J. Morgan Kousser, *The Shaping of Southern Politics: Suffrage Restrictions and the Establishment of the One-Party South, 1880–1910* (New Haven: Yale University Press, 1974), 76.

11. V. O. Key, *Southern Politics in State and Nation* (New York: Knopf, 1949), 209–10.

12. *Atlanta Journal*, 24 November 1905.

13. W. E. B. Du Bois, "Fifty Years After," preface to the Jubilee Edition of *The Souls of Black Folk* published in 1953 by Blue Heron Press, reprinted in *The Souls of Black Folk* (New York: Fawcett, 1961), xiv.

14. William H. Chafe, *Civilities and Civil Rights: Greensboro, North Carolina, and the Black Struggle for Freedom* (New York: Oxford University Press, 1980), 3.

15. Charles S. Johnson et al., *A Preliminary Report on the Survey of Racial Tension Areas* (Nashville, Tenn.: Julius Rosenwald Fund, November 1942), 119.

16. J. Melville Broughton, "Address by Governor J. Melville Broughton at the launching of the Liberty Ship *John Merrick* at Wilmington, N.C., Sunday, July 11, 1943, 5:15 P.M.," box 82, Race Relations folder, Governor J. Melville Broughton Papers, North Carolina State Archives, North Carolina Division of Archives and History, Raleigh.

H. Leon
Prather Sr.

We Have Taken a City

A Centennial Essay

It was hardly a revelation when W. E. B. Du Bois observed in 1901 that "the problem of the twentieth century is the problem of the color line."[1] Anyone committed to racial justice who had lived through the white supremacy campaigns of the late nineteenth century could see that a sea change had occurred that would take many years and much striving to reverse; indeed, a hundred years have passed without reversing it altogether. The violence in Wilmington in 1898 was the capstone of the white supremacy campaign in North Carolina and signaled its victory across the nation. With that in mind, I undertook almost twenty years ago to uncover the events in Wilmington and unravel their historical meaning in a work entitled *We Have Taken a City: Wilmington Racial Massacre and Coup of 1898.*

Since its publication in 1984, a number of gifted scholars have turned their energies to the momentous events in Wilmington, explaining their importance in terms of class, gender, and racial and electoral politics, among other perspectives. Essays by several of them appear in these pages, and their contributions speak for themselves. Though it is a procession that I have been proud to lead, I cannot help but conclude that we have all failed in a certain way; most Americans remember nothing of these events despite the enormous impact that they continue to have on racial politics in the United States. One hopes that this volume of essays will help a new generation of citizens and scholars find meaning in the past and hope for the future. As I look back at my labors of the decades past, weighing our predicament, it seems enough here simply to tell the story one more time.

H. Leon
Prather Sr.

On the Cape Fear River, about thirty miles from the Atlantic coast of North Carolina, rests the beautiful city of Wilmington. At the dawn of the twentieth century, the seaport was the largest and most important city of the Old North State. Country folk referred to it as "the big city" and admired its electric lights and streetcars at a time when North Carolina was still a predominantly rural state scattered with farm towns and a rapidly growing number of small textile mill villages, lumber camps, and tobacco markets. With a population of 20,055—blacks outnumbering whites by 11,324 to 8,731—Wilmington cast a long shadow over the state's political and commercial life.[2]

Ironically, Wilmington was one of the best cities for blacks in the American South in the years before the racial massacre of 1898. Compared to other communities in the South, blacks and whites more commonly walked the same streets, lived in the same neighborhoods, and patronized the same shops. Blacks also held considerable political power. In 1897, for example, there were three blacks on the ten-member board of aldermen, the city's most important elected body. Another black was a member of the powerful five-constituent board of audit and finance. Other public offices held by blacks included justice of the peace, deputy clerk of court, superintendent of streets, and even coroner. The city had two black fire departments and an all-black health board. To this list can be added a significant number of black policeman and, in federal patronage, the mail clerk and mail carriers.[3]

The most conspicuous of President William McKinley's black appointees was John Campbell Dancy, named collector of customs at the Port of Wilmington in 1897. In addition to being black, and a non-native of Wilmington, he replaced a prominent white Democrat. Dancy's salary as collector of customs was approximately $4,000 per year, which, as conservative editors often reminded the white public, was $1,000 more than the annual salary of the state's governor. An outsider who enjoyed an economic status far above most people in Wilmington, Dancy was understandably resented by many whites as well as some local blacks. Thomas M. Clawson, editor of the *Wilmington Messenger* (which was the official organ of the Democrats), made a practice of referring to Dancy as "Sambo of the Customs House."[4]

Blacks also figured centrally in Wilmington's business life. For example, only one in eleven of the city's eating house owners was white. More significant was the almost complete monopoly blacks enjoyed in the barber trade: twenty of the twenty-two barbers listed in the city directory were black, most pursuing their occupation in shops on the principal downtown streets. Blacks also greatly outnumbered whites as boot- and shoemakers. The black-owned establishment of Bell and Pickens was listed in the *Wilmington Business Directory* of 1897 as among the city's four dealers and shippers of fish and oysters. Among the butchers and meat sellers, three of nine were black. Two blacks were listed among the city's four tailors. Black Wilmingtonians were also conspicuous in such functions as dyers and scourers, druggists, and grocers and bakers. Both blacks and whites had a great deal of faith in the efficacy of medicinal roots, but the only person listed as a dealer under this heading was black, with an office located downtown, not in one of Wilmington's predominantly black neighborhoods such as Brooklyn. Many of Wilmington's most skilled craftsmen were also blacks. They included mechanics, furniture makers, jewelers and watchmakers, painters, plasterers, plumbers, blacksmiths, stonemasons, brickmasons, and wheelwrights. Frederick C. Sadgwar, a black architect, builder, and financier, owned a majestic two-story house that still stands as a monument to his handiwork.[5]

Thomas C. Miller, who plays a minor but memorable role in the story of the Wilmington racial massacre, was certainly the most unique of the black businessmen. He was one of Wilmington's three real estate agents and auctioneers, and the only pawnbroker listed in the city directory. In addition, he had extensive real estate holdings throughout the city. Miller did not seek public office; nevertheless, his affluence made his presence in the city undesirable to most whites. According to the black oral tradition, many whites owed him money. Typically, poor whites were envious of blacks who were successful in business, and in the countryside nightriders sometimes drove away prosperous blacks by burning them out. Whites did not torch Miller's home or business, but his fate in November 1898 reflected the plight of the Southern black middle class during this era.[6]

Wilmington was also one of the few Southern cities with a black newspaper, the *Daily Record*, purportedly the only black daily in the United States at the time. Owned and operated by the Manly brothers, the newspaper was headed by the militant and progressive editor Alexander Manly, whose fiery editorials would become at least the rhetorical center of gravity in the racial conflagration of 1898. Manly, a handsome "octoroon," was the acknowledged grandson of a former governor of North Carolina.[7]

Given that black Wilmington wielded enough economic and political power to defend its interests, race relations in the city tended to be relatively harmonious for many years after the Civil War. During the 1880s, however, class conflict in North Carolina ushered in momentous political changes. Many of the state's farmers were hard hit by plummeting agricultural prices, high railroad freight rates, and the laissez-faire economic approach of the Democratic Party. By 1892, thousands of white farmers had defected to the Populist Party. To break the Democratic stranglehold on the political system, the Populists placed class interests above racial solidarity and formed a working alliance with the Republicans, the preponderance of whom were African Americans.[8]

In 1894, this interracial "Fusion" ticket won control of both houses of the General Assembly. Here lay the wellspring of the racial massacre of 1898. Since Redemption in the 1870s, the Democratic Party had conspired successfully to deny political power to Wilmington's black citizens. This could not be accomplished with much grace or subtlety in a black-majority city, for it meant, in effect, that the Democrats had to suffocate local democracy for the sake of holding power. To that end, the Democrats had never been squeamish about resorting to electoral fraud and racial intimidation. At the same time, Democratic leaders vested control over city government not in Wilmington, but at the state level, where the lower percentage of blacks statewide and a voter registration system that discouraged black voting practically guaranteed that the General Assembly would be controlled by the Democrats. The state constitution created by the 1875–76 legislature, in fact, gave the General Assembly "full power by statute to modify, change or abrogate any or all" city ordinances and "substitute others in their stead."[9] The General Assembly allowed racial gerrymandering that ensured white Democrats at least seven of the Wilmington board of aldermen's seats and the

H. Leon
Prather Sr.

mayorship. The governor also appointed Wilmington's most powerful organ of government—the board of audit and finance, which held total control over all city spending. As a result, Wilmington's citizens, black and white, had little power over their own political affairs beyond the extent to which they had allies among the Democratic leadership in Raleigh.

The 1894 Fusionist legislature embarked on the task of dismantling the Democrats' election machinery. A new county election law was carefully designed to restore local self-government and home rule. Succinctly stated, it abolished the Democrats' policy of appointment of local offices, making them all subject to popular election. The law also brought a change uniquely of consequence to blacks. Under the Democratic interpretation of election laws, black North Carolinians had frequently been excluded from the polls, but the Fusionists began to enact new electoral laws and registration procedures that encouraged black voting. For Wilmington, in particular, the Fusionists abolished the board of audit and finance and gave its powers to Republican- and Populist-dominated local boards.

With the more liberal Fusion election laws, it appeared that the floodgates were thrown open for participation in government by black voters, estimated in some quarters at 120,000 Republican supporters. The Fusionist voter registration laws led to the democratization of the ballot throughout the Black Belt. Once again the black man constituted a formidable element within the Republican Party, and his voting power, which had been dormant since Reconstruction, reappeared as a force to be reckoned with. In 1896, mainly due to black voting, the Fusionist cause won every statewide race in North Carolina, increasing its majority in the legislature and putting white Republican Daniel L. Russell, of Wilmington, in the governor's mansion.[10]

Under the influence of Governor Russell, the Fusion-dominated legislature of 1897 amended the Wilmington city charter to take power away from Democratic appointees and make municipal elections more democratic. After the 25 March 1897 city elections, the mayor and six of Wilmington's ten aldermen (including two blacks) were Fusionists. Up to that point, the Democrats had held power in the city for more than fifteen years under the auspices of a local clique, which Benjamin Keith, a Wilmington alderman, dubbed the "Old Fox Crowd" or the "Old Pro Crowd." The municipal election gave public offices in Wilmington to new men, with a few of the lesser posts actually going to black candidates. Democrats contested the new election laws before the North Carolina Supreme Court, but failed to overturn them.[11] With the elections of 1898, it appeared, Wilmington's black majority would sweep Republicans into an era of political predominance. Defeated at the polls and in the courts, white Democrats resolved to take power by any means necessary.

Exactly when the Wilmington racial massacre was first conceived has long been shrouded in mystery. Thomas W. Clawson, Democratic editor of the *Wilmington Messenger*, wrote years later that "for a period of six to 12 months prior to November 10, [1898], the white citizens of Wilmington prepared quietly but effectively for the day when action would be necessary."[12] A white Wilmingtonian named Harry Hayden wrote that the coup originated with a "group of nine influential citizens": J. Alan Taylor, Hardy I. Fennell, W. A. Johnson, L. B. Sasser, William Gilchrist, P. B. Manning, E. S. Lathrop, Walter L. Parsley, and Hugh MacRae. It was Hayden, celebrating the triumph of white supremacy in Wilmington, who dubbed this self-styled committee of Democrats "the Secret Nine."[13]

The racial massacre in Wilmington almost certainly would not have occurred without the statewide white supremacy campaign of 1898, one unparalleled in American history. Alarmed by the rise of the Republican-Populist Fusion coalition, the Democratic leaders of North Carolina resolved that the political campaign of 1898 would be one of "redemption." They called for the restoration of what they considered good government and white supremacy. The weighty task of organizing the white supremacy campaign rested largely on the shoulders of the shrewd Furnifold M. Simmons, chairman of the state Democratic Executive Committee and later a United States senator. One of his contemporaries spoke of him as the grandest statesman that North Carolina had produced in half a century. He was recognized as "a genius in putting everybody to work—men who could write, men who could speak, and men who could ride—the last by no means the least important."[14]

Simmons was fully aware that his party would face defeat in the 1898 elections unless the campaign were waged on an issue that would cut across party lines. Southern political history had long demonstrated that the question of black participation in politics was a smoldering ember that could easily be fanned to full flame. Simmons decided, therefore, to make "Negro rule" and "white supremacy" the watchwords in the effort to return the Democrats to power. The Democrats leveled charges of corruption, scandals, and extravagance against the Republican-Populist coalition but always gave them secondary consideration. The campaign was to be increasingly centered around the issue of blacks' sharing government. The color line would be so sharply drawn that, ultimately, little else would be talked about.

To wage the white supremacy campaign, Simmons bypassed the old Democratic personalities—the men, many of them Confederate veterans, stilled steeped in nostalgia for the antebellum past—and recruited a group of aggressive, colorful, and dynamic young supporters. Among them was Josephus Daniels, editor of the *Raleigh News and Observer*, the Democrats' leading mouthpiece and a militant voice of white supremacy. (He was later secretary of the navy under President Woodrow Wilson.) In 1898, Daniels and other Democratic editors repeatedly portrayed blacks as "insolent" and accused them of displaying malice and disrespect for whites in public. They also complained of corrupt and brutal black police officers. Most especially, the Democratic editors focused on the supposed interest of black men in white women, perhaps the most sensitive subject in Southern race relations.[15]

Immediately following a key meeting of the Democratic Executive Committee in Raleigh on 20 November 1897, the first statewide call for white unity was issued. It was an eloquent address, written by Francis D. Winston of Bertie County. Winston called upon whites to unite and "reestablish Anglo-Saxon rule and honest government in North Carolina." He reported that evil times had followed as a consequence of turning over local offices to blacks: "Homes have been invaded, and the sanctity of woman endangered. Business has been paralyzed and property rendered less valuable. The majesty of law has been disregarded and lawlessness encouraged." Such conditions were "wrought by a combination of Republican and Populist leaders." The Democratic Party promised to correct these abuses and restore security once more to the "white women of the state."[16] In the 1898 campaign, the Democrats were to be the heroes, the saviors, the new redeemers, who would rescue the state from the villains, the Fusionist regime.

Now and then, the *Wilmington Messenger* depicted Fusion corruption and made attacks upon Governor Russell. Mostly, however, the conservative press pilloried blacks in the most sinister manner, with ugly cartoons cunningly drawn to provoke white racial fears. Simmons disseminated a large amount of racist propaganda, which preceded every Democratic orator across the state. Some of the Democrats' most effective speakers were Alfred M. Waddell (later mayor of Wilmington), Robert B. Glenn (later governor), and former governors Thomas J. Jarvis and Cameron Morrison. The king of oratory, however, was Charles B. Aycock, the Democratic Moses, who would lead North Carolina out of the chaos and darkness of "Negro domination." Early in the campaign, his cohorts began introducing him as the "idol of the east" and the next governor of North Carolina. Aycock's name became the magnet that attracted immense crowds: at Leesville, he addressed one of the largest groups ever assembled in Wayne County, comprised of men, women, and children—1,200 strong—"who came in buggies, in carts, in carriages, in wagons, on horseback and on foot." The Leesville performance was dwarfed by the Raleigh rally held in the Metropolitan House, where people had early "filled all seats, the windows, and occupied every inch of standing room in the rear of the hall." Aycock spoke for an hour and a quarter and swept the audience off its feet with his magnetism. As he was to do in all future addresses, he closed with an earnest appeal for white supremacy and the protection of white womanhood. Drawing his audience gradually to the dramatic climax, like a skilled evangelist entreating backsliders and sinners to come forward and be saved, he would ask the multitudes if they would come and rescue the state from "Russellism, Fusionism, and Black Domination." Rising and cheering, they shouted, "Yes, we will!" Not since the days of fire-eater William L. Yancey of Alabama had a political orator possessed such rustic appeal in North Carolina. To no avail, the Populists and Republicans warned that the Democratic machine was "crying nigger" with the purpose of diverting attention from the real political issues of the day.[17]

Early in the fall of 1898, organizers from the state's Democratic leadership visited Wilmington to spur the white supremacy campaign. They helped to organize a local campaign committee that successfully solicited funds from most of the white businesses in the city. They also helped to organize white supremacy clubs. As George Rountree, one of the Democratic organizers, later remembered, "Francis Winston came down and helped to organize these clubs, which by this time in October were spread over the state."[18] They urged every white man, regardless of party affiliation, to identify himself with the clubs. In the meantime, prominent political personalities abetted the membership drive in every city ward. Attorneys William B. McCoy, Iredell Meares, John D. Bellamy, and others permitted the White Government Union—as the white supremacy clubs in Wilmington were called—to use their offices for meetings, and on occasion they made lengthy addresses before its members. The clubs demanded that every white man in the city join. "Many good people," wrote white Wilmingtonian Benjamin F. Keith, "were marched from their homes, some by committees, and taken to headquarters, and told to sign. Those that did not were notified that they must

leave the city . . . as there was plenty of rope in the city."[19] Even Wilmington's ministers, who had first been outraged when they got word of the
impending coup d'état, eventually withdrew their opposition and sur-
rendered to the inevitable. To make matters worse, a racist labor movement also surfaced in Wilmington as part of the White Government
Union to oppose blacks' competing with whites for jobs. Endorsed by
the chamber of commerce, the goal of this anti-black labor group, as
stated at a mass meeting on 7 October, was "the substitution of white for
Negro labor."[20]

While the conspirators pressed to consolidate white working men and
business leaders against "Negro domination," the members of the Secret
Nine awaited their main chance. Opportunity came in the form of an
editorial by Alexander Manly, the black editor, which appeared in August 1898; his comments in response to the call of Georgia's Rebecca
Felton for white men to "lynch a thousand times a week if necessary" to
protect white women from black men had the effect of pouring gasoline
on the embers of white discontent. "If the alleged crimes of rape were . . .
so frequent as is ofttimes reported," Manly wrote, "her plea would be
worthy of consideration." But not every white woman who cried rape
told the truth, he argued, nor was every sexual contact between black
men and white women an act of rape. In fact, many black men were
"sufficiently attractive for white girls of culture and refinement to fall in
love with them, as is well known to all." Democratic reprints of the
article tended to end at this point, but Manly had continued. White men
also seduced and raped black women, he argued, and "carping hypo-
crites . . . cry aloud for the virtue of your women while you seek to
destroy the morality of ours." If white newspapers decried crime in
general rather than simply attacking supposed black criminality, "they
would find their strongest allies among the intelligent Negroes themselves," the editor insisted. "Tell your men that it is no worse for a black
man to be intimate with a white woman than for a white man to be
intimate with a colored woman."[21] Across the South, Democratic newspapers reprinted incendiary distortions of the Manly editorial. "Negro
Editor Slanders White Women," "Negro Defamer of White Women,"
"A Horrid Slander of White Women," and "Infamous Attack on White
Women" were just a few of the headlines arrayed against the editor and
his views.[22]

Manly and his family were the acknowledged offspring of Charles
Manly, Whig governor of North Carolina from 1849 to 1851. Governor
Manly, like many white men of his time, fathered two sets of children—
those born to his legal wife, who were white, and those born to a slave

woman, who were considered black. For anyone not acquainted with him, Alex Manly could have passed for a white man. "My father's family looked so much like whites," his son said later, "that sometimes I wondered myself."[23]

Although Manly's given name was Alexander, he was seldom called anything but Alex, even by his mother. Of average stature, he sported a mustache that matched his heavy black hair. Born 13 May 1866 in Wake County, about two miles from Raleigh, he attended Hampton Institute and mastered the painting trade. Finding little work near his home, Manly migrated to Wilmington, where he started a painting business. Soon followed by his brothers Frank, George, Grimes, and Laurin, Manly became a local political leader and taught Sunday school at the Presbyterian church. He served as register of deeds until he purchased a secondhand, but practically new, Jonah Hoe press from Thomas Clawson, the editor of the *Wilmington Messenger*, who had acquired it at an emergency sale. With the press, Manly began publication of a newspaper, which he called the *Record*, whose offices he established over a saloon directly across the street from the office of another local paper, the *Wilmington Star*. First published as a weekly, the *Record* soon blossomed into a daily under Manly's gifted editorial leadership. Clawson himself called it "a very creditable colored paper."[24] White business leaders encouraged the *Record* through liberal advertising in its pages. The paper soon achieved a wide readership among blacks across the state.

All of that ended with the publication of Manly's editorial, which gave the party of white supremacy all the political cover it could require for its conspiracy to seize power in Wilmington. Manly became the object of white men's wrath in bars, streets, and offices throughout the city and indeed across the South. No doubt one white man voiced the sentiments of many when he growled that "the impudent nigger ought to be horsewhipped and run out of town." Many spoke of smashing the paper's press. According to Walker Taylor, whose recollections appeared in 1905, "it required the best efforts we could put forth [to] prevent the people from lynching him. . . . Senator Simmons, who was here at the time, told us that the article would make it an easy victory for us and urged us to try and prevent any riot until after the election."[25]

The political impact of the editorial was already evident at a giant Democratic gathering in Fayetteville on 20 October 1898, the largest political rally ever staged by the party. Early in the morning, "vehicles filling all the streets and thoroughfares gave evidence that the white people of upper Cape Fear had left the plow, the machine shops, the kitchen, nay, the very neighborhood schoolroom," one account noted.[26] Here the Red Shirts, a terrorist wing of the Democratic Party, made their first appearance in North Carolina, accompanied by Senator "Pitch-fork" Ben Tillman, the fiery orator from Edgefield, South Carolina, who was the brightest star in the firmament of Southern white supremacy. A delegation from Wilmington led the parade, followed by 300 Red Shirts riding in military formation. A float carrying twenty-two beautiful young ladies in white trailed the Red Shirts, as if to justify the latter's claims of protecting the sanctity of white womanhood. Next came the carriage bearing Fayetteville's mayor and Democratic committee chairman, the editor of the *Fayetteville Observer*, and Senator Tillman himself. Arriving amid the boom of cannons, the great throng assembled at the speakers' stand and listened to the music of the Wilmington brass band. It would not be the last time that Wilmington set the rhythm of Democratic politics across the state.

Tillman, invited to speak on behalf of the white supremacy movement, was introduced as "the liberator of South Carolina."[27] Thanking the audience for its warm reception, Tillman inveighed against President Grover Cleveland, Alex Manly, African Americans, Republicans, and Fusion politics, lumping them all together under the rubric "negro domination." Noting the Red Shirts arrayed before him, Tillman recalled the days two decades earlier when the white people of South Carolina rose up in their wrath and crushed Negro domination forever. He had seen 5,000 Red Shirts in one audience, he said, and the crimson cloak had become the banner by which the white man was known.

The Manly editorial occupied a central place in Tillman's speech. Noting the "very beautiful girls" in his audience, the stemwinder from South Carolina remarked that they reminded him to say that "such articles as written by the negro editor in Wilmington were an insult to the women of North Carolina." "Why didn't you kill that damn nigger editor who wrote that?" he bellowed. "Send him to South Carolina and let him publish any such offensive stuff, and he will be killed."[28]

In the wake of Tillman's visit and the birth of the Red Shirt brigades in North Carolina, the Tarheel State produced its own prophet of white supremacy in Alfred M. Waddell. Noted for his blustery eloquence, Waddell was known in some circles as "the silver-tongued orator of the east." Born in 1834 on Moorefield, a plantation near Hillsborough, North Carolina, Waddell studied law and published a newspaper until the outbreak of the Civil War. During the war he served as a lieutenant colonel in the Confederate cavalry. After the fall of the Confederacy,

Waddell carried his ambitions into politics and served three terms in Congress from 1871 to 1877, losing his seat to Republican Daniel L. Russell, the future Fusionist governor.[29]

Unemployed in 1898, Waddell set himself to the cause of overthrowing the Fusion government. Scheduled to address "the white men of Wilmington" in the fall of 1898, Waddell packed the hall in which he spoke. He shared the platform with Thomas W. Strange, the chair of the Democratic Executive Committee of New Hanover County, and about fifty of the city's most prominent white citizens. Greeted by a deafening ovation, the old Confederate kept his audience enthralled. "We are reduced to the pitiful necessity of choosing whether we will live under the dominance of negroes led by a few unprincipled men, and see the ruin of all we hold dear, or prove ourselves worthy of the respect of mankind by restoring good government at all hazards and at every cost." White supremacy, he said, was the only issue in the coming election, and the shadow of race war hung over them. "I do not hesitate to say this publicly, that if a race conflict occurs in North Carolina, the very first men that ought to be held to account are the white leaders of the negroes who will be chiefly responsible for it," he declared. "To begin at the top of the list, I scorn to leave any doubt as to who I mean. . . . I mean the governor of this state who is the engineer of all the deviltry." Waddell would have his revenge. "We will never surrender to a ragged raffle of negroes," he vowed in closing, "even if we have to choke the Cape Fear River with carcasses."[30]

Waddell made his next appearance in Goldsboro, North Carolina, with "Special Trains From Wilmington," according to the *Messenger*, and discount tickets provided by the Seaboard and Southern Railroad from Greensboro and other cities. Some 8,000 white Democrats came to raise the cry of white supremacy. Furnifold Simmons, Charles Aycock, and William A. Guthrie, the mayor of Durham, shared the platform. Giving voice to a belief in manifest destiny and white supremacy that was sweeping the United States, Guthrie declared, "The Anglo-Saxon planted civilization on this continent and wherever this race has been in conflict with another race, it has asserted its supremacy and either conquered or exterminated the foe. This great race has carried the Bible in one hand and the sword [in the other]." Addressing the Fusionists, Guthrie warned, "Resist our march of progress and civilization and we will wipe you off the face of the earth."[31]

But it was Waddell who most electrified the crowd. The "insolence" and "arrogance" of black North Carolinians was overshadowed only by their inherent criminality, he declared, unfurling tales of black men using obscene language in the presence of white women and of white men "responsible for the evils of negro rule" because they had betrayed their race. "We are going to protect our firesides and our loved ones," the gray-bearded colonel assured the crowd, "or die in the attempt." Once more he concluded his lengthy oration with his promise that the white men of Wilmington would drive out the African Americans and their traitorous white allies, even if they had to throw enough dead black corpses into the Cape Fear to block its passage to the sea.[32]

The Red Shirts terrorized blacks and their white allies across the eastern part of North Carolina. Governor Russell warned that the Red Shirts had broken up political meetings in Richmond and Halifax Counties, and he reported that "in other cases property had been actually destroyed and citizens fired on in ambush; that several citizens have been taken from their homes at night and whipped; that several citizens have been intimidated and terrorized by threats of violence to their persons and their property, until they were afraid to register themselves preparatory to . . . the casting of a free vote at the ballot box."[33] The level of intimidation grew until Republican and Populist candidates for office were afraid to speak in Wilmington. Seeking to capitalize on the racial storm they had stirred up, the Democrats tried to suppress the Republican ticket in New Hanover County, arguing that a victory by any political ticket that opposed the Democrats in 1898 would surely result in a race riot. They convinced the business community of the danger, and business leaders, mainly Democrats, expressed their concern for the peace and welfare of the Wilmington community. Textile millionaire James Sprunt wrote to Governor Russell that the election "threatens to provoke a war between the black and white races . . . [and] will precipitate a conflict which may cost hundreds, and perhaps thousands, of lives, and the partial or entire destruction of the city." Reemphasizing the threat, Sprunt concluded, "We declare to you our conviction that we are on the brink of a revolution which can only be averted by the suppression of a Republican ticket."[34]

Soon the Red Shirts gathered in Wilmington in a series of marches and rallies organized by another unemployed agitator, Mike Dowling, an Irishman fired a few months earlier from his post as foreman of Fire Engine Company Number 2 for "incompetency, drunkenness, and continued insubordination." Dowling led the mounted white men through the streets of Wilmington as if they were ranks of cavalry. White women waved flags and handkerchiefs as the long columns of armed riders passed. The parade stopped in front of the Democratic Party headquarters in the old First National Bank Building, where Democratic politicians spoke to swelling crowds, after which the Red Shirts and others whooped it up far into the night. Headlines in all the white newspapers gave notice daily of white supremacy meetings, held by night in public buildings and by day on street corners. Often free food and moonshine whiskey appeared for the crowds as election day approached. On 2 November, Dowling and his Red Shirts led a "White Man's Rally" that featured free barbecue. At dusk, flaming barrels of tar spread brightly colored plumes of smoke across the city, creating a carnival atmosphere. The New Hanover County Horsemen, the Wilmington Red Shirts, and the Rough Riders—a group of white veterans fresh from the Spanish-American War—paraded through the downtown streets.[35] When leaders of the white supremacy movement spent the staggering sum of $1,200 to purchase a new, rapid-firing Gatling gun, however, it was clear that this was neither a barbecue nor a carnival.

In the days before the election, Wilmington was taunt with excitement and activity. Hearsay had it that blacks were buying guns and ammunition and preparing to fight. There were also reports that black leaders were using "churches to deliver incendiary speeches and impassioned appeals to blacks to use the bullet . . . and the kerosene and torch that would play havoc with the white man's cotton bale and warehouse."[36] At the suggestion of John R. Kenly, president of the Atlantic Coastline Railroad, the Democratic campaign committee hired a black detective to investigate the rumors. He concluded that blacks "were doing practically nothing," but two white Pinkerton detectives reported that black women servants had agreed to set fire to the dwellings of their employers and black men had openly threatened to "burn the town down" if the white supremacists prevailed in the election.[37] Blacks had, of course, become tense and apprehensive. A number of men attempted to purchase weapons, but since all merchants who stocked firearms were white and knew what was in the wind, they refused to sell guns or powder to African Americans. Blacks sought to order arms from a Northern manufacturer, but the company's local agent rejected the consignment. They had no arms for their defense, except for a few blacks who owned old army muskets or pistols.

Election day came and went without much of a stir. Black citizens avoided the polls in the hope that the bloodshed for which the Democrats clamored could somehow be avoided. The threat of violence suppressed the Republican turnout, and additionally the evidence strongly suggests a significant degree of election fraud. A journalist from the North reported that Wilmington's Republican majority of 5,000 in 1896 gave way to a Democratic majority of 6,000 in 1898—a gain of 11,000 votes.[38] In their determination to win, leading Democrats had declared their intention of doing so by hook or by crook, peacefully if possible but by revolution if necessary; and they did not falter in this resolve at any stage in the proceedings. But Jane Murphy Cronly, a white woman in Wilmington, expressed the sentiments of many ordinary citizens when she later wrote of the day after the election: "I awoke that morning with thankful heart that the election has passed without the shedding of the blood of either the innocent or the guilty. I heard the colored people going by to their work talking cheerfully together as had not been the case for many days now."[39] Before the day was out, it would be clear that Cronly had been overly optimistic.

On election day, Hugh MacRae of the Secret Nine had called the offices of the *Wilmington Messenger* and dictated a call for a mass meeting. That evening, the paper ran an eye-catching headline: "Attention White Men." The announcement asked that all white men gather at the courthouse at 10:00 A.M. and urged "full attendance as business of marked importance" would be transacted.[40] The next morning, a steady flow of white men from all walks of life could be seen entering the courthouse. Merchants, mechanics, farmers, bankers, clerks, and clergymen packed the meeting. On the rostrum sat Hugh MacRae, former mayor S. H. Fishblate, and other prominent white Democrats. Thomas Clawson, the editor of the *Messenger*, and his staff of reporters agreed to serve as secretaries. Fishblate chaired the meeting and called Alfred Waddell to the podium.

The moment had found the man. As Waddell made his way down the center aisle, the entire room broke into sustained applause. The former Confederate cavalry leader came to the meeting, he said, "entirely ignorant of its objective," but, he continued, he found it "always a pleasure, as well as a duty, to accept the call of the people of Wilmington."[41] Hugh MacRae handed Waddell a document. The Secret Nine had drawn up a "Wilmington Declaration of Independence," which Waddell began to read aloud to the throng.

The document's preamble asserted that "the Constitution of the United States contemplated a government to be carried on by an enlightened people . . . and its framers did not anticipate the enfranchisement of an ignorant population of African origin." The white men of North Carolina "who joined in forming the Union did not contemplate for their descendants a subjection to an inferior race."[42] Never again, the writers swore, would the white men of New Hanover County permit black men to participate in government. As Waddell completed his reading of the preamble, the crowd leapt to its feet and gave a thunderous ovation, yelling madly.

When the roar began to die down, Waddell proceeded to outline the declaration's eight resolutions. It was absolutely necessary that interracial politics end, they stated; the city was controlled by venal politicians who prevailed only by their affiliation with blacks, while white Democrats owned most of the property and paid a "like proportion" of taxes. The final two resolutions condemned Manly's editorial as "so vile and slanderous that it would, in most communities, result in the lynching of the editor" and demanded that his newspaper "cease to be published" and "its editor be banished from the city." The resolution set a twelve-hour deadline after which Manly would "be expelled by force."[43]

It is important to note here that Manly had already fled Wilmington and the *Record* had ceased publication. Even so, the politics of mob violence required a target. Twenty-five of the city's leading white citizens were appointed to a committee headed by Alfred Waddell, charged with carrying out the resolutions. The committee summoned thirty-two prominent African American citizens to the courthouse at six o'clock that evening.

The black contingent included Armond W. Scott (attorney), Thomas C. Miller (real estate agent and pawn broker), L. A. Henderson (attorney), David Jacobs (barber and county coroner), Cater Peamon (barber and political activist), Frederick C. Sadgwar (carpenter and architect), Thomas Rivers (mortician), Elijah Green (alderman), J. H. Alston (physician), the Reverend W. J. Leak, T. R. Mash (physician), John Goins (business manager of the *Wilmington Record*), John Holloway (postal clerk), the Reverend J. W. Telfair, William A. Moore (attorney), John H. Howe (member of 1897 North Carolina General Assembly), and Richard Ashe (financier). Most of those summoned met the committee at the courthouse at the appointed hour.[44]

There the black men saw arrayed against them the real financial powers of the city, backed by weapons superior in both number and firepower. It was clear, too, that the voice of white supremacy did not waver; there was murder in the air. The blacks knew this, even before they arrived; they came with their hats in their hands and appeasement on their minds, their heads bowed to the political reality before them. Cowed and terror-stricken, the black men focused on Alfred Waddell as he read them the declaration and explained it in firm language. Handing out copies, Waddell told them that no discussion was possible; the time had passed for words. They had been selected on the assumption that they were leaders of the black community, he said, and they were to receive and then deliver the ultimatum. He gave them until 7:30 the next morning to bring a reply to his house. One black man objected carefully, "Colonel, we are not responsible for this, and we have no authority." Waddell rose and made a terse reply: "The meeting stands adjourned," he said.[45]

The black men walked down the courthouse steps and proceeded immediately to David Jacobs's barbershop on Dock Street. After some deliberation, they drafted the following reply to the white ultimatum:

> We, the colored citizens to whom was referred the matter of expulsion from the community of the person and press of A. L. Manly, beg most respectfully to say that we are in no way responsible for, nor in any way condone, the obnoxious article that called forth your actions. Neither are we authorized to act for him in this manner; but in the interest of peace we will most willingly use our influence to have your wishes carried out.[46]

The men instructed attorney Armond Scott to deliver the reply in person to Waddell's home at Fifth and Princess Streets; instead, he placed it in a mailbox. This mistake may have cost a number of lives, though perhaps it only provided a convenient excuse for white leaders already bent on violence. In any case, since Scott had learned that his name was on a list of black politicians whom the Secret Nine intended to banish from Wilmington, he was no doubt reluctant to linger in Waddell's neighborhood.

On the streets of Wilmington the next morning, heavily armed white men streamed toward the city's stately white marble armory from all directions. Before eight o'clock, the armory was full of men awaiting the response of the black committee. "Every man brought his rifle," the *Messenger* reported, "and many had pistols also."[47] By 8:15, the throng began to grumble, but still they waited. A mob needs a leader.

Waddell volunteered. He lined up about 500 men in front of the building, with the committee of 25 at the head of the procession. Shouldering his Winchester, he assumed a position at the head of the column. Four abreast they set out around 8:30. "Under thorough discipline and under command of officers," one witness wrote, "capitalists and laborers marched together. The lawyer and his client were side by side. Men of large business interests kept step with clerks."[48] The procession passed up Market Street and threw the city into a state of excitement; schools let out, saloons closed their doors, and all business ground to a halt. People watched from sidewalks and windows, while men and boys poured into the streets. The line of march swelled to 2,000 strong.

As the column approached the vicinity of Love and Charity Hall, which housed Alexander Manly's press, African Americans could be seen fleeing in all directions. In front of the two-story frame structure on Seventh Street, between Nun and Church Streets, Waddell halted his hordes. Accompanied by several men, he knocked at the door a number of times. Getting no answer, the mob battered down the door and about twenty men ran inside, quickly smashing all the windows and demolishing the office fixtures. Hanging lamps fell onto the wooden floors and saturated the planks with kerosene; someone struck a match, and soon smoke rolled out of the upper windows.

The violence had only begun, although Waddell later wrote that after the destruction of Manly's press, he had immediately restored order. "I then marched the column back through the streets down to the armory, lined them up, and stood on the stoop and made a speech." He claimed to have told the crowd: "Now you have performed the duty on which you called on me to lead you to perform. Now let us go quietly to our homes and about our business and obey the laws, unless we are forced to defend ourselves otherwise."[49]

Black citizens, having heard about the destruction of Manly's printing press and office, assembled in other parts of Wilmington. Some talked of revenge and returning fire for fire. Rumors abounded that black men had organized themselves for armed retaliation. Roughly twenty-five black men assembled on the corner of Fourth Street, some of them carrying guns. Suspecting an attack, whites gathered on the west side of Fourth Street, between Brunjes's Store and St. Matthew's English Lutheran Church, armed and ready for confrontation. Police officer Aaron Lockamy, realizing the danger, moved among the black men and urged them to leave the scene. It is hard to say just what happened next. But a shot rang out. A young white man named William Mayo fell, blood crimson on his right arm. The bullet, according to the *Wilmington Messenger*, struck him in the left breast near the arm and exited through the right breast, piercing both lungs.[50] Then a crash of gunfire broke loose as whites fired a fusillade from their revolvers, shotguns, and Winchester rifles. Six black men fell under the heavy fire, two killed instantly.

A running gun battle broke out all along the street. The blacks ran in all directions, with whites in hot pursuit, firing as they went. Some blacks managed to fire back as they ran west on Harnett Street. Hearing

H. Leon
Prather Sr.

gunfire, whites emerged from houses along the way, exchanging volleys with the fleeing black men. On Third Street, an African American man named Sam Gregory ran into a hail of bullets and fell dead between Harnett and Swann Streets. Blacks who ran toward the scene were met by white men with guns, and shots were exchanged until the blacks were forced to scatter toward the railroad tracks. Another black man reached the rails before he fell dead of his wounds. Immediately, telegraphs flashed news of the racial violence across the state and beyond. Democratic leaders in other North Carolina towns—Oxford, Dunn, Monroe, Wilson, Mount Olive, Fayetteville, Macon, Winston-Salem, Clinton, Goldsboro—alerted their military forces, and major cities as far away as Atlanta and New Orleans offered to send help to the white insurgents in Wilmington.[51]

Somewhere out in the Dry Pond section of Wilmington, the Red Shirts gathered to await a signal, their horses pawing and ready for battle. The Rough Riders were also mounted and ready to fight, as was the Wilmington Light Infantry, led by Captain William Rand Kenan and Lieutenant Charles H. White. The Gatling gun, drawn on a truck by two fine horses, and two one-pound Hotchkiss cannons, drawn on a wagon, also stood ready to roll, commanded by Captain Henry McIlhenny. Colonel Roger B. Moore, a former Confederate officer and Ku Klux Klansman, buckled on a sword and rode with the ranks of white supremacy. At the sound of the firebell, all of these forces descended upon the poorly armed Brooklyn section of Wilmington.

Before the troops rolled into Brooklyn, bullets were already whistling along Bladen Street as blacks and whites skirmished intermittently. When the Red Shirts, Rough Riders, and Wilmington Light Infantry arrived, the sporadic gunfire changed to disciplined firepower. T. C. James, who commanded one group of foot soldiers, lined his men up and told them, "Now, boys, I want to tell you right now I want you all to load and when I give the command to shoot, I want you to shoot to kill."[52] At Fourth and Harnett, the troops unleashed their initial barrage. With military precision, the soldiers fired to the cool orders of their commander, ceasing only when no shots came in answer. Editor Thomas Clawson, standing with other journalists just behind the firing line, reported that "a volley tore off the top of a [black] man's head and he fell dead about 20 feet in front of the news-hawks."[53]

After the initial confrontation, the white vigilantes met only intermittent resistance, mainly occasional sniper fire from behind fences, trees, buildings, and other sheltered places. A shot that seemed to come from a shanty near Sixth and Bladen Streets drew heavy fire from the white

ranks but no response. Diagonally across the street, a high fence surrounded Manhattan Park, inside of which was a dance hall frequented
by a rough crowd, some of whom appeared at the sound of gunfire with
their own guns. They were no match for the dozens of white men who
rushed to the scene, firing wildly, as planks in the fence were literally cut
in half by .44 caliber rifle bullets and the walls of the dance hall became
pitted with gunshots. One defenseless black man ran out the rear of the
hall. The white men cut him down with a fusillade of fifteen to twenty
bullets. As one of the shooting party exclaimed mockingly, "When we
tu'ned him ove', Misto Niggah had a look of s'prise on his count'nance, I
ashore you!"[54]

Any semblance of a battle soon gave way to the atmosphere of a
manhunt. Daniel Wright, an active and intrepid black politician, was
the object of a vigorous search by the Red Shirts; he was accused of
shooting William Mayo, the first white man who had fallen wounded,
though it is far from clear what role he may have played in the clash. A
howling mob surrounded Wright's house, demanding that he surrender.
The men fired a number of shots into the attic, thinking that he was
hiding there. Suddenly, one of the Red Shirts reeled and fell from his
horse; another soon followed. Determined to sell his life as dearly as
possible, Wright, wielding a smokeless and noiseless rifle, had fired into
the group, killing Will Terry and George Bland in rapid succession.

By the time the Red Shirts finally captured Wright, a large crowd had
gathered. Someone knocked the prisoner down with a length of pipe,
bloodying his head. When he got up, one of his captors yelled, "String
him up to a lamp post." Another insisted that Wright be permitted to run
the gauntlet, and the men turned him loose, yelling, "Run, nigger, run!"
When he had gotten fifty feet or so, Wright fell in a hail of at least forty
rounds. "He was riddled with a pint of bullets, like a pigeon thrown from
a trap," one observer wrote.[55] Wright lay bleeding in the street for an
hour and a half before anybody dared to carry him to the city hospital,
where he lingered for a day before dying.

The manhunt grew less and less specific; Red Shirts and Rough Riders moved into the black sections to "hunt niggers," as one said, or, as
another put it, to "kill every damn nigger in sight."[56] One witness testified that he had seen six black men shot down near the Cape Fear
Lumber Company, their bodies buried hurriedly in a nearby ditch.
Another described the killing of nine African Americans by a lone white
marksmen who reputedly set fire to their shanty in Brooklyn and picked
them off one by one as they fled the flames. Still another witness told of
the murder of an innocent deaf black man, shot by the mob because he

failed to obey a command to halt that he never heard. Other observers related seeing an African American slain after he approached two white men on the wharf; his killers threw the carcass into the Cape Fear. Jane Murphy Cronly later accused the Wilmington Light Infantry of shooting down blacks "right and left in a most unlawful way, killing one man who was simply standing at a corner waiting to get back to his work."[57] Indeed, some whites used the racial violence to settle old feuds. A Philadelphia editor wrote that "there was not one white man under arms who did not have some score to settle with a Negro rankling in his breast." That was one reason, observed the *Atlanta Constitution*, "why so many farmers went into Wilmington. . . . They had long awaited for an opportunity of this kind."[58]

The conservative *New York Times* put the death toll at nine black men, compared with fifteen reported in the *New York Herald* and sixteen in the *Richmond Daily Times*. Writing in his memoirs, Alfred Waddell recalled that "about 20 [blacks] were killed." Historian J. G. de Roulhac Hamilton, relying largely on Democratic Party sources, set the death toll at twelve, while Josephus Daniels of the *News and Observer*, writing years later, said there were eleven deaths. More reliable, in all likelihood, was the report of the black coroner, David Jacobs, who impaneled fourteen coroner's juries, all of which reached the same verdict: the deceased died as a result of gunshot wounds inflicted by unknown persons. An uncertain number of other victims, Coroner Jacobs reported, had been buried secretly.[59] When one goes beyond the standard historical accounts and explores the oral traditions, claims for the level of killing take on bizarre dimensions, with some witnesses who contend that "over 100 were killed in the internecine street fighting."[60] The Reverend J. Allen Kirk, in "A Statement of Fact Concerning The Bloody Riot in Wilmington, N.C., November 10, 1898," wrote that hundreds of black citizens were killed and their bodies thrown into the river. "Wagon loads of Negro bodies were hauled through the streets of Wilmington," another eyewitness reported, while a black schoolteacher wrote a relative in Boston that she "saw carts pass with men thrown up there like dead animals they were taking . . . out to bury."[61] Persisting even today are legends of the mouth of the Cape Fear clotted with black bodies; these stories probably echo the oft-quoted vow of Alfred Waddell to "choke the Cape Fear River with carcasses" if necessary. It is unlikely that we will ever know exactly how many black citizens died in the violence of 1898.

While the human toll is hard to tally, the political, social, and economic impact is more clear. An exodus of black and white citizens began almost as soon as the violence erupted. Many upper-class white men had already sent their families out of the city, and whites who lived in and around Brooklyn found shelter at designated schools and churches, well guarded by citizens' committees. But black citizens were on their own. The *Messenger* reported that "a crowd of at least 500 men, women and children were on the road and in the woods beyond Smith's Creek Bridge."[62] The *Caucasian*, a Raleigh newspaper, wrote that "the roads were lined with [blacks], some carrying their bedding on their heads and whatever effects could be carried."[63]

November nights in the Lower Cape Fear were cold enough to cause considerable suffering for the hundreds of blacks who fled to the woods. "It was pitiable to see the children hurrying in fright after their parents," the *Caucasian* reported.[64] Many had dashed from their homes without blankets or coats; they huddled unprotected and slept on the ground. The forest would be their refuge for two days. "Bone-chilling, drizzling rain falls sadly from a leaden sky," Charles Francis Bourke of *Collier's Weekly* wrote from the scene. "Yet in the woods and swamps," he continued, "innocent hundreds of terrified men, women and children wander about, fearful of the vengeance of whites, fearful of death, without money, food, insufficient clothes." The little children "whimpered in the darkness and rain," their parents "fearful to light fires, listening for chance footsteps crushing fallen twigs, shuddering and peering gray-faced into the darkness, wailing, waiting—they knew not for what." The scene was almost too much for the correspondent to bear, and the sound that drifted through the trees haunted Bourke: "In the blackness of the pines, I heard a child crying and a hoarse voice crooning softly a mournful song, the words of which fell into my memory with the air: 'When de battle over we kin wear a crown in the new Je-ru-sulum.' "[65]

But the new Jerusalem that emerged on the Lower Cape Fear would have no crown for the descendants of slaves. The Secret Nine and their allies made of the riot a rather thin smokescreen for their violent and revolutionary seizure of power from the legally elected Fusionist government. The gunfire had not ceased before Alfred Waddell called a meeting of his cohorts to select a new city government. The cabal sent Frank H. Stedman and Charles W. Worth to City Hall to demand the resignations of Mayor Silas Wright, the aldermen, and the Populist chief of police. Though Wright demurred at first, he relented as the crowd around the building swelled into a dangerous mob supporting the demands of the Democratic delegation. Stedman, Worth, and J. Alan Taylor (a member of the Secret Nine) took Wright's resignation and assumed authority; one by one, the aldermen also resigned and were replaced by white Democrats. Likewise, the entire police department was forced to resign so that it could be taken over by white Democrats. Not surprisingly, the new board of aldermen unanimously elected Alfred Waddell to serve as mayor of Wilmington.

Like all triumphant revolutionaries, Waddell quickly announced that he intended to use all his powers to "preserve peace and order." He asked for all citizens to "cooperate with the municipal authorities in every way possible to secure the permanent establishment of good government." Finally, he claimed that "the law will be rigidly enforced and impartially administered to whites and blacks alike."[66] He even sent parties into the woods around the city to encourage refugees to return to their homes. The coup plotters had assumed control and moved quickly to legitimate their authority by restoring a semblance of stability.

The second and equally predictable chore of the victorious insurgents was to remove any residual challenge to the revolution. Immediately after Waddell became mayor, the Secret Nine furnished him with a list of prominent Republicans, both white and black, who must be banished from Wilmington. The next morning at dawn, white Democrats began to congregate at the city jail and then to line the streets leading to the railroad station. As the whites jeered, soldiers with fixed bayonets, under the command of George L. Morton, walked six of the most prominent of the black Republicans who had not already fled town to the train station. There they were ordered never to return, loaded on a "northbound train and placed in a special car with a guard under orders to carry them beyond the limits of the state."[67]

At two o'clock that afternoon, the Democrats assembled a still larger crowd for the separate but equal banishment of the city's leading white Republicans. The mob dragged one of them, a former congressman and postmaster named G. Z. French, to a telephone pole on Front Street, where they threw a noose over his head and started to lynch him. Only the intervention of Stedman saved French from death. French fell on his knees but then hastily got up and ran toward the train, where he cringed on the floor beneath the seats of the coach. The train pulled away to a great cheer from the crowd; the coup d'état was complete and the Democrats were in complete control of the largest city in the state.

The black exodus was not limited to those who fled immediately or were banished by the victors. As a result of the terror and the unemployment that soon followed as whites took over jobs once held by African Americans, hundreds of black citizens packed their bags and left Wilmington. The black entrepreneurial and professional class departed the port city in droves. Blacks lost their local majority: in 1890 the black population was larger than the white population by 2,593, but by 1900 whites represented a small majority that was destined to grow steadily. Wilmington's black heyday had ended.[68]

If white working people had believed that putting an end to black political participation and crushing black economic power would lift them up, they were sorely disappointed. On the one hand, Mayor Waddell and his cronies quickly established white preference for municipal jobs (dismissing all of the black police officers, for example), and white labor representatives circulated among private employers, urging merchants, manufacturers, contractors, and railroads to substitute white workers for black. But on the other hand, much to the chagrin of white employees, city authorities also lowered municipal wages. If white men wanted black jobs, they would have to work for black wages. Jobs formerly considered black jobs soon became lily white; white men trucked the bales of cotton, operated the cotton compresses, and hoisted containers from the holds of ships that docked in Wilmington. White men in North Carolina's largest city proved willing to accept "nigger work" and "nigger wages," so long as black exclusion persisted as the quid pro quo. Business leaders like Hugh MacRae, Walter Parsley, and Thomas Clawson spoke regularly on behalf of white labor's right to exclude blacks, as well they might since it deflected attention from white workers' right to decent wages. The exclusion of black workers provided more jobs for whites but undermined the dignity and value of their labors.[69]

The political meaning of events was equally clear. Both locally and statewide, Democratic leaders envisioned a complete and permanent elimination of blacks from the political process. To ensure what Josephus Daniels called "permanent good government by the party of the White Man," they resolved to checkmate both the African American voters in the Black Belt and the white Republicans who allied themselves with blacks. The conspirators planted George Rountree in the state legislature expressly for that purpose. "The chief reason for my accepting the nomination in '98 to the legislature," Rountree wrote much later, "was to see if I could do something to prevent a re-occurence of the 1898 political upheaval by affecting a change in the suffrage law." When the next General Assembly convened, Rountree was selected to chair a special joint committee in charge of the disfranchisement amendment. "I, as chairman, did all the work," he claimed later.[70]

Since amendments to the United States Constitution clearly established African American voting rights, ways had to be found to circumvent the Constitution. In Mississippi, in 1890, state authorities contrived an "understanding clause" that provided the principal technique for blocking black ballots. The constitutions of South Carolina and Louisiana incorporated modifications of the scheme in 1898. North Carolina Democrats finally seized upon the infamous "grandfather clause," first devised in Louisiana, to disenfranchise black citizens of the Tar Heel State.

In the gubernatorial campaign of 1900, Charles Brantley Aycock and the Democratic machine made the suffrage amendment the major issue. They pulled out all the stock themes of "Negro domination" and built another statewide white supremacy campaign. Aycock used the violence that Democrats had orchestrated in Wilmington as an argument for giving the Democratic Party full sway over state politics; disenfranchisement, he argued, would prevent future bloodshed. Wilmington itself was rather quiet during the campaign. Though only two years earlier blacks had held a strong voting majority, the entire city tallied only two votes against the disenfranchisement of black North Carolinians.[71] White Democrats had "taken a city," to be sure, and across the state of North Carolina had drawn with the blood of the innocent the color line to which Du Bois consigned our century.

Notes

1. W. E. B. Du Bois, *The Souls of Black Folk* (New York: Fawcett, 1961), 23.

2. U.S. Bureau of the Census, *Eleventh Census of the United States*, 1890, 1:473. For an overview of Wilmington's history and social character prior to the racial massacre, see H. Leon Prather, *We Have Taken a City: Wilmington Racial Massacre and Coup of 1898* (Cranbury, N.J.: Associated University Presses, 1984), 17–31.

3. *Wilmington Business Directory*, 1897 (Richmond, Va.: Hill Directory Co., 1897), 11, 271.

4. Helen G. Edmonds, *The Negro and Fusion Politics in North Carolina, 1894–1901* (Chapel Hill: University of North Carolina Press, 1951), 89; John Campbell Dancy Collections, Private Papers and Correspondence, Andrew Carnegie Library, Livingstone College, Salisbury, N.C.; *Charlotte Star of Zion*, 10 November 1898.

5. *Wilmington Business Directory*, 1897, 261–77 passim.

6. Ibid., 274; Prather, *We Have Taken a City*, 24; Felice Sadgwar and Mabel Sadgwar, interview with the author, Wilmington, N.C., 6–8 April 1977.

7. *Wilmington Business Directory*, 1897, 11; June Nash, "The Cost of Violence," *Journal of Black Studies* 4 (December 1973): 159.

8. See Prather, *We Have Taken a City*, 30–34.

9. *Constitution of the State of North Carolina*, 1875–76, art. 7, sec. 14; Prather, *We Have Taken a City*, 34–35.

10. Prather, *We Have Taken a City*, 30–34.

11. Benjamin F. Keith, *Memories* (Raleigh: Bynum Printing Co., 1902), 79–82; Prather, *We Have Taken a City*, 36–48.

12. Harry Hayden Papers, 7, Special Collections Library, Duke University, Durham, N.C.

13. Ibid.

14. Josephus Daniels, *Editor in Politics* (Chapel Hill: University of North Carolina Press, 1936), 284; Prather, *We Have Taken a City*, 55.

15. Prather, *We Have Taken a City*, 55–56.

16. Fred Rippy, ed., *Furnifold Simmons, Statesman of the New South: Memoirs and Addresses* (Durham, N.C.: Duke University Press, 1936), 17–19; Prather, *We Have Taken a City*, 56.

17. *Raleigh News and Observer*, 4 August 1898; Prather, *We Have Taken a City*, 59.

18. George Rountree, "Memorandum of My Personal Recollection of the Election of 1898," 2, Henry G. Connor Papers, Southern Historical Collection, Wilson Library, University of North Carolina at Chapel Hill.

19. Keith, *Memories*, 99.

20. *Wilmington Messenger*, 8 October 1898.

21. H. Leon Prather, *Resurgent Politics and Educational Progressivism in the New South: North Carolina, 1890–1913* (Rutherford, N.J.: Fairleigh Dickinson University Press, 1979), 152–53; Thomas W. Clawson, "Exhibit A" copy of a controversial editorial in the *Wilmington Record*, 18 August, Clawson Papers, Louis T. Moore Collection, North Carolina Department of Archives and History, Raleigh; Prather, *We Have Taken a City*, 73–80.

22. *Wilmington Messenger*, 21, 23, 25, 27 August 1898.

23. Beth G. Crabtree, *North Carolina Governors, 1585–1974* (Raleigh: State Department of Archives and History, 1974), 82, 87; Samuel A. Ashe, Stephen B. Weeks, and Charles L. Van Noppen, eds., *Biographical History of North Carolina* (Greensboro, N.C.: C. L. Van Noppen, 1905–17), 6:354–55; William S. Powell, *The North Carolina Gazetteer* (Chapel Hill: University of North Carolina Press, 1968), 311.

24. *Wilmington Daily Record*, mutilated copies on microfilm, New York Public Library, New York, N.Y.; *Collier's Weekly*, 23 October 1898, 5.

25. Association of the Wilmington Light Infantry, Minutes, 14 December 1905, Personal Accounts of Members' Experiences in the Wilmington Riot, 1, North Carolina Collection, Wilson Library, University of North Carolina at Chapel Hill.

26. *Fayetteville Observer*, 22, 27 October 1898; *Raleigh News and Observer*, 22 October 1898.

27. *Raleigh News and Observer*, 22 October 1898.

28. *Fayetteville Observer*, 22, 27 October 1898; *Raleigh News and Observer*, 22 October 1898.

29. Alfred M. Waddell, *Some Memories of My Life* (Raleigh: Edwards & Broughton, 1908), 51.

30. *Wilmington Messenger*, 25 October 1898; *Wilmington Morning Post*, 25 October 1898.

31. *Raleigh News and Observer*, 29 October 1898.

32. *Asheville Daily Gazette*, 30 October 1898.

33. *Charlotte People's Paper*, 19 August, 9 September 1898.

34. Sprunt to Russell, 24 October 1898, Alexander Sprunt and Sons Papers, office files 6138–6410 (1898), Special Collections Library, Duke University, Durham, N.C.

35. Prather, *We Have Taken a City*, 94–95.

36. *Raleigh News and Observer*, 1 November 1898; *New York Herald*, 1 November 1898; Henry L. West, "The Race War in North Carolina," *Forum* 26 (January 1899): 580.

37. Rountree, "Memorandum," 4–5.

38. *Progressive Farmer*, 29 November 1898.

39. [Jane Murphy Cronly?], "An Account of the Race Riot in Wilmington, N.C., in 1898," 5, Cronly Family Papers, Special Collections Library, Duke University, Durham, N.C.

40. Anonymous letter, 9 November 1898, Hinsdale Family Papers, Special Collections Library, Duke University, Durham, N.C.

41. *Wilmington Messenger*, 10 November 1898.

42. *Appleton's Annual Cyclopaedia*, 1898, s.v. "Race Troubles and State Election."

43. Harry Hayden, *The Story of the Wilmington Rebellion* (Wilmington, N.C.: n.p., 1936), 10.

44. Hayden Papers, 15; Prather, *We Have Taken a City*, 108–10.

45. *Wilmington Messenger*, 19 November 1898; West, "Race War in North Carolina," 584.

46. *New York Herald*, 11 November 1898.

47. *Wilmington Messenger*, 11 November 1898.

48. Ibid.

49. Alfred M. Waddell, "The Story of the Wilmington, N.C., Race Riots," *Collier's Weekly*, 26 November 1898, 4; Prather, *We Have Taken a City*, 112–15.

50. *Wilmington Messenger*, 11 November 1898.

51. *Raleigh News and Observer*, 27 April 1900.

52. Wilmington Light Infantry, Personal Accounts, 8.

53. Thomas W. Clawson, "The Wilmington Race Riot of 1898," 8, Clawson Papers, Louis T. Moore Collection, North Carolina Department of Archives and History, Raleigh.

54. Charles Francis Bourke, "The Committee of Twenty-Five," *Collier's Weekly*, 26 November 1898, 16; Prather, *We Have Taken a City*, 122–25.

55. *Wilmington Messenger*, 11 November 1898.

56. Prather, *We Have Taken a City*, 126–27.

57. [Cronly?], "Account of the Race Riot," 2–3.

58. *Atlanta Constitution*, 11 November 1898.

59. *Wilmington Morning Star*, 11 November 1898; *New York Times*, 11, 12 November 1898; *New York Herald*, 20 November 1898; *Richmond Daily Times*, 11 November 1898; Waddell, *Some Memories of My Life*, 243; *Wilmington Messenger*, 11 November 1898.

60. Hayden Papers, 22.

61. Ibid.; Nash, "The Cost of Violence," 164–65.

62. *Wilmington Messenger*, 11 November 1898.

63. *Raleigh Caucasian*, 17 November 1898.

64. Ibid.

65. Bourke, "The Committee of Twenty-Five," 6.

66. *New York Herald*, 11 November 1898; *New York Times*, 11, 12 November 1898.

67. *New York Herald*, 12 November 1898.

68. Prather, *We Have Taken a City*, 136–47.

69. Ibid., 147–49.

70. George Rountree, "Memorandum of My Personal Reason for the Passage of the Suffrage Amendment to the Constitution (Grandfather Clause)," 1–2, Henry G. Connor Papers, Southern Historical Collection, Wilson Library, University of North Carolina at Chapel Hill.

71. See Prather, *We Have Taken a City*, 179–81.

David S.
Cecelski

Abraham H. Galloway

Wilmington's Lost Prophet and the Rise of
Black Radicalism in the American South

In the spring of 1863, a recruiting agent for the Union army walked the
streets of New Bern, North Carolina, looking for Abraham H. Galloway.
The seaport was usually a town of 5,500 inhabitants, but at that moment
it was overflowing with thousands of fugitive slaves who had escaped
from the Confederacy. The setting was one of excess in all things: hardship, disarray, fear, heartbreak, joy. Federal troops crowded into colonial
homes and antebellum manors. Downtown buildings lay in charred
ruins: retreating Confederates had burned some of them, and a Union
general torched the others after snipers shot at his sentries. The Confederates had fled so quickly that they left doors banging in the wind, family

portraits in front yards, a piano in the middle of a street. The murmur of sawmills could be heard across the Trent River, the sound of the former slaves building a new city. The days clattered noisily by, and even the stillness of evening was broken by short bursts of ecstasy: slave sisters reunited after a lifetime apart or a slave family that had survived a journey of 150 miles. No one breathed easy. New Bern was a sliver of sanctuary for African Americans in the slave South, and the Confederate army could have recaptured the city at any time.[1]

Edward W. Kinsley, the recruiting agent, had not come to New Bern with the intention of looking for Galloway. He had arrived there as an emissary of Governor John Albion Andrew of Massachusetts, an abolitionist leader seeking to recruit an African American regiment. Kinsley had expected the former slaves to throng into the army's ranks; instead, they avoided him nearly to a man. "Something was wrong," he realized, "and it did not take [me] long to find out the trouble." All pointed him to one individual, the man whom the slave refugees considered their leader. "Among the blacks," he learned, "was a man of more than ordinary ability, a coal black negro named Abraham Galloway."[2]

In 1863 Galloway was only twenty-six years old, a prodigy who had already lived three men's lives. Born into enslavement by the Cape Fear River, Galloway had grown up in Wilmington. He had become a fugitive slave, an abolitionist leader, a Union spy. He was tall, strong, and handsome, with long wavy hair and flashing eyes. He was not, as Kinsley remembered, "coal black," but light-skinned. He consented to see Kinsley but even after several meetings refused to help recruit former slaves into the Union army. Then, for unknown reasons, Galloway changed his mind. He sent a message to Kinsley to meet him at the home of a black leader named Mary Ann Starkey. When the New England abolitionist arrived that night at midnight, somebody blindfolded him and led him into an attic room. When the blindfold came off, as Kinsley later recounted, "he could see by the dim light of the candle that the room was nearly filled with blacks, and right in front of him stood Abraham Galloway and another huge negro, both armed with revolvers."[3]

That night the convocation of liberated slaves did not mince words. If the Union intended to make the war a crusade for black freedom, then Kinsley would find no shortage of recruits in New Bern. But if the Federal army planned to use black men like chattel and wage a war merely for the preservation of the Union, that was another story. Kinsley had to know that Galloway was serving the Union army—wild rumors of his exploits as a Union spy were whispered on every street corner—and must have wondered, was Galloway really willing to hurt the Union

David S.
Cecelski

cause by withholding black troops or was this merely a negotiating tactic to improve the lot of black soldiers and their families? Galloway and his lieutenants did not let Kinsley know, and we will probably never know either. Instead, they bluntly listed their demands: equal pay, provisions for black soldiers' families, schooling for soldiers' children, and assurances that the Union would force the Confederacy to treat captured blacks as prisoners of war rather than execute them as traitors.

Kinsley later described the next few moments as the most harrowing of his life. Galloway had not brought him to that dark attic to negotiate terms, but to guarantee them. Holding a revolver to Kinsley's head, he compelled the Union recruiter to swear a personal oath that the Federal army would meet these conditions. After Kinsley did so, the former slaves released him into the night air. "The next day," he remembered later, "the word went forth, and the blacks came to the recruiting station by [the] hundreds and a brigade was soon formed."[4] The more than 5,000 African Americans eventually recruited in New Bern, most of them former slaves, became the core of the 35th, 36th, and 37th Regiments, United States Colored Troops, known originally as the African Brigade.[5]

Rarely have we glimpsed what the tens of thousands of black Southerners who found asylum in Federal territory during the Civil War did with their new freedom. Instead, historians have tended to see the "freedpeople," or "contrabands" (as the Union army called blacks under Federal occupation), either as if through the eyes of so many New England missionaries, as downtrodden, helpless souls entirely reliant on white goodwill, or, just as misleadingly, as patriotic "good soldiers" blindly devoted to the Union cause and serving unquestionably under the terms and conditions that Union commanders offered them. This scene in New Bern hints at a different story: instead of docility, we see militancy; instead of unquestioning loyalty to the Union cause, we see former slaves attempting to shape the Union cause; instead of imbibing the politics of white abolitionists or Republicans, we see black Carolinians charting their own political course; instead of the contrabands looking to Northern blacks for political guidance, we glimpse a new politics emerging out of the struggle against slavery in the South.

For all of the story's broader implications about the former slaves and the Civil War, the center of its intrigue is Kinsley's portrayal of that "man of more than ordinary ability . . . named Abraham Galloway." The young black leader comes to mind particularly now, as we contemplate the various meanings of the Wilmington "race riot" a hundred years ago. Galloway spent most of his life in Wilmington, but he has been utterly forgotten there, as elsewhere. He became arguably the most important black leader in North Carolina during the Civil War and Reconstruction. Yet, except for brief entries in a few biographical dictionaries and short passages in broader scholarly works about Reconstruction, this mercurial figure has received little notice, having never been the subject of a book, a journal article, or a magazine feature.[6] The white supremacists of 1898 drew a veil of forgetfulness over the black militancy and political radicalism that Galloway embodied. They revised the history of the Civil War and Reconstruction into a fable of "Negro domination" and black sexual predation. In the history books they replaced black radicals such as Galloway with images of shiftless, deferential, and primitive blacks, so unable to recognize their own best interests that they needed white guidance at every step.[7] Galloway and the black insurgents who followed in his footsteps were purged from the Southern past, victims of the white supremacists of the post-Reconstruction generation no less than those who died in Wilmington in 1898. Galloway, son of Wilmington, personified a different path into the twentieth century, a democratic politics that was sown in slavery, grew into first light during the Civil War, and flowered in Reconstruction. Here, then, is the story of Abraham H. Galloway: slave, fugitive, abolitionist, Union spy, special agent, leader of the freedpeople, women's suffragist, state senator.

Galloway was born on 13 February 1837 in Smithville (later Southport), the seat of Brunswick County, North Carolina, twenty-five miles south of Wilmington at the mouth of the Cape Fear River.[8] His mother, Hester Hankins, was a slave born in 1820.[9] His father, John Wesley Galloway, the son of a Brunswick County planter, was white.[10] Relatively little is known about Abraham's mother: she was likely, but not certainly, owned by planter William Hankins of Town Creek, and she married Amos Galloway, one of John Wesley's slaves, in or about 1846.[11] As we will see later, she and her son remained close throughout his life. Not surprisingly, the life of Abraham's father is better documented. The Galloways included some of the wealthiest planters and merchants in Brunswick County, but John Wesley was only a small farmer, later a ship's pilot and, sometime after 1850, captain of the federal lightship off Frying Pan Shoals. He seems to have shared the aristocratic values of his wealthier cousins, but he never owned much property beyond four African Americans.[12] The circumstances of his relationship with Abraham's mother are altogether murky. We know only that Abraham later recalled that

John Wesley "recognized me as his son and protected me as far as he was allowed so to do."[13]

A well-off railroad mechanic in Wilmington named Marsden Milton Hankins owned Galloway from infancy.[14] How the mulatto child came into the Hankins household is not clear; Hankins may have owned Abraham's mother, or, if she was owned by John Wesley Galloway, Abraham may have been sold for discretion's sake when John Wesley first married in 1839. Galloway later recalled that Hankins "was a man of very good disposition who always said he would sell before he would use a whip." His wife Mary Ann evidently was not so even-tempered; Galloway remembered her as a "very mean woman" who "would whip contrary to his orders."[15] Trained as a brickmason, young Galloway was hiring out his own time before his twentieth birthday, a common practice for slave artisans in antebellum Wilmington. Hankins, a skilled laborer himself, could not supervise a slave closely. He left Galloway to seek out brickmasonry jobs when, where, and how he pleased so long as the slave continued to bring into the Hankins household a steady $15.00 a month.[16]

In 1857 Galloway escaped from Wilmington. He later explained that he fled the port city because he could no longer earn the $15.00 a month that Hankins required of him. This may seem a rather uncompelling motivation for such a risky undertaking, especially if we take his word that Hankins was not a malicious master. But if the failure to earn money might lead to Galloway's sale in the local slave market—a fate that could have marooned him on one of the rice fields or turpentine orchards of the Lower Cape Fear—then it makes sense. No matter his gentle nature, Hankins clearly saw Galloway primarily as a financial investment—and every investor sometimes has to cut his losses. At any rate, Galloway and a friend, a slave named Richard Eden, found a schooner captain willing to conceal them among the turpentine barrels in his cargo hold.[17]

An abolitionist underground of free and slave residents of Wilmington helped fugitive slaves to escape by ship throughout the 1850s.[18] The seaport's political leaders seemed to find solace in blaming free black sailors from ports outside of the South for such antislavery activity. "They are of course," wrote the *Wilmington Aurora*'s editor, "all of them, from the very nature of their position, abolitionists."[19] Local whites seemed reluctant to acknowledge subversive elements within the local slave community. Typically, when copies of David Walker's *Appeal to the Coloured Citizens of the World*—one of the primary documents in American antislavery thought—appeared in Wilmington in 1830, the town's leaders struck out brutally at black sailors, but they apparently did not consider the fact that Walker had been born and raised a free black in Wilmington. Though Walker had traveled extensively after leaving the South, his call for armed resistance to slavery had its roots in the intellectual culture of African Americans in the Cape Fear. Sustained by strong linkages to maritime black communities across the Western Hemisphere, this intellectual culture was grounded in the egalitarian ideals of the Enlightenment, an evangelical theology that stressed the "natural rights" of all peoples before God, and a particular brand of abolitionism born of African American slavery. Slave literacy had been outlawed in North Carolina in 1830, but this political vision was preserved among a predominately illiterate people in song, sermon, and saying, eventually, with David Walker and others, to make its way onto the page at first flush of formal learning.[20] Galloway left Wilmington, as Walker had, with a political vision far more defiantly egalitarian than that of most of the abolitionists he would meet north of the Mason-Dixon Line.

Galloway arrived in Philadelphia in June of 1857. Perhaps with the help of black sailors, he and Eden reached the Vigilance Committee of Philadelphia. They met with William Still, an African American coal merchant who was the committee's executive secretary, and they were soon forwarded to its contacts in Canada in order to evade the fugitive slave laws of the United States. On 20 July 1857, Eden wrote one of the committee's directors that he and Galloway had arrived in Kingston, Ontario, in "good health" and that Galloway had found employment, presumably as a brickmason, at $1.75 a day.[21] Over the next four years, Galloway immersed himself in the abolitionist movement and quite likely in aiding other African Americans to flee the South. As the nearest part of Canada for most fugitive slaves who fled the South, Ontario had a large African American community with a strong stake in the abolitionist cause. The black fugitives founded relief societies, newspapers, political groups, and even secret militias that supported the "Underground Railroad" in the United States and helped black refugees get established in Canada.[22] Galloway seems to have devoted himself to the abolitionist cause in a serious way. Several newspaper reports later indicated that he left Canada and gave antislavery speeches in the United States and was especially active in the abolitionist movement in Ohio, which, if true, he did at risk of being prosecuted under the Fugitive Slave Act of 1850.[23] During these years, Galloway also built extensive ties among the abolitionist leaders of Boston, though the exact character of his relationship with the Bird Club and other Boston antislavery groups remains uncertain.

Whatever else Galloway accomplished in the abolitionist movement or the Underground Railroad, he convinced George L. Stearns, the Boston industrialist who bankrolled John Brown's military raids in Kansas and sponsored the 54th Regiment, Massachusetts Volunteers (the black regiment featured in the 1989 movie *Glory*), that he would serve the Union army well as a spy. This is the single most compelling reason for believing that Galloway was involved in covert activities in the abolitionist movement. Stearns was a serious man who recruited thousands of black soldiers from Maine to Texas, and Galloway would have made a fine Union enlistee. By the outbreak of the Civil War, however, Stearns had seen something in Galloway that suggested a far more decisive role.[24]

Galloway returned south at the beginning of the Civil War. Stearns had brought the young mulatto to the attention of a Boston acquaintance, Colonel Edward A. Wild, who evidently introduced Galloway to General Benjamin F. Butler at Fortress Monroe, Virginia. Galloway was soon recruited into the Union's secret service under Butler. Working out of Fortress Monroe, Galloway undertook special missions in the coastal portions of Virginia and North Carolina that had been captured by Federal troops during General Ambrose E. Burnside's campaign of 1861–62.[25] We will probably never know more than a hint of what Galloway did in his capacity as an intelligence agent for the Union army. Mystery shrouds much of his life, and none more than his service under Butler.[26] He reportedly answered directly to Butler and was said to "possess the fullest confidence of the commanding General."[27] It is quite likely that Galloway returned to North Carolina even prior to the Federal occupation; a Union corporal stationed in the occupied seaport of Beaufort, North Carolina, later noted in his diary that Galloway was "in the detective service of Gen. Butler" and had scouted marine landings for Union troops, presumably during the Burnside campaign.[28] That is quite plausible. Union commanders depended heavily on local slaves to identify landing sites during the Burnside expedition. Somebody had to recruit the slave pilots or somehow elicit the necessary piloting knowledge from African American watermen. One report indicated that Galloway also investigated claims of Union sympathy among Confederate prisoners of war near Norfolk and recruited white Unionists into a military regiment.[29]

Galloway began working out of New Bern soon after its capture by Federal forces in March 1862. The colonial-era port became the headquarters of the Federal regiments in North Carolina and the Union blockading fleet. During the remainder of the war, the Union kept a precarious hold on the city, using it as a base for military raids into eastern North Carolina and for a nasty war with Confederate guerrillas. Thousands of runaway slaves poured into the city. One can only imagine the different ways that Galloway might have been, as a Northern journalist later wrote of him, "of some service to the Union army." The slaves who flocked to New Bern brought with them a wealth of information about the Confederacy that had to be culled. Guides for reconnaissance missions and raids into the state's interior had to be recruited, as did spies willing to move across Confederate lines on espionage and intelligence-gathering missions. Familiar with the terrain, Confederate defenses, and local slave communities, the former slaves were especially well situated to perform these challenging tasks. "Upwards of fifty volunteers of the best and most courageous," wrote Vincent Colyer, superintendent of Negro affairs in New Bern in 1862–63, "were kept constantly employed on the perilous but important duty of spies, scouts, and guides." Colyer reported that the black operatives "were invaluable and almost indispensable. They frequently went from thirty to three hundred miles within the enemy's lines; visiting his principal camps and most important posts, and bringing us back important and reliable information."[30] More than likely, Galloway was the chief intelligence agent working among the fugitive slaves in North Carolina. He worked closely with the Union commanding officers in New Bern, including Brigadier General Edward A. Wild (promoted from colonel in 1863), Brigadier General John J. Peck, and Major General John C. Foster.[31]

Whatever duties Galloway carried out as a spy for the Union army, they gave him a unique vantage point to organize among the great crowds of former slaves congregating behind Federal lines. As soon as New Bern had fallen in March 1862, the city was, in Burnside's words, "overrun with fugitives from the surrounding towns and plantations." Hundreds, then thousands, of African American men, women, and children fled from bondage in Confederate territory to freedom in New Bern. "It would be utterly impossible . . . to keep them outside of our lines," an overwrought Burnside reported to the secretary of war, "as they find their way to us through woods and swamps from every side."[32] Situated in New Bern, Galloway built strong contacts among the fugitives there as well as among the smaller, outlying contraband camps in

David S.
Cecelski

Beaufort, Plymouth, and Washington and on Roanoke Island. In these camps congregated the most ardent radicals, the most incorrigible troublemakers, the most militant artisans, the most defiant slave preachers—in short, the black Carolinians who had most ardently dared to defy or deceive slavery. Inevitably, these insurgents saw the nature of power in the slave South with the clarity characteristic of outlaws. They saw its inherent violence, its paternalist veneer, its pathological foundations in ideas of racial purity, sexual domination, and social hierarchy. They bore scars that they had acquired the hard way, as they negotiated plantation discipline and eluded slave patrols and the Home Guard. It was no accident that Galloway emerged as a leader among this self-selected assembly of liberated slaves. Many, including Galloway himself, moved back and forth between occupied and Confederate territory, venturing into the latter even as far as Wilmington, working as Union agents or searching for families and friends still in bondage. Out of New Bern's contraband camps, then, black men and women extended lifelines deep into Confederate territory, expanding and informing the radical political culture that was emerging in New Bern.

By the spring of 1863, Galloway had become more than a Union spy. He had become the most important political leader among the more than 10,000 former slaves who resided in the contraband camps and seaports occupied by the Federal army. The liberated slaves had erected their largest shanty towns along the outskirts of New Bern. Out of those roughhewn villages arose a great revival of African American political culture, a ferment comparable in ways to the black freedom movement that would come a century later. Unfettered by slavery, the black multitude exulted in the free expression of worship, family life, even music. Moreover, they looked to politics both as a weapon against their outlandishly racist treatment by the Union occupying forces and as a tool to shape their destiny after the Civil War.[33] They organized schools, relief societies, self-help associations, and churches, including St. Peter's, the first African Methodist Episcopal Zion church in the South.[34] These institutions became cornerstones of black political life.

Confronted by the dangers of Confederate guerrillas and the depredations of Union soldiers, they also organized a black militia. William H. Singleton, the only black veteran who wrote a memoir of the New Bern occupation, indicated that the refugees had been drilling on their own during the early spring of 1862, well before President Lincoln permitted African Americans to serve in the army. Singleton suggests, in fact, that this militia formed the heart of the black brigades recruited in

New Bern in the summer of 1863. If that is true, then on the night that Galloway negotiated the terms of black enlistment, he had a stronger hand than merely the revolver aimed at Edward Kinsley's head; he had a fighting force of at least several hundred black soldiers anxiously waiting to join the fray.[35] The fact that hundreds of black men showed up almost instantly at a word from their leader certainly suggests a high degree of existing organization. Galloway had also clearly begun to mark an independent political course that placed his first loyalty to the former slaves, not the Union army.

This was the milieu in which Galloway grew into political prominence. No matter how much his radical politics had been shaped by his own life in slavery, in the abolitionist movement, or as a Union spy, Galloway was home. He was of this society, knew its people, knew its horrors. He could scarcely help but play a leadership role in the black political movements emerging within New Bern, and he developed a close relationship to the black women organizing support for the slave refugees. He worked especially closely with Mary Ann Starkey, at whose home Edward Kinsley met Galloway that night. Starkey had turned her home into a meeting place for a small adult "reading school" and a Bible school class. She also led a black women's relief society that solicited funds and supplies among both the former slaves and Northern abolitionists for refugee families and, later, for black soldiers.[36]

Working with black groups like Mary Ann Starkey's relief society and William Singleton's militia, Galloway seems to have discovered a new maturity. Prior to this moment, the twenty-six-year-old had lived the kind of rebel's life that required talents for subterfuge: guile, restraint, dissemblance, patience, the ability to act boldly but carefully under pressure and in solitude. These gifts served Galloway well as a fugitive, an abolitionist, and a spy. Now Galloway developed a genius for politics. He became a grassroots organizer, a coalition builder, and an inspiring orator. As a secret agent and political leader, he seemed to pop up everywhere in Federal territory—and he struck quite a figure. He was already renowned for a severe sense of honor and a fearless readiness to defend it, a trait that could only have endeared him to former slaves, for whom honor had always been a white man's prerogative. Galloway may already have gotten into the habit that he developed later of always carrying a pistol where people could see it in his belt. Yet he could not have seemed reckless or foolhardy. For all his bravado, there was a disarming quiet about Galloway; patience, tact, and wariness had helped him to survive too many dangers not to be a part of him. Still, he laughed loud and often, and he must have had a sweet side, for everywhere the young man went black Carolinians crowded around him as if he were a prophet.[37]

The recruitment of North Carolina's former slaves into the Union army began in May of 1863. In the seaport of Beaufort, thirty-five miles east of New Bern, a Confederate sympathizer named Levi Pigott groused in his diary that "the black traitors are gathering in considerable numbers" to join the army. Pigott described the "horror, or the fiery indignation that burns in [the Rebels'] bosoms . . . when they think of their husbands and brothers and sons who may fall at the hands of the black savages."[38] Galloway did nothing to allay such Confederate hostility. Prior to President Lincoln's approval for former slaves to join the Union army, Galloway had made black military service the issue about which he was most outspoken. He not only recruited black soldiers when the time came, but he also articulated a political rationale for armed struggle that unnerved die-hard Rebels such as Pigott. At black political rallies held during the Federal occupation, Galloway argued that the former slaves would fight harder and better than white Union soldiers. At one point, he was quoted as saying that although McClellan "failed to take Richmond with 200,000 white soldiers, Butler would soon take it *with twenty thousand negroes*."[39]

More fervently, Galloway contended that the black regiments would compel a victorious Union to grant the former slaves both freedom and political equality—that is, the right to vote, serve on juries, and run for elected office, all issues around which no political consensus had yet been reached, even in the North. Galloway's linkage of military service and political equality reflected a growing accord among African American leaders. "Once let the black man get upon his person the brass letters U.S., let him get an eagle on his button and a musket on his shoulder and bullets in his pocket," Frederick Douglass had said, "and there is no power on earth which can deny that he has earned the right to citizenship in the United States."[40] Galloway shared Douglass's conviction. During a speech at a rally celebrating the first anniversary of the Emancipation Proclamation, Galloway told Beaufort's freed men and women, as Levi Pigott remembered it, "that their race would have not only their personal freedom, but political equality, and if this should be refused them at the ballot box[,] they would have it at the cartridge box!"[41]

With more than 50,000 blacks fighting in the Union army by the end of 1863, Galloway shifted his priorities toward the achievement of black political equality after the Civil War.[42] He was still seen frequently among the liberated slaves in North Carolina: he moved to Beaufort and married Martha Ann Dixon, the eighteen-year-old daughter of two former slaves, on 29 December 1863.[43] He was active with pro-Union political groups and local organizations that defended the rights of black soldiers in Beaufort and New Bern. He spoke frequently at the black churches that had become the heart of political education and community organizing in the contraband camps, as well as at the mass rallies held by the freedpeople on Independence Day and the anniversary of Emancipation Day. He assisted Union officers in recruiting black soldiers in Beaufort and New Bern, and probably over a much wider area.[44] Brigadier General Wild referred to him at this point not as a Union spy but as his "confidential recruiting agent," a term that suggests that Galloway was recruiting former slaves for special missions, presumably in Confederate territory. Galloway's contacts among slaves even in the most heavily fortified cities of the Confederacy were extensive by the fall of 1863. Their extent can be measured by his success that November, in Wild's words, at "manag[ing] to get his *mother* sent out of Wilmington, N.C." Wilmington was one of the most heavily guarded cities in the Confederacy, yet Galloway somehow arranged for his slave mother to escape to New Bern. Three Union generals—Wild, Peck, and Foster— felt so beholden to Galloway that they promised their former spy and "confidential recruiting agent" that they would play a part in getting his mother from New Bern to the home of one of Galloway's contacts in Boston. "I would like to do all I can for Galloway, who has served his country well," Wild wrote Edward Kinsley on 30 November 1863.[45]

The scope of Galloway's political leadership grew as he represented the liberated slave communities of North Carolina at the national level. In May of 1864, he was part of a five-man delegation of black leaders who met with President Lincoln to urge him to endorse suffrage for all African Americans. He also began to travel extensively to Boston and New York, where he met with abolitionist leaders about the political fate of former slaves after the war.[46] In addition, Galloway was one of 144 black leaders who answered the call to "the strong men of our people" and attended the National Convention of Colored Citizens of the United States, on 4 October 1864, in Syracuse, New York. Presided over by Frederick Douglass, the convention was the most important gathering of American black leaders during the Civil War. Skeptical of the commitment to racial equality in both the Democratic and Republican Parties, the convention delegates articulated a black political agenda that called for the abolition of slavery, the end of racial discrimination, and political equality.[47] They also founded the National Equal Rights

League and pledged themselves to organize state chapters to advocate political equality. Though his political organizing in the freedpeople's camps must have tailed off at the end of 1864—many of his most militant lieutenants were fighting with Grant in Virginia, and a yellow fever epidemic had swept New Bern and Beaufort—Galloway had organized a state chapter and five local chapters of the Equal Rights League in North Carolina by January 1865.[48]

New Bern and Beaufort remained the central points for black political organizing in North Carolina immediately after the Civil War. New Bern and its adjacent freedpeople's camp, James City, were especially important. The Federal forces had compelled the state's other contraband camps to disband and return the lands on which they were situated to their antebellum owners, but the former slaves in James City had refused to surrender their new homes. They and other black residents of the Federal occupation area had developed political, educational, and religious institutions that gave them a long head start in confronting postwar life. For all its hardships (or perhaps because of its hardships), the Federal occupation had been a very effective "rehearsal for Reconstruction," to borrow the title of Willie Lee Rose's landmark study of black freedpeople in South Carolina.[49] While former slaves elsewhere struggled to disentangle themselves from the web of slavery, fitfully trying out new rights and testing their new limits for the first time, the freedpeople whom Galloway had helped to politicize during the Federal occupation of the North Carolina coast moved steadfastly to make an impact on Reconstruction politics. Galloway remained in the thick of this political ferment, exhibiting, as one journalist said, an "exceedingly radical and Jacobinical spirit" that resonated deeply among African Americans.[50] When, in 1865, more than 2,000 former slaves celebrated the Fourth of July with a Beaufort parade organized by the Salmon P. Chase Equal Rights League, Galloway delivered the keynote address, calling for "all equal rights before the law, and nothing more."[51]

Not surprisingly, a few weeks later, on 28 August, Galloway emerged, as a correspondent for the *New York Times* put it, as the "leading spirit" of a mass meeting of New Bern's black citizens, organized to shape a political agenda for the postwar era. It was the first such gathering of former slaves held in the South. In a long keynote address, Galloway called for voting rights and public schooling. "We want to be an educated people and an intelligent people," he told the crowd. In a double-edged declaration that echoed his words of two years before, he also declared that "if the negro knows how to use the cartridge box, he knows how to use the ballot box."[52]

Beyond endorsing black suffrage, the mass meeting in New Bern addressed the white backlash against the freedpeople and the violent, undemocratic nature of the postwar society that had emerged during Presidential Reconstruction. The black New Bernians, led by Galloway, resolved "that the many atrocities committed upon our people in almost every section of our country . . . clearly demonstrate the immense prejudice and hatred on the part of our former owners toward us." They protested "the enforcement of the old code of slave laws that prohibits us from the privileges of schools, that deny us the right to control our families, that reject our testimony in courts of justice, that after keeping us at work without pay till their crops are laid by and then driving us off, [refuse] longer to give us food and shelter." In great detail, the delegates described white terrorism—"whipping, thumb-screwing and not infrequently murdering us in cold blood"—against blacks who challenged the antebellum racial code. "In our judgement," they concluded, with something more than a measure of understatement, North Carolina "comes far short of being a republican form of government and needs to be remodeled."[53]

The New Bern assembly appointed Galloway and two other men, John Randolph and George W. Price, to head the call for a statewide freedpeople's convention in Raleigh on 29 September. The organizers appealed to the state's black citizens soon thereafter with newspaper announcements under the banner: "Freedmen of North Carolina, Arouse!" The three New Bern leaders instructed black Carolinians to assemble in every township to "speak their views" and to organize district meetings where delegates would be nominated to the freedpeople's convention in Raleigh.[54] On the same day that Governor William Holden called to order a state constitutional convention dominated by the antebellum aristocracy, Galloway called to order 117 black delegates representing 42 counties at an African Methodist Episcopal church in Raleigh. Few dressed so finely as their white counterparts across town, some had passed the collection plate to obtain a railroad ticket, and many had slipped out of their hometowns quietly in order to avoid violence at the hands of local white conservatives.[55] While the white conservatives drafted the so-called Black Codes to bar African Americans from political life, the black delegates articulated a profoundly more democratic vision of Southern society. They demanded the full rights of citizenship, public schools, equal protection under the law, regulation of working hours, and the abolition of all laws "which make unjust discriminations on account of race or color."[56]

The black delegates represented a wide range of political views, from strident nationalists to fearful accommodationists, but the more radical delegates from New Bern, Beaufort, and Roanoke Island dominated the convention in large part because they had refined their political ideology and gained practical experience in political argument and strategy during the years of Federal occupation. Several black leaders from the Federal occupation shone with special brilliance in Raleigh. The Reverend James W. Hood, an AME Zion leader in New Bern, was elected chairman of the convocation, for instance. His moderate willingness to appeal to white goodwill and his cautious advice for the freedpeople to move slowly carried a great deal of influence. But none of the delegates made a deeper impression on the black participants or white observers than Galloway. "Perhaps the most remarkable person among the delegates," a Northern journalist, John Richard Dennett, observed, was "a light-yellow man whose features seemed to indicate that there was a cross of Indian blood in his veins." In Dennett's description of Galloway one can imagine why white conservatives found the former slave so unsettling and why he held so powerful an appeal for so many freedpeople. The ex-slaves had been born into a Southern society that upheld white supremacy and tried to deny the existence of interracial sex, that associated blackness with ugliness, that compelled black men to carry themselves with great deference, and punished any black who dared to challenge a white man's superior intelligence. Politically and personally, Galloway would have none of it. "His hair was long and black and very curly," Dennett wrote.

> He appeared to be vain of its beauty as he tossed it carelessly off his forehead, or suffered it to fall heavily and half conceal his eyes. These were twinkly and slippery, and nearly always half shut, for he laughed much, and then they partly closed of themselves, and at other times he had a way of watching from under his dropped lids. He was a well-shaped man, but it was hardly to be discovered as he lolled in his seat, or from the insufferably lazy manner of his walking. When he spoke, however, he stood erect, using forcible and graceful gestures. His voice was powerful, and, though an illiterate man, his speaking was effective.

We can hear Dennett trying to fit Galloway into an antebellum racial stereotype—"the insufferably lazy manner of his walking," his "slippery" eyes—but neither Galloway's force of will nor Dennett's grudging admiration allows him to do it. "His power of sarcasm and brutal invective," Dennett conceded, "and the personal influence given him by his fearlessness and audacity, always secured him a hearing."[57] Galloway's defiance of white authority alarmed more cautious black delegates, and the freedpeople's convention as a whole struck a more conciliatory posture when they presented their demands to the white convention. But few would forget Galloway or fail to tell stories about him when they returned to homes besieged by white terror. He may have frightened them, for they knew how white conservatives might react to such an insurgent, but he also gave voice to the vision of freedom born in bondage.

Galloway left New Bern for Wilmington late in 1866 or early in 1867. He may have moved to rejoin his mother—she probably returned to Wilmington soon after the Civil War (she was definitely there by 1870)—or he may have returned home because he recognized that Wilmington would again become the capital of African American political life in North Carolina.[58] Wilmington was the state's largest city and had a majority-black population; its large number of black artisans and maritime laborers formed the core of a politically militant class that would have attracted Galloway. By 3 January 1866, the North Carolina office of the Equal Rights League had also conspicuously opened in downtown Wilmington. Galloway's relocation to Wilmington and the opening of the Equal Rights League's office may not have been unrelated.[59]

Galloway tried to give his life a semblance of normalcy in Wilmington. He and his wife went about raising their two sons and attended St. Paul's Episcopal Church, while he joined the Masons. Reconstruction was not an ordinary time, however, and a quiet life was not his destiny. The Wilmington that Galloway returned to was in the throes of a violent conflict over the shape of postwar society. Nothing was guaranteed— certainly not the freedpeople's right to vote, to own land, to receive schooling, to earn decent wages, to enjoy the normal privileges of civil society, and to have equal protection under the law. These issues were all being worked out on the streets of towns like Wilmington just as surely as in the halls of the U.S. Congress. Every encounter between a black person and a white person was fraught with danger. "They perceive insolence in a tone, a glance, a gesture, or failure to yield enough by two or three inches in meeting on the sidewalk," a visitor noted of Wilmington's white citizens.[60] Cape Fear conservatives sought to re-establish their antebellum power at the same time that blacks sought to assert their new rights of freedom and citizenship. The talents for covert organizing and self-defense that Galloway had honed as a runaway slave, a fugitive abolitionist, and a Union spy would be put to good use in Reconstruction Wilmington.

By the beginning of 1866, conservatives had regained power in Wilmington, in large part due to Union military commanders who sympathized more with the Cape Fear aristocrats than with former slaves. "The true soldiers, whether they wore the gray or the blue are now united in their opposition . . . to negro government and negro equality," gloated a local newspaper, adding, "Blood is thicker than water."[61] Nightriders and white militias brutally beat, killed, and otherwise terrorized African Americans who dared to act like free citizens, and they strove to reimpose control over the freedpeople's lives—including control over whom they worked for, what wages they commanded, where they lived, and how they raised their children. The presence of black troops among the Federal occupying force in Wilmington had momentarily restrained conservative violence, but Union commanders showed a lack of resolve in supporting the black troops, even refusing to intervene when Confederate militia groups targeted them. Increasingly, the black troops realized that they were on their own in postwar Wilmington. They mutinied against their white officers in September 1865, and in February 1866 they laid siege to the city jail in order to halt the public whipping of black prisoners convicted in a trial in which the conservative judge had not allowed black testimony. After that, Union commanders withdrew all black troops from the Lower Cape Fear and replaced them with white soldiers.[62] White terror reigned throughout the Cape Fear. "The fact is," a freedman reported, "it's the first notion with a great many of these people, [that] if a Negro says anything or does anything that they don't like, [they] take a gun and put a bullet into him."[63] Not far from Wilmington, in Duplin County, a police captain named J. N. Stallings gave orders to shoot without trial blacks who had been accused of minor theft.[64]

With passage of the Reconstruction Acts by the Radical Congress of 1867, Wilmington blacks gained a crucial new political opportunity. The Reconstruction Acts restored federal military authority in the South and required states in the former Confederacy to pass a constitution that guaranteed universal male suffrage before they could be readmitted to the Union. The acts also opened the polls to black voters while banning from political life any antebellum officeholder who had taken an oath to uphold the U.S. Constitution but sided with the Confederacy. Galloway was soon looking toward the constitutional convention that would occur in Raleigh early in 1868. On 4 September 1867, he addressed a mass meeting of the state's Republican Party at Tucker Hall in Raleigh, delivering a conciliatory address aimed at building broad, biracial support for the Republicans. He exhorted his audience to "go everywhere there is a black man or a poor white man and tell him the true condition of the Republican Party."[65] Later that month, "after loud calls for 'Galloway,'" he addressed a torchlit procession of black citizens from the top of Wilmington's market house. "My people stand here tonight fettered, bound hand [and] foot by a Constitution that recognizes them as chattel," Galloway exclaimed.[66] That fall he was elected one of thirteen delegates from seven Cape Fear counties to serve at the constitutional convention.

Galloway was, in the words of historian W. McKee Evans, one of "a small group of active delegates who largely dominated the life of the convention."[67] During the constitutional convention, which ran from January to March of 1868, Galloway served on the judiciary committee, and alongside white reformer Albion Tourgée on the committee for local government. As one of only 13 blacks among the 120 persons elected to the constitutional convention, however, he felt a special responsibility to represent the political concerns of the state's African American population. At one point, on 20 February, Galloway explained his support for the popular election of the judiciary by saying, in a reporter's paraphrase, that "the Judiciary in New Hanover was a bastard, born in sin and secession." "In their eyes, it was a crime to be a black or a loyal man," he continued, and he denounced conservative judges who had allegedly imprisoned blacks solely to keep them from voting.[68] At another point, Galloway vehemently opposed public support of a railroad that, in his words, "did not employ a single colored man," and he also refused to support a YMCA request to use the convention hall unless "no distinction be made between the races."[69]

Galloway routinely endured arguments about black inferiority from conservative delegates and their newspaper editors, as he would later in the state senate. Every day that he spent in Raleigh, he heard comments such as the Sentinel's, that true North Carolinians would blush "that a set of apes and hybrids should be holding a brutal carnival in her halls of legislation."[70] Much to their dismay, conservative delegates discovered that such remarks inspired Galloway's most cutting rhetoric. Following one harangue on the unfitness of blacks for suffrage, Galloway responded by saying "that the best blood in Brunswick County flowed in [my] veins," a reference to his own mixed-race heritage, "and if [I] could do it, in justice to the African race, [I] would lance [my]self and let it out."[71] Despite the rancor, conservatives were a small minority at the constitutional convention. On 16 March 1868, the delegates signed a new state constitution that introduced universal male suffrage, removed all religious and property qualifications for officeholding, endorsed the popular election of county officials, increased public school support, and made the state's penal code more humane.[72]

When he returned to Wilmington, Galloway discovered that the conservatives had launched a vicious campaign to intimidate black voters from ratifying the new constitution or electing Radical leaders in the upcoming April election. Galloway himself was running for the state senate, in the first election in which blacks were eligible to hold state office. Under the leadership of Colonel Roger Moore, one of the Cape Fear's most celebrated aristocrats, the Ku Klux Klan attempted to frighten blacks away from the polls. Klan terrorism prevailed in other parts of North Carolina but collided with a stubborn militancy among African Americans in Wilmington. Black men patrolled the city's streets, firing their guns in the air and wielding fence rails to intimidate Klansmen. Shots and scuffles shattered the evening quiet on the downtown streets repeatedly on the nights between 18 and 21 April in 1868, and while exactly what happened in the darkness is unknown, after that the Ku Klux Klan was never a force in Wilmington during Reconstruction.[73] Even without documentary proof, one feels confidant that Galloway was not sitting quietly at home with his family. In the spring 1868 election the Republicans carried two-thirds of the electorate in New Hanover County, and voters chose Galloway to represent New Hanover and Brunswick Counties in the state senate. That fall, he was also voted the first black elector to a presidential convention in North Carolina history.[74]

Galloway realized that armed self-defense was crucial to political survival in Wilmington. Conservative leaders held him in contempt, Democratic editors parodied him mercilessly, and the threat of assassination followed his every step. Wherever he went in the port city, Galloway conspicuously wore a pistol in his belt, a noteworthy symbol of defiance only two years after Wilmington conservatives had organized house searches to disarm the black population. The rise of the Republican Party helped to back up Galloway's lone firearm. Later in 1868, a local militia, one of several organized by Wilmington blacks to defend themselves against white terrorists, elected Galloway their commander. Led most commonly by Union veterans, the black militias—like their ubiquitous white counterparts—supposedly existed to fight off foreign invasion or to quell insurrections, but they acted during Reconstruction as a military wing of the Republican Party.[75] Nobody understood better than former slaves and Union veterans that a constitution was only as

61

Abraham H.
Galloway

strong as the military power available to defend it. The Klan would rage out of control in the Carolina Piedmont from 1868 to 1870 but remained prudently quiet in Wilmington.[76]

Galloway was one of three black senators, joined by seventeen black representatives, in the North Carolina General Assembly of 1868. He was only thirty-one years old, poor, and still could not read or write.[77] He was, however, an extraordinary orator and an influential legislator. He was an intelligent, ferocious debater, the kind of man whose biting sense of humor and sharp eye for hypocrisy inspired most of the senate conservatives to steer away from a direct argument with him. Few of his fellow senators had ever been compelled to confront a black man as an equal, much less a black man as fearless and battle-tested as Galloway. The *Wilmington Daily Journal*, a Democratic newspaper that was apparently still squeamish about Galloway's mixed-race parentage, once referred to him as "the pugilistic 'Indian Senator.' "[78] On one occasion, after a white senator from Craven County had insulted him in the midst of a floor debate over the racial makeup of New Bern's city council, Galloway declared "that he would hold the Senator from Craven responsible for his language, outside of this Hall; and . . . that, if hereafter, the Senator from Craven insulted him, he would prove to him the blood of a true Southron."[79] That was by no means the only incident in which Galloway reminded conservative Democrats that he was at least as aristocratic by birth as them. He not only claimed to be "a true Southron," but he also brazenly touted his parentage by a black woman and a white man.[80] No senate floor debate could examine the "color line" or anti-black laws without Galloway taunting his Democratic colleagues for their hypocrisy in language that reminded them that they were ultimately talking about family. Repeatedly, when a conservative called black men sexual predators posing threats to "white womanhood," Galloway reminded the senators how commonly white men pursued black women—and, knowing Galloway, he was probably well enough acquainted with the conservative Democrats' private lives to make more than a few of them nervous with a wink or a whisper. No wonder Galloway attracted venomous editorials in Democratic newspapers. The *Wilmington Journal* referred to Galloway's flaunting of his "bastardy" as "disgusting vulgarity [that is] a disgrace to any civilized community." Another time, the *Daily Journal*'s editors could barely bring themselves to acknowledge Galloway's having mentioned his parentage and interracial sex, referring obliquely to "some indelicate remarks [by Galloway] in regard to . . . white men mingling with negroes which we omit for the sake of decency."[81]

The codifying of a new color line occupied the senate repeatedly during Galloway's first term. This was true even with respect to the conduct of the General Assembly itself. On 8 July 1868, as a typical example, Galloway successfully amended a proposal to segregate the senate galleries by race to allow for a middle section that could be occupied voluntarily by blacks and whites.[82] Such a racial "middle ground" would become unthinkable after the Wilmington massacre of 1898, but for a generation black activists such as Galloway drew a more fluid boundary between black and white North Carolinians. It required constant diligence, however, as can be seen from a floor debate over racial segregation in public schools on 26 February 1869. When a Senator Love introduced an amendment requiring that no black teacher be employed in a school that had white students, a Senator Hayes, with Galloway's support, moved to amend Love's amendment to say, "or employ white teachers to serve in any school wherein colored children are to be instructed." This second amendment unnerved conservatives, who feared the political implications of black control over black schooling. To make the point stronger, Galloway moved next to amend Love and Hayes's amendment, facetiously adding a provision "that no white Democrat should teach any colored girl." Ruled out of order, Galloway had won the day if not the war. The full senate rejected Love's amendment and later created a state board of education and the first statewide system of public schooling. Yet not even white Republicans supported the call by Galloway and his fellow black legislators for racially integrated public schools or for equal funding of black schools.[83]

Much of Galloway's brief senate career addressed the most fundamental rights of the freed men and women. He voted for the Fourteenth and Fifteenth Amendments to the U.S. Constitution, introduced a successful bill to help former slaves hold onto land and homes given them while in bondage, and supported several measures to curtail the Ku Klux Klan, including a bill to create a state militia to combat white terrorism. Galloway strongly supported Governor Holden's ill-fated attempts to crack down on the Ku Klux Klan in the Piedmont, where by mid-1870 at least 260 KKK terrorist acts had been documented. He also pushed to guarantee that blacks serve on juries, a right granted by the 1868 constitution, but one that Galloway contended was often ignored by county commissioners.[84]

More than any other elected leader in North Carolina, Galloway also fought for women's rights. The rights of women had become an important political issue in the Reconstruction South, with Radicals and suffragists briefly finding common cause in an advocacy of universal suffrage. Black Southerners supported women's suffrage far more strongly than whites, perhaps a sign of the relatively higher status that black women had held in slave families and of a more collective sensibility toward voting among the ex-slaves.[85] Twice Galloway introduced bills to amend the state's constitution to allow women's suffrage, once in 1868 and again in 1869. Outraged by an 1868 state supreme court ruling that men had a right to beat their wives, he sought unsuccessfully to force the senate judiciary committee to report a bill against domestic violence. He also supported a bill that gave women a greater right to sign deeds, and another to protect married women from willful abandonment or neglect by their husbands.[86] Women's suffrage and many of the other pioneering women's rights measures advocated by Galloway would not become law in North Carolina for half a century.

With respect to his support for women's suffrage, as for most issues for which he fought, we should resist the temptation to see Galloway as ahead of his time. The fiery young activist had emerged out of a politically vibrant slave culture deeply committed to egalitarian democracy and communitarian values in the Cape Fear. His years as a fugitive slave, Northern abolitionist, and Union spy had strengthened his commitment to the African American men and women among whom he had grown up. He had also been deeply influenced by his experience in the freedpeople's camps of North Carolina. Galloway embodied the black radicalism that emerged in the Cape Fear during Reconstruction, but he did not invent it; this tradition grew from a collective experience. To his credit, he found within himself the strength of spirit and the raw courage to carry that collective vision of racial justice and political equality out into a world that was not ready for it.

Galloway died unexpectedly of fever and jaundice on 1 September 1870 at his mother's home in Wilmington.[87] He was only thirty-three years old. He had just been reelected to the state senate, still held together a fragile biracial coalition in the local Republican Party, and had recently survived an assassination attempt.[88] He died on the cusp of a conservative resurgence that would prevail across North Carolina between 1870 and 1877. Racial violence, official corruption, and the Republican Party's own internal divisions paved the way for the Democratic triumph. Compared to the rest of North Carolina, however, Wilmington remained a stronghold of African American political power and working-class militancy. W. McKee Evans has argued, in fact, that the unique ability of Wilmington Republicans to maintain significant numbers of black policemen and militia units preserved the relative peace of Cape Fear society from 1868 to 1877. At one point, in 1875, the *Wilmington Journal* even alleged that "there are now nearly, or quite as many negro [militia] companies in this city, as there are white companies throughout the limits of North Carolina."[89] This was an exaggeration, but it does suggest that Wilmington blacks continued to embrace the political militancy personified by Galloway long after his death.

Though he died a pauper, an estimated 6,000 mourners gathered at Galloway's funeral on 3 September 1870. They came from every Wilmington neighborhood and from the countryside for many miles around. The funeral procession stretched half a mile through a downtown Wilmington draped with American flags at half-mast. The Masons in their finery, the black firemen's brigades, the political and fraternal societies, a hundred carriages, and throngs of people on horseback and on foot marched down Market Street to St. Paul's Episcopal Church. The multitude could not fit into the church and crowded the streets nearby. One newspaper called it the largest funeral in the state's history.[90] As the vast mass of black men, women, and children accompanied Galloway's coffin to the cemetery, they could not possibly have imagined that his life would so quickly seem like a half-forgotten dream. Indeed, Galloway's story is a familiar saga, and one that cuts across the ages. It is the oft-told story of the rebel hero who lives a life so deeply unreconciled to tyranny that it inspires even the most downtrodden and despised to suspect, at least for a brief instant, that freedom and justice may not be just a dream. That we have forgotten him says as much about our day as his.

65

Abraham H. Galloway

Notes

I would like to express my deepest gratitude to the following individuals for their help in researching and writing this essay: Tim Tyson, Paige Raibmon, George Stevenson, Richard Reid, Margaret Rogers, Beverly Tetterton, John David Smith, John Haley, Glenda Gilmore, Peter Wood, Laura Edwards, Kelly Navies, Stephen Kantrowitz, Jeffrey Crow, Rev. Vernon Tyson, William Harris, Laura Hanson, and Raymond Gavins.

1. The broad picture that I have drawn of occupied New Bern and the specific incidents that I have mentioned are derived from a variety of primary and secondary sources. See John Barrett, *The Civil War in North Carolina* (Chapel Hill: University of North Carolina Press, 1963), 93–113; Joe A. Mobley, *James City: A Black Community in North Carolina, 1863–1900* (Raleigh: North Carolina Department of Cul-

tural Resources, Division of Archives and History, 1981), 1–25; and David Cecelski, "A Thousand Aspirations," *Southern Exposure* 18, no. 1 (Spring 1990): 22–25. Among the most interesting of the many published reminiscences and diaries written by Union soldiers in New Bern, see W. P. Derby, *Bearing Arms in the Twenty-seventh Massachusetts Regiment of Volunteer Infantry during the Civil War, 1861–1865* (Boston: Wright & Potter, 1883), esp. 94–95; James A. Emmerton, *A Record of the Twenty-third Regiment Mass. Vol. Infantry in the War of the Rebellion, 1861–1865 . . .* (Boston: William Ware & Co., 1886); "Corporal" [Z. T. Haines], *Letters from the Forty-fourth Regiment M.V.M.: A Record of the Experience of a Nine Months Regiment in the Department of North Carolina in 1862–3* (Boston: Herald Job Office, 1863); Vincent Colyer, *Report of the Services Rendered by the Freed People to the United States Army, in North Carolina, in the Spring of 1862, After the Battle of New Bern* (New York: Vincent Colyer, 1864); J. Waldo Denny, *Wearing the Blue in the 25th Mass. Volunteer Infantry* (Worcester, Mass.: Putnam & Davis, 1879); Thomas Kirwan, *Soldiering in North Carolina* (Boston: n.p., 1864); John J. Wyeth, *Leaves from a Diary, Written While Serving in Co. #44 Mass. From September, 1862, to June, 1863* (Boston: L. F. Lawrence & Co., 1878); J. Madison Drake, *The History of the Ninth New Jersey Veteran Vols.* (Elizabeth, N.J.: Journal Printing House, 1889); Herbert E. Valentine, *Story of Co. F, 23d Massachusetts Volunteers in the War for the Union, 1861–1865* (Boston: W. B. Clarke & Co., 1896); D. L. Day, *My Diary of Rambles with the 25 Mass. Volunteer Infantry, with Burnside's Coast Division: 18th Army Corp and Army of the James* (Milford, Mass.: King and Billings, 1884); and Albert W. Mann, *History of the Forty-fifth Regiment Massachusetts Volunteer Militia* (Jamaica Plain, Mass.: 1908.)

2. Mann, *History of the Forty-fifth Regiment,* 446–49.

3. Ibid.

4. Ibid., 301–2, 446–49. Kinsley later related this story to a reunion of the 45th Regiment, Massachusetts Volunteer Infantry, which had been stationed in New Bern in 1863. The essential parts of Kinsley's story—including his role in the recruitment of African American soldiers in New Bern, his acquaintance with Galloway and Starkey, Galloway's involvement in Union recruitment despite his devotion to independent black organizing, and Starkey and Galloway's having worked together—are confirmed in a series of letters among Kinsley, Brigadier General Edward A. Wild, and Mary Ann Starkey in the Edward W. Kinsley Papers, 1862–89, Special Collections Library, Duke University, Durham, N.C. (hereafter, DU).

5. For an excellent overview of the recruitment of the African Brigade in New Bern, and for references to more general works on the recruitment of black soldiers into the Union army, see Richard Reid, "Raising the African Brigade: Early Black Recruitment in Civil War North Carolina," *North Carolina Historical Review* 70, no. 3 (July 1993): 266–97.

6. The few published works that discuss Galloway refer mainly to his political life during Reconstruction. See W. McKee Evans, *Ballots and Fence Rails: Reconstruction on the Lower Cape Fear* (Chapel Hill: University of North Carolina Press, 1966), 87–91; Leonard Bernstein, "The Participation of Negro Delegates in the Constitutional Convention of 1868 in North Carolina," *Journal of Negro History* 34, no. 4 (October 1949); Elizabeth Balanoff, "Negro Legislators in the North Carolina General Assembly, July, 1868–February, 1872," *North Carolina Historical Review* 49, no. 1 (January 1972): 23–24, 27; William S. Powell, ed., *Dictionary of North Carolina Biography* (Chapel Hill: University of North Carolina Press, 1979–96), 2:271–72;

and Eric Foner, *Freedom's Lawmakers: A Directory of Black Officeholders during Reconstruction* (New York: Oxford University Press, 1993), 81–82.

7. For background on this literature of the "Age of Reaction" in North Carolina, see David S. Cecelski, "Oldest Living Confederate Chaplain Tells All? Or, James B. Avirett and the Rise and Fall of the Rich Lands," *Southern Cultures* 3, no. 4 (Winter 1997/98), 5–24.

8. *New National Era*, 4 September 1870.

9. Martha A. Little deposition, 22 September 1927, Celie Galloway Pension Application File (1927), U.S. Department of the Interior: Bureau of Pensions, Veterans Administration Hospital, Winston-Salem, North Carolina (hereafter, VA); 15 October 1866 entry, New Hanover County: Record of Cohabitation, 1866–68, North Carolina State Archives, Raleigh (hereafter, NCSA); Ninth Federal Census: New Hanover County, North Carolina, Population Schedule, 1870, National Archives, Washington, D.C (hereafter, NA). In 1927 Celie Galloway, the widow of another Abraham (or Abram) Galloway, also of Brunswick County, applied for veterans benefits based on her husband's military service in the Union army. To establish that her husband was not the better-known Abraham H. Galloway, the subject of this essay, her attorney visited Beaufort, North Carolina, to take depositions from the surviving family of Abraham H. Galloway in order to ascertain details about his personal appearance, military career, and death that would distinguish the two men and justify the widow's claims for pension benefits. The attorney interviewed Abraham H. Galloway's widow, Martha Ann Little, who still lived in her native Beaufort; she had remarried in 1887.

10. William Still, *The Underground Railroad: A Record of Facts, Authentic Narratives, Letters, etc., Narrating the Hardships, Hair-Breadth Escapes, and Death Struggles of the Slaves in their Efforts for Freedom* (Philadelphia: Porter & Coates, 1872), 150–52; Petition of Lewis A. Galloway for Division of Negroes (March 1837), Lewis A. Galloway Estate Record, Brunswick County Estate Records, NCSA; Lewis Galloway Will (1826), Brunswick County Wills, 1765–1912, NCSA.

11. William Hankins is the only member of the Hankins family in Brunswick County or New Hanover County who owned slaves in 1850. In that year, he owned twenty-four slaves, including two female slaves of Hester's age. The 1850 census does not list slaves by name, only by age and gender. Seventh Federal Census: Brunswick County, North Carolina, Population and Slave Schedules, 1850, and New Hanover County, Population and Slave Schedules, 1850, NA.

Amos Galloway belonged to Lewis Galloway at the time of his death in 1826 and was apportioned to his son John Wesley legally by 1837 and in practice some time before that date. Amos and Hester Hankins considered themselves married as of April 1846, though it is doubtful that they shared a household at that time. They were living together in Wilmington as of the 1870 federal census. See Petition of Lewis A. Galloway for Division of Negroes (March 1837), Lewis Galloway Estate Record, Brunswick County Estate Records, NCSA; 15 October 1866 entry, New Hanover County Record of Cohabitation, 1866–68, NCSA; Ninth Federal Census: New Hanover County, North Carolina, Population Schedule, 1870, NA.

12. Sixth, Seventh, and Eighth Federal Censuses: Brunswick County, North Carolina, Population and Slave Schedules for 1840, 1850, and 1860, NA; Seventh and Eighth Federal Censuses: New Hanover County, North Carolina, Population and Slave Schedules for 1850 and 1860, NA; John W. Galloway (1864), Brunswick County Estate Records, NCSA; John W. Galloway died at the age of fifty-three of

yellow fever, evidently while serving in the Confederate coast guard in Bermuda on 27 September 1864. See *Wilmington Daily Journal*, 15 October 1864. Cited in Helen Moore Sammons, *Marriage and Death Notices from Wilmington, North Carolina Newspapers, 1860–1865* (Wilmington, N.C.: North Carolina Room, New Hanover County Public Library, 1987), 76.

13. Quoted in Still, *Underground Railroad*, 150–52.

14. William Still indicates that a Milton Hawkins owned Galloway, but the deposition of Galloway's wife and the listings of a locomotive mechanic named Milton Hankins in the 1860 and 1870 federal censuses confirm his owner as Milton Hankins. The mistake was presumably a typographical error. See Martha A. Little deposition, Celie Galloway pension file, VA; Still, *Underground Railroad*, 150–52; Eighth and Ninth Federal Censuses: New Hanover County, North Carolina, Population Schedules for 1860 and 1870.

15. Still, *Underground Railroad*, 150–52; Fugitive Slave Ledger, William Still Papers, Historical Society of Philadelphia, Philadelphia, Pa.; *Wilmington Daily Journal*, 20 July 1869.

16. Still *Underground Railroad*, 150–52. For background on slave life in antebellum Wilmington, see esp. Peter P. Hinks, *To Awaken My Afflicted Brethren: David Walker and the Problem of Antebellum Slave Resistance* (University Park, Pa.: Pennsylvania State University Press, 1997), 1–21; David S. Cecelski, "The Shores of Freedom: The Maritime Underground Railroad in North Carolina, 1800–1861," *North Carolina Historical Review* 71, no. 2 (April 1994): 174–206; Alan D. Watson, *Wilmington: Port of North Carolina* (Columbia, S.C.: University of South Carolina Press, 1992), 46–52; and James Howard Brewer, "Legislation Designed to Control Slavery in Wilmington and Fayetteville," *North Carolina Historical Review* 30, no. 2 (April 1953): 155–66. There are also two indispensable autobiographies written by former slaves who grew up in Wilmington. See Rev. William H. Robinson, *From Log Cabin to the Pulpit; or, Fifteen Years in Slavery*, 3rd ed. (Eau Claire, Wis.: James H. Tifft, 1913), and Thomas H. Jones, *The Experience of Thomas H. Jones, Who Was A Slave for Forty-Three Years* (Boston: Bazin & Chandler, 1862).

17. Still, *Underground Railroad*, 150–52.

18. For a detailed examination of slave runaways and maritime culture in antebellum Wilmington, see Cecelski, "The Shores of Freedom," 174–206.

19. Guion Griffis Johnson, *Ante-Bellum North Carolina: A Social History* (Chapel Hill: University of North Carolina Press, 1937), 577–78.

20. Hinks, *To Awaken My Afflicted Brethren*, 1–21, 173–236; Julius S. Scott, "The Common Wind: Currents of Afro-American Communication in the Era of the Haitian Revolution" (Ph.D. diss., Duke University, 1986); W. Jeffrey Bolster, *Black Jacks: African American Seamen in the Age of Sail* (Cambridge: Harvard University Press, 1997), esp. 190–214; David Walker, *Appeal to the Coloured Citizens of the World, But in Particular, and Very Expressly, to Those of the United States of America*, rev. ed. with intro. by Sean Wilentz (New York: Hill & Wang, 1995).

21. Still, *Underground Railroad*, 151–52.

22. David G. Hill, *The Freedom-Seekers: Blacks in Early Canada* (Agincourt: Book Society of Canada Ltd., 1981), 24–61; Ken Alexander and Aris Glaze, *Towards Freedom: The African-Canadian Experience* (Toronto: Umbrella Press, 1996), 51.

23. The abolitionist movement in Ohio seems a likely field for Galloway's labors. Secret, militant black abolitionist groups with strong ties to Canada operated out of Ohio throughout the 1850s, among them a military group known as the Liberators that had close ties to John Brown. There is some evidence that these clandestine

groups served the Union army in an intelligence capacity in the early stages of the Civil War, which, if true, makes it an enticing possibility that it was from one of these groups that Galloway was recruited into the spy service. See Richard Hinton, *John Brown and His Men* (New York: Funk & Wagnalls, 1894), 171–75, and William Cheek and Aimee Cheek, *John Mercer Langston and the Fight for Black Freedom, 1829–65* (Urbana: University of Illinois Press, 1989), 350–52.

24. Wild to Kinsley, 30 November 1863, Edward W. Kinsley Papers, DU; *National Cyclopaedia of American Biography* (New York: James T. White & Co., 1898), 8:231; Frank P. Stearns, *The Life and Times of George Luther Stearns* (Philadelphia: J. B. Lippincott Co., 1907), esp. 276–320; Charles E. Heller, *Portrait of an Abolitionist: A Biography of George Luther Stearns, 1809–1867* (Westport, Conn.: Greenwood Press, 1996), 123–59.

25. Wild to Kinsley, 30 November 1863, Edward W. Kinsley Papers, DU; *New National Era*, 4 September 1870.

26. Union military records occasionally refer to spying activities, but no official records have yet been found that discuss Galloway's duties as an intelligence agent. The following National Archives records have been consulted for mention of Galloway without success: RG 110, Scouts, Guides, Spies, and Detectives; Secret Service Accounts; RG 109, Union Provost Marshal's Files of Papers Relating to Citizens or Business Firms (M345); RG 92, index to scouts in Reports of Persons and Articles Hired and the index to Quartermaster Claims; RG 59, Letters of Application and Recommendation During the Administrations of Abraham Lincoln and Andrew Johnson; RG 94, indexes to Letters Received by the Adjutant General's Office, 1861–65 (M725); and General Information Index.

27. *Raleigh Weekly Standard*, 7 September 1870.

28. Edmund Cleveland diary, 24 November 1864, Southern Historical Collection, University of North Carolina Library, Chapel Hill.

29. *New National Era*, 22 September 1870.

30. Colyer, *Report of the Services Rendered by the Freed People*, 9–10. Colyer describes a number of intelligence missions conducted by former slaves in Confederate territory. See pp. 10–22.

31. Wild to Kinsley, 30 November 1863, Edward W. Kinsley Papers, DU.

32. Gen. Ambrose E. Burnside to Hon. E. M. Stanton, Secretary of War, 21 March 1862, U.S. War Department, *The War of the Rebellion: A Compilation of the Official Records of the Union and Confederate Armies* (Washington, D.C.: Government Printing Office, 1880–1901), ser. 1, vol. 9, 199–200.

33. The racist conduct of the Union army is one of the strongest themes in both the private papers and published works by Federal soldiers stationed in North Carolina during the Civil War. See, among many others, Arthur M. Schlesinger, ed., "Letter of a Blue Bluejacket," *New England Quarterly* I, no. 4 (October 1928), 562, 565; Emmerton, *A Record of the Twenty-Third Regiment, Mass. Vol. Infantry*, 135–36; Levi W. Pigott diary, 15 August 1863, 17 August 1864, Levi W. Pigott Papers, NCSA.

34. See esp. Colyer, *Report of the Services Rendered*, 29–51; Mobley, *James City*, 5–13, 29–46; Cecelski, "A Thousand Aspirations," 22–25.

35. William H. Singleton, *Recollections of My Slavery Days* (New York: n.p., 1922), 8–9. Copy in the New York Public Library, New York, N.Y.

36. Andrew J. Wolbrook to Edward W. Kinsley, 3 September 1863, and Wolbrook to Kinsley, 12 September 1863, Edward W. Kinsley Papers, DU. Starkey and Galloway worked closely throughout the Civil War, and Starkey clearly held Galloway in

great esteem. After the war, however, the two seem to have had at least a momentary falling out over financial matters. See Mary Ann Starkey to Edward W. Kinsley, 27 July 1865, Edward W. Kinsley Papers, DU.

37. Evans, *Ballots and Fence Rails*, 111–12; John Richard Dennett, *The South As It Is: 1865–1866*, ed. Henry M. Christman (New York: Viking, 1965), 151–53.

38. Pigott diary, 30 May, 1, 18 June 1863, L. W. Pigott Papers, NCSA.

39. Ibid., 1 January 1864; *Proceedings of the National Convention of the Colored Citizens of the United States, 1864*, reprinted in Herbert Aptheker, ed., *A Documentary History of the Negro People in the United States* (New York: Citadel Press, 1951), 1:511–13.

40. Aptheker, *Documentary History*, 1:522–23.

41. Pigott diary, 1 January 1864, L. W. Pigott Papers, NCSA.

42. The Lincoln administration first considered the use of black troops in mid-1862. "Limited and unauthorized" use of black troops had actually occurred in at least Kansas, Louisiana, and South Carolina before August 1862, when the War Department finally authorized the recruitment of the first slave regiment—the 1st South Carolina Volunteers, recruited from the occupied portion of the Sea Islands—into the Union army. In September 1862, Lincoln issued a "Preliminary Proclamation of Emancipation" that stated that as of 1 January 1863 slaves in the Confederate states would be "forever free." Once the proclamation went into effect, blacks were recruited on a mass scale. Six months later, thirty black regiments had been organized. More than 186,000 blacks enlisted in the Union army, and roughly one-third of them would eventually be listed as dead or missing. See Leon F. Litwack, *Been in the Storm So Long: The Aftermath of Slavery* (New York: Knopf, 1979), 69–71, 98.

43. Galloway married Martha Ann Dixon at the Beaufort home of her parents, Napoleon and Massie Dixon. Martha A. Little deposition, Celie Galloway pension file, VA; Marriage Register: Carteret County, N.C., 1850–1981, NCSA; Eighth Federal Census: Carteret County, N.C., Population and Slave Schedules, 1860.

44. Pigott diary, 4 August 1863, L. W. Pigott Papers, NCSA; Cleveland diary, 24 November 1864, Southern Historical Collection, University of North Carolina Library, Chapel Hill.

45. Wild to Kinsley, 30 November 1863, Edward W. Kinsley Papers, DU. In this letter, Wild refers to Galloway's Boston contact as a "Mr. Stevenson of 7 Hull St." This was presumably John Hubbard Stephenson (1820–88) of 9 Hull Street, of the millinery firm of Stephenson & Plympton. He is not known to have been a part of the city's abolitionist movement. See *Boston Directory* (Boston: George Adams, 1862) and *Boston Evening Transcript*, 22 December 1888.

46. *North Carolina Times* (Raleigh, N.C.), 21 May 1864; Mary Ann Starkey to Edward W. Kinsley, 21 May 1864, Edward W. Kinsley Papers, DU.

47. *The Liberator*, 9 September 1864, reprinted in Aptheker, *Documentary History*, 1:511, 516.

48. Horace James, *Annual Report of the Superintendent of Negro Affairs in North Carolina, 1864, With an Appendix, Containing the History and Management of the Freedmen in this Department up to June 1st, 1865* (Boston: W. P. Brown, n.d.), 6–18; *Old North State* (Beaufort, N.C.), 7 January 1865; John Niven, ed., *The Salmon P. Chase Papers*, vol. 1, *Journals, 1829–1872* (Kent, Ohio: Kent State University Press, 1993), 542–44.

49. Willie Lee Rose, *Rehearsal for Reconstruction: The Port Royal Experiment* (Indianapolis: Bobbs-Merrill, 1964).

50. Sidney Andrews, *The South Since the War; As Shown by Fourteen Weeks of Travel and Observation in Georgia and the Carolinas* (Boston: Ticknor & Fields, 1866), 125.

51. Roberta Sue Alexander, *North Carolina Faces the Freedmen: Race Relations during Presidential Reconstruction, 1865–67* (Durham, N.C.: Duke University Press, 1985), 16; Pigott diary, 4 July 1865, L. W. Pigott Papers, NCSA.

52. *New York Times*, 17 September 1865.

53. Ibid.

54. *Wilmington Herald*, 8 September 1865.

55. Evans, *Ballots and Fence Rails*, 87–91.

56. Aptheker, ed., *Documentary History*, 1:546.

57. Dennett, *The South As It Is*, 151–53.

58. *New National Era*, 22 September 1870. Galloway is not listed in the city directories of New Bern or Wilmington in 1865–66. See Frank D. Smaw Jr., *Smaw's Wilmington Directory* (Wilmington, N.C.: Frank D. Smaw Jr., ca. 1866), and R. A. Shotwell, *New Bern Mercantile and Manufacturers' Business Directory and North Carolina Farmers Reference Book* (New Bern, N.C.: W. I. Vestal, 1866).

59. Evans, *Ballots and Fence Rails*, 93.

60. Dennett, *The South As It Is*, 42.

61. Quoted in Litwack, *Been in the Storm So Long*, 271.

62. Evans, *Ballots and Fence Rails*, 64–81; Litwack, *Been in the Storm So Long*, 289.

63. Dennett, *The South As It Is*, 110.

64. Evans, *Ballots and Fence Rails*, 83–85.

65. *Tri-Weekly Standard* (Raleigh, N.C.), 7 September 1867.

66. Wilmington *Evening Star*, 25 September 1867; *New National Era*, 22 September 1870.

67. Evans, *Ballots and Fence Rails*, 95–97.

68. *Wilmington Journal*, 21 February 1868.

69. *The Standard* (Raleigh, N.C.), 25 January, 17 February 1868, cited in Bernstein, "The Participation of Negro Delegates," 399, 407.

70. Quoted in Evans, *Ballots and Fence Rails*, 98.

71. *Wilmington Weekly Journal*, 28 February 1868.

72. Evans, *Ballots and Fence Rails*, 95–97.

73. Ibid., 98–102.

74. Linda Gunter, "Abraham H. Galloway: First Black Elector," *North Carolina African-American Historical and Genealogical Society Quarterly* (Fall 1990): 9–10.

75. *The Christian Recorder*, 24 September 1870. For background on the black militias in the Reconstruction South, see Otis A. Singletary, *Negro Militia and Reconstruction* (Austin: University of Texas Press, 1957).

76. Allen W. Trelease, *White Terror: The Ku Klux Klan Conspiracy and Southern Reconstruction* (Baton Rouge: Louisiana State University Press, 1971), 189–225; Evans, *Ballots and Fence Rails*, 101–2, 145–48; William C. Harris, *William Woods Holden: Firebrand of North Carolina Politics* (Baton Rouge: Louisiana State University Press, 1987), 287–307.

77. Balanoff, "Negro Legislators," 23–24, 27.

78. *Wilmington Daily Journal*, 20 July 1869.

79. *Wilmington Weekly Journal*, 2 April 1869.

80. See, for example, *New York Times*, 17 September 1865.

81. *Wilmington Daily Journal*, 20 July 1869; *Wilmington Journal*, 4 August 1870,

Bill Reaves Collection, New Hanover County Public Library, Wilmington, N.C. (hereafter, NHCPL).

82. *Senate and House Journals, 1868*, 41–42.

83. *Senate and House Journals, 1869*, 360–61; Balanoff, "Negro Legislators," 34–36.

84. Balanoff, "Negro Legislators," 41–42, 44–48; *North Carolina Standard* (Raleigh, N.C.), 21 January 1868, 10 February 1870; *Laws of North Carolina, 1868–69–70*, chap. 77; A. H. Galloway George Z. French, and J. S. W. Eagles to Governor Holden, 10 August 1869, Governors Letter Book 60, NCSA.

85. For an informative discussion of the collective outlook on voting held by Reconstruction blacks, see Elsa Barkley Brown, "Negotiating and Transforming the Public Sphere: African American Political Life in the Transition from Slavery to Freedom," *Public Culture* 7 (1994): 107–46.

86. *Senate and House Journals, 1868–1869*, 209, 223, 648; *1869–70*, 466; *Wilmington Journal*, February 1869, Bill Reaves Collection, NHCPL; Balanoff, "Negro Legislators," 42–44.

87. Galloway grew ill so suddenly that his wife and two young sons, John L. and Abraham Jr., were not able to return from a trip to New Bern before his death. "Widow's Declaration of Pension for Martha A. Little," 29 January 1894, Celie Galloway pension file, VA.

88. *Raleigh Weekly Standard*, 7 September 1870; *Wilmington Daily Journal*, 2–4, 10 September 1870, 23 April 1871, Bill Reaves Collection, NHCPL; *The Christian Recorder*, 24 September 1870.

89. Evans, *Ballots and Fence Rails*, 137–41.

90. *The Christian Recorder*, 24 September 1870; *Wilmington Journal*, 2–4 September 1870, Bill Reaves Collection, NHCPL; *Raleigh Weekly Standard*, 17 September 1870.

Here's an idea: Name a women's running shoe after a mythical demon who preyed on sleeping women. Reebok did. . . . The dictionary defines incubus as an evil spirit that in medieval times was thought to descend upon women and have sex with them. . . . "I'm horrified and the company is horrified [said a Reebok spokeswoman]. We are a company that has built its business on women's footwear, so to do anything that's denigrating to women is not what we're about."
— *New Orleans Times-Picayune*, 20 February 1997, C1

**Glenda E.
Gilmore**

Murder, Memory, and the Flight of the Incubus

My first word of Susan Smith's missing children in Chester, South Carolina, came as I pulled into my son's preschool in Charlotte, North Carolina. The stunning radio report grew worse with every "fact." Horrible images washed over me: a carjacking, a menacing black attacker, two towheaded tykes, a frantic young blond working mother. I hugged my own little guy and stumbled out of the car. Some of the other mothers were crying. We said lingering goodbyes that morning and arrived early that afternoon to gather our children. That evening the television news broadcast a composite sketch of the alleged kidnapper. On the screen before me appeared a caricature of a black criminal:

a powerfully built man with very dark skin, crazed eyes, a menacing mouth, a tight stocking cap on the small dome of his head.

Susan Smith was lying, I realized in a rush. For I had "seen" this man before, in sources almost one hundred years old. He was the incubus: in mythology, he is a winged demon that has sexual intercourse with women while they sleep; on the ground in 1898, he represented the black beast rapist. White politicians created him to seize political power and to extend white male "protection" to white women of the lower classes. This figure gave the Wilmington racial massacre of 1898 its force; it haunted white women's dreams and pushed white men to reach deep inside themselves to fan a rage that became murderous. A century later, when all else failed Susan Smith—parents, marriage, career, love—she used the one morsel of status left to her as a poor white Southern woman with a past. If threatened by a black man, she could become beloved again, cleansed in the blood of her lambs. She could even use the power of the black male rapist myth to get away with murder. Or so she thought.

The incubus I spotted that night on television first flew about North Carolina in the spring and summer of 1898, after Furnifold Simmons, chairman of the Democratic Party, met with Charles Brantley Aycock and Josephus Daniels at the Chatawka Hotel in New Bern in March.[1] Aycock was a young man on the make, a struggling attorney in the eastern part of the state. Daniels edited the *Raleigh News and Observer*, the state's preeminent Democratic newspaper. They holed up at the Chatawka in a desperate attempt to find a way back to power after the Democratic Party had lost the governor's seat and the legislature in 1896 to a biracial coalition of Populists and Republicans known as Fusionists. The Democrats found their ploy in the idea of "home protection."[2]

They would use a rape scare to pull white apostates back into the Democratic Party. Simmons dispatched his agents around the state. Headlines screamed: "An Incubus Must Be Removed."[3] Democrats founded White Government Leagues, embellished local accounts of African American "outrages" for statewide broadcast, and even tried their hands at song. These lyrics appeared on the front page of the *Wilmington Messenger* two days before the massacre:

Rise, ye sons of Carolina!
Proud Caucasians, one and all;
Be not deaf to Love's appealing—

Hear your wives and daughters call,
See their blanched and anxious faces,
Note their frail, but lovely forms;
Rise, defend their spotless virtue
With your strong and manly arms.[4]

Daniels was perfectly willing to publish fabrications of "Negro atrocities" on a daily basis. The actual facts of the matters seemed difficult to pin down. If the situation appeared calm locally, reports circulated that the white people in the next town had suffered outrages. If conditions in that town looked sleepy enough when one arrived, news came that trouble had broken out farther down the road. Local correspondents sent in reports of street altercations, of sassy black women pummeling innocent white virgins with umbrellas, of "assaults with attempt to rape," and of rapes. Simmons and Daniels concentrated on stories about the eastern black-majority counties, which they fed to the Piedmont, where white Democrats had recently voted Populist, and to western North Carolina, where whites most often voted Republican. It was a brilliant strategy.

The Democrats charged that as the white man slumbered, allowing African Americans to take political power, the incubus of black power had visited their beds as well. The "safety of the home" became the Democrats' campaign slogan. White men must "restore to the white women of the state the security they felt under the [previous] twenty years of democracy."[5] The Populist white man who valued his class interests above his race learned with a shock that he had opened the gates of hell for some distant white woman. The Democrats' pressure swelled white men's egos and honed their indignation. An explosion seemed imminent.[6]

In fact, there was only a rape scare, not a rape epidemic. Available crime statistics show no appreciable increase in either rapes or "assaults with intent to rape" in either 1897 or 1898.[7] Black men were not inspired to rape by the hope of political power, nor were those African American men in law enforcement and the judiciary negligent in carrying out their duties toward black criminals. The rape scare was a politically driven wedge powered by the sledgehammer of white supremacy.

Charles Aycock described Wilmington as "the storm center of the White Supremacy movement."[8] As a black-majority city, Wilmington became emblematic of the problem of "Negro rule" and provided fertile ground for stories of "Negro outrages." Tales of woe issued forth from Wilmington's outnumbered whites, reprinted and embellished by Josephus Daniels up in Raleigh. The problem in Wilmington was not rape; it was the practice of democracy. After the Republicans and Populists won control of the state legislature in 1894, they had returned county and local offices to "home rule." As a result, African Americans, white Republicans, and Populists won election to local posts previously held by Democrats who had been appointed on the state level. In other words, the Fusionists restored local democracy to heavily black towns and counties.

In 1897, Wilmington Republicans won a majority on the board of alderman and elected a white Republican as mayor. White Democrats promptly protested, and the previous Democratic city administration refused to yield city hall to the newly elected Republicans. Before it was over, yet a third board of aldermen constituted itself and elected yet another mayor. Ultimately, the state supreme court decided in favor of the duly elected Republicans. Wilmington's white Democrats, accustomed to ruling without majority support by state appointment, would not abide by the decision; they vacated their offices but immediately began to undermine the new government.[9] Thus, in the beginning, the roots of the Wilmington racial massacre grew in political soil, but the Democrats' sexually slanderous depiction of black men rained down on those roots to nourish a mutant growth.

In Wilmington, the discontent of deposed officeholders quickly blended with that of frustrated white workers. Businessmen organized a "white man's labor bureau" to take jobs away from black men. The point was never to drive much-needed black labor out of Wilmington, but rather to skim off the best jobs as an object lesson. As a contemporary put it, "Of course, enough white laborers to supply the demand cannot be secured, but it is thought that after a few negroes have been turned adrift, the rest will need no further warning."[10] The chamber of commerce boldly declared "against Negro Domination," arguing that officeholding by black officials "arrests enterprise, hampers commerce and repels capital."[11] Many characterized the white supremacy campaign as a "business men's movement" arguing that even the "democratic political leaders are simply trailing behind." It did not bode well for the peacefulness of the community when the leading newspaper became a "veritable arsenal, a large closet being stored with revolvers and rifles," or when a "business men's committee . . . purchased a Colt rapid-firing gun with which to protect the cotton wharves and other property from incendiary mobs."[12]

The sources of white men's discontents were political and economic, but the language of "home protection" gave that discontent a powerful psychosexual charge. Without the hysteria that swelled from the belief that their wives and daughters lived in danger, it is unlikely that otherwise average white men could find it within themselves to commit mass murder, as they ultimately did in Wilmington. A white man might protest an election or gripe about the prosperity of his black neighbors while he had trouble finding work, but it took Furnifold Simmons's incubus hovering over the city to incite him to kill. Asserting manhood and protecting womanhood—upholding "family values" one might say—provided a rationale for self-defense. To be remade into killers, white men had to connect gender and race; they had to believe that one duty—the exercise of patriarchy—prevailed over all other commandments, including the biblical injunction against murder. Manipulated by propagandists elsewhere in the state, encouraged by their own ministers, inflamed by leading white men in their own community, they came to believe that black men's very presence in public affairs threatened white women. The lie of the incubus became their reality.

Looking back on the racial massacre in 1936, a Wilmington resident recalled the compelling power of the incubus. Colonel John D. Taylor, a one-armed Confederate hero, and his son, J. Alan Taylor, allegedly talked in the weeks just prior to the 1898 election. "Alan," the old veteran warned, "we are a conquered people. . . . The day is coming, however, when Northerners will regard our cause, 'State's Rights,' as just. . . . Meanwhile, we must continue to grin and bear it." To which his son, a rising young man, was said to have replied, "But my little daughter, Mary, and young son, Douglas, now in their 'teens are representative of a new generation; and I am going to do my utmost to make Wilmington a clean, safe, and happy place. . . . I do not want them, and their little friends growing up . . . [among] rapists!"[13] Together with eight other white men, J. Alan Taylor organized an armed militia to patrol each of the city's five wards, block by block. This group, known among themselves as "the Secret Nine," refashioned their identities. From the clay of upstanding businessmen, they remolded themselves into murderous "revolutionaries."[14]

Given the lack of real, live black rapists, Wilmington's white men, now organized and armed in secret militias, began to see all around them signs that pointed to tears in the social fabric, that seemed to be portents of the incubus lurking just out of sight. It was in this tense atmosphere that Alexander Manly, editor of the only black daily newspaper in the state, the *Daily Record*, tried to counter the rape scare in August. Manly felt he must answer the unfounded charges that lay thick on the ground, and he took the opportunity to do so when the white-owned *Wilmington Messenger* resuscitated a year-old speech that Rebecca Latimer Felton had given in Georgia. According to Felton, neglectful Southern white men had let things deteriorate to the point that lynching of black rapists was the only remedy, a pronouncement that fit perfectly with the white supremacists' campaign.[15]

To answer the Democrats' dangerous revitalization of Felton's command to "lynch 1,000 weekly," Manly fought fire with fire.[16] First, he argued that often white women cried rape after illicit affairs across the color line came to light. Then Manly pointed out that white men both raped and seduced black women. Why, he wondered in print, was it worse for a black man to be intimate with a white woman than for a white man to be intimate with a black woman? "We suggest that the whites guard their women more closely, as Mrs. Felton says, thus giving no opportunity for the human fiend, be he white or black," Manly chided. "You leave your goods out of doors and then complain because they are taken away. Poor white men are careless in the manner of protecting their women." Thus, Manly played directly into the "home protection" campaign and brushed up against white men's bruised patriarchy.[17]

It was the sexually charged political climate that gave Manly's words their explosive effect. Manly dared to equate the morals of poor white and poor black people. For Manly, class trumped race; poor white women were no better than poor black women. Manly's best-aimed blow was the suggestion that some white women freely chose black men as lovers, which shook the monolithic power of whiteness. All white women were pure, regardless of their class or circumstances. All black men were animals or children. Therefore, no white woman could prefer a black man over a white man.

Reaction to the August editorial came swiftly. Felton declared: "When the negro Manly attributed the crime of rape to the intimacy between negro men and white women of the South the slanderer should be made to fear a lyncher's rope."[18] The *Wilmington Messenger* reprinted the statement each day until the election, often as the lead-in for a new "outrage" report, and the *Raleigh News and Observer* often ran parts of the column.[19] Manly, very handsome himself, had commented that some black men were "sufficiently attractive for white girls of culture and refinement to fall in love with." To this one editor added, "Here he tells of his own experience, and he has been holding 'clandestine meetings' with poor white women, wives of white men." But others, realizing the problem of alleging that any white women sought trysts with black men, simply called Manly's editorial "a dirty defamation," a "sweeping insult to all respectable white women who are poor," and a "great slur."[20]

Glenda E.
Gilmore

Tensions ran high as rumors circulated that whites were plotting to burn Manly's press and lynch him.

Ten days before the racial massacre, Furnifold Simmons seized upon Manly's editorial as if it had inspired the home protection campaign rather than answered it. Manly, Simmons told white Wilmingtonians, had "dared openly and publicly to assail the virtue of our pure white womanhood." All other political issues paled by comparison to this attack on the home. Politics "passed out of the public mind, and in a whirl of indignation, which burst forth like the lava from a pent up volcano, there was thrust to the front the all absorbing and paramount question of White Supremacy." The "sturdy manhood" of North Carolina should not "submit" to a "mongrel ticket" backed up by "federal bayonnets," Simmons warned, even as he reminded white men that "the issues involved are pregnant with momentous consequences."[21]

We don't know if Furnifold Simmons read Sigmund Freud, but we can be sure that Simmons read his audience perfectly. His barely concealed sexual references—pent up volcanos, lava bursting forth, thrustings to the fore, federal bayonnets, mongrel tickets, and pregnant issues—struck white men where they lived. Such language linked the most intimate issues of home and family to local politics and federal law in a bond that Southerners would take a century to uncouple.

While Manly's editorial provided fodder for fully sexualizing the home protection campaign, John C. Dancy's vice presidency of the newly formed National Afro-American Council illustrated to Wilmingtonians the direct connections between black political power and home protection. Dancy had been born a slave in Tarboro, North Carolina, where his father thrived as a builder after Emancipation. He attended Howard University and then taught and worked in journalism. As a lay leader of the African Methodist Episcopal Zion Church, he was a staunch temperance man who had traveled the world in support of the cause. Now, at forty-one, Dancy stood at the peak of his ambition, since the national Republican administration had appointed him collector of customs for the Port of Wilmington, one of the few salaried appointments available in the fledgling federal bureaucracy.[22] At its first meeting in Rochester, New York, the National Afro-American Council adopted a resolution to "secure uniform marriage laws in all the states, and revision of the laws in the twenty four States where inter-marriage between whites and blacks is not allowed."[23]

Here, thought white Democrats, was an astoundingly bold use of black political power to undercut white patriarchy through legal reform. By passing such a resolution, white men could argue, the new organization of black men declared its members' desire to marry white women. The legal right to marry white women, however, was probably not at all what the resolution meant to those present. In truth, black delegates addressed an entirely different but very pressing issue for their constituents. Their proposals sought to extend statutory protection to black women who were in long-term liaisons with white men, a common occurrence, particularly in the South.

In Wilmington, whites used the resolution as an object lesson for the damage that could ensue if blacks held political power. Dancy held one of the highest paid and most coveted appointments in the state. He had enjoyed the respect of many whites. A scant eight months earlier, before the statewide white supremacy campaign, the *Wilmington Messenger* said of him, "He has never been an extremist and numbers his personal friends among both races. He is true to his convictions, but always courteous and conservative in their expression."[24] Suddenly, Dancy represented everything wrong with the Fusion takeover two years earlier; there was no longer such thing as a "courteous and conservative" black leader. Indeed, white Democrats argued, political success had licensed Dancy's personal desire to marry white women, as evidenced by his vice presidency of an organization promoting interracial marriage. The white Democrats argued that "the success of the combination [of Republicans and Populists] in this State . . . has evidently emboldened the race, specially [sic] those in this State led by Dancy."[25] In less than a year, politics had led Dancy straight into white men's homes; soon he would stand beside their beds with the force of law propping him up. Whites ignored Dancy's protest that he personally had opposed the resolution.[26]

In such a heated racial climate, each stroll down the street suggested to white people fresh evidence of the incubus that lurked in their midst. They began to turn incidents that might have earlier gone unnoticed or been seen as individual encounters into evidence of an African American plot on the safety of white homes. Some of these confrontations involved black and white men only. When, for example, Hugh MacRae, a prominent white man, stood in the street several feet from the curb deep in conversation with a friend, he simply expected traffic to move around him. Accustomed to deference, MacRae assumed that he literally owned the street. When a two-wheeled cart, pulled by "a fast-stepping horse," came toward him, he probably never thought of moving. But the black driver surged "defiantly" onward, and Hugh MacRae jumped up on the sidewalk, grievously offended. MacRae recounted the incident that evening to his uncle, Walter MacRae, who is said to have exclaimed, "If something is not done to put down this surly and rebellious attitude of the Negroes towards the whites, we will have a repetition of the Sepoy rebellion, which ended only after the British had shot some of the mutinous leaders at the very mouths of cannon, to which they were lashed."[27]

Even childish pranks proved fodder for news accounts of what could go wrong when African Americans had full civil rights. The *Daily Charlotte Observer* reported in all earnestness the ignoble experience of "two of Wilmington's most prominent and respected businessmen." One day, while out driving, the two men encountered a "dozen little negro boys." The children chased the white men's carriage and "made vulgar remarks about the horse and the men."[28] Finding themselves compared to the nether regions of a horse simply undid the white men. Respect and prominence depended not on one's accomplishments, but on the deference one commanded in public. For whites a hundred years ago character did not exist apart from reputation, apart from what others thought of you. Of the two—character and reputation—reputation mattered more. Self-respect reflected public opinion—not inner worth—in a way that is difficult for us to imagine today.

The leading white men of Wilmington, so accustomed to deference, could not abide a world in which black men failed to stop for them or little boys teased them in the streets comparing them to horses' asses. To whites such minor occasions seemed justification for murder because they reflected an attitude that could easily undermine white men's unquestioned right to be at the top of the social, political, and economic order and, just as important and all but inseparable, the right to rule in their homes. If indignity was a slippery slope down which they refused to slide, true democracy was out of the question. When Simmons's emissary, Francis Winston, arrived in Wilmington to organize the official White Supremacy Leagues, he pulled out his usual incubus speech "to inflame the white men's sentiment." But this old tune played *too* resoundingly: Winston found Wilmington's white men "already willing to kill all of the office holders and all of the negroes." In a curious reversal of his usual role, Winston claimed that he "immediately reacted and became a pacifist."[29]

If white men could not abide a lack of deference from black men, they certainly were not going to tolerate it from black women. The patriarchy of the white man and its theoretical sheltering capacities never stretched to black women. If white men were to protect womanhood, what did it mean that they would not extend chivalry to black women? Black women in Wilmington made this a public issue through an informal campaign of their own: they demanded that white streetcar conductors extend their arms to help them on and off the cars. Our evidence is fragmentary on this point; we must imagine the individual occurrences: a well-dressed middle-class black woman, heading home from shopping, attempting to juggle her burdens and mind her skirts as she jumped up on the car's high step. The white conductor must have stood there passively, watching her struggle, although his job was literally to conduct people on and off the car. The cars remained unsegregated at this point, but these moments of boarding and disembarking became a portent of the Jim Crow racial structure to come. Black women must have protested on the spot, demanding assistance; the conductors must have reacted with confusion. Some African Americans likely took the issue up with the car company or local officials. One white supremacist reported that an "audacious Negro grudge [was] developing against the streetcar conductors because they did not help black women on and off the conveyance as they did white women."[30]

The importance of this cryptic reference rests on our ability to imagine the world black women envisioned: a world in which women of certain classes, black and white, enjoyed white male protection in public places. In 1898 black women in Wilmington tried to hold chivalry to its word. They imagined a future in which white men's much-vaunted protection would transcend race. The failure of their attempt reveals that patriarchy's allure to white men lay not in its duties, but in its benefits: in the power that the heights of social hierarchy conferred upon white men. That power gave them control over white women, over white children, and over black people of all ages and both sexes. It led them to take their proper places in government and to rule in the home. White men would risk much to preserve their status, even if they refused to follow the responsibility that their power was said to carry.

Moreover, black women's autonomy in public challenged the idea of female deference. Black and white women had met each other on the streets day in and day out since Emancipation, but the political climate that put sexuality and home protection at the center of electoral decisions reordered daily encounters between women of different races. We have only the flimsiest strands of evidence rendered by white sources to recover black women's outrage at the white supremacy campaign. The white newspapers began to report street confrontations between black and white women as signs of "Negro outrages." The stories suggest that black women struck back in the language of the streets.

The most infamous of these confrontations came in Wilmington. One morning, several white women encountered a black woman standing in their way on the sidewalk. One of the white women, forgetting for a moment her "frail but lovely form," seized the black woman and shoved her out of the way. The black woman raised her umbrella and began to strike back at her assailant. A black man, watching the fight, shouted encouragement to the umbrella-wielding woman: "That's right; damn it, give it to her."[31] A street fight between a black woman and a white woman so confounds our notions of white women's delicacy and black women's deference, it is difficult to know what to make of it. Josephus Daniels knew, however. "Such exasperating occurrences," the editor argued about a similar incident, "would not happen but for the fact that the negro party is in power in North Carolina."[32] Wilmington's white men also read such incidents as political and formed an organization of "Minute Men," vowing to put an end to three things: rising crime, poor policing, and "negro women parad[ing] the streets and insult[ing] men and ladies." Invoking Manassas and Chancellorsville, they armed themselves and let it be known that they "would welcome a little unpleasantness."[33]

Black women understood that while electoral politics excluded them as actors, the system included them as objects. They formed organizations to aid the Republican Party and used their power to mount a campaign of nerves to counter the white supremacists. They backed Manly publicly, calling his newspaper "the one medium that stood up for our rights when others have forsaken us." The women's political group conducted its own registration campaign of black husbands, fathers, and sons, warning "every negro who refuses to register . . . we shall make it our business to deal with him in a way that will not be pleasant." They too used the language of patriarchy—"we shall teach our children to love the party of manhood's rights"—but with a twist. If a black man failed to live up to his duty by failing to vote, women would mind their duty and see him "branded a white-livered coward who would sell his liberty."[34]

White women entered the fray as well, most directly on the streets when they punched and shoved black women, more symbolically at rallies where they appeared on the stump as shining virgins to support white supremacist rallies. Women glided by in political parades, fashioned banners, peppered editors with letters, and decried "Negro rule" to audiences at party rallies. The *Wilmington Messenger* gushed that women had become a "potent factor" in the campaign.[35] They joined the White Government Leagues, which Francis Winston dubbed a haven for the "home loving" as he pointed out that the "white good women in North Carolina are unusually aroused."[36]

When election day dawned in Wilmington, voters crowded into the polling places, but in many ways, the occasion was anticlimactic, since Fusionists had been afraid to campaign in New Hanover County, and Republican-held municipal offices were not up for election that year. The only offices for which Wilmingtonians could vote were one congressional seat, a place in the state senate, and a sprinkling of judgeships and county positions. When the polls closed that afternoon, the Democrats claimed a "glorious victory," yet the Democratic congressional candidate won within the city by a mere 54 percent of the vote. It was important to portray the election as a political triumph for white supremacy to confer legitimacy on its unfinished business. Alongside the election results, the *Wilmington Messenger* ran a boxed advertisement: "ATTENTION WHITE MEN. There will be a meeting of the White Men of Wilmington this morning at 11 o'clock at the Court House. A full attendance is desired, as business in the furtherance of White Supremacy will be transacted." Thus the white men of Wilmington served notice that a democratic victory would not satisfy them; they wanted more.[37]

This unfinished "business in the furtherance of White Supremacy" explains why white men ran amok in the streets of Wilmington two days after the election, murdering some black leaders and driving others from town. The massacre testifies both to the larger purposes of the campaign and to the inexorability of hatred unleashed. What happened in Wilmington was about more than party politics or economic jealousy. It was about how political rhetoric can license people to do evil in the name of good. By now, Furnifold Simmons's machine could boast of a statewide Democratic victory. By now, the Secret Nine knew that there was no threat to their homes from black rapists; they knew that no incendiary mobs of black men gathered to burn the cotton sitting on the wharves. Yet these white men wanted more than an electoral victory: they wanted their honor back. They wanted revenge for being considered, even for a moment, as black men's equals.

Hundreds of white men arrived at the courthouse the morning after the election ready to finish what the white supremacy campaign had started. The crowd clamored for Alfred Moore Waddell to mount the stage. Two days earlier, Waddell had uttered the most infamous get-out-the-vote speech in North Carolina history, taking Simmons's vague rhetoric of home protection to its logical, and violent, conclusion. "You are Anglo-Saxons," Waddell had told the men as they prepared to vote. "You are armed and prepared, and you will do your duty. . . . Go to the polls tomorrow, and if you find the negro out voting, tell him to leave the polls, and if he refuses, kill him. We shall win tomorrow, if we have to do it with guns."[38] Indeed, the Anglo-Saxons had won, but now they still itched for the chance to use the guns. From the meeting after that victory came a "White Declaration of Independence." It urged employers to fire black help and ordered Alexander Manly out of the city. Then whites demanded resignations from the chief of police and the Republican mayor, who had another year to serve, and terrified them into giving up their offices.[39]

The next day, black leaders failed to respond in a timely fashion to an ultimatum issued by the writers of the White Declaration of Independence ordering Alexander Manly to leave the city. Five hundred angry men demanded that the captain of the Wilmington Light Infantry lead them to burn Manly's press, to which he retorted, "What, me lead a mob? Never!" So the group turned to Alfred Waddell, who shouldered his Winchester, his white hair flowing in the breeze, and marched out toward Love and Charity Hall, the black mutual aid society building that housed Manly's newspaper.[40]

When the rampage came, the black targets of white wrath reflected the three objects of the white supremacy campaign: black women, black politicians, and black prosperity. An army of white men rampaged through the city. They strip-searched black women, looking for weapons.[41] Then the white men hunted down prominent black leaders and white Republican officeholders, including John Dancy, and either shot them or chased them out of town. The Wilmington Light Infantry, mobilized to keep the peace, just jumped into the fray.[42]

Manly had long since escaped the city, but the mob burned Love and Charity Hall to the ground, igniting several other structures. The Colt rapid-firing gun proved terrifyingly effective, as effective as lashing rebellious Indians to cannons had been in the Sepoy rebellion. Black men were shot in the back as they ran. Black barber Carter Peamon, who had saved the lives of two white men earlier in the day, found himself forcibly deported on a switch engine. When he jumped off the train, an "unknown white man" shot him dead.[43] The Secret Nine arrested Robert Bunting, the United States Commissioner; John Melton, the chief of police; and two other white men, planning to banish them from the city the next morning.[44] "What have we done, what have we done?" one African American man screamed. George Rountree, a white man who moments before had telephoned to have the rapid-firing gun sent over, found himself unable to answer since "they had done nothing."[45]

At the end of the day, no one knew how many had died. Alfred Waddell seized the mayor's office, and his cronies demanded the "resignations" of Republican officeholders, filling the positions themselves.[46]

Subsequently fourteen coroner's juries met, and all found that the black victims had died "at the hands of unknown persons." Waddell thought around twenty African Americans had died. George Rountree, J. Alan Taylor, and Hugh MacRae bragged of ninety dead.[47] It is doubtful that the terrified family members of the slain would have presented their loved ones' dead bodies to the Democratic city officials for a coroner's inquest.

Sometimes, murder does its best work in memory, after the fact. Terror lives on, continuing to serve its purpose long after the violence that gave rise to it ends. During the massacre, hundreds of Wilmington's African Americans left and huddled in the woods surrounding the city. In the next month, 1,400 blacks left Wilmington. Six months later, prosperous African Americans were still departing by the scores in special rented cars attached to regular passenger trains going north and west.[48]

Some who lacked the means to flee appealed to the federal government for assistance. Three days after the Wilmington massacre, an anonymous African American woman sent a letter to Republican president William McKinley begging for help. Why had he not sent troops? Why had he left Wilmington's black citizens unprotected "to die like rats in a trap"? "We are loyal, we go where duty calls," she said, noting that many of Wilmington's young black men served in the 3rd North Carolina Volunteer Regiment mobilized for the Spanish-Cuban/American War. Now, with the damage done, McKinley could at least send a ship for the survivors, perhaps working out a way to take them to Africa, where "a number of us will gladly go." Then she hurled the rhetoric of patriotism back at the president of the United States: "Is this the land of the free and the home of the brave? How can the Negro sing my country tis of thee?" "Why," she asked her president, "do you forsake the Negro?"[49]

Why indeed? There is evidence that the administration at least dithered before deciding to leave the unpunished murderers holding office in Wilmington. Several of the deposed white officeholders fled to Washington, where black congressman George White tried to get them an audience with the president.[50] When that failed, on Christmas Eve, R. H. Bunting and John Melton penned a pathetic appeal to McKinley, begging for help. According to Bunting and Melton, the Wilmington press warned them if they returned home to collect their belongings or settle their affairs, they would be killed.[51]

Even before Bunting and Melton wrote to McKinley, the United States attorney general demanded that the U.S. Attorney for the Eastern District of North Carolina look into prosecuting the perpetrators of the riot. The U.S. Attorney, C. M. Bernard, seemed to be the very picture of bureaucracy as he professed his willingness to cooperate on the one hand, while putting obstacles in his superiors' path on the other. Bernard was "not only ready and willing, but anxious" to bring the perpetrators to trial, but what would he use for proof? Despite the fact that murder has rarely been so well-documented or boasted of, Bernard argued that his case was weak, with "no information reliable from any witnesses except from news paper reports" and Bunting and Melton's letters. Moreover, he needed a "complaint from somebody, or a witness or witnesses," and Bunting and Melton had fled to Washington. By April, Bernard apparently had investigated further and wrote to the attorney general that, with more information, he could indict the white supremacists for violating election laws across the state. Bernard might have been an inept or unwilling investigator, but he was quite cunning when it came to escaping the responsibilities of his office. Rather than proceed with the case, he outlined a long list of information he would have to obtain before he could prosecute and demanded federal assistance to get it. He asked for an undercover man from the Secret Service and two fearless attorneys from out of state to try the case. Without this commitment of federal resources, it was best not to risk prosecuting, the U.S. Attorney cautioned his Washington bosses. If they prosecuted and failed to convict, the authority of the federal government would be undermined in North Carolina for generations to come.[52]

The likelihood of an acquittal is what ultimately convinced the men in Washington to drop the matter. Within living memory, a war had been fought to establish federal authority. But thirty-eight years later, that "authority" still did not include enforcement of the U.S. Constitution's guarantee of civil rights—even though the same authority was often used to check labor union uprisings. From the end of the Civil War until Dwight D. Eisenhower sent federal troops into Little Rock in 1957, no president dared to prove the power of the Reconstruction amendments on Southern soil. The federal government's failure to act in the aftermath of the Wilmington racial massacre became a pattern it followed for another fifty years.

Since the federal government refused to take action to punish Alfred Waddell, George Rountree, J. Alan Taylor, Hugh MacRae, and others of their ilk, the cultural work of the Wilmington racial massacre spread from its intensely local context to serve as an object lesson for African Americans across the nation. Publicity washed over Wilmington. The white supremacists who led the riot bragged in the national press about their success and justified their actions.[53] As far away as Omaha, Nebraska, African Americans held a mass meeting to condemn "the criminal collusion of the Government and State authorities" with the leaders of the massacre.[54]

Alexander Manly helped spread the word of what had happened in Wilmington as he toured the nation telling "the story of his flight from Wilmington."[55] When he spoke to a New York audience of 200 people, mostly black women, he stated unequivocally what he could not say in North Carolina. The white man, Manly argued, had been trying "for years . . . to obliterate all traces of virtue and morality from the negro race," by seducing and attacking "colored women of the South." Felton's protection of white women was misplaced, Manly pointed out, since "negro girls were the unprotected females more than the whites." Wilmington's whites had seen successful black men as a "menace to the white man's commerce," and therefore wanted to rob them of political rights. Condemning McKinley for his inaction, Manly also pointed out that while the black 3rd North Carolina Volunteer Regiment was "away fighting for the flag, the white man in the South rose up to drive the colored man from the ballot box."[56]

If the terror that murder inspires lives on to do its work, at other times its legacy is the way that memory blurs the facts, tangling story lines, balling up separate strands of the tale so that they become only kernels of truth. The truth of Wilmington fell away. It went unmemorialized; indeed, it was even reversed. For example, in one ridiculous reversal of good and evil, Harry Hayden, a 1936 chronicler of the massacre who glorified the white supremacists, changed the name of the African Americans' Love and Charity Hall to Free Love Hall.[57]

When I began writing about the Wilmington racial massacre, I was curious about how white Wilmingtonians remembered it. Most, it turned out, knew nothing of it. But one white man I asked, a prominent racial liberal, had heard of it. He gave it the gloss of a late 1960s race riot. In 1898, he told me, black people in Wilmington revolted against their abject poverty and lack of civil rights, rioting in their neighborhoods and burning some businesses. They did this, he argued, with some justification, although he could not remember what it was. Even in his relatively sympathetic rendering, the lesson of the 1898 massacre vanished. In his tale, poor blacks created social disorder with cause. The truth—that upper-class whites led a racial massacre against middle-class blacks—is so obscured that deeds of which white Wilmingtonians boasted for a half-century astound us today. The very name that adhered to the violence—"riot"—misleads, as the black woman who begged McKinley for help predicted it would. "There was not any rioting," she told the president, "simply the strong slaying the weak."[58]

It is important for us to be clear about what happened in Wilmington in November 1898, to state it plainly, and to memorialize it honestly. The explanatory power of the Wilmington racial massacre is found in the ways that white leaders murdered to uphold their class position, their manhood, and their whiteness. The point of the lesson lies in the murderers' very ordinariness. It does no good to demonize the white men who killed or led others to kill and then went on to be good citizens, loving husbands, and caring parents and grandparents. What we must do is understand them, as did one man reflecting at the time on the massacre: "I suppose anything must be justifiable to preserve a woman's virtue, a man's honor, and our Christian Civilization. . . . The late unpleasantness was simply natural evolution, an evil preventing a much greater evil."[59] If such thinking led everyday men to commit unspeakable acts, then we must stand forever in awe of the power of rhetoric to incite murder.

The political and economic facts of the white supremacy campaign and the Wilmington racial massacre died in 1898, but the rhetorical power of the black incubus lived on. As complicated as life is, we are rarely able to untangle our own cultural legacies; rather, we tend to accept them as a matter of course, to call them our "feelings," sometimes to name them our "prejudices." First, the politics of the massacre faded; then even its memory faded. But the most powerful legacy of the Wilmington racial massacre lived on: the idea that black men represent the greatest danger against which white women must be constantly vigilant. Now, as one hundred years ago, this simply is not true. All statistics show that rapes and assaults are overwhelmingly more likely to be committed on women by men of the same race and the most likely perpetrator is someone known to the victim.

Of course, white women are not taught to fear their acquaintances, lovers, and family members. They are taught to fear black men. Growing up as a white girl in the South, I learned an intricate racial etiquette that served to isolate me from black men even as I moved around them in public places. Never look a black man in the eye. Never sit down on a park bench beside a black man. Move to the other side of the sidewalk, or better yet the other side of the street, if a black man comes toward you. If the elevator doors open and a black man is inside, stand there and look distracted—do not enter. The racial choreography to which I moved served to prevent me from coming face to face with black men, but the dance itself always reminded me of the danger. I might never see the incubus, but everywhere I went, I could feel the brush of his wings.

That is why Susan Smith conjured up a black criminal to cover up a heinous crime. It seemed logical to her, foolproof even. It was as if nothing much had changed in the South.

In fact, much has changed. Collectively and individually, white and black Southerners have tried to shed the horrors of their past and build an integrated society. We have not succeeded completely, but then we have powerful memories to face. Once we face them, their lessons bear down on us, causing us to question ideas that seem apolitical, and sometimes, at first glance, unrelated to race.

In the end, the case of Susan Smith can comfort us. That she falsely accused a black man of two monstrous murders she had committed is deplorable, outrageous . . . and ultimately understandable. It was the lesson that Susan Smith learned from her culture. The miracle is that she did not succeed. While Smith had simply to pluck the mythology of the black criminal from her intellectual surroundings and use it in her own defense, the ubiquitous nature of the tale did her in. The white South Carolina sheriff who heard her story knew that he had heard it before. And he knew that his daddy and his granddaddy had heard it too. He did not believe her. It took a century, but he did not believe her. This time, the flight of the incubus came to ground.

Notes

Thanks, as always, to Jacquelyn Hall and Karen Leathem for a thousand readings and brilliant editing. Thanks to David Cecelski and Tim Tyson for encouraging me to allow humanity to creep into my history.

1. Of course, there had been discussion in the press about the possibility of black men raping white women and accounts of such crimes prior to 1898. But using such possibilities in a statewide political campaign to link black political power and rape was a fresh strategy to win back offices from the interracial coalition of Populists and Republicans. For an assessment of the gradual politicization of rape after the Civil War, see Martha Hodes, *White Women, Black Men: Illicit Sex in the Nineteenth-Century South* (New Haven: Yale University Press, 1997). For the connections between politics and sexuality during Reconstruction, see Laura F. Edwards, *Gendered Strife and Confusion: The Political Culture of Reconstruction* (Urbana: University of Illinois Press, 1997).

2. *New Berne Journal*, 3 December 1897.

3. "An Incubus Must Be Removed," *New Berne Journal*, 10 August 1898.

4. *Wilmington Messenger*, 8 November 1898, 1.

5. "An Incubus Must Be Removed," *New Berne Journal*, 10 August 1898; *New Berne Journal*, 3 December 1897.

6. The strategy is well documented, even boasted of, in James Fred Rippy, ed., *F. M. Simmons, Statesman of the New South: Memoirs and Speeches* (Durham, N.C.: Duke University Press, 1936), 25–30, and Josephus Daniels, *Tar Heel Editor* (Chapel Hill: University of North Carolina Press, 1941).

7. *Biennial Report of the Attorney-General of the State of North Carolina, 1897–*

1898 (Raleigh: Guy V. Barnes, 1899), 71–72, 73, 96–97, and *Biennial Report of the Attorney-General of the State of North Carolina, 1899–1900* (Raleigh: Edwards and Broughton and E. M. Uzzell, 1901), 34–35, 37, 42, 60, 84, 85. For a discussion of the criminal statistics and documented crimes, see Glenda Elizabeth Gilmore, *Gender and Jim Crow: Women and the Politics of White Supremacy in North Carolina, 1896–1920* (Chapel Hill: University of North Carolina Press, 1996), 82–89. For recent criticism of historians' acceptance that there actually was a rape epidemic, see Daniel Levering Lewis, "Referee Report," *Journal of American History* 83 (March 1997): 1262.

8. H.L.W., "The Wilmington Rebellion" (typescript in the author's possession), 9. The typescript, originally in the possession of a Wilmington family, was written by H.L.W. around 1946 and sent to me by a North Carolinian in 1996. Written ten years after Harry Hayden's "Story of the Wilmington Rebellion" (Wilmington: privately published, 1936), the H.L.W. typescript includes names of men who committed illegal acts that are absent in Hayden's account. H.L.W.'s treatise invoked the Wilmington massacre as a warning to black North Carolinians against pushing for integration in the post–World War II period.

9. The best account of these events is H. Leon Prather, *We Have Taken a City: Wilmington Racial Massacre and Coup of 1898* (Cranbury, N.J.: Associated University Presses, 1984), 30–48.

10. *Washington Post,* 31 October 1898, quoted in H.L.W., "The Wilmington Rebellion," 2.

11. *Wilmington Messenger,* 3 November 1898, 6.

12. *Washington Post,* 29 October 1898, reprinted in *Wilmington Messenger,* 1 November 1898, 4.

13. The story is recounted in Hayden, "The Story of the Wilmington Rebellion," and again in H.L.W., "The Wilmington Rebellion," 6–7.

14. The other eight men were Hugh MacRae, W. A. Johnson, P. B. Manning, L. B. Sasser, E. S. Lathrop, Hardy Fennell, William Gilchrist, and Walter L. Parsley, according to H.L.W., "The Wilmington Rebellion," 7.

15. "Lynch 1,000 Weekly, Declares Mrs. Felton," n.p., n.d., "Newspaper Clippings," Mss. 81, Felton Collection, Hargrett Rare Book and Manuscript Library, University of Georgia, Athens. Robert Howard Wooley, "Race and Politics: The Evolution of the White Supremacy Campaign of 1898 in North Carolina" (Ph.D. diss., University of North Carolina at Chapel Hill, 1977), 186.

16. "Lynch 1,000 Weekly, Declares Mrs. Felton."

17. Manly's editorial was reprinted in white newspapers across the state. It originally ran on 18 August 1898 in the African American *Wilmington Daily Record,* but no copy of this issue exists. The *Wilmington Morning Star* reprinted it on 25 August and the *New Berne Journal* and the *Raleigh News and Observer* on 26 August. The *Wilmington Messenger* seems to have reprinted it every day until the elections, often as a preface for news of other black "outrages" against white women. See, for example, *Wilmington Messenger,* 5 November 1898, 6.

18. Felton's comment appeared in the *Literary Digest* 17, no. 22 (26 November 1898) but must have been written before she had knowledge of the events that took place earlier in the month in Wilmington. Clipping in "Newspaper Clippings," Felton Collection, Hargrett Rare Book and Manuscript Library, University of Georgia, Athens.

19. The *Wilmington Messenger* reprinted the column throughout October.

20. *Wilmington Messenger*, 1 November 1898, 6.

21. Ibid., 3 November 1898, 5.

22. "Honorable John C. Dancy," in William J. Simmons, *Men of Mark* (Cleveland: Leo M. Rewell & Co., 1887), 1101–1104; John C. Dancy, *Sands against the Wind: Memoirs of John C. Dancy* (Detroit: Wayne State University Press, 1966). On the limitations of federal power and patronage positions, see Steven Skrowronek, *Building a New American State: The Expansion of National Administrative Capacities, 1877–1920* (New York: Cambridge University Press, 1982).

23. "Comments by the State Democratic Committee on the Hand Book Issued by the Peoples Party State Executive Committee," n.p., [1898], North Carolina Collection, Wilson Library, University of North Carolina at Chapel Hill.

24. *Wilmington Messenger*, 1 March 1898, 1.

25. "Comments by the State Democratic Committee," 21.

26. On Dancy's distancing himself from the call for marriage reform, see *Charlotte Observer*, 13 October 1898, 6. Dancy later told John Edward Bruce that he thought T. Thomas Fortune actually favored mixed marriages, and Dancy had argued in opposition to the resolution. Fortune had very little knowledge of Southern politics, and Bruce seemed to harbor a lifelong dislike for mixed-race people. See John C. Dancy to John Edward Bruce, 30 January 1899, Salisbury, N.C., reel no. 1, mss. autograph letters no. 311, John Edward Bruce Papers, Schomburg Center, New York, quoted in Hodes, *White Women, Black Men*, 276.

27. H.L.W., "The Wilmington Rebellion," 5.

28. *Daily Charlotte Observer*, 7 September 1898, 2.

29. George Rountree, "Memorandum of My Personal Recollection of the Election of 1898," folder no. 41, box 3, Henry G. Connor Collection, Southern Historical Collection, Wilson Library, University of North Carolina at Chapel Hill.

30. A. J. McKelway, "The Cause of the Troubles in North Carolina," *Independent* 50 (November 1898).

31. *Wilmington Messenger* article, reprinted in *Raleigh News and Observer*, 8 September 1898, 4.

32. *Winston Free Press* article, reprinted in *Raleigh News and Observer*, 22 September 1898, 3.

33. *Wilmington Messenger*, 5 November 1898, 4.

34. Proclamation in the *Daily Record*, n.d., reprinted in *Raleigh News and Observer*, 22 October 1898, 2; H. L. West, in *Washington Post*, quoted in *Wilmington Messenger*, 1 November 1898, 2.

35. *Wilmington Messenger*, 4 November 1898, 1.

36. *Raleigh News and Observer*, 23 August 1898, 6.

37. *Wilmington Messenger*, 9 November 1898, 8.

38. Frank Weldon, "North Carolina Race Conflict," *Outlook* 60 (19 November 1898): 707.

39. Copy of speech, 9 November 1898, folder 2B, Alfred Moore Waddell Papers, Southern Historical Collection, Wilson Library, University of North Carolina at Chapel Hill; *Wilmington Messenger*, 10 November 1898, 8; Prather, *We Have Taken a City*, 107–11.

40. H.L.W., "The Wilmington Rebellion," 21–22.

41. Anonymous to Wm. McKinley, 13 November 1898, file 17743-1898, Record Group R660, Department of Justice, National Archives, Washington, D.C.; David Fulton [Jack Thorne], *Hanover; Or, The Persecution of the Lowly: A Story of the*

Glenda E.
Gilmore

Wilmington Massacre ([New York]: M. C. L. Hill, n.d.), 95–96. *Hanover* is a fictional account that depicts the strip search of Lizzie Smith.

42. Anonymous to Wm. McKinley, 13 November 1898.

43. Hayden, "The Story of the Wilmington Rebellion," 17.

44. Ibid., 19.

45. Rountree, "Memorandum."

46. Prather, *We Have Taken a City*, 96–124; Thomas Clawson, "The Wilmington Race Riots in 1898," Clawson Papers, Southern Historical Collection, Wilson Library, University of North Carolina at Chapel Hill; Weldon, "North Carolina Race Conflict"; Rountree, "Memorandum"; *Wilmington Messenger*, 11 November 1898, 1, 4.

47. Hayden, "The Story of the Wilmington Rebellion," 20.

48. *Star of Zion*, 15 December 1898, 4; 4 May 1899, 4. Hayumi Higuchi, "White Supremacy on the Cape Fear: The Wilmington Affair of 1898" (M.A. thesis, University of North Carolina at Chapel Hill, 1980), documents this out-migration for several years after the massacre.

49. Anonymous to Wm. McKinley, 13 November 1898.

50. *Star of Zion*, 17 November 1898; Eric Anderson, *Race and Politics in North Carolina, 1872–1902: The Black Second* (Baton Rouge: Louisiana State University Press, 1981), 284–95.

51. R. H. Bunting and John R. Melton to Hon. William McKinley, 24 December 1898, file 17743-1898, Record Group R660, Department of Justice, National Archives, Washington, D.C.

52. C. M. Bernard to Hon. John W. Griggs, Atty. Gen'l, 5 December 1898; Bernard to Griggs, 1 April 1899, file 17743-1898, Record Group R660, Department of Justice, National Archives, Washington, D.C.

53. See, for example, McKelway, "The Cause of the Troubles in North Carolina."

54. "Negroes Demand Protection," n.p., [7 December 1898], microfiche 394, Hampton University Clipping Files.

55. "Manly to Start a Paper Here," n.p., 8 December 1898, microfiche 394, Hampton University Clipping Files.

56. "Demand Justice," [New York], n.d., microfiche 394, Hampton University Clipping Files.

57. Hayden, "The Story of the Wilmington Rebellion," 15.

58. Anonymous to Wm. McKinley, 13 November 1898.

59. George Howard to Henry Groves Conner, 14 November 1898, folder no. 40b, box 3, Henry G. Connor Collection, Southern Historical Collection, Wilson Library, University of North Carolina at Chapel Hill.

**Stephen
Kantrowitz**

The Two Faces of Domination
in North Carolina, 1800–1898

In the days following the Wilmington massacre of 1898, Colonel Alfred M. Waddell was at pains to emphasize how restrained he and his
men had been. According to an article he wrote for *Collier's Weekly*,
published barely two weeks after the insurrection had made him mayor,
the white men of Wilmington had been faced with a distasteful task;
they had accomplished it soberly and conservatively. After destroying
the press of Alexander Manly's *Daily Record*, Waddell claimed, he had
told his troops to "go quietly . . . and obey the law, unless . . . forced, in
self-defense, to do otherwise." When jailed black Republicans were
threatened with lynching, he wrote, "I stayed up the whole night myself,

and the forces stayed up all night, and we saved those wretched crea-tures' lives." Anxious black men who came to see him were informed, "Never a hair of your heads will be harmed."[1]

In late 1898 federal intervention remained a possibility, and Waddell knew better than to speak directly about how many men his troops had murdered—a number he later estimated at "about twenty."[2] Yet amid all these portrayals of his self-restraint and concern for black Wilming-tonians' welfare, Waddell could not resist alluding to the terror and slaughter of those November days: though the actual victims were hard to find in his article, Waddell made sure that no one could mistake his restraint for squeamishness or lack of manliness. He began the article with two quotations from a speech he had given earlier that year to kick off the white supremacy campaign in Wilmington: first, he repeated having suggested that if there were a "race conflict," its first victims should be the state's white Fusionist leaders; and second, he quoted his own utterly unambiguous threat to "choke the current of the Cape Fear with carcasses."[3] Acknowledging, in print and after the violence, some of the most inflammatory and potentially self-incriminating statements he had made over the course of the campaign, Waddell hinted at the death toll and his own part in it.

Waddell was hardly the first elite white North Carolinian to present himself as capable of both paternalistic concern and murderous threat, for violence and restraint were the two faces of the Southern master class. Over a century and more, powerful white men maintained their dominance by constantly reminding their potential enemies—slaves and abolitionists, Republicans and Populists—how quickly one mask could be exchanged for another. The Waddell who had spoken those murder-ous words could present himself as the peacemaker, pouring oil on trou-bled waters. But all potential adversaries had to understand also that the man who poured the oil would, if provoked, be the first to set it aflame.

These two masks—of violence and of self-restraint—matter because they enabled the men who wore them to retain power throughout most of the nineteenth century. Between 1800 and 1898 North Carolina's elite white men dominated a slave society, overthrew Reconstruction, and de-stroyed the interracial Fusion regime. Slaveholding, we will see, taught these men the necessity of a double-edged approach to domination, and they continued to apply that lesson even after slavery was destroyed. The Wilmington white supremacy revolution of November 1898, far from being exceptional, irrational, or inexplicable, grew directly out of the nineteenth-century history of North Carolina and the South.

The Anxiety of Slaveholding

Slaveholding taught North Carolina's white elite how complicated it could be to hold a large population in bondage. As workers, kinfolk, believers, and rebels, in fields, cabins, and clearings across fifteen states, enslaved African Americans set their own wills against those of their masters. They demonstrated every day that they were much more than instruments of their owners' wishes, making the practice of slaveholding a constant battle. Slaveholders lived with the knowledge that the people they owned might well kill them if doing so would bring freedom. They therefore hesitated to speak too often or too directly about the possibility of slave insurrection. The prospect was too real, too catastrophic, to be articulated openly as a part of daily life. Alexis de Tocqueville noted both this fear and this reticence in his 1835 work, *Democracy in America*, describing the "danger of a conflict between the blacks and whites of the South of the Union" as "a nightmare constantly haunting the American imagination." He noted, too, that while Northerners spoke of this danger constantly, white Southerners did not; for Tocqueville, there was "something more frightening about the silence of the South than about the North's noisy fears."[4]

North Carolina elites feared such revolts as much as any of the South's planter class. At the turn of the nineteenth century, black slaves in the French colony of Saint-Domingue (Haiti) overthrew and killed their white rulers, establishing a black-ruled republic. The fact that no insurrection had gone so far on the North American mainland was small comfort, especially to those who lived in the black-majority areas of the coastal South—areas such as the Lower Cape Fear. In the wake of the Haitian revolution, the white citizens of Wilmington were among many local elites who wanted their port closed to blacks from the West Indies: these people were feared to be the vectors of revolutionary freedom, a virus particularly dangerous to slaveholders' authority.[5]

Two years after the abortive 1800 uprising planned by the Virginia slave Gabriel, planters uncovered insurrection plots in North Carolina's Albemarle region. Based on a few scraps of paper and testimony beaten out of slave suspects, whites in Bertie, Halifax, Washington, and other counties became convinced that slaves and free blacks planned to march on Elizabeth City, where they would join with rebels from elsewhere in North Carolina and Virginia. Twenty-four slaves were hanged and dozens more whipped or deported during the late spring and summer of 1802.[6] Countless local scares and rumors circulated in the ensuing decades, lent credibility by the periodic discovery of large-scale conspiracies. Denmark Vesey's 1822 plot against Charleston terrified white Southerners because of its scope and degree of organization. A decade later, Nat Turner went much further in Southampton, Virginia, as he and his party of rebels murdered the families of the people who held them in slavery.[7]

The slave regime had developed institutions to confront such dangers, notably the slave patrol. In moments of crisis, moreover, white men frequently mobilized volunteer militias and sped to the scene of reported danger. But at times even these kinds of policing seemed insufficient to make whites secure; indeed, slaveholders in the Cape Fear counties occasionally hesitated to use the police powers they legally had. Apparently, even the two faces of domination had not succeeded fully in establishing white authority over North Carolina's black population: in 1830, some patrollers feared that undertaking their legal responsibilities would bring retaliation, including arson, from slaves who moved about "when and where they please."[8]

In the midst of the great fear that followed Nat Turner's rebellion in 1831, a rumor spread that insurrectionary bands of slaves were converging on Wilmington. It was assumed that their intentions matched those of conspirators such as Gabriel and Vesey: to murder slaveholders, burn the city, and turn the slaveholding world upside down. The scare sent many white citizens of nearby Duplin County fleeing into the swamps.[9] When no revolutionary black army arrived to destroy Wilmington, the tired and filthy white people emerging from the swamps had to acknowledge that their information had been wrong. That growing awareness, however, was less a revelation than a respite: though Governor Montfort Stokes assured them that "nothing like a concerted or extensive plan has been discovered," their terror had hardly been irrational.[10] It had also brought the deaths of countless black residents of the tidewater, people thought to be participants in insurrectionary schemes: their bloody skulls, fixed atop a long line of poles, may well have given a rural lane near Wilmington the horrifying name it bore into the second half of the twentieth century: "Niggerhead Road."[11]

Paternalism and Punishment

But the slave South was not quite an armed camp, with two sides perpetually braced for a racial battle to the death. Though the slave system rested upon a bedrock of violence, masters primarily sought the orderly production of rice and tobacco and cotton; they wanted to work their slave laborers, not kill them.[12] Slaves, split up into relatively small groups on isolated plantations, found it difficult enough to meet together for worship or celebration; they spent more of their energy holding together families and communities than plotting elaborate revolts that inevitably ended in failure and death.[13]

And so slaves pressed masters indirectly and individually. They worked more slowly than they could; they "lay out" in the woods for days at a time; they stole chickens and hams to supplement meager rations of corn and salt pork. Masters complained endlessly about the problems of slave discipline. They explained these difficulties in large part by defaming the moral and intellectual character of black people as a whole: if it was in the nature of Africans to malinger and steal, slaveholders reasoned, then it was not the fault of an individual master that his slaves were less than perfectly reliable.

Slaveholders argued that slaves were essentially childlike, incapable of higher reasoning and only haltingly responsive to moral tutelage. Such "children," they declared, needed the combination of kindness and discipline that only a "parent," usually a father, could provide. Thus the slaveowners articulated a language of paternalism, a language that sought to recast the plantation not as a place of brutality and exploitation, but as the home of familial devotion and reciprocal obligation. A slaveholder representing himself in this way might refer, without apparent irony, to his "family, white and black";[14] the plantation household became, in his imagination, a peaceable kingdom in which subject and sovereign alike had important roles to play. Paternalism provided masters with a language they could use to justify leniency toward slaves who committed minor infractions against plantation discipline. A slave who ran away, or who stole, or who talked back to an overseer, might be treated as an erring child in need of moderate correction, not as a potential revolutionary. Masters hoped that if the rules of life and work— and the punishments for minor violations—were clearly established, slaves would accept the system as at least provisionally just.

But the world the slaveholders made in their imaginations was a simpler, less violent place than the world in which they actually lived. Though many slaveholders liked to think of themselves as patient and benevolent patriarchs, the terms of their patience and benevolence were not up for negotiation. Slaves might be part of a "family," but in fact masters frequently threatened slaves with being sold away from their families as a way of coercing their obedience.[15] The reciprocal terrors of punishment and insurrection—not paternalist myths of reciprocal obligation—lay at the heart of antebellum Southern life: very few masters and even fewer slaves ever forgot that the essence of slavery was physical domination, or that a bullwhip carried in a velvet bag was a bullwhip just the same. Thirty or forty strokes of the lash were common as a punishment for crimes of theft or disobedience; such a beating could leave even a healthy adult physically incapacitated and permanently scarred. More serious punishments included whippings of a hundred strokes or more, bodily mutilation, and execution.[16] Few slaves mistook paternalist rhetoric for reality or made more than provisional peace with its underlying coercion. Such flowers of mutuality as did develop therefore had shallow roots, for they rested on the rock of coercive force.

The two faces of domination presented slaves with a cruel but simple choice: apparent acceptance of the master's terms or brutal retribution at his hands. This savage dilemma made the price of open rebellion extremely high and opened up a breathing space in which masters could experiment with paternalist forbearance. This paternalism remained hollow, however, for it could not survive without force to back it up. A master who acted with restraint in every extremity could hardly expect to turn a profit. He needed to be able, in the space of a heartbeat, to exchange one face for another, to abandon paternalism for coercion, fear, and violence.[17]

The slave who approached a master deferentially, seeking a favor, might or might not gain it. But the slave who seriously overstepped the bounds of submission would face no such uncertainty. On an isolated plantation, on a hot July afternoon, the master facing a recalcitrant or rebellious slave did so alone, and he could have only one aim: to make an example of that person by bringing him or her brutally to heel. Slaveholders never forgot for more than passing moments that, above all, their dominance required fear.

White Abolitionists and Black Soldiers

As the Northern abolitionist movement gained strength during the 1830s, the Southern master class turned both of its faces on this new threat. The perceived insurrectionary potential of abolitionism seemed to require a preemptive, muscular response, from new laws to local vigilante activity against those perceived to be abolitionist provocateurs. Southern elites protested in ever more strident terms against what they perceived as Northerners inciting Southern slaves to rebel. Of course, this "outside agitation" had deep local roots: before the white New England radical William Lloyd Garrison shocked slaveholders with his newspaper *The Liberator* in the 1830s, the black Wilmingtonian David

Walker had laid out the unequivocal terms of the black freedom struggle in his *Appeal to the Coloured Citizens of the World*.[18] But it was the penetration of antislavery ideas into national politics that frightened slaveholders most: they sought to muzzle slavery's enemies by denying them a hearing in Congress, by increasing the number of slaveholding states in the Union, and finally by threatening to secede if their rights to slave property were not guaranteed absolutely and irrevocably.

As long as the federal government generally deferred to slaveholders' wishes, no secessionist consensus emerged. Some slaveholding intellectuals countered abolitionist arguments with defenses of slavery as a moral and social good; more important, leading politicians from all regions attempted to cement compromises or coalitions that would ensure the security of slave property. They spoke the language of regional compromise and mutual interest. But the threat of secession—and, if need be, war—was never far behind. John Brown's raid at Harpers Ferry, Virginia, in 1859 demonstrated to the satisfaction of most slaveholders that abolitionists sought the destruction of their regime through bloodshed. The election of Abraham Lincoln without a single Southern electoral vote confirmed the slaveholders' worst fears.

Part of the reason so many Southern states seceded before Lincoln had even taken office was that Southern leaders had come to see the nation as a plantation writ large: if their authority was not explicitly recognized, it stood in serious jeopardy. There was little room for compromise. Having persuaded themselves—despite explicit denials—that Abraham Lincoln and the Republican Party would make the Union unsafe for slavery, most slaveholders treated his election as the opening salvo of a war against them, a war that would culminate in the bloody insurrection Tocqueville had sensed looming in their imaginations.[19]

The Civil War did not bring a hellish replay of the Haitian revolution; indeed, after the war, planters rhapsodized about the loyalty and devotion their slaves had shown. But it was only in comparison to what would have happened in the deeply feared race war that the actions of Southern slaves could be considered "loyal." Nearly 200,000 black men served in the war, many of them slaves, and practically all of them on the side of the Union.[20] And Confederate "chivalry" recognized this fact. Although Southern soldiers generally fought their white Union opponents according to the contemporary rules of war, respecting flags of truce, exchanging prisoners, and paroling enemy officers, this manly restraint in the midst of bloody Civil War quickly gave way to outright savagery when black men marched in blue. It was Confederate policy to treat black soldiers as agents of insurrection, not legitimate combatants. At Fort

Pillow on the Mississippi River and at dozens of other battlegrounds during the conflict—including Plymouth, North Carolina—victorious Confederate troops massacred captured or surrendering black Union troops—former slaves and Northern-born free blacks alike.[21] The existence of a black soldiery, the closest thing the slave South had ever seen to a systematic slave revolt, demanded a response that no one could possibly misunderstand.

Reconstruction and "Redemption"

At the end of 1865, a panic began to spread among white Southerners. Convinced that their black neighbors were plotting to rise up and kill them at Christmas, they once again mobilized against the long-feared onslaught.[22] Though no black uprising ensued, the fear of slave revolt had been reborn in a world without slaves. What is more, that world presented the defeated ruling class with challenges that were in many ways as daunting as an actual rebellion. An occupying army made up of both black and white soldiers administered the peace, and within and outside this army's ranks there emerged Union League and Republican Party organizations, some of which were biracial. Once Congress took over Reconstruction policy in 1867, black citizenship followed black freedom; with laborers in a position to help make laws, it became infinitely more difficult for the old ruling class to reconstitute the basis of its rule—its dominance over the agricultural economy.

It also became increasingly difficult to reestablish the white solidarity that had preserved slavery for so many generations. Only a decade before, slaveholders had labeled as wild-eyed fanatics the Northern abolitionists who sought to ally with Southern blacks. Now it appeared that a significant fraction of white Southerners were willing to do the same. The Republican Party, made up of both blacks and whites, emerged as a biracial alternative to the former slaveholders' Democratic Party, and in the 1868 elections the new party won a majority of North Carolina's votes.[23]

Democrats went to great lengths to head off this political revolution. That former slaves should have any part in governance was already an intolerable situation: mere freedom, properly constrained by an enforced racial hierarchy and a white conservative legislature, might, under the circumstances, be tolerable, but black participation in government was itself an act of rebellion. As far as the former slaveholders were concerned, such a rebellion sounded the call for white mobilization as clearly as any slave revolt. The Republican legislature and the Union

Leagues plotted, Democrats claimed, to make a mockery of free elections and bring about racial conflict: Democrats claimed in their campaign literature that if their party won the 1868 election, Republicans were "resolved to make *war*" to ensure their continued rule.[24]

In fact, it was not the Republicans but the Democrats who made war in 1868. The Ku Klux Klan, a terrorist network serving the interests of landlords and the Democratic Party, threatened, beat, and killed the postwar descendants of both slaves and abolitionists. Klansmen selectively targeted and punished black and white people who sought to open up the state's economic, political, and social life to the strivings of poorer men and women.[25] Albion Tourgée, the Ohioan whose experiences as a judge in Reconstruction North Carolina became the basis for his novel *A Fool's Errand*, recognized that the Klan was the logical successor of the slave patrol.[26] Antebellum patrollers had borne legal responsibility for maintaining discipline over enslaved black people; their postbellum counterparts beat, whipped, or killed freedpeople who sought to exercise their political, economic, and civic rights. Many counties saw hundreds of separate incidents of violence.[27] Klansmen in Alamance County gave freedman Joseph Harvey 150 lashes and beat his infant child to death with clubs as part of a general campaign of intimidation and terror on the part of more than 600 members of the "White Brotherhood." By 1870, the terror had spread to every corner of the state and encompassed everything from veiled threats to political assassination.[28] In Lenoir and Jones Counties, a Klan-like organization forbade white men to labor alongside blacks and set a "maximum wage" for black workers.[29] Vigilantes also took aim at white North Carolinians who voted Republican, taught in freedpeople's schools, or rented land to former slaves: the Lenoir County terrorists assassinated both a white Northern-born sheriff and his black traveling companion.[30]

Freedpeople resisted the Klan when they could. In December 1870, Klansmen broke into the Chatham County house of a former slave named Essic Harris in order to seize his gun; a week later, they returned to attack him again. Harris had rearmed, and he fought off his assailants, wounding two.[31] Although Harris was momentarily successful, broader attempts to mobilize collective resistance to the Klan frequently backfired. Republican William Holden, North Carolina's Reconstruction governor, lost support when he sent white troops against the Klan. Most whites were not Republicans, and a federally supported military intervention in North Carolina reopened wounds that had scarcely begun to heal.

Black self-defense in the 1870s, whether locally organized or within state militias, inspired the same terror among many whites as had slave revolts in previous decades. Indeed, some newspapers printed stories—always from other states—of actual insurrectionary plots. In 1875, the *Monroe Enquirer* reported that squads of black men in nineteen Georgia counties were drilling in preparation for an "uprising" in which they would divide "the land and the spoils" among the state's freedpeople.[32] Whether or not the newspaper's editor actually found this story credible is less relevant than his belief that his readers would take it seriously.

In the end, the Reconstruction Republican experiment, rooted in a faith in democratic rules and institutions, could not counter the terrorist challenge.[33] By consistently targeting local Republican leaders, North Carolina Klansmen undermined the tenuous political coalition that held the party's diverse membership—Northerners and Southerners, rich and poor, black and white—together. The former slaveholders' ruthlessness, forged in the fire of slavery, was a sword that came readily to hand even after Emancipation.

The men who "redeemed" North Carolina from the Republicans, like their counterparts throughout the South in the 1870s, had only two major items on their agenda: to restore their own fortunes and to reduce the freedpeople to a dependent labor force. What they did not know how to do was to bring prosperity to the mass of the state's white men. Moreover, it quickly emerged that some black men remained determined to vote and prosper, and that some white men shared the Republican Party's commitment to poor people's subsistence rights and public education. Some white men clearly thought that Redemption had promised a future where white farmers could prosper, not just one in which they were white; some would even trade the wages of whiteness for a less exclusive prosperity.[34] As they faced hard times in the post-Reconstruction era, they grew increasingly skeptical of Redeemers' claims that white supremacy was all that mattered; they proved willing to join opposition movements and even biracial coalitions, so long as those seemed to offer them some hope of economic independence.

Throughout the 1870s and 1880s, as substantial numbers of white men continued to join black men in voting Republican, Democrats sought to enforce the supposedly "natural" racial segregation of political life.[35] They attempted to humiliate white Republicans by denying them access to white-only bars and restaurants, demanding first that they be "white men in principle as well as color."[36] If social slights did not affect white Republicans' allegiances, Democrats turned to a concerted campaign to ostracize such men, seeking to drive them from the public arenas necessary for their social, political, and economic lives. Even here, however, the Democratic elites frequently hinted that although white men had everything to lose by remaining Republicans, they could quickly regain their status if they renounced those ties. "There are a great many honest, upright good citizens . . . in the Radical party," declared one conservative newspaper. These were the sort of men whose whiteness—whose respectability and social fitness—might be regained by joining the Democratic Party.[37] The savage face of proscription and terror could be exchanged for respectful amity, but only if these white men would act as white supremacists demanded. The two faces of domination, it appeared, could be turned on whites as well as black.

Fusion and Its Destruction

The Democrats' uneasy rule was further shaken in the late 1880s by the appearance of the Farmer's Alliance. The Alliance provided hard-pressed farmers with an economic analysis of their hardship, and it suggested remedies that included cooperative economics and expansion of the money supply, both of which threatened the entrenched power. Democrats sought to neutralize the Alliance by keeping it out of politics, but soon the more radical members of the group, unsatisfied with Democratic responses to their demands, organized a new political party.

The People's Party, widely known as the Populists, sought a degree of federal intervention in the agricultural economy that even Reconstruction Republicans had not envisioned. Its most determined members fought for a world without middlemen, a world where corporate power was strictly limited, a world in which basic economic matters were decided democratically. Some recognized that in the South such a fight could succeed only if all farmers worked together; these Populists sought to break down the racial hierarchy that the Democrats had worked so hard to reinforce. These were the men who pioneered the "Fusion" strategy that in 1894 brought North Carolina's Republicans and Populists together in a reinvigorated biracial coalition that won the election and ended two decades of white supremacist Democratic control. In 1896 they sealed that victory by winning every single statewide office in North Carolina; their coalition, it appeared, was beginning to develop a life of its own, one that might bear fruit in new fiscal and social policies, and possibly—as black and white Fusionists worked together—in a climate of diminished racial hostility and hierarchy.

In 1898, when the Democrats concluded that the time was ripe for an assault on the Fusion government, they employed the same combination of sober persuasion and violent coercion that they had learned over the preceding generations. Just as they had once used their control of the law, they now used their near monopoly of the state's newspapers to lay out a stark set of alternatives: black and white Fusionists could either return to their proper places in the social order—blacks to social and economic subservience, whites to the party of white supremacy—or they would be subjected to murderous violence. Alexander Manly could either leave town or face the mob; similarly, as the *Wilmington Messenger* warned white Fusionist B. F. Keith, in the coming "magnificent fight for 'civilization vs. barbarism' . . . there is no middle ground upon which white men may stand."[38]

Violence, together with the credible threat of violence, proved successful. Democrats organized military companies, dubbed "White Leagues" or "Red Shirts," to give credibility to their threatening face. They imported speakers such as South Carolina's Ben Tillman, who spoke in Fayetteville and Red Springs near the end of the campaign. Famous for his pugnacity and his boast that he had helped in the bloody overthrow of Reconstruction in South Carolina, Ben Tillman was a symbol of Democrats' determination to win at all costs.[39] For the once and future ruling class, domination still meant offering stark and unmistakable alternatives. In parts of the state, Democrats' threats were sufficient to create Democratic majorities in an "orderly"—or at least relatively bloodless—election. But where Democrats could not win at the ballot box—and especially in Wilmington, where the city government had not been up for election in 1898—they proved entirely willing to demonstrate that political power in November 1898 came from the barrel of a gun.

Through Red Shirt terror and intimidation, Democrats suppressed Fusionist voting and won most of the contests in the 8 November election. But Wilmington's city government, since it was not up for election that year, remained in Republican and Populist hands. On 10 November, as part of a well-organized plan, Alfred M. Waddell led an army of white men into a predominantly black Wilmington neighborhood. They claimed that their purpose was to punish Alexander Manly, an editor who had published an angry editorial rebutting white men's sexual slanders against black people; but they were more than ready for a fight. They destroyed Manly's press and set the building that housed it ablaze. When black men appeared, having witnessed or got word of the mob's activities, Waddell's troops opened fire. Perhaps they believed that a black mobilization—and therefore "race war"—was inevitable, and they wanted to have the upper hand. Perhaps they were simply discharging years of frustration at having been denied the political and social authority to which they felt entitled. Within hours, white Democrats had mobilized a formidable fighting force from Wilmington and surrounding communities, including military units recently returned from service in the Spanish-American War. With a Gatling gun, a cannon, and hundreds of Winchester rifles, they scoured the city for their enemies: they fired on and disarmed black men; they combed black houses and neighborhoods for Fusionist city officials and gave those they found the choice of death or exile. White Fusionists like B. F. Keith, a city alderman, learned their lessons as well: "should one disapprove publically" of the massacre and coup, he wrote to a leading Populist, "he would have to leave [North Carolina] at once." Keith concluded, "I think it will be best for us not to say anything at present."[40]

The official death toll came to seven black men, but even Waddell acknowledged the actual total to be three times higher.[41] As one of the participants in the massacre wrote to a female acquaintance, "We have not killed enough negroes. Two or three white men were wounded and we have not gotten enough to make up for it." He concluded his letter with a description of the killing of one of the black men held responsible for wounding a white man: "He was caught and got on his knees, begging for mercy, saying he had five little children home, but the crowd of citizens who had him said *go* and he hadn't gone ten feet before the top of his head was *cut off* by bullets." For the self-defined white "citizens" of Wilmington, this was perhaps "enough to make up" for four years of Fusion rule.[42]

Alfred M. Waddell might not have wanted to speak directly about such violence when he addressed the readers of *Collier's* after the Democratic seizure of power. He understood, as clearly as any slaveholder had at the beginning of the century, that no class could profitably remain in power if it relied only on force. The violence necessary to overthrow the elected government had to be followed immediately by an appeal for social peace and harmony, an opportunity for both defeated opponents and potentially hostile outsiders to draw back from confrontation with white supremacist terror and accept the new order of things. And so once the forces subverting racial hierarchy and elite white rule had been beaten and shot back into line, Waddell could— indeed, had to—trade his Winchester rifle for expressions of tender concern, donning the paternalist face that had served previous generations so well.

Even as the Democratic forces disarmed the African American population and drove out the black political and economic elite, Waddell's self-transformation had begun: in a matter of hours, according to his article, he moved from being "the head of the procession" that attacked black Wilmington to being the leader of the force protecting black prisoners. "My position has been radically changed," he reported explaining to the victorious mob. In the closing lines of his *Collier's* article, Waddell expressed the satisfaction he felt at having restored "the negroes" to an appropriately grateful, subservient position: "They have seen my proclamation," he wrote with satisfaction, "and they feel secure, and they are rejoiced over it."[43] From murder had come the comforting stability of renewed paternal authority.

Black North Carolinians were not fooled. As one Wilmington woman wrote, pleading anonymously for a federal response to the white supremacy revolution, "The man who promises the Negro protection now as Mayor is the one who . . . said the Cape Fear should be strewn with carcasses." "Today," she concluded, "we are all mourners in a strange land with no protection near."[44] But for victorious white Democrats, whose new era of "progress" and "civility" rested on this foundation of white supremacist terror, the two faces of domination had once again brought proper order to North Carolina.[45]

Notes

1. Alfred M. Waddell, "The Story of the Wilmington, N.C., Race Riots," *Collier's Weekly*, 26 November 1898, 4–5.

2. Alfred M. Waddell, *Some Memories of My Life* (Raleigh: Edwards & Broughton, 1908), 243.

3. Waddell, "Story of the Wilmington, N.C., Race Riots," 4.

4. Alexis de Tocqueville, *Democracy in America*, trans. George Lawrence, ed. J. P. Mayer (New York: Harper, 1988), 358.

5. R. H. Taylor, "Slave Conspiracies in North Carolina," *North Carolina Historical Review* 5 (January 1928): 20–34.

6. John Scott Strickland, "The Great Revival and Insurrectionary Fears in North Carolina: An Examination of Antebellum Southern Society and Slave Revolt Panics," in *Class, Conflict, and Consensus: Antebellum Southern Community Studies*, ed. Orville Vernon Burton and Robert C. McMath Jr. (Westport, Conn.: Greenwood Press, 1982), 57–95.

7. Douglas R. Egerton, *Gabriel's Rebellion: The Virginia Slave Conspiracies of 1800 and 1802* (Chapel Hill: University of North Carolina Press, 1993); Edward Pearson, "From Stono to Vesey: Slavery, Resistance, and Ideology in South Carolina, 1739–1822" (Ph.D. diss., University of Wisconsin–Madison, 1992); Stephen Oates, *Fires of Jubilee: Nat Turner's Fierce Rebellion* (New York: Harper, 1975).

8. Taylor, "Slave Conspiracies," 24.

9. Ibid., 32.

10. N.C. Gov. Montfort Stokes to S.C. Gov. James Hamilton, 18 November 1831, in Eric Foner, ed., *Nat Turner* (Englewood Cliffs, N.J.: Prentice-Hall, 1971), 64–65.

11. Diary entries, 9–13, 21 September 1831, Personal Diary for 1830–36, Moses

Ashly Curtis Papers, Southern Historical Collection, University of North Carolina, Chapel Hill; Stephen Kantrowitz, personal communication with Vernon C. Tyson, 15 July 1997, Raleigh, N.C.

12. The social and intellectual world of a large planter is illuminated in Drew Gilpin Faust, *James Henry Hammond and the Old South: A Design for Mastery* (Baton Rouge: Louisiana State University Press, 1982).

13. The last generation of historical writing on American slavery has been in large part a dialogue with Eugene Genovese's *Roll, Jordan, Roll: The World the Slaves Made* (New York: Vintage, 1974). The following paragraphs of this essay suggest that Genovese, in describing the day-to-day management of Southern slave society, does not give sufficient emphasis to the violence and fear that pervaded that society.

14. Eugene Genovese, " 'Our Family, White and Black': Family and Household in the Southern Slaveholders' World View," in *In Joy and in Sorrow: Women, Family, and Marriage in the Victorian South*, ed. Carol Bleser (New York: Oxford University Press, 1991), 69–87.

15. Norrece T. Jones Jr., *Born a Child of Freedom, Yet a Slave: Mechanisms of Control and Strategies of Resistance in Antebellum South Carolina* (Hanover, N.H.: University Press of New England, Wesleyan University Press, 1990).

16. Ibid.; Paul A. David et al., *Reckoning with Slavery: A Critical Study in the Quantitative History of American Negro Slavery* (New York: Oxford University Press, 1976), 55–93; Clarence Poe, "Indians, Slaves, and Tories: Our Eighteenth Century Legislation Regarding Them," *North Carolina Historical Review* 9 (July 1909): 1–21.

17. Dependent for their survival and prosperity on the credibility of the masks they wore, slaveholders ultimately extended this sensitivity to appearances into other areas of their lives. By the last generations of slavery they often seemed willing to risk death at one another's hands rather than endure even minor slights. Their "honor," in other words, was inextricably rooted in the exigencies of slaveholding. See Kenneth Greenberg, *Honor and Slavery: Lies, Duels, Noses, Masks, Dressing as a Woman, Gifts, Strangers, Humanitarianism, Death, Slave Rebellions, the Proslavery Argument, Baseball, Hunting, and Gambling in the Old South* (Princeton: Princeton University Press, 1996); Steven Stowe, *Intimacy and Power in the Old South: Ritual in the Lives of the Planters* (Baltimore: Johns Hopkins University Press, 1987); and Bertram Wyatt-Brown, *Southern Honor: Ethics and Behavior in the Old South* (New York: Oxford University Press, 1982).

18. *David Walker's Appeal, in Four Articles; Together with a Preamble, to the Coloured Citizens of the World, but in particular, and very expressly, to those of the United States of America*, rev. ed. with intro. by Sean Wilentz (New York: Hill & Wang, 1995).

19. The slaveholders' faith in their own physical mastery may also have caused them to overestimate the ability of their primarily agricultural region to win a war against the industrializing North; however, this martial self-confidence seems to have inspired wariness and, at times, even crippling terror among many Union officers, especially in the early years of the war: see Michael C. C. Adams, *Our Masters the Rebels: A Speculation on Union Military Failure in the East, 1861–1865* (Cambridge: Harvard University Press, 1978).

20. For documents and analysis of the experiences of nearly 200,000 black Union troops, see *Freedom: A Documentary History of Emancipation, 1861–1867*, Series 2, *The Black Military Experience*, ed. Ira Berlin, Joseph P. Reidy, and Leslie S. Rowland (New York: Cambridge University Press, 1982). Recent scholarship has argued

that slaves, by their actions, helped force the Union to adopt emancipation (and black enlistment) as part of its overall strategy; see Ira Berlin et al., *Slaves No More: Three Essays on Emancipation and the Civil War* (New York: Cambridge University Press, 1992). The Confederate government refused officially to enlist black men until the last weeks of its existence, but individual black soldiers did fight with Confederate armies, primarily as the body servants of their owners. It should not surprise us that enslaved Southerners, generally forbidden to organize as a group, pursued their freedom through complex individual calculuses of risk and benefit that occasionally included Confederate military service; nor should this cause us to doubt that a Confederate victory would have kept most Southern blacks in slavery long after 1865.

21. Richard L. Fuchs, *An Unerring Fire: The Massacre at Fort Pillow* (Rutherford, N.J.: Fairleigh Dickinson University Press, 1994).

22. Dan T. Carter, "The Anatomy of Fear: The Christmas Day Insurrection Scare of 1865," *Journal of Southern History* 42 (August 1976): 345–64.

23. Paul D. Escott, "White Republicanism and Ku Klux Klan Terror: The North Carolina Piedmont during Reconstruction," in *Race, Class, and Politics in Southern History: Essays in Honor of Robert F. Durden*, ed. Jeffrey J. Crow, Paul D. Escott, and Charles L. Flynn Jr. (Baton Rouge: Louisiana State University Press, 1989), 5, 30.

24. "Tracts for the People," number 6: "The Radical Scheme of War and Treason," Democratic pamphlet, 1868, in *North Carolina Political Tracts, 1865–1898*, microfilm at the North Carolina Collection, University of North Carolina, Chapel Hill.

25. Allen W. Trelease, *White Terror: The Ku Klux Klan Conspiracy and Southern Reconstruction* (1971; reprint, Baton Rouge: Louisiana State University Press, 1995).

26. Albion Tourgée, *The Invisible Empire* (1883; reprint, Baton Rouge: Louisiana State University Press, 1989), 123–24.

27. Escott, "White Republicanism and Ku Klux Klan Terror," 30.

28. Trelease, *White Terror*, 194, 198–207.

29. Ibid., 189.

30. Ibid., 190.

31. Ibid., *White Terror*, 337.

32. *Monroe Enquirer*, 31 August 1875, p. 3.

33. This is a major theme of Eric Foner's *Reconstruction: America's Unfinished Revolution, 1863–1877* (New York: Harper, 1988).

34. David Roediger, *The Wages of Whiteness: Race and the Making of the American Working Class* (New York: Verso, 1990).

35. Escott, "White Republicans and Ku Klux Klan Terror," 34.

36. *Monroe Enquirer*, 14 August 1876.

37. Ibid.

38. *Wilmington Messenger*, 7 September 1898, 1.

39. *Fayetteville Observer*, 13, 20 October 1898.

40. Keith to Butler, 28 November, [14 November] 1898, Marion Butler Papers, Southern Historical Collection, University of North Carolina, Chapel Hill.

41. See reports in the *Wilmington Messenger*, 11 November 1898, and the *Washington Post*, 11 November 1898; see also Prather, *We Have Taken a City: Wilmington Racial Massacre and Coup of 1898* (Cranbury, N.J.: Associated University Presses, 1984), and other essays in this volume.

42. Jack Metts to Miss Elizabeth, 12 November 1898, Cronly Family Papers, Manuscript Department, Perkins Library, Duke University.

43. Waddell, "Story of the Wilmington, N.C., Race Riots," 14–16.

44. Anonymous to William McKinley, 13 November 1898, file 17743-1898, Department of Justice, Record Group R660, National Archives, Washington, D.C.

45. As late as the 1940s, state leaders continued to alternate declarations of paternalist obligation with reminders of the deadly consequences of black political or economic mobilization; see Timothy B. Tyson's essay in this volume.

111

**The Two
Faces of
Domination**

Laura F.
Edwards

Captives of Wilmington

The Riot and Historical Memories
of Political Conflict, 1865–1898

For a century, myth and legend have shrouded the Wilmington racial massacre. Only recently have Southern historians stopped justifying the 1898 white supremacy campaign and the violent takeover of Wilmington as a necessary evil. For the most part, historians long repeated the story constructed and perpetuated with frightening effectiveness by Democratic newspaper editors such as Josephus Daniels of the *Raleigh News and Observer*, by four governors who made political capital of their leading roles in the 1898 white supremacy campaign, and by supporters of U.S. senator Furnifold Simmons, the campaign's architect and, afterward, North Carolina's political kingmaker for nearly thirty years. Public avenues, state buildings, and university halls named in honor of them bear witness to these political leaders' success.

Among the most influential of the historians who accepted the Democratic version of events in 1898 was J. G. de Roulhac Hamilton, whose state history informed the content of school textbooks for generations. Writing in 1919, Hamilton interpreted the Democratic Party's takeover of Wilmington as the dramatic conclusion of a historical conflict between the forces of good and evil. His story began in the dark days following the Confederacy's defeat when, according to Hamilton, Northern radicals in Congress unleashed their vengeance on the prostrate South. These misguided policies, he explained, allowed corrupt Republican leaders to dupe ignorant black voters and to gain control of the state in the late 1860s. Just when the resulting disorder threatened complete destruction, the Democrats rallied to save the day. Hamilton admitted that they resorted to questionable tactics, such as violence and fraud. But, he insisted, the end justified the means. The Democratic victory in the mid-1870s, however, was incomplete, because the Republican Party still remained strong in the eastern part of the state, where blacks were a majority of the population. According to Hamilton, evil still lurked there in the form of "violence, injustice, dishonesty" as well as "inefficiency, incompetence, and partisanship, accompanied by a deadly blight upon all progress." The Democratic Party managed to contain the "blight" in a few counties during the 1880s. But it grew in strength and threatened to infect the rest of the state by the 1890s. The final showdown came in Wilmington. Encouraged by designing demagogues, the conduct of blacks in the city had grown "indescribably bad" and was getting worse. With "murder, burglary, arson, [and] the threat of rape" staring them "in the face," the victimized white citizenry had no choice but to organize and take back the city. As in the 1870s, the methods were regrettable. But, Hamilton argued, whites in Wilmington were acting in the best interests of the entire community. They were actually protecting the mass of blacks by destroying the evil forces leading them astray and establishing order, security, progress, and "good government" for everyone.[1]

Although obviously sympathetic to the political goals of the Democratic Party, Hamilton did not simply fabricate a history to serve his own political purposes. He took pride in his professional status and based his work on archival sources, newspaper accounts, and oral testimony, clearly documenting all his conclusions. Not surprisingly, these sources tended to confirm his political views. They also supplied the key narrative elements that structured his analysis. For Wilmington, Hamilton relied primarily on local newspapers from eastern North Carolina, published by whites who were sympathetic to the Democratic Party. The *Washington Post*'s North Carolina correspondent, who gave Wilmington extensive coverage, agreed with the local Democratic press. So did many other newspapers across the country. Even the *New York Herald*, which attempted a more objective tone, concluded that whites had been forced to take drastic steps because of "outrageous abuses" of power under "black domination." In fact, the press used the Democratic takeover of Wilmington to capture complicated political conflicts and condense them in a single, bold narrative—a conventional moral drama played out on a set stage, with clearly identifiable heroes and villains and an unambiguous ending. What happened in Wilmington became an affirmation of white supremacy not just in that one city, but in the South and in the nation as a whole.[2]

Although celebratory and apologetic accounts of the 1898 white supremacy campaign remain at the center of North Carolina's white political culture and popular understanding, a new generation of Southern historians has overturned the fallacy of the "heroic" tale of white supremacy. After the Civil War and Emancipation, these historians have argued, North Carolina's Democratic Party successfully institutionalized a conservative agenda at odds with the interests of most state residents by methodically crushing the opposition. While particularly blatant and brutal, the violence in Wilmington was a logical extension of tactics used commonly by Democratic leaders throughout the late nineteenth century. This reappraisal of Wilmington has won the day among scholars and will presumably "trickle down" to a younger generation as school texts are rewritten and new popular accounts appear. Yet, in many ways, these new historical accounts remain trapped in the same problematic narrative confines that structured J. G. de Roulhac Hamilton's work. To be sure, the conclusions are reversed: Wilmington is now a tragedy in which evil triumphs over virtue. But the story is still told as a conventional moral drama that unfolds on the same stage, with the same actors, and the same kind of plot.[3]

The similarities raise some of the same problems for current historians as they did for Hamilton. Specifically, accounts both old and new tend to cast working-class African Americans as passive figures, buffeted about by events beyond their control. These people receive rights. Rights are taken away from them. But even sympathetic versions rarely depict them as active participants in securing or defining those rights. Ironically, recent historical treatments of Wilmington, with their powerful portrayals of raw Democratic force, perpetuate this view. The drama captures our historical imagination so completely that we find it difficult to think of African Americans, particularly working-class blacks, as anything but politically marginal. To retell the story, we need to abandon the familiar stage, props, and script. In fact, we need to distance ourselves from Wilmington altogether. We must go back in time to Reconstruction to recover a different history of struggle—one that centered on issues never articulated by any political party, that never reached the pages of any newspaper, that unfolded in obscure places, and that was spearheaded by people whose names have long since been forgotten. The voices, actions, and aspirations of these black, primarily working-class people break down the confining assumptions that have trapped previous work on Wilmington and allow us to see both the racial violence and its legacy in different ways.

Josh Green, a dockworker who died fighting in Wilmington, provides our first clue to this forgotten world of political conflict. Green was not an actual person, but a character in Charles Chesnutt's thinly fictionalized account of the Wilmington riot, *The Marrow of Tradition*. Chesnutt, an African American writer who grew up near Wilmington, knew the region, its people, and its politics. Appalled at the way national reports uncritically accepted local Democratic interpretations, he presented the event from an African American perspective. *The Marrow of Tradition* thus follows the facts closely—although Chesnutt's facts are different from those of contemporary white reporters, politicians, and historians.

Josh Green represents a strong undercurrent of militancy that Chesnutt saw among working-class blacks in the South at the turn of the century. Chesnutt attributes this militancy to the "younger generation" who had been raised in freedom and expected more than their parents. A part of this new generation, Josh Green demands respect and refuses to accept the injustices forced upon his race in the past. He also knows the price of acquiescence, for he watched the Ku Klux Klan murder his father and frighten his mother into insanity. The racial massacre becomes Green's pivotal moment. Faced with the violence of whites, he decides on open, armed resistance and dies a violent death. Although he knows what the outcome will be, the choice is clear. "I would rather be a dead nigger any day," he announces, "dan a live dog!" Green's character had a basis in fact. As literary scholar Richard Yarborough suggests in another essay in this volume, he is actually a composite of Josh Halsey and Daniel Wright, two black Wilmingtonians who died fighting white supremacy in 1898. Other African Americans resisted as well. On the day of the slaughter, unidentified blacks confronted white rioters and attempted to protect themselves and their communities. Among them were several hundred cotton compress workers who poured out the factory doors onto the streets when they heard about the violence.[4]

Yet, even as Chesnutt corrected the racial biases of white-authored accounts, he wrote other biases into his version of Wilmington, misrepresenting the source, substance, and accomplishments of black working-class militancy. A middle-class intellectual who had settled in the urban North, he tended to see political action in terms of incremental reform initiated from above by an organized, formally educated elite. He also valued middle-class respectability as a strategy for racial uplift, while simultaneously romanticizing and dismissing the culture of poor Southern blacks as authentic but misguided and counterproductive. Drawing on these views, Chesnutt was in part critical of Josh Green. Although sympathetic to Green's rage, Chesnutt believed that direct action hurt African Americans by reinforcing negative racial stereotypes of black criminality and irrationality.[5]

The historical record provides another way to situate people like Josh Green. As local records from across the state reveal, black militants did not just begin to appear at the turn of the century. Nor were they just members of the "younger generation." Nor were they only men. To the contrary, working-class African American women and men had been publicly claiming and defining their rights as free people since Emancipation. Often overlooked because they took place during the ordinary business of daily life, their stands were undertaken at great risk and at great personal cost. They also resulted in important, tangible victories. In this sense, the fictional Josh Green and his real life counterparts in 1898 were actually part of a long tradition of political struggle.[6]

This struggle has remained hidden largely because historians have tended to define politics narrowly in terms of elections, policies, and public institutions. To be sure, the Reconstruction Acts, the Thirteenth, Fourteenth, and Fifteenth Amendments, and the new state constitutions swept aside the public, institutional impediments that kept African Americans from enjoying full civil and political rights. But these same measures transformed private life as well. In fact, as I have argued in my recent book *Gendered Strife and Confusion: The Political Culture of Reconstruction*, "private" and "public" life in the late nineteenth century South were connected. More than that, the relationship between the two was crucial to the very structure of Southern society. Before Emancipation, private and public were literally linked in the figure of a white male household head who assumed economic, legal, and moral responsibility for a range of dependents, including African American slaves as well as white women and children. Private authority translated directly into public power, giving household heads the right to represent their dependents' political interests. White men thus claimed power through their ability to fulfill the duties of household head, not on the ascriptive basis of their race and sex alone. Not every man measured up. White men who lacked sufficient property to maintain households of their own were also politically marginalized. Nevertheless, the position of propertyless white men was always different from that of white women and African Americans, who might step out of their proper places and even step into the role of household head but could never fully embody the power of that role.[7]

By contrast, law and social convention denied both private and public power to all dependents—women as wives, African Americans as slaves, and children as minors. Of course, these groups occupied distinctly different positions. Equating the subordination of slaves, which was legally absolute, with the subordination of white wives and children would constitute a serious misrepresentation of Southern society. But the status of these groups overlapped in the sense that they were relegated to the private sphere, where they were subject to the governance of a household head. There, slaves endured the most extreme form of dependency, legally categorized as their masters' property. They had no recognized claims to their families, personal possessions, or even their own bodies. They could be sold at any time. They could not read and write, assemble freely, own property, or enter into contracts, including legal marriage. Anything that they used or produced, including their children, belonged to their masters. Physically tied to their owners' households, they could not leave without written permission. This did not mean that slaves had no belongings, families, or private lives outside their masters' control. But it did mean that all these things were "privileges" that masters could revoke at any time.[8]

War and Emancipation shook the antebellum household to its foundations, destabilizing the configuration of power it supported. Even the simplest acts took on political meaning. Bringing family members together to form their own households, demanding wages for their work, or resisting corporal punishment—in all these ways African Americans rejected their former position as dependents within households headed by whites. Such acts, moreover, were understood by African Americans and whites as overt political claims connected to larger structural changes in Southern society. This was the experience of Maria Mitchell, a black woman from Edgecombe County, in 1869. As her son later described it, "his Mama was talking loud." B. D. Armstrong, a white man, probably her employer, asked her what all the "fuss" was about. Mitchell responded that "she was talking for her rights and would as much as she pleased and as loud as she pleased." Irritated, Armstrong said that "if she did not hush he would make her hush." Then he "struck her in the face five licks and broke out a piece of her tooth." Not so easily silenced, she kept "talking for her rights," filed charges of assault against Armstrong, and succeeded in obtaining an indictment against him.[9]

By itself, Maria Mitchell's case seems odd and inconsequential. But it was only one among hundreds of similar cases from across North Carolina during the 1860s, 1870s, and 1880s. In this context, Maria Mitchell's claims and the way she made them offer insights into working-class African Americans' political concerns and the politics of daily life in the post-Emancipation South. Generally, these cases involved common interactions that just happened to end in extraordinary ways. When conflict erupted between blacks and whites, it was usually because African Americans refused to defer to whites in authority. Cases like Mitchell's thus reveal the daily battles that ordinary African Americans continually fought to realize freedom in both their private and public lives. At the same time, legal proceedings themselves upped the public stakes by bringing in the state to settle conflicts that had formally been within the private purview of white masters. Some African Americans, like Maria Mitchell, initiated suits themselves, claiming public personas that had been denied them in slavery. But even when they simply answered charges, working-class African Americans still participated in a fundamental reworking of state governance by defending themselves in court. Their very presence there countered the aims of the Democratic Party, which sought to limit access to rights and public space on the basis of race and class. And poor African Americans did not merely mouth Republican Party principles or insist that existing laws apply equally to everyone. Instead, they turned the courtroom into their own political forum, demanding recognition of concerns ignored in party politics and advancing interpretations of their rights that were far more radical than those in any party platform.[10]

Emancipation theoretically transferred the power of masters to former slaves, making African Americans masters of their own bodies and their own lives. Maria Mitchell acted on this new autonomy by talking "as much as she pleased and as loud as she pleased," even when it offended a prominent white man. With these words, Mitchell announced that she could express her own ideas, however, whenever, wherever, and to whomever she wanted. Filtered through the categories of the law, her words sound like a simple endorsement of free speech. But Mitchell was actually claiming something much more fundamental: she was now her own person, not a legal extension of some white master's estate, and had the right to conduct herself and her life as she saw fit. B. D. Armstrong's reaction suggests why Mitchell's actions were so important. Ordering her to "hush" because her words irritated him, he rejected Mitchell's right to self-expression. Then he went one step further, denying her right to control her own body. With five blows to her mouth, Armstrong tried to obliterate the new boundaries Mitchell had drawn and to force her back into submission.[11]

B. D. Armstrong's reaction was typical among white Southerners after the Civil War. For most, black skin had been so thoroughly conflated with slavery's complete denial of civil status that the two were difficult to disentangle. In fact, it was common for whites to attribute the effects of legal subordination to the biological "nature" of African Americans. By this logic, African Americans were not just people who had been enslaved and therefore happened to occupy the position of slave. They *were* slaves: dependent, irrational, and lazy by nature, African Americans were physically unable to understand or to exercise civil or political rights. Racial imagery popular among whites threw these assumptions into sharp relief. When African Americans were under the supervision of their masters, whites depicted them as happy, ineffectual minors who could not survive without guidance. But once Sambo and Mammy ventured out on their own, their characters changed dramatically. They became the menacing, oversexed black male rapist and black female Jezebel, images that conveyed the extent to which whites believed African Americans were incapable of self-governance. Physical discipline, according to many whites, was the only way to compel social responsibility.[12]

After Emancipation, such efforts took both legal and extralegal forms. North Carolina's Black Code, passed during Presidential Reconstruction in 1866 and similar to Black Codes in other Southern states, legally limited all African Americans' civil status. It did recognize freedpeople's right to enter into contracts and allowed them to initiate suits in the criminal and civil courts. But these rights meant little within the context of the code's other provisions. African Americans were given more severe punishments than whites for similar offenses. They were not allowed to testify against whites, except in cases that directly involved their own interests. The vagrancy section required them to work and limited their freedom of movement, while other provisions denied them the right to bear arms and encumbered their ability to enter into contracts and to buy and sell property. The Black Code even undercut the institutional integrity of African American families by allowing whites to bind

Laura F.
Edwards

out black children without consulting their parents. The terms used to refer to African Americans in the Code suggest its intent: they were "negroes," "persons of color," men and women who were "lately slaves," and "inhabitants of this state," but African Americans were not full citizens. Nor did they have the civil status necessary to protect themselves, their property, or members of their families, as white citizens did.[13]

The sentiments embodied in North Carolina's Black Code had existed before the code was passed in 1866 and continued after it was abolished in 1868. For some whites, even the few rights allowed to African Americans in the Black Code were too much. They saw the smallest, simplest acts as threatening reminders of African Americans' new civil status. Uncertain of the law's ability to contain the threat, they took it on themselves to respond. Klan attacks, for instance, went beyond attempts to destroy the Republican Party or to release pent-up personal frustrations. The predations described by a group of beleaguered blacks in Granville County were common. In their neighborhood, the Klan had gone "to a Colored mans house and Got him out and Beet him [illegible word] and beet his wife and cut her Dress open and tied her to a tree. . . . They then went to another ones house and comence tarring [tearing] the top of his house off. . . . [They] Got hold of his wife . . . and she Got Loose and ran and they shot her In the back and by [the] side of the face." The terror might keep African American men from voting for the Republican Party. If not, the Klan still made its point. Bursting into houses, destroying cherished belongings, and then beating, torturing, and murdering, the Klan graphically reduced its victims to the position formerly allotted to slaves—a people without rights to property, family, or even their own bodies.[14]

The Klan and other organized vigilante groups were not the only ones who tried to teach this lesson. Violence against African Americans was a chillingly common part of everyday life in late nineteenth-century North Carolina. The most minor encounters could end violently. In 1868, when Jordan Overby took a few pieces of bark from a tree in Granville County to dye cloth, he did not even think to ask permission. But George Watkins, the white man who owned the land, flew into a rage, overwhelmed Overby, tied him down, and threatened to give him 500 lashes if he did not pay—and pay dearly—for the bark. Open defiance almost inevitably drew blows from whites. James Peace initiated and won a settlement against his white employer in 1866. But when he returned with the authorization to receive his back wages, his employer shot him. Fortunately, the employer's aim was as bad as his temper, and Peace survived his wounds.[15]

Just as Maria Mitchell refused to "hush" and then filed charges, so did Jordan Overby and James Peace. Given the particular historical context, their actions were remarkable. As slaves, none of these people could have charged their masters or anyone else with assault. If their masters beat them, there was no crime at all because the law granted masters the right to "discipline" their slaves as they saw fit, stepping in only when punishment resulted in death. If someone else beat them, the law labeled it a crime against the master. Emancipation wiped away these inequalities only in theory. In practice, African Americans had to continually assert their new civil status. In the cases of Maria Mitchell, Jordan Overby, and James Peace, they fought to make what had been acceptable corporal punishment against slaves into the illegal act of assault. In other cases, they fought to receive wages for their labor,[16] to protect their property,[17] and to keep their family members together.[18] In all these ways, African Americans not only asserted their rights, but also forced whites to acknowledge them. However much they might resist the idea, whites had to deal with African Americans' new civil status the moment they were hauled into court and made to justify their actions. Of course, the outcomes of these cases did not always support African Americans' claims. But the process itself was still important. By continually trying to realize civil rights in practice, poor blacks kept this political promise from dwindling into empty rhetoric. Not surprisingly, many whites found African Americans' legal claims profoundly disturbing. It was an experience they neither forgot nor forgave.

Maria Mitchell's claims to speak in public were also significant. The political implications of slavery had gone far deeper than the denial of suffrage. Relegating slaves to a private sphere and placing them under the direct dominion of their masters, the law kept African Americans out of all formal public arenas. They could not sue, bring criminal charges, make contracts, or testify against whites. Even more insidious, the law categorized all their concerns as "private" matters unsuitable for "public" consideration. The law found expression in white Southerners' concern about African Americans' public presence. Local white authorities dispatched patrollers to enforce the laws prohibiting slaves from assembling or going abroad on their own. When blacks met up with whites, they were forced into established patterns of deference. Certain that all blacks needed constant supervision, whites explained the constraints in terms of African Americans' alleged irresponsibility. It never occurred to them that what they considered "disorderly behavior" might stem from legitimate complaints about the existing social order.[19]

After Emancipation, white Southerners complained loudly and regularly about African Americans' new access to public space. They tried to restrict unsupervised meetings, whether religious, social, or political. Whites also tried to curtail freedpeople's mobility. In Edgecombe County, William Royster swore out a complaint against Green Gay in 1868 for visiting the black workers on his plantation. As Royster explained, he told Gay "that he did not belong on the farm, and that unless he kept order and quiet he should not visit the farm." Gay replied "that he would come whenever he wished to and that [Royster] could not keep him away." Whites also demanded that African Americans maintain a deferential demeanor. Not surprisingly, William Royster was as concerned about Gay's "defiant and desperate manner" as his mobility. Royster was not alone. Whites took offense when black people looked them directly in the eye, stood tall and squared their shoulders, or otherwise assumed a noticeably assertive physical stance. When the races came in contact on city streets and in other public areas, whites expected African Americans to step out of the way and tip their hats. In fact, one of the most common complaints among whites after Emancipation was that African Americans defied established racial conventions and refused to cede public space to whites.[20]

African Americans' access to electoral politics and the legal system troubled white Southerners even more. Many believed African Americans to be dishonest and deceitful by nature. As such, they were a race of people whose public statements could never be trusted. In fact, the issue of black testimony provoked some of the most heated exchanges among whites debating the state's Black Code. The code ultimately allowed blacks to testify in cases where their immediate interests were involved. But conservative whites thought even this gave African Americans too great a public voice. They never accepted the practice of unrestricted black testimony instituted after the code's abolition. Black manhood suffrage, from their perspective, was completely out of the question. Like B. F. Moore, conservative Democrat and principal architect of the Black Code, many whites forecast doom if African American men could vote: "The race, long degraded by servitude, ignorant of the politics of government, very low in its grade of morals, and wholly dependent for a living on the ability of the wealthier class of society, would, if allowed to vote, consult their material aid, and speadily [sic] engender among the whites, hosts of vile and reckless demagogues." Republicans who received the votes of blacks were "vile and reckless demagogues" by definition. When these candidates won election to state and local offices, white conservatives were convinced that their worst fears had been realized.[21]

But poor blacks like Maria Mitchell determinedly claimed a political presence with or without the vote. In "talking for her rights," Mitchell made public her discontent with B. D. Armstrong in a way common among poor people during this period. One year later, Dock Baker made a similar stand at the door of Collins T. Cross's house in Edgecombe County, cursing him loudly and refusing to leave. When ordered to do so, he spat back that "he would be God d—d if he went home until he got ready." After John F. Knight accused Virginia Barlow's daughter of stealing from him in 1871, Barlow followed Knight's buggy down the road for two miles verbally "abusing" him all the while. Hurling words like punches, Mitchell, Baker, and Barlow talked loud in places where others could not help but hear.[22]

B. D. Armstrong, Collins T. Cross, and John F. Knight ordered the African Americans who had offended them to be quiet and then assaulted them when they refused. But violence did not silence Maria Mitchell, Dock Baker, or Virginia Barlow. Instead, these blacks went to another public forum and filed charges, affirming their right to speak publicly. The court amplified their demands with the authority of the law and the power of the state. Needless to say, this was not the outcome that Armstrong, Cross, Knight, or other white conservatives desired. Of course, some African Americans had verbally abused white men in the days of slavery. But they had no public recourse if the incidents ended in violence. Their masters mediated the conflicts and meted out punishments themselves, reasserting authority over all their slaves in the process. After Emancipation, African Americans could contest that authority in ways that they had not been able to do before. And they did. Where men like Armstrong, Cross, and Knight had once acted with virtual impunity, they now had to defend themselves before an outside authority—the state. The actions of Scott Wilkerson, who guarded a black employee's house to keep him from filing a complaint with the local magistrate, threatening to "split [his] head open with a rail" if he did, suggests how disturbing the experience could be for whites. To add insult to injury, state authority during Republican rule was often represented by a jury including the very people whom these elite white men had so recently commanded at will. Occasionally, African Americans even won. But if they did not, their cases still undermined the authority that all whites had formally exercised over all African Americans.[23]

No wonder some whites tried so hard to silence African Americans and bar them from public arenas. Democrats moved to restrict access to the local courts as soon as they seized control of the state legislature. Their new state constitution, ratified in 1876, gave the legislature the power to appoint all magistrates and other key officials in county government. Over the remainder of the century, the legislature slowly expanded the jurisdiction of magistrates, who already exercised broad discretionary power to accept or dismiss certain complaints at will. As Democratic appointees tried a wider range of cases without outside oversight, the legal position of African Americans deteriorated. By 1880, one African American labeled the Granville County Inferior Court the "infernal court." Warming to the subject, he joked with bitter humor that presiding Democratic justices would lock up black people just for showing their faces at the courthouse. Nonetheless, African Americans continued to use the legal system in counties and municipalities (like Wilmington) with large black populations where Republicans managed to retain a foothold. In 1877, when Granville County's John Bobbitt tried to file charges against his white employers, the Democratic justice in his township flatly refused to hear his complaint. Not so easily discouraged, Bobbitt walked to the county seat in search of the Republican sheriff. Bobbitt's trek underscored both the importance and the fragility of African Americans' access to the public arena of the courts.[24]

Working-class African Americans' position as propertyless people who had to sell their labor for a living also compromised their ability to talk "as much as [they] pleased and as loud as [they] pleased," as Maria Mitchell had done. In the antebellum South, unskilled laborers had not enjoyed the same social or political standing as landowners and craftsmen, who possessed the land, tools, or skills to establish households and maintain control over their own and their families' labor. If anything, wage work implied a certain amount of dependency. North Carolina law classified common laborers as domestic dependents—menial servants who were subject to their masters' governance. Not only did the law give employers complete control over the production process, but neither law nor cultural practice clearly limited the amount of power employers could assume over their workers' private lives. Antebellum courts even placed some renters within this category, distinguishing between tenants and sharecroppers. Legally, antebellum tenants paid a specified amount to work the land for a given time, but they maintained control over their labor, the production process, and the final product. Even before the Civil War, however, sharecroppers were common laborers who worked under the direct control of their landlords and possessed no property rights to the goods they produced.[25]

Once released from slavery, African Americans faced these entrenched laws and customs that positioned all propertyless laborers as dependent servants. Racial ideology only compounded freedpeople's problems, reinforcing the associations between black skin and economic subordination. The advent of Republican rule in 1868 did little to buttress their position. Republicans strengthened workers' ability to collect wages through laborers' lien laws. Nevertheless, these measures still restrained workers' mobility and fixed their obligations to employers by specifying that a laborer had to work out "the full term for which he shall have contracted" or be fired by the employer through no legally recognized fault of the laborer. In 1874, the state supreme court affirmed that all common laborers were governed by their masters in the same manner as other domestic dependents. By extension, labor conflicts were private matters outside the scope of state governance. "There is a certain analogy among all the domestic relations," the presiding justice wrote, "and it would be dangerous to the repose and happiness of families if the law permitted any man under whatever professions of philanthropy or charity, to sow discontent between the head of a family and its various members, wife, children and servants. Interference with such relations can only be justified under the most special circumstances." When Democrats reclaimed the statehouse, they used this opening to undercut the position of laborers still further. In 1877, the legislature went so far as to collapse all tenants into the same category with sharecroppers and common laborers. Afterward, all propertyless people legally shared the same burdens of dependency.[26]

Looking back fondly to the control they exercised over labor in slavery, many white employers and landlords tried to push these legal openings to their most extreme limits. B. D. Armstrong, for instance, did not hesitate to order Maria Mitchell to stop "making a fuss" or, when she refused, to use physical force to coerce compliance. His response was common among white employers and landlords in the decades following Emancipation. Like Armstrong, other whites insisted on broad supervisory powers over their laborers' lives on and off the job, including the right to "discipline" workers with physical force. In fact, employers and landlords refused to recognize African American laborers' and tenants' right to direct any aspect of their own lives. They paid wages so low that black workers fell into debt and, unable to get ahead, became locked into menial labor. They interfered with black workers' social gatherings and religious meetings. They obstructed poor African Americans' efforts to keep family members together and set up their own households. They even tried to regulate modes of individual expression, such as "talking loud." And they loudly protested any public regulation of their actions or the labor relationship as an infringement on their own privacy.[27]

African Americans often refused such demands, as Maria Mitchell's actions suggest. Even before Armstrong slapped her in the face, he had done something to make Mitchell confront him and "talk for her rights." So certain was she that he had violated her basic rights that she was willing to endure physical violence to make her point. The court defined her confrontation with Armstrong as an assault case. But when Maria Mitchell was "talking for her rights," she probably had something different in mind. Conflicts like hers generally grew out of black laborers' efforts to obtain some control over working conditions, payment of wages, or personal prerogatives.[28]

Less tangible, but no less important, many black laborers also insisted that they be treated with the respect they thought all free people deserved. Usually, black workers who felt aggrieved simply moved in hopes of finding better positions elsewhere. But some confronted their employers directly, giving expression to thoughts that often went unsaid. In 1884, for instance, William Allen of Granville County finally tired of his employer's peremptory tone and tight control. After announcing that he was neither treated "right" nor like a "man," Allen charged at his employer with a large stick. Another Granville county man, Allen Oakley, finally reached his limits as well. The local newspaper, the *Torchlight*, featured Oakley as one of the county's most successful black farmers in 1879. Yet his landlord, Fielding Knott, still demanded that Oakley "work by [his] orders" and "be obedient and respectful." For all the economic benefits of his position, Oakley could not bring himself to meet these demands. One day in 1881, when Knott rebuked him, Oakley "seemed to fly into a passion," picked up a nearby chair, and threatened to smash Knott on the head with it. While perhaps neither Allen nor Oakley received satisfaction, other African American workers did. They won compensation for their work, meager though it often was. They kept their families together. They set up their own community institutions. They found ways to control the work process. And, like Maria Mitchell, they maintained their dignity, even if they could not always force their employers to acknowledge it. In all these ways, black working people challenged the idea that the need to labor for others translated directly into powerlessness. Although not completely successful, they did resist the most extreme forms of dependency. Still, even their small victories were never secure. With little institutional backing, African American laborers had to continually fight the same battles to maintain what little ground they had managed to seize.[29]

Together, Maria Mitchell's claims provide the larger political backdrop against which the events behind the Wilmington massacre were played out. In fact, Josh Green articulates them all early in Charles

Chesnutt's novel, long before Democratic leaders begin plotting the takeover of the city. First, he declares his civil status as a free person: "I ain' no w'ite folks' nigger," and "I don' call no man 'marster.'" Then, in the same impassioned speech, he claims his right to control his labor and the fruits earned thereby: "I don' wan' nothin' but w'at I wo'k fer, but I wants all er dat." And finally he insists on his right to defend his interests publicly: "I never moles's no wi'te man, 'less'n he moles's me fus'."[30] Later, when the rioting begins, he puts these principles into action. "De w'ite folks are killin' de niggers, an' we ain' gwine ter stan' up an' be shot down like dogs," he announces. "We're gwine ter defen' ou' lives, an' we ain' gwine ter run away f'm no place where we've got a right ter be; an woe be ter d w'ite man w'at lays han's on us!"[31] But neither the character's words nor his actions were new or unique to 1898. Chesnutt spoke through him from an established, venerable tradition of black working-class protest. Josh Green was "talking for his rights." And like Maria Mitchell, he was willing to take great risks to be heard.

In 1898, Democrats reacted to claims such as those made by Mitchell and Green. The whites who seized power in Wilmington wanted to do more than simply eliminate African Americans from local and state government. After all, if electoral politics had been their only concern, there would have been no reason to stage the violent takeover of Wilmington. African Americans had never dominated state or local governance, not even in eastern North Carolina, where they formed the majority in many counties. The Democratic Party, moreover, had just swept the November election two days earlier, securing white supremacy in electoral politics by assuring passage of a disfranchisement amendment.[32] But electoral victory addressed only part of Democrats' concerns. White men still had to deal with people like Maria Mitchell, who could "talk for their rights" even if they could not vote. In fact, these black workers' political claims were much more difficult to silence because they were not confined to party politics. To be sure, white rioters specifically targeted Alexander L. Manly, the black editor of the *Wilmington Record*, destroying the newspaper's offices in retaliation for an editorial they deemed to be disparaging to white women. Later, the mob also sought out other prominent black leaders. But their violence was also directed at the black working class.

Behind the virulent racial rhetoric of the 1898 Democratic campaign were specific complaints about black working-class militancy. That fall, local newspapers were filled with stories complaining of African Americans' assertive public presence. In one incident, reported by the *Wilmington Messenger*, a black woman refused to cede her half of the sidewalk to a white woman and then struck her with an umbrella. According to the newspaper, a nearby black man urged the black woman on, calling out, "'That's right, d—n it, give it to her.'" Other reports accused African American men, women, and children of verbally criticizing whites, approaching them in a threatening manner, or physically assaulting them.[33] Of course, these incidents may have been figments of the rather active imaginations of Democratic newspaper editors. Even so, the press's obsession reveals that Democratic political concerns reached beyond the ballot box and extended to African Americans' access to public space more generally. As Glenda Gilmore has argued, many of these newspaper reports were probably based in fact. After all, poor blacks like Maria Mitchell had regularly and openly asserted their right to move and express themselves in public areas since Emancipation. In fact, the newspaper reports may reflect an actual increase in the number of public confrontations between blacks and whites. Had African Americans had a chance to present their side of the story, some might have explained that they were simply going about their business without acknowledging the presence of whites or giving them the deference they expected to receive. Others might have admitted openly shaming whites or claiming their share of streets and sidewalks. In short, the unnamed blacks in the newspaper reports may have been "talking for their rights . . . as much as they pleased and as loud as they pleased," in the same way Maria Mitchell had done a generation earlier.[34]

But whatever the reality of events, reports in the Democratic press indicate that the ways African Americans interacted with whites in public spaces were still highly contested. The rumors that circulated among whites in 1898 about an African American plot to take over the state and make it a black colony suggest how deeply threatened they felt. The resolutions issued at the mass meeting held by Democrats immediately before the riot were even more specific. "The white men," they announced, "expect to live in this community peacably, to have and provide absolute protection for their families, who shall be safe from insult from all persons whomsoever." In the violence that followed, Wilmington's whites made their move to take back the streets, the city, and the state.[35]

Another chief Democratic complaint during the 1898 campaign was "lawlessness." "The majesty of the law has been disregarded and lawlessness encouraged," bemoaned white Democrats in Goldsboro. "In many localities," they continued, "men no longer rely upon the officers of the law for protections, for they are known to be incompetent or corrupt." Of course, the men they referred to were white men, while the incompetent officers were either black or elected with the help of black votes, and the crimes constituting the lawlessness of which they complained were perpetrated by blacks. Democratic governor Charles B. Aycock later claimed that African Americans had unleashed a crime wave in 1898 that whites had no means of stopping. In his words, "lawlessness stalked the State like a pestilence": "ladies were insulted on the public streets," "burglary in our chief city became an every night occurrence," and "more guns and more pistols were sold in the State than had been in the preceding years." Aycock could point to innumerable reports of black crime to "prove" his point. But the crime wave in 1898 was a Democratic creation, whipped up by sympathetic editors who continually printed incendiary reports in an effort to woo white votes. Many reports were fabrications. Some were only loosely based in fact. And others turned black "insolence" into criminal behavior.[36]

The underlying political concern was not black crime, but the tenacity with which African Americans had claimed their legal rights. Many whites still could not accept the idea that African Americans had their own independent identities and civil status, as clearly indicated by the resolutions of a Democratic mass meeting in Wilmington just before the riot. The resolutions accused the African American of "antagonizing our interest in every way, and especially by his ballot." In other words, African Americans had asserted and acted on their own interests instead of "realizing that [their] interests are and should be identical with those of the community." Ballots were not the only source of antagonism identified. One resolution placed a moratorium on African Americans' civil rights as well: "We are prepared to treat the negroes with justice and consideration in all matters which do not involve sacrifices of the interest of the intelligent and progressive portion of the community." Recognition was extended to African Americans' civil rights only insofar as they did not conflict with the racial privilege of whites. When this happened, Wilmington's white Democrats vowed, they would place the law aside to "enforce what we know to be our rights." They made good on this threat in the violence that soon followed.[37]

Finally, the white Democrats of Wilmington turned the small gains that African American laborers had made into a threat to whites' livelihoods. During the 1898 campaign, the Democratic Party had repeatedly complained that the "lawlessness" of "black domination" had retarded the state's economic growth. "Business has been paralyzed," Goldsboro Democrats declared, "and property rendered less valuable." Not stopping with appeals to the propertied elite, Democrats reached into the homes of embattled white farmers and laborers. "White mechanics by the dozens have walked our streets without money and without work," claimed the *Wilmington Messenger*, while "negroes are given steady employment."[38]

North Carolina was in the midst of economic upheaval in 1898. But the source of the problem was the long, slow transition to an industrial economy, not "black domination." White farmers were only now beginning to experience the changes that black workers had been living with since Emancipation. Unable to negotiate the fickle swings and devastating dips of the cotton and tobacco markets, many white farmers were teetering on the brink of collapse in 1898. The condition of propertyless rural whites had gone from bad to worse, as they slid into an inescapable cycle of debt and destitution. For these white men, the transition was about more than poverty. Thrown off their land, they were also thrown out of a traditional way of life in which property ownership had secured their authority over family members. With the land went a man's control over his own labor and that of his wife and children. Gone was the means by which he fulfilled his obligations as a husband and father to provide and protect. Gone was the basis on which he claimed political power. Gone was his independence and his very identity as a man.[39]

Present and former white landowners yelled the loudest as the state's economy lurched away from its agrarian roots. They began organizing and ultimately threatened Democrats' economic and political plans. In the late 1880s, white farmers joined together in the Farmer's Alliance, a cooperative organization that built its own warehouses, factories, and purchasing cooperatives with the intent of keeping profits that went to middlemen in the hands of growers themselves. To be sure, desperate tenants also joined the Alliance. But the organization's platform addressed the concerns of landowners who faced the loss of their land through mortgage and the crop-lien system. Tenants and agrarian wage workers, who did not legally own property in the crops they produced or control their own labor, could not fully participate in or benefit from the organization's cooperative schemes. In fact, tenants could be prosecuted for stealing if they tried to sell their crops on their own. Nonetheless, the Alliance did provide some hope for the state's rural poor at a time when the Democrats and even the Republicans offered none. So did Populism, the political movement that grew out of the Alliance. Addressing the problems of small growers across the country, the Populist platform included government regulation of the railroads, antitrust legislation, an inflationary monetary policy to boost stagnant farm prices, and an inventive scheme to stabilize volatile agricultural markets. Not only was Populism inimical to the economic policies favored by the Democratic

Party's leaders; its politics also threatened Democratic control by striking a political alliance of convenience (known as Fusion) with the Republican Party in 1896.[40]

Democratic leaders tried to crush this coalition, luring disgruntled whites with appeals to racial supremacy and white masculinity. Democratic rhetoric directly addressed the economic concerns of common whites, pointing the finger at African Americans. If white North Carolinians were experiencing difficulties, the Democrats argued, it was because African Americans monopolized jobs, lowered wage levels, brought down property values, and slowed economic growth generally. The continual charges of black-on-white rape literally brought the argument home. Declining economic fortunes meant that white men were also losing the authority they once exercised over their wives and children as heads of household. Democratic leaders capitalized on these fears and directed them in particular ways by playing on white men's sense of emasculation and on their racial prejudices. It was not structural economic changes promoted by Democrats that were undermining white men's authority; it was black men, by raping and sexually assaulting white women.[41]

Democratic candidates and newspapers across the state hurled these accusations at African Americans during the 1898 campaign. The force and velocity was particularly strong in eastern North Carolina. In October, whites rallied to call for "white labor for white men" and the "substitution of white for Negro labor." By November, whites were even more convinced of the logic behind Democratic explanations of their economic woes. The resolutions issued before the Wilmington massacre insisted that "giving nearly all of the employment to negro laborers has been against the best interests of the city" and explained why Wilmington's economy had not grown more in recent years. One resolution concluded that, henceforth, white men would be given preference in employment because "we realize that white families can not thrive here unless there are more opportunities for employment for the different members of said families." Another resolution proclaimed the right of white men to protect their families from the threat of black lawlessness. Collectively, the resolutions thus identified the small victories of black workers seeking to achieve respect, independence, and adequate compensation as a dangerous threat to whites. More than that, they used the bodies of black men to stand in for the complicated economic changes that were transforming gender roles in working-class families. In this way, Democrats effectively severed blacks and whites at the very moment when dispossessed whites were becoming landless laborers in large

Laura F.
Edwards

numbers. In their efforts to place themselves above the African American laborers, white rioters and their supporters only assisted in creating a future at odds with their own economic interests—a future where they too would be common laborers and where they too would endure the powerlessness that Democrats had built into that labor relation.[42]

Democratic leaders fueled the fury. But their tactics resonated among whites in North Carolina because they were already willing to listen. Sadly, they had more to learn from African Americans. In the decades following Wilmington, working-class whites would be economically and politically marginalized. Labeled a problematic population in need of expert aid and occasional discipline, they would find it increasingly difficult to affect public debate. Poor African Americans had been there already. They had been wage workers since Emancipation, battling the same labor problems that whites were only now beginning to face. They had been struggling to obtain control over their private lives. And they had not let their political marginality keep them from making their voices and their concerns public. Instead of listening, whites in Wilmington unleashed their frustration and rage on African American workers and whites elsewhere in the state cheered them on. In the process, they became captives of Wilmington, the event that supposedly marked their victory but really marked their own defeat.

Historians became captives of Wilmington as well. They made Wilmington into good drama, but not good history. Even recent accounts oversimplify complex historical conflicts, forcing them into existing channels and closing off promising alternatives for understanding the past and the present. Retelling the Wilmington massacre to include working-class African Americans as central political actors opens up lost alternatives. In some ways, the event becomes more ominous. Instead of an incident pivotal and peculiar because of its violence, Wilmington becomes yet another example of the violence endemic to politics in the post-Emancipation South generally.

At the same time, events in Wilmington also offer new hope and a useable past for us to draw on today. After all, a history told in terms of the all-powerful forces of evil arrayed against the heroic but vulnerable forces of good can be paralyzing. It tends to diminish the capacity of human beings to shape the course of events by casting history in terms of absolute defeat or absolute victory. Restoring human agency and contingency reveals a history of uneasy truces and continual negotiation. From this perspective, what happened in Wilmington was not an end, but a beginning. To be sure, the *Wilmington Messenger* triumphantly proclaimed victory on 12 November 1898. "The tables are turned now forever," it crowed. "Never more shall Sambo and Josh ride rough shod over the white men who befriended and helped them." But victory would never be so easy or so complete. The newspaper's stock images of Sambo and Josh did not represent working-class African Americans. Not even Charles Chesnutt's militant Josh Green captured the strong tradition of political protest that had sustained African Americans through decades of conflict. In Chesnutt's fictionalized account, Josh Green dies. But the political tradition that he represented was not extinguished in the flames and bloodshed of 1898. White Democrats might congratulate themselves on their manly heroism. But political struggle did not require the presence of the Republican Party or even the vote: it predated events in Wilmington, and it would continue after Wilmington. For it would take much more than one day of violence in one city to silence the descendants of Maria Mitchell.

Notes

I would like to thank Kirsten Fischer, Bob Ingalls, Giovanna Benadusi, and Fraser Ottanelli for their comments. Tim Tyson and David Cecelski have been model editors; their incisive readings have greatly strengthened the presentation of this essay's main themes. The University of South Florida provided research funds; the University of California, Los Angeles, allowed time off for writing; and the Newberry Library generously provided workspace and a stimulating intellectual environment during revisions of this essay. But my biggest debt is to Sheila Cohen, whose crack research assistance made this piece possible.

1. J. G. de Roulhac Hamilton, *History of North Carolina*, vol. 3, *North Carolina Since 1860* (Chicago: Lewis Publishing Co., 1919), quotes from 280, 284, and 297.

2. Quote from *New York Herald*, 14 November 1898; see also 11, 12, 13 November 1898. For the tone of the *Washington Post*'s coverage, see, for instance, 1, 7, 11, 12 November 1898. The *Henderson Gold Leaf*, 23 November 1898, reprint of an article from the *North Carolina Presbyterian*, linked the racial situation in Wilmington to that in the rest of the country. For other national newspapers supportive of the takeover, see those mentioned by the *Wilmington Messenger*, 13, 18 November 1898. There were exceptions; for examples of national press coverage critical of the Democratic takeover of the city, see *Wilmington Messenger*, 15 November 1898. See also Herbert Shapiro, *White Violence and Black Response: From Reconstruction to Montgomery* (Amherst: University of Massachusetts Press, 1988); Glenda Elizabeth Gilmore, *Gender and Jim Crow: Women and the Politics of White Supremacy in North Carolina, 1896–1920* (Chapel Hill: University of North Carolina Press, 1996).

3. Even the most critical recent discussions of Wilmington tend to have these assumptions embedded within them. See, for instance, Edward L. Ayers, *The Promise of the New South: Life after Reconstruction* (New York: Oxford University Press, 1992), 300–304; Paul D. Escott, *Many Excellent People: Power and Privilege in North Carolina, 1850–1900* (Chapel Hill: University of North Carolina Press, 1985), 253–55; Gilmore, *Gender and Jim Crow*, 91–118; John Haley, *Charles N. Hunter and Race Relations in North Carolina* (Chapel Hill: University of North Carolina Press,

1987), 105–34; H. Leon Prather, *We Have Taken a City: Wilmington Racial Massacre and Coup of 1898* (Cranbury, N.J.: Associated University Presses, 1984).

4. Charles Chesnutt, *The Marrow of Tradition* (1901; reprint, Ann Arbor: University of Michigan Press, 1969), quote from 284. The Democratic press highlighted African Americans' resistance in a self-serving way to justify the violent actions of whites. Nonetheless, these reports still indicate the presence of black militancy during the violence. See, for example, *Wilmington Messenger*, 11 November 1898; *Henderson Goldleaf*, 17 November 1898; *Oxford Public Ledger*, 17 November 1898; *Greensboro Patriot*, 16 November 1898; *Washington Post*, 11 November 1898; *New York Herald*, 11 November 1898. There were also reports of militant black resistance to various kinds of white aggression during and immediately after the 1898 campaign. In three separate incidents, blacks gathered in Wilson, Wilmington, and Ashpole (Lumberton County) to protect individual African Americans who had been accused by whites of various "crimes" and threatened with mob violence; see *Wilmington Messenger*, 23, 25 October, 6, 10 November 1898.

5. For discussions of this perspective among black leaders at the time, see Gilmore, *Gender and Jim Crow*; Evelyn Brooks Higginbotham, *Righteous Discontent: The Women's Movement in the Black Baptist Church, 1880–1920* (Cambridge: Harvard University Press, 1993).

6. The following analysis is based on hundreds of cases in local court records and the Freedmen's Bureau records. In this article, I focus specifically on the Criminal Action Papers, 1865–90, of Granville, Orange, and Edgecombe Counties, North Carolina Department of Archives and History, Raleigh (hereafter, NCDAH). The cases in these three counties are not unusual; the court records from other counties in North Carolina contain very similar kinds of patterns and conflicts. The Records of the U.S. Bureau of Refugees, Freedmen, and Abandoned Lands (hereafter, RBRFAL) are located in two places. Those in the National Archives, Record Group 105, contain the records of local bureau agents; I have used those from the Warren District, containing Granville, Warren, and Franklin Counties. The Records of the Assistant Commissioner for the State of North Carolina are in the same National Archives record group, but have been microfilmed, National Archives Microfilm Publication M843. They contain the reports and correspondence of local agents as well as petitions from freedpeople and cases that were forwarded to the assistant commissioner's office for consideration. I am drawing conceptually on my own work, *Gendered Strife and Confusion: The Political Culture of Reconstruction* (Urbana: University of Illinois Press, 1997). I am also drawing on work that emphasizes everyday forms of resistance among poor and politically marginalized people; see, for instance, Robin D. G. Kelley, *Race Rebels: Culture, Politics, and the Black Working Class* (New York: The Free Press, 1994); James C. Scott, *Weapons of the Weak: Everyday Forms of Peasant Resistance* (New Haven: Yale University Press, 1985), and *Domination and the Arts of Resistance: Hidden Transcripts* (New Haven: Yale University Press, 1990).

7. Edwards, *Gendered Strife and Confusion*. See also Peter Bardaglio, *Reconstructing the Household: Families, Sex, and the Law in the Nineteenth-Century South* (Chapel Hill: University of North Carolina Press, 1995); Nancy Bercaw, "The Politics of Household: Domestic Battlegrounds in the Transition from Slavery to Freedom in the Yazoo-Mississippi Delta, 1850–1860" (Ph.D. diss., University of Pennsylvania, 1995); Victoria Bynum, *Unruly Women: The Politics of Social and Sexual Control in the Old South* (Chapel Hill: University of North Carolina Press, 1992);

Elizabeth Fox-Genovese, *Within the Plantation Household: Black and White Women in the Old South* (Chapel Hill: University of North Carolina Press, 1988), 192–241; Stephanie McCurry, *Masters of Small Worlds: Yeoman Households, Gender Relations, and the Political Culture of the Antebellum South Carolina Low Country* (New York: Oxford University Press, 1995); LeeAnn Whites, *The Civil War as a Crisis in Gender: Augusta, Georgia, 1860–1890* (Athens: University of Georgia Press, 1995).

8. For discussion of the legal position of slaves, see Eugene D. Genovese, *Roll, Jordan, Roll: The World the Slaves Made* (New York: Vintage Books, 1976); Thomas D. Morris, *Southern Slavery and the Law 1619–1860* (Chapel Hill: University of North Carolina Press, 1996); James Oakes, *Slavery and Freedom: An Interpretation of the Old South* (New York: Alfred A. Knopf, 1990); Mark V. Tushnet, *The American Law of Slavery, 1810–1860: Considerations of Humanity and Interest* (Princeton: Princeton University Press, 1981).

9. *State v. B. D. Armstrong*, 1870, Criminal Action Papers, Edgecombe County, NCDAH. For an elaboration of these general points, see Edwards, *Gendered Strife and Confusion*.

10. As long as the court system remained open to them, African Americans flooded courts with complaints against a wide range of offenders, including those from their own families and communities. Even when they filed charges against other blacks, African American were still asserting their new civil status as people with rights that everyone—whether black or white, relatives or strangers—had to respect.

11. *State v. B. D. Armstrong*, 1870, Criminal Action Papers, Edgecombe County, NCDAH.

12. For racialized images, see Winthrop D. Jordan, *White Over Black: American Attitudes Toward the Negro, 1550–1812* (Chapel Hill: University of North Carolina Press, 1968). Some whites went so far as to argue that African Americans' racial makeup made them so inferior that they could not feel pain in the same way as whites and thus required more punishment. For the way whites mapped racial ideology onto black bodies, see Elizabeth B. Clark, "'The Sacred Rights of the Weak': Pain, Sympathy, and the Culture of Individual Rights in Antebellum America," *Journal of American History* 82 (September 1995): 463–93; Kirsten Fischer, "Embodiments of Power: Slavery and Sexualized Violence in Colonial North Carolina," paper given at the Tenth Berkshire Conference on the History of Women, Chapel Hill, North Carolina, June 1996.

13. *Public Laws of North Carolina* (1866), chap. 40. Also see Roberta Sue Alexander, *North Carolina Faces the Freedmen: Race Relations during Presidential Reconstruction, 1865–67* (Durham: Duke University Press, 1985), 39–51; Eric Foner, *Reconstruction: America's Unfinished Revolution* (New York: Harper and Row, 1988), 198–216; Charles Brantner Wilson, *The Black Codes of the South* (Tuscaloosa: University of Alabama Press, 1965).

14. Silas L. Curtis et al. to Gov. William W. Holden, 11 October 1868, Governor's Papers, Holden, NCDAH. Such incidents are voluminously documented in U.S. Congress, *Testimony Taken by the Joint Select Committee to Inquire into the Condition of Affairs in the Late Insurrectionary States* (Washington, D.C.: Government Printing Office, 1872). Also see W. McKee Evans, *Ballots and Fence Rails: Reconstruction on the Lower Cape Fear* (Chapel Hill: University of North Carolina Press, 1966), 69–73; Otto H. Olsen, "The Ku Klux Klan: A Study in Reconstruction Politics and Propaganda," *North Carolina Historical Review* 39 (Summer 1962): 340–62; Albion Winegar Tourgée, *The Invisible Empire* (New York: Fords, Howard, and Hulbert, 1880; reprint, Baton Rouge: Louisiana State University Press, 1989);

Allen W. Trelease, *White Terror: The Ku Klux Klan Conspiracy and Southern Reconstruction* (New York: Harper and Row, 1971). Martha Hodes, "The Sexualization of Reconstruction Politics: White Women and Black Men in the South after the Civil War," *Journal of the History of Sexuality* 3 (January 1993): 402–17, argues that the Klan targeted households, raped women, and sexually mutilated black men specifically to "unman" black men and thus push them out of the political arena.

15. Jordan Overby to General Miles, 30 August 1867, Assistant Commissioner's Records, RBRFAL; *James Peace v. Harmon Puryear*, May 1866, Records Relating to Court Cases and Complaints, Assistant Superintendent's Office, Oxford, RBRFAL. For examples of similar cases of white-on-black violence where African Americans prosecuted, see *State v. Robson*, 1866; *State v. Johnson*, 1868; *State v. Cardin*, 1868; all in Criminal Action Papers, Orange County, NCDAH. *State v. Taylor and Taylor*, 1866; *State v. Overton*, 1869; *State v. Lloyd*, 1869; *State v. Cross*, 1870; *State v. Sparkes*, 1872; *State v. Nettles*, 1873; *State v. Pippin*, 1887; all in Criminal Action Papers, Edgecombe County, NCDAH. *State v. Horner*, 1867; *State v. Edmunds*, 1867; *State v. Noblin*, 1870; *State v. Rice*, 1871; *State v. Kirkland*, 1872; *State v. Wilkerson*, 1873; *State v. Mitchell*, 1877; *State v. Regan*, 1878; all in Criminal Action Papers, Granville County, NCDAH. For cases likely involving challenges to Klan violence, see *State v. Thompson, Gibson, and Gibson*, 1869; *State v. Lattamore, Miller, and Blackwood*, 1871; both in Criminal Action Papers, Orange County, NCDAH.

16. The Freedmen's Bureau, charged with overseeing the institution of free labor, was the only government institution to handle labor disputes in the South. Before, during, and after Republican rule, Southern courts refused to consider such conflicts, labeling them "private" disputes between employers and employees and thus outside their jurisdiction. As a result, such cases appear only sporadically and in unusual contexts after the bureau ceased adjudicating these matters, around 1868. Until then, however, the records of the Freedmen's Bureau are filled with labor disputes, suggesting how persistent African Americans were in contesting their employers' power. Most disputes involved the nonpayment of wages. Individual cases heard by local superintendents are too voluminous to list individually here. But the superintendent in Warren district, which included Granville, Warren, and Franklin Counties, heard thirty-eight complaints brought by African Americans against their employers between January and September of 1867; see Thomas W. Hay to Jacob W. Chur, 25 September 1867, Annual Reports of Operations Received from Staff and Subordinate Officers, RBRFAL. If his report had included the months from September through December, the number would have been far higher, since these were the months when crops were harvested and accounts were settled. For further discussions of this issue, see Jonathan M. Bryant, *How Curious a Land: Conflict and Change in Greene County, Georgia, 1850–1885* (Chapel Hill: University of North Carolina Press, 1996); Barbara J. Fields, *Slavery and Freedom on the Middle Ground: Maryland during the Nineteenth Century* (New Haven: Yale University Press, 1985); Eric Foner, *Nothing but Freedom: Emancipation and Its Legacy* (Baton Rouge: Louisiana State University Press, 1983); Joseph P. Reidy, *From Slavery to Agrarian Capitalism in the Cotton Plantation South: Central Georgia, 1800–1880* (Chapel Hill: University of North Carolina Press, 1992); Julie Saville, *The Work of Reconstruction: From Slave to Wage Laborer in South Carolina, 1860–1870* (New York: Cambridge University Press, 1994); Leslie A. Schwalm, *A Hard Fight for We: Women's Transition from Slavery to Freedom in South Carolina* (Urbana: University of Illinois Press, 1997).

17. Cases where African Americans prosecuted whites for theft are less common, largely because most African Americans had so little property to steal. The property they had worked to create during slavery was judged to be their masters' and thus freedpeople were often prosecuted for taking what they saw as their own. Reclaiming withheld wages was far more common; see n. 16. But some African Americans did prosecute whites for theft: see *State v. Blackwood, Guttenburg, and Markham*, 1866, Criminal Action Papers, Orange County, NCDAH; *State v. Bragg et al.*, 1867, Criminal Action Papers, Granville County, NCDAH. The cases listed in n. 15, regarding Klan violence, also involved the protection of property. The most dramatic example of African Americans' statements of their rights to property ownership, however, can be found in the testimony presented at congressional hearings on the Klan. There African Americans found an outlet to express their sense of outrage at the way some whites felt so comfortable in destroying their belongings. See U.S. Congress, *Testimony Taken by the Joint Select Committee to Inquire into the Condition of Affairs in the Late Insurrectionary States*.

18. The most vivid examples of African Americans' efforts to establish the institutional legitimacy of their families comes in their resistance to whites' attempts to apprentice their children at will. The Freedmen's Bureau records contain a running discussion of this issue. Yet even the most sympathetic bureau officers would not have been very well aware of the blatant inequities of the system if not for the freedpeople themselves, who kept agents' attention riveted on the issue, whether they liked it or not. Thomas Hay, bureau superintendent for the subdistrict of Warren, which included Granville County, canceled seventy-seven indentures in the first eight months of 1867 alone. Representing successful complaints, this figure gives only a partial accounting of freedpeople's opposition. Across the state, freedpeople deluged the bureau with complaints; see Alexander, *North Carolina Faces the Freedmen*, 117. The reaction of African Americans elsewhere in the South was similar; see Ira Berlin, Stephen F. Miller, and Leslie S. Rowland, eds., "Afro-American Families in the Transition from Slavery to Freedom," *Radical History Review* 42 (1988): 107–11; Fields, *Slavery and Freedom on the Middle Ground*, 148–49; Foner, *Reconstruction*, 201; Herbert Gutman, *The Black Family in Slavery and Freedom*, 1750–1925 (New York: Pantheon, 1976), 402–12.

19. For discussions of these issues for slaves, see John W. Blassingame, *The Slave Community: Plantation Life in the Antebellum South* (New York: Oxford University Press, 1972); Genovese, *Roll, Jordan, Roll*; Charles Joyner, *Down by the Riverside: A South Carolina Slave Community* (Urbana: University of Illinois Press, 1984); Lawrence Levine, *Black Culture and Black Consciousness: Afro-American Folk Thought from Slavery to Freedom* (New York: Oxford University Press, 1977). For free blacks, see Ira Berlin, *Slaves without Masters: The Free Negro in the Antebellum South* (New York: Pantheon, 1974); Bynum, *Unruly Women*; John Hope Franklin, *The Free Negro in North Carolina*, 1790–1860 (Chapel Hill: University of North Carolina Press, 1943).

20. *State v. Gay*, 1868, Criminal Action Papers, Edgecombe County, NCDAH. Jane Dailey, "Deference and Violence in the Postbellum Urban South: Manners and Massacres in Danville, Virginia," *Journal of Southern History* 63 (August 1997): 553–90. Also see William Cohen, *At Freedom's Edge: Black Mobility and the Southern White Quest for Racial Control*, 1861–1915 (Baton Rouge: Louisiana State University Press, 1991); Fields, *Slavery and Freedom on the Middle Ground*; Gilmore, *Gender and Jim Crow*; Martha Hodes, *White Women, Black Men: Illicit Sex in the Nineteenth-Century South* (New Haven: Yale University Press, 1997); Tera W.

Hunter, *To 'Joy My Freedom: Southern Black Women's Lives and Labor after the Civil War* (Cambridge: Harvard University Press, 1997); Saville, *The Work of Reconstruction*; Schwalm, *A Hard Fight for We*.

21. *Raleigh Sentinel*, 29 August 1865. The debate over freedpeople's right to testify in court all but eclipsed discussions of the code's other provisions. Editorializing about the issue, the *Raleigh Sentinel* identified the testimony as "the great question of the session" (2 February 1866). The evidence supports this conclusion. For a summary of the session, see the *Sentinel*, 1, 2, 9, 22, 27 February 1866. Governor Jonathan Worth spoke frequently of the subject in his correspondence; see, for instance, J. G. de Roulhac Hamilton, ed., *The Correspondence of Jonathan Worth* (Raleigh: Edwards and Broughton, 1909), 1:467, 509, 571–72. So did common whites; see John Richard Dennett, *The South As It Is, 1865–1866*, ed. Henry M. Christman (New York: Viking Press, 1965; reprint, Athens: University of Georgia Press, 1986), 132–34, 168–69, 181. For discussions of conservatives and their political ideology, see Escott, *Many Excellent People*; Evans, *Ballots and Fence Rails*; Michael Perman, *Reunion without Compromise: The South and Reconstruction, 1865–1868* (New York: Cambridge University Press, 1973).

22. *State v. Armstrong*, 1870; *State v. Collins T. Cross*, 1870; *State v. Knight*, 1872; all in Criminal Action Papers, Edgecombe County, NCDAH. For similar cases, see *State v. Lazina Sherond*, 1868; *State v. Bettie Lloyd*, 1883; both in Criminal Action Papers, Edgecombe County, NCDAH; *State v. Noblin*, 1870; *State v. Allen*, 1884; both in Criminal Action Papers, Granville County, NCDAH. Whites also used such tactics; see *State v. Sparkes*, 1872, Criminal Action Papers, Edgecombe County, NCDAH.

23. *State v. Wilkerson*, 1873, Criminal Action Papers, Granville County, NCDAH. Other historians have also noted that African Americans sought out the court system as a validation of their rights as citizens; see Jonathan M. Bryant, " 'We Have No Chance of Justice before the Courts': The Freedmen's Struggle for Power in Greene County, Georgia, 1865–1874," in *Georgia in Black and White: Explorations in the Race Relations of a Southern State, 1865–1950*, ed. John C. Inscoe (Athens: University of Georgia Press, 1994), 13–37; Donald G. Nieman, "Black Political Power and Criminal Justice: Washington County, Texas, 1868–1884," *Journal of Southern History* 55 (August 1989): 391–420; Foner, *Nothing but Freedom*; Christopher Waldrep, "Substituting Law for the Lash: Emancipation and Legal Formalism in a Mississippi County Court," *Journal of American History* 82 (March 1996): 1425–51. Of course, as the title to Bryant's essay suggests, they were not always successful, particularly after Democrats regained control over state and local government.

24. Quotes from *Torchlight*, 20 July 1880; *State v. Mitchell*, 1877, Criminal Action Papers, Granville County, NCDAH. For changes in the local courts, see *Laws of North Carolina* (1876–77), constitution, art. 4, sec. 27, chap 154; *Laws and Resolutions of North Carolina* (1879), chap. 92; *Public and Private Laws of North Carolina* (1889), chap. 504. For discussions of the importance of these changes, see Escott, *Many Excellent People*, 166–70; Michael Perman, *The Road to Redemption: Southern Politics, 1869–1879* (Chapel Hill: University of North Carolina Press, 1984), 193–220.

25. Edwards, *Gendered Strife and Confusion*, 66–80. For nineteenth-century employment relations, see Christopher L. Tomlins, *Law, Labor, and Ideology in the Early American Republic* (New York: Cambridge University Press, 1993); Robert J. Steinfeld, *The Invention of Free Labor: The Employment Relation in English and American Law and Culture, 1350–1870* (Chapel Hill: University of North Carolina

Press, 1991). For antebellum tenancy in North Carolina, see Marjorie Mendenhall Applewhite, "Sharecropper and Tenant in the Courts of North Carolina," *North Carolina Historical Review* 31 (April 1954): 134–49.

26. Quoted material from *Public Laws of North Carolina* (1868–69), chap. 117; *Haskins v. Royster* 70 N.C. 601 (1874). The decision in *Haskins v. Royster* was upheld in *Morgan v. Smith* 77 N.C. 37 (1877). The laborers' lien laws include *Public Acts and Resolutions of North Carolina* (Special Session, 1868), chap. 41; *Public Laws of North Carolina* (1869–70), chap. 206. For the 1877 tenant act, see *Public Laws of North Carolina* (1876–77), chap. 283. After they overthrew the Republicans, Democratic legislators across the South passed a series of measures that undercut the position of laborers and sharecroppers even more; see especially Harold D. Woodman, *New South, New Law: The Legal Foundations of Credit and Labor Relations in the Postbellum Agricultural South* (Baton Rouge: Louisiana State University Press, 1995). Also see Cohen, *At Freedom's Edge*; Alex Lichtenstein, *Twice the Work of Free Labor: The Political Economy of Convict Labor in the New South* (New York: Verso, 1996); Reidy, *From Slavery to Agrarian Capitalism*, 221–27, 232–33.

27. See, for example, Bryant, *How Curious a Land*; Edwards, *Gendered Strife and Confusion*, 92–106; Fields, *Slavery and Freedom on the Middle Ground*; Foner, *Nothing but Freedom*; Reidy, *From Slavery to Agrarian Capitalism*; Saville, *The Work of Reconstruction*; Schwalm, *A Hard Fight for We*.

28. Such confrontations appeared as "assaults," not as legitimate conflicts over the terms of the labor relation because of the court's refusal to recognize, let alone adjudicate, such matters. In the first few years following Emancipation, the Freedmen's Bureau dealt with such cases (see n. 16). Sometimes it was the white employer who ended up filing charges. See, for instance, *State v. Sherond*, 1868; *State v. Gay*, 1868; both in Criminal Action Papers, Edgecombe County, NCDAH; *State v. Rice*, 1871; *State v. Harris*, 1877; *State v. Mitchell*, 1877; *State v. Barnett*, 1879; *State v. Oakley*, 1881; *State v. Allen*, 1884; all in Criminal Action Papers, Granville County, NCDAH.

29. *State v. Allen*, 1884; *State v. Aclu*, 1881; both in Criminal Action Papers, Granville County, NCDAH.

30. Chesnutt, *The Marrow of Tradition*, 114.

31. Ibid., 281.

32. See, for instance, Eric Anderson, *Race and Politics in North Carolina, 1872–1901: The Black Second* (Baton Rouge: Louisiana State University Press, 1981); Helen G. Edmonds, *The Negro and Fusion Politics in North Carolina, 1894–1901* (Chapel Hill: University of North Carolina Press, 1951); Escott, *Many Excellent People*; Gilmore, *Gender and Jim Crow*.

33. For the umbrella incident, see *Wilmington Messenger*, 7 September 1898. The same article lists similar incidents; also see *Wilmington Messenger*, 9, 16, 21 October, 3, 6 November 1898. Also see Prather, *We Have Taken a City*, 53–55.

34. Gilmore, *Gender and Jim Crow*, 102–5. Also see Dailey, "Deference and Violence in the Postbellum Urban South."

35. *Washington Post*, 10 November 1898; see also *Wilmington Messenger*, 10 November 1898. For rumors of the plot to make the state a black colony, see Prather, *We Have Taken a City*, 63–64.

36. Quotes from Hamilton, *History of North Carolina*, 290; R. D. W. Connor and Clarence Poe, *The Life and Speeches of Charles Brantley Aycock* (New York: Doubleday, Page and Company, 1912), 229. For other references to and discussions of a black crime wave in Wilmington and eastern North Carolina generally, see *Wil-*

mington Messenger, 22 July, 23 August, 7 October 1898; *Henderson Goldleaf*, 23 November 1898; *Oxford Public Ledger*, 17 November 1898. Such reports were so widespread and so readily accepted among whites that J. G. de Roulhac Hamilton took them at face value and incorporated them into his study as "fact." For the Democratic creation of this crime wave, see Gilmore, *Gender and Jim Crow*.

37. Quote from *Washington Post*, 10 November 1898; see also *Wilmington Messenger*, 10 November 1898. Such concerns were also articulated clearly in a *North Carolina Presbyterian* article, reprinted in the *Henderson Gold Leaf*, 23 November 1898.

38. Quotes from Hamilton, *History of North Carolina*, 290; Prather, *We Have Taken a City*, 61. The Wilmington chamber of commerce also expressed these concerns in a series of resolutions before the riot; see *Wilmington Messenger*, 7 October 1898. The *Messenger* applauded the sentiments, but also criticized them for not being forceful enough (*Wilmington Messenger*, 8 October 1898).

39. Historians have usually focused on the economic component of this transition; see, for instance, Escott, *Many Excellent People*; Lawrence Goodwyn, *The Democratic Promise* (New York: Oxford University Press, 1976); Reidy, *From Slavery to Agrarian Capitalism*. For the gendered implications of Southern white men's economic position, see Edwards, *Gendered Strife and Confusion*; Gilmore, *Gender and Jim Crow*; McCurry, *Masters of Small Worlds*.

40. Anderson, *Race and Politics in North Carolina*; Edmonds, *The Negro and Fusion Politics*; Escott, *Many Excellent People*; Gilmore, *Gender and Jim Crow*. Much of the work on the Alliance and Populism in the South has emphasized their broad appeal to poor Southerners, white and black. But this literature assumes that tenants were simply poorer versions of landowners and that the problems of both groups were the same. In reality, all tenants in North Carolina were legally wage laborers. Tenants and agricultural day laborers could identify with the Alliance's and Populism's promise to stabilize agricultural markets. But neither organization spoke to their most pressing concern—namely an asymmetrical labor relation that placed power in the hands of their employers and denied them any public means of redress. In fact, the Alliance and the Populist Party denied the legitimacy of this issue. For instance, the *Progressive Farmer*, the official voice of the Alliance in North Carolina, insisted that interests of farmers and laborers were "identical" and that "whatever benefits one will benefit the other" (7 February 1887).

41. The continual reprint and discussion of Alex Manly's denunciation of lynching is typical. Manly, the black editor of the *Wilmington Daily Record*, had charged poor white women with consenting to sexual relations with black men and criticized white men for not protecting their womenfolk better. But Democratic newspapers turned his argument into a justification of black-on-white rape and a slur on white womanhood. See, for example, *Wilmington Messenger*, 21, 23, 25, 28 August, 9 October 1898. For increased reports of black-male-on-white-female rape, see Gilmore, *Gender and Jim Crow*.

42. Quotes from Prather, *We Have Taken a City*, 63; *Washington Post*, 10 November 1898. This argument relies heavily on the work of W. E. B. Du Bois, *Black Reconstruction: An Essay toward a History of the Part Which Black Folk Played in the Attempt to Reconstruct Democracy in America, 1860–1880* (New York: Russell and Russell, 1935), and David Roediger's application of Du Bois's insights in *The Wages of Whiteness: Race and the Making of the American Working Class* (New York: Verso, 1991).

LeeAnn
Whites

Love, Hate, Rape, Lynching

Rebecca Latimer Felton and the
Gender Politics of Racial Violence

In the long, hot summer of 1897, the headlines of the Southern press screamed out the news of seemingly ever escalating incidents of violence, mayhem, and race hatred. Front-page headlines of the *Atlanta Constitution* read, "In Hot Pursuit. Clayton County Men Will Lynch. The Negro is Caught." The *Atlanta Journal* added, "Hunting Him to Death. Several Counties are Up in Arms to Avenge the Crime of the Negro Oscar Smith." And only days later, the headlines read, "This Black Brute Will Be Burned. Anthony Williams, Who Murdered Miss Williams at West Point, Tenn. Caught in Alabama. Will be Taken to the Scene." Wrapped around this lurid reportage was a running commentary on the innocence and vulnerability of white women, the looming threat posed by black men, and the apparently uncontrollable mob violence of white men.[1]

The actual reportage always began with the white man: white men in hot pursuit, white men lynching black men, white men worrying about the safety of white women, white men discussing the mob behavior of other white men. The actions of those in the lead roles, however, the roles of the virginal "victim" and the black "beast," always preceded the actual newspaper coverage and were left to the assumptions and the imagination of the reader. While the question of the morality of mob violence by white men was discussed, the Southern press never questioned the innocent virginity of the woman victim or the violent passion of the black man. When and if the stories of the black men and white women actually involved were told, the account was secondhand, after the fact, shaped by rumor and innuendo. After all, at the point that many of these stories were told, the key participants were not able to testify. The black man was maimed, burned, dead; the white woman was shamed, humiliated, mute.

The way these stories were told in the press reflected the social location of their white male writers or the white male participants they chose to interview. There were virtually no white women reporters in the Southern press in the summer of 1897, and it was unusual for any coverage of women's accounts of events to appear as front-page news. In the case of the lynching controversy, newspaper editors almost never solicited black men's opinions. At best they found deferential ministers willing to confirm the white man's story, apologizing for the apparent immorality of some members of the Negro race and pledging their support for swift punishment. As a result, we will probably never know what actually transpired between Oscar Smith and Jewel Campbell or Anthony Williams and Rene Williams in the summer of 1897. At least we will never know how they would freely and openly tell us their story if they were with us today.

It stands as a testament to how much race and gender relations have changed in the last hundred years that today, even without Oscar Smith's or Rene Williams's testimony, we can read much of this 1897 news coverage and imagine a very different scenario from that which was envisioned by many readers at the time. Take, for example, the story that appeared in the *Atlanta Constitution* on 25 July 1897. The headline read, "Negro Finds Safety in Jail. Insulted a Lady and Her Neighbors were Aroused." The story was reported as follows. The "Negro" (who remained nameless) went to his employer's house to ask his employer's wife, Mrs. W. Anderson (who has only her husband's name) for a lock of her hair to make a watch charm. "Fortunately," as this account put it, the husband came upon the two, and the "Negro" beat a hasty retreat. When the "incident" became known to the neighbors, they were so infuriated by the "impudence" of the black man that by nightfall some fifty men were searching for him. Had they found him they would have lynched him on the spot.[2]

We read this story today and we wonder how the simple request for a lock of a white woman's hair by a black man could enrage fifty white male neighbors to the brink of lynching. We wonder whether Mrs. Anderson really thought the request was "impertinent," as the press recounted, or whether her husband decided it was, and she simply stood by, in her "proper" place as his wife: shamed, humiliated, and mute. Perhaps, we could conjecture, it was really Mr. Anderson who was the brute, or at least the neglectful and unappreciative husband, and perhaps the unnamed black man was actually an engaging and admiring companion of Mrs. Anderson. We will never know. What we do know is that something very intense was going on between black men and white women in the summer of 1897. It may have been violence, or it may have been love, or perhaps it was both. Whatever it was, it was so intense that it disrupted the white-male-dominated Southern social order, and the white-male-dominated press. It put the story of the relationships between black men and white women, however distorted, however filtered through dominant racial and gendered lenses, on the front page of the daily news.

While the discussion of lynching in the Southern press was dominated by white male writers, and the actual actors were never able to tell their own story directly, the very violence of white men's response opened the way for at least some black men and some white women to be heard in public. The result was explosive when the position of one white woman—Rebecca Latimer Felton, a well-known advocate of white women's issues—and one black man—Alex Manly, a prominent black newspaper editor and officeholder in Wilmington, North Carolina—were picked up and widely circulated on the front pages of the major newspapers of the South, serving to further inflame white male supremacist sentiment and leading ultimately to the Wilmington racial massacre in the fall of 1898. Historians of white racial violence, whether that violence be lynchings or massacres, have been inclined to emphasize the economic and political motivations behind white men's behavior. Feeling threatened by the political and economic accomplishments of black men and the black community more generally, white

Southern men increasingly resorted to violence in order to perpetuate the white supremacist social order of the South in the 1890s. From this perspective, lynchings for the alleged reason of rape of white women played an obfuscatory role, serving to legitimate white men's repression of black men for the "real" reasons of economic and political competition. In tracing out the connection, however twisted and distorted, between sexual relations between black men and white women and the Wilmington racial massacre, this essay attempts to contribute to our understanding of the role that sexuality, particularly efforts to regulate white women's sexuality, played in the racial violence of the 1890s and in the consolidation of white supremacy in the South of Jim Crow.

Not surprisingly, the black voice that was first taken up by the white press of the South in the discussion of racial violence in the summer of 1897 at least tacitly accepted the description of sex across the color line as being the "rape" of white women. On 28 July, the *Atlanta Constitution* reported on a series of resolutions adopted by the Bannister Baptist Association. The headlines read, "Negro Preachers Condemn the Crime. Assaults upon Defenseless Women are Severely Censured. Lynching is made a Side Issue. The Offense and Not the Work of the Mobs the Great Wrong." This group of ministers committed themselves to "cooperate with the whites to bring to justice any and all who may be guilty, and to use their influence in the larger community to create sentiment against the crime." They commended the governor for affirming the power of the law to "mete out full justice and punishment to those who have or may attempt to outrage it."[3]

In their resolutions, these ministers took a stance against rape, describing it as "the most dastardly, cowardly and infamous crime known to humanity." They pledged their resources to cooperate in hunting down the alleged perpetrators of such crimes. They did not directly condemn lynching, but instead tried to wrap their own position in the authority of the governor, who opposed lynching on the grounds that the regular workings of the legal system were sufficient to bring rapists to justice. They apparently hoped that they could reduce the incidence of the lynching of black men by conceding the possibility that some black men might have perpetrated violent crimes against some white women, thus reassuring whites that the black community would support the effective working of the rule of law. The closest any black man came to actually being able to condemn violence against black men in the white-dominated Southern press was a sermon by an Atlanta minister, the Reverend Proctor. He pointed out that there was a natural tendency to look to the faults of others rather than to seriously consider one's own.

He argued that both lynching and rape were crimes, and that the white community should take care of their problem and the black community would take care of theirs.[4]

While, by August of 1897, a few black men did gain at least some space for their perspective on white mob violence, however hedged about, white women were still mute. Indeed Southern newspapers actively reinforced the appropriateness of their silence, particularly on "political" matters. In July, for instance, the press covered the story of the Atlanta Woman's Christian Temperance Union (WCTU), which had just been kicked out of its long-standing meeting place in the basement of the Trinity Methodist Church for advocating woman suffrage. The church's minister charged the membership of the group with turning the church into a "town hall" by speaking to a Sunday school class on the Anti-Barroom Bill that was currently pending in Atlanta. "Men," according to the minister, "lose respect for women who dabble in politics." Women, he went on to assert, were not suited to public, political activities because their brains were "smaller than men's, lighter and finer in structure."[5]

On 3 August, however, in the face of the relentless press coverage of lynchings for the alleged crime of rape, Bill Arp, who wrote a regular column for the *Atlanta Constitution*, actually went so far as to call directly for the opinion of white women on mob violence. In a lengthy commentary, Arp indicated that he had very little confidence in the seemingly endless discussion in the daily press from clergy, judges, lawyers, and, as he put it, "young unmarried men who lived in rock built cities." None of these men, Arp claimed, had any real-life experience in the "dangers" of isolated country living. For himself, he recounted how he had moved his family out of the countryside some years earlier and into the "rock built" city in order to "protect" his wife. According to Arp, lynching for what he termed the "nameless crime" had nothing to do with the ineffectiveness of the legal system, as some lawyers, ministers, and politicians had been claiming. Instead, he argued that mob violence by white men constituted a "spontaneous outburst of emotions long felt and long smothered and those emotions are based on love—love for the home and wife and children, love and respect for wives and daughters of neighbors."[6]

Arp called upon white women to step forward and take a public stand on the question, a question that he had framed as a matter of white men's love for white women. This was presumably an issue on which white women were well qualified to speak. From the vantage point of one hundred years later, we might choose to frame the question in a more open way, and rather than simply asking white women to affirm white men's loving behavior toward them, we might think that the more appropriate question to ask would be, who is really loving whom here? Was rape really the act of hate, while lynching was the act of love, as Bill Arp and the white press more generally asserted? Or, was the alleged "rape" really the act of love, and lynching the act of hate, as the story of Mrs. Anderson, the lock of hair, and the unnamed black farmhand might suggest?

Bill Arp did not have to wait long to receive an answer from white women, or at least from one white woman. On 12 August, at the annual meeting of the Georgia State Agricultural Society, Rebecca Latimer Felton gave a speech entitled, innocuously enough, "Woman on the Farm." This was not the first time she had given this speech. It was not even the first time she had given it before the Georgia State Agricultural Society. Indeed, by the summer of 1897, Rebecca Latimer Felton was already one of the most publicly outspoken members of her sex in the American South. She began her political career over twenty years earlier, as the campaign manager for her husband, William Harrell Felton, in his two successful bids for a seat in the U.S. Congress. At that time it was rumored that not only did she manage his campaign but she also wrote many of his speeches. Whatever the truth or falsity of that rumor, she certainly did write biting editorials in his defense, which she sent to the local press, never actually signing with her own name, but instead employing pseudonyms, like "Bartow" (the name of her upcountry county), or "Plowboy" (a reference to the Feltons' political alliance with the white yeomanry of the region). It was not until Rebecca Felton joined the WCTU in 1886 that she actually entered the political arena in her own right. Already well known for her powerful editorial style, she became even better known for her oratorical talents, as she stumped the state in defense of what she understood to be women's interests, especially temperance reform.[7]

Felton gave her speeches over and over again, revising them somewhat to suit her particular audience or changing social conditions. Amid the lengthy discussion of rural violence and lynching that occurred in the daily press in the summer of 1897, Felton added two new issues to her "Woman on the Farm" speech. She added a call for improved educational opportunities for white women, including their admission to the University of Georgia, and she advocated the lynching of black men if it would "protect" white women from rape. Not surprisingly, it was her advocacy of lynching that dominated the front pages of the state's newspapers the next day. The first line of the *Atlanta Constitution* headline simply read, "'Lynch,' Says Mrs. Felton," followed by, "She Makes a Sensational Speech Before the Agricultural Society at Tybee." In the speech's most widely quoted passage, Felton was reported as taking to task the churches, the courthouse, and the very "manhood" of the white South for failing to "put a sheltering arm about innocence and virtue." If, she concluded, "it needs lynching to protect woman's dearest possession from the ravening human beasts—then I say lynch, a thousand times a week, if necessary."[8]

The one sentence—"if it will save one white woman, I say lynch a thousand black men"—would be repeated endlessly in the press commentary, and by Rebecca Latimer Felton herself in the months and years that followed. She claimed to have been driven to this position after reading the news coverage of five lynchings of black men (sometimes she claimed it was six, other times seven) for the rape of white women in the week preceding her 12 August lecture. And exactly how did she read these press accounts? At first consideration, it would appear that she read them with the same underlying assumptions as the white men who wrote them. That is, the victimization of the white woman is a given, the guilt of the black man is assumed, and the question is apparently simply whether the retaliatory actions of the white male mob were justified. Here Felton would appear to be much more a tool of the white-male-dominated press, at least of that faction, exemplified by Bill Arp, which advocated white mob behavior, than the black ministers, some of whom at least attempted to deconstruct the white male telling of the story by suggesting that lynching was as much of a crime as was rape, or at least by suggesting that the law would suffice to mete out retribution for criminal acts.[9]

Indeed, when Felton was moved in her speech to discuss the "crimes" on both sides, she focused not on lynching in conjunction with rape, but rather on what might initially appear to be an unlikely parallel: the "crime" of lynching and the "crime" of election fraud. She argued that lynching belonged in the same category of lawlessness as encouraging crimes against the electoral process, such as registration fraud, ballot box stuffing, and false counting. According to Felton, white men's crime was in having "initiated" black men as voters into these "mysteries" by bribing and otherwise corrupting the black man's vote in order to ensure their own political party's victory at the polls. In her speech at Tybee Island, she argued that it was not surprising that once black men came to understand that they could break the election laws with impunity, they would also come to assume that they could engage in "theft, rape and murder" without fear of legal retribution.[10]

While Bill Arp claimed that the "crime" of lynching was the result of the "frustrated love" that white men felt for white women, Felton made it sound as though lynching was a result of a misplaced "embrace" between black and white men at the polls. As she put it, "as long as your politicians take the colored man into their embrace on election day and make him think that he is a man and brother, so long will lynching prevail, for familiarity breeds contempt." In one of the most critical responses to Felton's speech, the *Boston Transcript* severely criticized this condemnation of brotherhood on her part. In an editorial, the paper charged that rather than being a problem of misplaced love, the problem was one of misplaced hate on the part of white Southerners for black Southerners. "If," the *Transcript* editorial queried, "the colored man is made to feel that he is not a man and a brother, how can he be blamed for acting the part assigned him in some times being a brute?" Perhaps, the editorial suggested, what was notable about the Southern black man's behavior was that in the midst of such "fiendish sentiment," he should continue to "adhere to progressive human standards."[11]

With the front-page publication of Felton's speech, it appeared that a new stage in racial violence had opened in Georgia. According to the *Transcript* editorial, while mob violence had already reached the point of casting "reproach and blight upon the state," the entry of white women into the debate as its militant advocates could only intensify the levels of already horrific behavior. Indeed, the *Transcript* even went so far as to charge that the real hatemongers in the South were in fact white women like Felton. As the editor put it, "When it comes to declaring who are the wild beasts of Georgia society, the black man would not get all the votes."[12]

Felton read this criticism of her speech by the *Transcript* as a particularly clear manifestation of Northerners' general attitude of "hatred" for all things Southern—and by "Southern" she obviously meant the white South. According to Felton, the North felt such deep animosity for the white South, and for Southern white women in particular, that Northern editors actually lined up with the "perpetrator of the crime." Felton argued that the Northern press was so antagonistic toward white Southern women that it did not even consider these assaults upon "defenseless" white women to be criminal acts, not, that is, when they were committed by what she termed the North's "pet political favorite," the black man. Here Felton reiterated her underlying position regarding who was doing the loving and who was doing the hating in the summer of 1897. There was too much "love" for the black man by the white man, on the one hand, according to Felton, and not enough love for the white woman by the white man, on the other. While Northern men were clearly the most guilty in this regard, white Southern men were at least complicitous, as could be seen by their fraternization with black men at the polls.[13]

While Felton clearly took offense at this manifestation of "brotherhood" between black and white men, she was actually more concerned about what she assumed was a fairly direct connection between this political "embrace" and a social embrace between black men and white women, a social embrace that she refused to understand as anything other than rape. This was a concern that she assumed the "abolitionist" Northern press, like the *Boston Transcript*, did not share. To the contrary, as she pointed out in her response to the *Transcript* editorial, Northern laws actually "appear to encourage and promote the mixture of the white and black races—because these laws authorize and permit marriage between the two races." She went on to suggest, undoubtedly somewhat tongue in cheek, that perhaps this was the reason the editor of the *Transcript* did not understand why such miscegenation was forbidden by the laws of Georgia. While she graciously "declined to comment" on the question of Northern law and custom with regard to mixed-race marriage, she felt fully empowered to speak for the South. "Let the editor of the Boston *Transcript* remember," she threatened, "that the irrevocable edict has gone forth from every farm house in Georgia and from every true man's heart, that the black fiend who lays unholy and lustful hands on a white woman in the state of Georgia shall surely die!"[14]

Here was the core of the social illness that led to mob violence in the summer of 1897. Felton could not understand an embrace between a black man and a white woman as being anything other than rape. As a result, she frequently conflated the rape of white women by black men with marriage between white women and black men, as she did in this response to the *Transcript* editorial. The fact that the love of some black men for some white women had to be hate in the minds of many white Southerners stood at the center of the radical distortions of who was loving whom, who was hating whom, and what was the "real" meaning of "rape" and "lynching" in the summer of 1897. It helps to explain why a loving request for the lock of a white woman's hair could be read by many white Southerners as essentially a "rape" of the white woman, a "rape" that then called for a lynching.

The whole question of who was doing the loving and who was doing the hating became a quagmire in the late nineteenth-century South because love for the white supremacist social order as a whole required turning the individual love of some black men for some white women into an act of hate, into rape, as surely as it required that brotherhood between black men and white men be understood as a veritable "crime." It had to be hate because, as Felton was inclined to put it, white women were the "coming mothers of the white race." As such, they were more than simply individual women who loved individual men, they were literally the carriers of white supremacy. Even if some individual black men genuinely loved some individual white women, such a love was at the same time an act of hate against the larger white supremacist social order of the South as a whole.[15]

There was, however, more than one way to maintain white supremacy. At least this was Felton's response to what she perceived as the crisis of the racial order in the summer of 1897. If white men were going to fall down on the job, and black men were going to aspire to social as well as political equality, white Southern women could still be expected to hold the line. They, after all, had it within their power never to understand the social advances of a black man as anything besides an act of hatred. They could singlehandedly transform love into hate in the way that the white supremacist social order required in order to perpetuate itself. The problem that Felton faced, however, was that her shock troops in the battle for white supremacy, white women themselves, also appeared to be in some danger of giving way. So while Bill Arp and the white male press in general referred to the "nameless crime" and meant to indicate rape, it was the actual or potential "falling down" of white women that constituted the truly "nameless crime" for Felton. A "crime" that she could never actually bring herself to name but which nonetheless stood at the center of her proposals for the reform of white rural women's condition.[16]

The intensity of the debate that surrounded Felton's advocacy of racial violence in the white male press tends to obscure the fact that she actually added two new points, not just one, to her speech on farm women. Along with advocating the lynching of black men, she also advocated improved educational opportunities for white women. She demanded improved access to a common school education for white farm women, and, for more privileged white women of the middle and upper classes, like herself, she asked for admission to the University of Georgia. In the case of the poorest of white rural women, Felton assumed that a common school education would allow them to pull themselves up faster in class terms than any black man could possibly rise up to meet them. She liked to tell a story in her speeches to illustrate this point. She would tell her audience about a train ride she had recently taken. While walking through the cars to the smoker, she tells of passing a neatly dressed black woman who was busy reading a book in Greek. She asked the woman why she was reading the book, and the woman answered that she was on her way to teach summer school and was refreshing her mastery of the subject she would teach. Arriving at her own seat in the rear coach, Felton happened to gaze out the window at a nearby cotton field, only to see four young white women hoeing cotton, "shabbily dressed—in the same field with negro men and boys." For Felton, it was a moving scene: "I have never been so heart sick . . . These are unwholesome conditions. . . . These are the coming mothers of our race."[17]

In earlier versions of her "Woman on the Farm" speech—for instance, the version that she gave at the 1891 meeting of the Georgia State Agricultural Society—Felton held white men solely responsible for the deplorable conditions of white women on the family farm. Who, after all, was responsible for these young white women being "reduced" to working in the fields beside black men, if not their white male relations? In her earlier versions of the speech, she castigated the white men in her audiences for failing to appreciate properly the contributions of white women on the family farm. Men who went to town on Saturdays to hold forth about the state of "my crop," "my house," and "my farm" with their fellow farmers, elicited Felton's particular wrath. According to Felton, gender relations on the family farm provided at least one case in which the old adage, "the man and his wife are made one," was realized, and, in the realization, "that one is the man." White men needed to recognize, Felton repeatedly argued, that the most important "crop" they would ever raise was their children and that in that business their wives were their best asset.[18]

From Felton's perspective in 1891, white men had it within their power to mend whatever ailed the family farm and the position of white women on it. They had it within their power to love their women as they should, or at least as Felton thought they should. They could acknowledge their partnership with their wives by coming to understand that they would "never raise a more important crop than their children." In this way, they could put their women, and domesticity more generally, at the center of what should properly be referred to as "our farm" and "our house." In 1891, Felton suggested to her farm audience that they could manifest concretely their advocacy of a gender reformed farm family by setting aside a portion of their crop as the "Wife's Farm," the idea being that just as the wife made the husband's breakfast in the morning, so should the husband work in the wife's fields. Felton must have been pleased when, at the 1891 meeting of the Georgia State Agricultural Society, her proposal was adopted and she was made state president of the "Before Breakfast Clubs."[19]

By 1897, however, Felton no longer considered reforms internal to the family farm and white gender relations sufficient to ameliorate the condition of white farm women. Now she added external "threats" and external "solutions"—the external "threat" of violence by the black man and the external "solution" of the lynch mob. At the same time, however, she also called for another external solution, the expanded education of white women. By empowering women in their own right, Felton hoped to put white women in a position to protect themselves against the potential abuse of both black and white men. As long as women could be educated to do what Felton considered to be right on their own, the dangers that the shortcomings of men of both races posed to the maintenance of a "constructive" social order could be reduced.[20]

All this is not to say that Felton envisioned no role for white men in the reform of white women's condition. After all, it was white men whom she continued to petition for support, in this case for improved educational opportunities for their women. Felton also assumed that improved educational opportunities, and the increased autonomy for white women that accompanied them, created another "new" role for white men. For as white women became more integrated into public life, they also became more "vulnerable" to the designs of strange men. White men's "new" role, then, was to "clear the path" of other men who blocked white women's way to the schoolhouse, the university, and ultimately even the voting booth. The most extreme form of this new kind of "protection" that white men were now being called upon to provide was that of lynching black men for the alleged rape of white women. From this perspective, however, Felton's call to "lynch a thousand black men if it would save one white woman" appears to be only the tip of the iceberg. Felton was in fact grappling with a far larger structural problem: how to empower white women to "protect" themselves without at the same time granting them the power to make choices that would undercut the white racial hierarchy.

Historians have long wondered why Rebecca Latimer Felton, one of the leading advocates for women's rights in the South, should also have been one of the region's most outspoken racists—why the "protection" of one group, white women, became fused in her thinking with the advocacy of the violent repression of another, black men. The key to this question is not to be found in an examination of either Felton's race or gender politics alone, but rather in the way that her increasingly reactionary race politics were created by, and in turn nourished, her increasingly progressive gender politics, through the medium of sexual relations, itself perhaps the ultimate form of fusion. It was the horror of this fusion that drove Felton on, that propelled her ever more militant advocacy of racial violence and gender "protection" in order to secure a segregated domestic integrity, where both black and white women would be properly recognized and empowered as the "coming mothers" of their respective races.[21]

For this reason, the greatest threat to Felton's project was sexual relations across the color line, and it is the primacy of her opposition to miscegenation that provides the key to her race politics and her gender politics. Indeed, her initial motivation for entering the political arena in her own right had little to do with either white women or black men. It did, however, have everything to do with miscegenation. It was during William Felton's second term in office that Rebecca Felton came upon a report concerning the convict lease system in Georgia. The Feltons were horrified at the extent to which the lease appeared to recapitulate the system of slavery, with the vast majority of the prisoners assigned to the lease being black, and the lessees being white. What particularly appalled Rebecca Felton was the way in which criminals were thrown together on the chain gang, regardless of their age or sex, or the seriousness of their crime. The presence of mixed-race children on the chain gang, fathered by the white guards and black women prisoners was, in Felton's estimation, the bitterest fruit of this obscene system.[22]

This issue galvanized Rebecca Felton. As she explained it, when she looked around Georgia in the mid-1880s for organized women's groups who might be concerned about the treatment of women and children on the convict lease, she found only one statewide organization outside the churches, the Woman's Christian Temperance Union. In 1886 she joined the WCTU in order to organize support for a petition to the state legislature opposing the lease. With her heart pounding in her chest at her own temerity, as she related later, she gave her first public address before the WCTU, urging the organization to sponsor her petition against the conditions of the lease. The WCTU adopted her petition, and in 1887 she presented it to the state legislature. Even for simply presenting the petition—she did not actually address the state legislature—she was nonetheless thoroughly excoriated. The state's elected leaders roundly denounced her as the "political She" of Georgia.[23]

It is perhaps hard to understand how a woman who got her own independent start in politics by trying to improve the conditions of black women and children, and who withstood considerable social opprobrium for her inappropriate behavior in doing so, could a short ten years later advocate the lynching of black men. What is critical to realize, however, is that in her mind, the problem posed by black women on the lease and white women in rural areas was the same. They were both examples of the basic wrong of miscegenation. The difference, however, was that when it came to black women, Felton was more than capable of naming the "nameless crime." It was here, then, that she could begin a crusade directly against miscegenation. Indeed, Felton had a long-standing opposition to white men's sexual abuse of black women for the way that it undercut the position of white women as their wives and as the mothers of their children. She railed against the way that white men, in the days of slavery, had "kept two households under one roof." She charged that the "crime that made slavery a curse lies in the fact that unbridled lust placed the children of bad white men in slave pens, on auction blocks." For this "crime" against their "parental responsibility," "the retribution of wrath was hanging over this country and the South paid penance in four years of bloody war."[24]

The defeat of the Confederacy and the emancipation of the slaves thus held forth the possibility that white women could finally command the first attention of their men, an attention that had always been threat-ened under slavery. The real horror of the convict lease system in Fel-ton's mind was that it represented the return of the worst of the slave owning South, where, as Felton put it, "mulattos were as common as blackberries." In the 1880s, Felton took up the reform of white men by organized white women with a vengeance. Under the auspices of the WCTU, she went after a whole complex of white men's "sins," includ-ing drinking, gambling, and prostitution. In 1891, when she gave her first farm speech, she was hopeful that white men could be induced or, at worst, forced—through prohibition, as well as through the reform of the convict lease—to commit to a new form of segregated domesticity. Then white women would finally be at the center of white men's lives and would finally be loved and appreciated as they never had been under the old slaveholding, staple crop system of the antebellum South of her birth.[25]

Instead, just as white women and the "white life for two"—as the WCTU dubbed the single sexual standard—appeared to be gaining some public and political advocacy, the bottom of the white supremacist social order seemed to be sliding out in the other direction. Sexual relations between black men and white women were considerably more threatening to Felton than those between white men and black women. As painful as white men's philandering might be to white women, it was still within the power of the white race to control. Granted, some white men seemed entirely unwilling to control their behavior, but by the 1890s, some white women seemed at last to be acquiring enough public power to force or convince white men to straighten up. Black men were, however, outside of Felton's control, and most frightening of all was the possibility that white women themselves would, with their newfound empowerment, choose black men rather than choosing white men as their "partners" in a "white life for two."

Racial violence and gender mutilation: these were Felton's answers to the possibility of love between white women and black men in the summer of 1897. Black men would have to be exterminated, and white women who had been with them would have to be seen as "ruined," as Felton put it, a fate that any respectable woman would regard as worse than death itself. And yet, even in the face of this mounting racial and gender violence, some black men and some white women refused to keep their place in the Southern social order. Indeed, Felton's own outspoken discussion of the need to lynch black men in order to protect white women opened the door for a more militant public statement on sexual relations across the color line. It was not until August of 1898, almost a year after the initial publication of Felton's speech, that Alexander Manly, the editor of the *Wilmington Record*, a popular black-owned daily in the South, decided to respond to Felton's allegations against black men in her "Woman on the Farm" speech. Unfettered by the constraints placed upon black men in the white male press, Manly published a reply that finally named the nameless, an act that was like throwing gasoline on the smoldering embers of the previous summer's mayhem of lynching and mob violence.[26]

Manly began his editorial by agreeing with many of Felton's positions on white women, though he was inclined to include black women as well. He thought that lower-class women of both races were sorely in need of moral uplift and that improved educational opportunities would indeed "protect" them on the farm. Not only did Manly concur with Felton's suggested reforms for white women; he also agreed with her assessment of the shortcomings of white men. "We suggest that the white men guard their women more closely," he wrote, "thus giving no opportunity for the human fiend, be he white or black." He suggested that poor white men were "careless" about their women: "You leave your goods out of doors and then complain because they are taken away." It was at this point that Manly parted company with Felton, however, for while Felton was only too willing to detail the various ways that white men abused their position of power—whether that was in their failure to respect and empower their women sufficiently or in their fatal "embrace" of black men at the polls—she was unable to grant white women any agency in their own predicament. Manly had no such compunctions. He suggested that poor white men were so careless toward their women that "their women were not any more particular in the matter of clandestine meetings with colored men, than are the white men with colored women." He asserted that "meetings of this kind go on for some time, until the woman's infatuation or the man's boldness bring attention to them and the man is lynched for rape."[27]

As if it were not enough to suggest in cold, hard print that the whole matter was a result of white women's "infatuation" with black men, Manly went on—well past the point of endurance for most Southern whites—to point out that while every black man who was lynched for the alleged crime of rape was described in the white press as a "big, burly, black brute," many were actually the sons of white fathers. They not only were not "black" and "burly," but they were "sufficiently attractive for white girls of culture and refinement to fall in love with them, as is well known to all." Alexander Manly was himself the acknowledged offspring of Charles Manly, governor of North Carolina from 1849 to 1851, and one of his slave women. From Felton's perspective, Alexander Manly represented all the errors of the white man, beginning with his mixed-race background, extending to the Fusion politics in North Carolina that had put him into public office as the register of deeds, and ending with his position as editor of an independent black newspaper. The initial ill-founded "embrace" of the white man had in this case borne fruit in the form of a mixed-race man, now in a position not only to embrace the white woman, but to write about it for all the world to read.[28]

In Alexander Manly, Rebecca Latimer Felton had indeed met her match. For if Felton was the white woman who gained the most public space to speak in the race crisis of the 1890s, Manly was the black man who found himself most empowered to represent the experience of black men. If Felton emerged as one of the leading New White women of the turn-of-the-century South, Manly epitomized the New Black man. If Felton was the "political She" of Georgia, notorious for her outspoken criticism of white men and white gender relations, Manly, as an editor and officeholder, was an equally outspoken advocate of the interests of his race. From their common condition as members of groups subordinate to the power of the white man, they could and did concur on many aspects of what they saw as his abusive behavior. In his editorial, for instance, Manly suggested that Felton should "begin at the fountainhead if she wishes to purify the stream." He pointed out that white men needed to be taught "purity" by their women. This was one of Felton's main arguments for admitting white women to the University of Georgia in her Tybee Island speech. She assumed that the presence of young women would improve the moral environment for the young men there. But, as with Manly's discussion of poor white women, he once again carried the matter one step further than Felton, across the color line. "Tell your men," he advised Felton, "that it is no worse for a black man to be intimate with a white woman than for a white man to be intimate with a colored woman." Manly's argument was once again color blind. *All* men should live by the single sexual standard advocated by Felton and the WCTU. Moreover, Felton should realize, and white people more generally should acknowledge, that the "sin" cut both ways. White men were clearly in no position to be passing judgment on black men, much less lynching them, for "sins" that they so frequently committed themselves.[29]

Not surprisingly, Manly's speech set the state of North Carolina on fire. In the summer and fall of 1898, the white supremacist Democratic press used the speech as a centerpiece of the campaign to organize popular opposition to the Fusion coalition of the Republicans and Populists, which had put black men into public offices and had thereby contributed to giving them the power to name the unnameable. After successfully using racial intimidation and appeals to white solidarity to capture the elections in the fall of 1898, mob sentiment moved beyond the lynching of one man to the massacre of the race. Manly's press was burned as the starting point of a conflagration that left at least eleven blacks dead, and promoted a general exodus of the black population, led by Manly himself, who had fled to New Jersey sometime before the racial massacre.

Felton wrote a reply to Manly's editorial and to the massacre that followed upon it. She read both as a graphic confirmation of the truth of the stance that she had taken on mob violence in her Tybee Island speech the previous summer. In her reply to Manly's editorial, she claimed that since the delivery of her Tybee speech the incidence of lynchings in the state of Georgia had decreased by half. In North Carolina, however, what she described as "corruption in politics and undue familiarity with North Carolina negroes at the polls" had instead created the conditions for a general racial massacre. In what was for her a typical slide from politics to social life, she charged that "the black race will be destroyed by the whites in self defense unless law and order prevail in regard to the crime of rape and lynching that follows." She revealed the real bottom line of her politics by arguing that when "the negro Manly attributed the crime of rape to intimacy between negro men and white women of the South, the slanderer should be made to fear a lyncher's rope rather than occupy a place in New York newspapers."[30]

As much as Felton's speech gave Manly the ground to stand on, Manly's speech forced Felton to reveal that the real problem was not violence against white women, but rather the possibility of intimacy between black men and white women. The real threat to the social order was not hatred, but love. And as Felton opened the door to Manly, so Manly opened the door for a white woman to acknowledge that love. But it could not happen—not, at least, within the geographical confines of the South. The Wilmington massacre made the whole question of Southern race relations front-page news across the nation. In the North, African Americans held meetings to protest the massacre. At one such meeting, at the Cooper Union in New York City, a white woman, Mrs. Elizabeth Grannis, "set the audience wild" when she claimed, "I am only here tonight to represent womanhood. Now we all know that white women and white girls of the South are full of colored blood." Infuriated, Rebecca Felton penned a reply charging Elizabeth Grannis with "telling a willful and venomous untruth." According to Felton, Grannis was purposefully playing on the "basest passions of that ignorant audience." The North, according to Felton, could keep Elizabeth Grannis. Not even "colored citizens" of Georgia would tolerate her presence with such "base falsehood on her lips."[31]

There was no place in the South for white women who openly affirmed their relationships with black men. Indeed by the next year, after the vehement reaction of Southerners to her remarks, Elizabeth Grannis had decided to leave the country altogether and set sail for Europe. There was no place for black men either, at least if Alexander Manly's experience was any indicator. He decided to resettle permanently in the North. Felton, however, remained in the South. The events of the late 1890s, her exchanges with Manly and Grannis, and her proposed "solutions" to the threat of the likes of Oscar Smith and Rene Williams propelled her ever further into public prominence and political power. In 1901, she became the first woman to address the state legislature in Georgia. Clark Howell, the state senator who introduced her, noted that while there is a "great deal of discussion and contention as to who is the smartest man in Georgia, it is universally conceded that the woman who is to address you today is the brightest and the smartest woman in the state." Felton had come a long way since 1887, scarcely more than a decade earlier, when simply for presenting a petition in the very same statehouse, she had been roundly condemned as the "political She" of Georgia.[32]

By the end of her long life, Rebecca Latimer Felton would see many of the reforms she advocated in the summer of 1897 made into law: disenfranchisement of the black population, the admission of white women to the University of Georgia, the passage of prohibition and compulsory education legislation, the abolition of the convict lease and the establishment of a separate system of juvenile correction. As her politics of racially segregated domesticity became law throughout the South, so too did she continue to ride the political wave, becoming the first U.S. woman senator in 1923. Years later, she reveled in the changes in the status of white Southern women that her appointment to the U.S. Senate indicated. "It meant that a woman reared in the sheltered security of an antebellum plantation was to be the first of her sex to sit in the U.S. Senate. It was hard to realize. Who in that day would have had the hardihood to predict that the time would come when Georgia women would hold public office?" she wondered. Perhaps only the unnamed, the silenced, the mute men and women, whose lives and deaths nonetheless drove her story, as surely as she was empowered by theirs, could have answered her question.[33]

Notes

1. *Atlanta Constitution*, 12 July 1897; *Atlanta Journal*, 12 July 1897; *Atlanta Journal*, 14 July 1897. Reports of lynching for the alleged crime of rape were frequent. See also, *Atlanta Constitution*, 15, 25 July, 3, 12 August 1897, and *Atlanta Journal*, 16, 22 July, 4 August 1897.

2. *Atlanta Constitution*, 25 July 1897.

3. Ibid., 28 July 1897.

4. Ibid., 3 August 1897.

5. Ibid., 2 July 1897.

6. Ibid., 1 August 1897. For a further discussion of the issue by Bill Arp, see ibid., 4 July 1897.

7. On Rebecca Latimer Felton, see John E. Talmadge, *Rebecca Latimer Felton: Nine Stormy Decades* (Athens: University of Georgia Press, 1960); Josephine Bone Floyd, "Rebecca Latimer Felton: Political Independent," *Georgia Historical Quarterly* 30 (March 1946): 14–34, and "Rebecca Latimer Felton, Champion of Women's Rights," *Georgia Historical Quarterly* 30 (June 1946): 81–104.

8. As published in the *Macon Telegraph*, 18 August 1897. I cite the newspaper version of this speech because the various handwritten versions of the speech in her papers do not include the notorious sentence that made the speech so incendiary. Either the versions in her papers are not the version she gave at Tybee, or, more likely, she added the call for the lynching of black men in the heat of the delivery of the speech. See her speech, "Southern Women and Farm Life," Rebecca Latimer Felton Papers, Hargrett Library, University of Georgia, Athens (hereafter, HL), reel no. 15. Here she discusses the "fear of outrage" but does not advocate lynching as the solution.

9. In her Tybee Island speech, Felton claimed to have read of five lynchings in the press the week before; as the debate heated up, the number increased to six, and eighteen months later she claimed it was seven; see *Atlanta Constitution*, 22 December 1898.

10. Ibid.

11. As reprinted in the *Macon Telegraph*, 20 August 1897.

12. Ibid.

13. Ibid.

14. Ibid.

15. For more on the "coming mothers of the white race," see "Duty of Mothers" and "The Duty and Obligation that Lies on Southern Women," in Felton Papers, HL, box 14, and "Mrs. Dr. W. H. Felton On Heredity" and "The Problems that Interest Mothers," in Rebecca Latimer Felton, *Country Life in Georgia in the Days of My Youth* (1919; reprint, New York: Arno Press, 1980), 264–70 and 279–84.

16. For some examples of the centrality of sexuality to Felton's reform proposals for white women, see "The Education of Veterans Daughters," "The Ladies of the Home Missionary Society," and "Rescue Work," in Felton Papers, HL, box 15, and "The Industrial School For Girls," in Felton, *Country Life*, 270–72.

17. "Address Before the Georgia Legislature, November, 1901," in Felton, *Country Life*, 170–92.

18. "Mrs. Felton's Addresses to Farm Institutes in the Early Nineties," Felton Papers, HL, box 15.

19. "Southern Chivalry: The Wife's Farm—The Husband's Pledge," Felton Papers, HL, reel no. 13.

20. For example, see Talmadge, *Rebecca Latimer Felton*, 125.

21. "Mrs. Dr. W. H. Felton on Heredity," in Felton, *Country Life*.

22. Felton, *Country Life*, 120.

23. Ibid.

24. Ibid., 93.

25. Ibid., 79.

26. See H. Leon Prather, *We Have Taken a City: The Wilmington Racial Massacre and Coup of 1898* (Cranbury, N.J.: Associated University Presses, 1984), esp. 47–80, for the most complete discussion of Manly's editorial and the racial massacre that followed.

27. Ibid., 72–73.

28. Ibid., 68–69.

29. Ibid., 73.

30. "Mrs. Felton vs. Manly," Felton Papers, HL, reel no. 13.

31. "Grannis Answered: Mrs. WH Felton Pays Her Respects to a Slanderer," Felton Papers, HL, reel no. 18.

32. Felton, *Country Life*, 171.

33. Rebecca Latimer Felton, *The Romantic Story of Georgia's Women* (Atlanta: Atlanta Georgian and Sunday American, 1930), 45.

Not logic but a hollow social distinction has separated the races. The economically depressed white accepts his poverty by telling himself that, if in no other respect, at least socially he is above the Negro. For this empty pride in a racial myth he has paid the crushing price of insecurity, hunger, ignorance, and hopelessness for himself and his children.

—Martin Luther King Jr., *Stride toward Freedom*, 1958

Michael Honey

Class, Race, and Power in the New South

Racial Violence and the Delusions of White Supremacy

In *Black Reconstruction*, W. E. B. Du Bois observed how white workers after the Civil War sold their birthrights as citizens in a free republic for a mess of pottage, going against their own long-term class interests by supporting white supremacy. Observing conditions in his native South many years later, Martin Luther King Jr. likewise saw the poor wages, terrible working conditions, and general poverty and lack of power among most white Southerners as proof that racism had served their interests poorly, if at all.

Why did they do it? And how did it happen? We still ask questions posed by Du Bois and King: whose interest does racism really serve? Why did events such as the Wilmington massacre happen? Who is responsible? Such questions remain relevant today in a society that still has not overcome the historical legacies left by slavery, segregation, lynch law, and black disfranchisement. Such historical questions need to be asked, for they lead into a reconsideration of the roots and character of an American racism that we still struggle to overcome today.

Particularly in the South, no matter how poor white workers might have been, Du Bois argued, most of them supported white supremacy because it provided "a sort of public and psychological wage" of economic and social advantages over African Americans. In supporting white supremacy, however, poorer whites aligned themselves with a white ruling class whose interests were quite at odds with their own. In this sense, white supremacy was a snare and a delusion. Slavery exploited blacks and marginalized white workers, and though Reconstruction's experiment in democracy momentarily drove the hereditary ruling class out of power, white supremacy eventually divided and conquered Southern workers. According to Du Bois, "every problem of labor advance in the South was skillfully turned by demagogues into a matter of interracial jealousy." Instead of an alliance between black and white laboring people a "deep, awful and ineradicable cleft" emerged between them, creating "a solid South impervious to reason, justice or fact." Not just in the South, but on the national stage, Du Bois observed, racism undermined labor solidarity at every turn.[1]

Since Du Bois, numerous labor historians have documented how white workers, based on their perceptions of economic self-interest, acted as historical agents in the creation of white supremacy.[2] Indeed, in the context of the South, some historians have viewed the white people at the bottom of society rather than those at the top as the primary carriers of racism. One line of thought has always viewed poorer Southern whites as the main enemies of progress for African Americans and paternalistic white elites as their main allies. Considering the great wave of racist violence that swept the white South in the late nineteenth century, with its rabid obsession with interracial sex, it might be tempting for us to see the Wilmington pogrom and other racial terror as products of a kind of generalized white psychic illness—a mentality of extremism, an "unnamed hysteria," or "rage for order," as one historian has called it.[3]

Du Bois, however, did not think lynch law and racial violence emanated primarily from the white working class or from some primal urge or psychological crisis among Southern whites in general. Du Bois saw the Atlanta race riot of 1906 with his own eyes, and later he watched the brutal imperialism of the Western capitalist nations take its toll on Africa, Asia, and Latin America; he thus saw the racial violence of the South as part of a global system, in which a few enriched themselves at the expense of the many. He saw white terror, mad as it might be, as part of the struggle over wealth and power in an era of capitalist expansion. "The color line" became the preeminent problem of the twentieth century because the world's economic and social systems were marked by both class and color, Du Bois concluded.[4] The Wilmington racial massacre was part of that world and ushered in the century.

There is no secret about the fact that the "best white men," as Glenda Gilmore has called North Carolina's up-and-coming landed and business elites, engineered and led the white supremacy campaign of the 1890s. Through state and national media they trumpeted their role in the "revolution" from above as a great step forward, claiming to have freed the economy, politics, and the affairs of society from the grasp of indolent, rapacious blacks and corrupt, conniving whites. In an age of Social Darwinism, they saw the educated and rich, namely themselves, as the natural leaders of a "progressive" business society. In the view of white business elites, the exercise of power at the ballot box or in the halls of government by African Americans and lower-class whites violated the natural order. Fighting for their own place in this order, many white women joined the crusade to disfranchise black men. Without the civilizing influence of slavery, they claimed, black men were retrogressing back to a state of barbarism from which white women had to be protected. The "best white men" and the women who joined them in the white supremacy campaign thus did not see the murder of black people in the streets of Wilmington as an atrocity, but as an act of defense by white people. The "best" whites for the most part saw the Wilmington massacre as the crowning event in a long battle to keep power and civilization in the hands of the well-bred and wealthy.[5]

Their struggle for control, of course, went back to the origins of North Carolina society. White elites had used slavery to exploit black labor and marginalize white workers, and they used white supremacy to do much the same thing after slavery ended. In their pursuit of power, white elites cloaked their class politics in racial and sexual appeals. White plantation owners, financiers, manufacturers, merchants, lawyers, and newspaper editors, along with other white professionals and, of course, politicians, continually vied for power, but these economic elites always realized they were a small minority of the population. They thus recognized the signal importance of dividing their lower-, middle-, and working-class opposition, and racism provided the key to doing this. Ruling elites constantly diverted white lower-class resentment and demands for expanded democratic rights, and they often did it by "crying nigger."[6]

White supremacy maintained its signal importance in North Carolina because, perhaps more than any other Southern state, North Carolina had a bitter history of class divisions, expressed largely through contests over government: who controlled it, whose interests it would serve, and how democratic it would be. In the colonial era, class conflict broke into the open during the Regulator revolt, while in the antebellum period it was most evident when white mechanics, yeoman farmers, and nonslaveholders fought to tax slaveholders at full value for their slaves. Class conflict then revolved around the fact that most white people did not own slaves and probably never would, yet the richest slaveholders, a small fraction of the population, had always controlled North Carolina's political and economic life.[7] Class conflict over whose interests government should serve appeared even more openly during the Civil War, as common whites engaged in widespread revolt against the Confederacy, using armed guerrilla warfare and a variety of other forms of resistance to what they called "a rich man's war and a poor man's fight."[8]

Class conflict, struggles over political power, and the question of race always remained intertwined. Both during and after slavery, the soundness of planter and entrepreneurial investments rested on keeping an abundant supply of cheap labor, whether free or enslaved. But controlling labor, given the level of white lower-class discontentment and contestation, required firm control over state power. For workers, slavery had made it difficult to conceive of labor-based alliances across the boundaries of color. The post–Civil War era, however, offered the possibility that transracial, class-based voting alliances could reconfigure Southern society to the benefit of people at the bottom. During Reconstruction, a nascent Republican Party gained significant support from white artisans, wage workers, farmers, and businesspeople alienated from former slaveholders and their Confederate allies.[9] These dissatisfied whites allied with the emancipated slave population at the ballot box to reform the system that had for so long favored the landed upper classes over the common people.

Reconstruction's political leaders created the basics of "modern government"—public schools, public welfare institutions, property rights for women, tax exemptions for small homesteaders, and universal male suffrage. These accomplishments cost the old elites money and power and upset their aristocratic notions of hierarchy and privilege. A new system of democracy at the local level created an even greater threat. In 1868, the Radical Reconstructionists replaced the previous system by which elites had controlled the law through local officials appointed by the legislature. With an expanded male suffrage and the right to make their own decisions, local people elected new judges, sheriffs, and other county officials and created a much more responsive and representative government than that which had prevailed under the old appointive system. Backed by Union Leagues filled with middling and poor men of both races, the state Republican Party made local government an active, if still hesitant, force by which ordinary people might address their needs. Newly enfranchised African American men provided the most unified voting bloc within the Reconstruction era's movement toward self-government, while black families and the black community struggled at all levels to create a new economic, civil, and political framework for the exercise of freedom.[10]

The trend toward more democratic government set off decades of struggle by white elites to turn back the clock. During the "white terror," as historian Allen Trelease has called it, the Ku Klux Klan acted basically as a terrorist wing of the Democratic Party. Led by some of the state's most prominent men, the Klan specialized in assassinating vulnerable Republicans, white and black, in areas far from those—like Wilmington or eastern North Carolina's Second Congressional District—with the largest concentrations of black population. In black strongholds, the triumph of white supremacy would require stronger measures to succeed.[11]

During Reconstruction, Democrats perfected the arts of demagoguery and race-baiting. In the election of 1876 they seized control of both the governorship and the legislature through violence, ballot tampering, and their control of the news media, which replaced economic issues in the campaign with concern over "the Negro in politics." They split white westerners in the mountains and the Piedmont from the Republicans, and, once in power, they replaced elective local government with local government appointed by the legislature. Through racial politics, they created a regime, according to historian Helen G. Edmonds, of "Democratic election law, Democratic control of county governments, gerrymandering, intimidation, manipulation, and corruption."[12]

Under the banner of "white supremacy," Democrats used tax breaks and the fiscal power of the state to aid their favored enterprises and consolidate the power of a landed, commercial, entrepreneurial upper class. They undercut debtor support laws and adopted fence and stock laws that enclosed grazing lands and helped drive subsistence farmers off the land. Textile and lumber mill owners exploited the labor of dispossessed white farmers who migrated into "public work," while ex-slaves also became wage workers at the lowest rates of pay. Low wages, widespread use of child labor, night work, hazardous conditions, company towns, abusive foremen, peonage, underfunded public schools, high rates of illiteracy, and poverty all marked the advent of industrial capitalism in North Carolina.[13]

As North Carolina became part of a "New South" led by entrepreneurs such as those in the textile, tobacco, railroad, and banking industries, labor exploitation accelerated. In the 1890s, the number of cotton mill, lumber, furniture, and tobacco workers doubled or in some cases even tripled.[14] As profits rose, wages stayed largely the same or got worse. Factory workers in New Hanover County, as elsewhere, averaged ten to twelve hours of work per day in 1890, with bare subsistence wages for unskilled adult factory labor typically ranging from 50 to 75 cents a day, and for children ranging from 30 to 50 cents.[15] The Knights of Labor and craft unions attempted to organize, but racial intimidation and the threat of firing forced them to work in conditions of secrecy and fear. They made little headway. Where they could organize unions, workers gained far higher wages than their unorganized counterparts. Yet only twenty unions existed in the state in 1890, representing a handful of white male railroad engineers and conductors, bricklayers, carpenters, and printing trades workers. By 1900, labor unions existed in only three or four of the state's larger cities. In New Hanover County, none of the nearly 2,000 factory workers were unionized, and only a few locomotive engineers belonged to unions, according to the state's labor bureau. Not surprisingly, legislation to support workers' rights to organize or to limit the working hours of children and women got nowhere.[16]

At the same time, the plantation regimes in the eastern part of the state fastened onto a one-crop economy and a system of tenantry and sharecropping that led to debt peonage for countless agricultural workers. Far from being a land of independent small farms, North Carolina saw tenants and sharecroppers, the great majority of them black, operating more than two-thirds of its farms by 1880. White landowners used racial segregation as a means of forcing unfair labor contracts and indebtedness on black agricultural workers, who became easily expendable and suffered under conditions little better than slavery. Black women in particular found themselves increasingly drawn into distasteful domestic and personal service for whites because the wages of their own men remained extremely low. White small farmers also faced increasing impoverishment. The market price of their crops continually declined while their costs rose, as railroads, bankers, and merchants took an ever greater share of the farmers' profits. Meanwhile, state government gave the entrepreneurial classes tax breaks and other advantages that eluded the common people.[17]

The economic depressions of the 1890s led more and more North Carolinians to contest Democratic rule. The propaganda of white supremacy, terror and intimidation, top-down control of county government by the Democratic legislature, gerrymandering, and electoral fraud had suppressed democratic aspirations in the 1870s and 1880s. As lower-class dissatisfaction increased in the 1890s, even these restraints could not hold back reform movements. Through a series of state and local elections, an organized Populist Party and a newly resurgent Republican Party mobilized small farmers, mountaineers, workers, and virtually the entire African American voting population against the vested interests of wealthy Democrats who controlled the state. Some 90,000 members of the white Farmer's Alliance turned against the Democratic Party, recognizing that it had betrayed them in favor of railroad, banking, and other corporate interests.[18]

When these farmers voted for the Populist Party in 1892, they realigned the political landscape, as farmers did all over the South. As the economic depression of 1893 and 1894 swept the country, North Carolina Populists went further still and "fused" with the Republican Party. By supporting common candidates, these two parties took over the legislature in 1894 and 1896, elected Populists to fill both of the state's positions in the U.S. Senate, and placed Republican Daniel Russell in the Governor's mansion in 1896. Virtually all African American voters and many whites hostile to corporate interests had a common cause.[19]

The problem for the Democrats once again became too much democracy. The Fusion legislature enacted laws putting ceilings on interest rates, raising new taxes to support public schools, guaranteeing all men the right to vote, and reducing the privileges of the railroads. By controlling interest rates, it undercut the investments of bankers, and by threatening to repudiate debts accumulated at the local level (due to tax breaks given to industries), it threatened the profits of merchants and textile, lumber, and tobacco factory owners. Worst of all, Fusion abolished the appointive system of the Democrats and restored popular elections at the local level. As a result of these actions, said the chairman of the state Republican Executive Committee, "every business interest in the state representing capital was arrayed against us." Businessmen wanted a government that would provide tax breaks and otherwise subsidize their enterprises, keeping wages and public expenditures low—not one that would advance the education and welfare of small farmers and workers.[20]

Not "Negro domination," but too much democracy, through the fusion of Republicans and Populists, set off the white supremacy campaign that led to the Wilmington massacre; and every Democrat, Republican, and Populist throughout the state knew it. African Americans had never made up more than one-fifth of the North Carolina General Assembly, and the state had elected only four blacks to Congress in fourteen years—and they all came from one district, which was 70 percent black.[21] If the absurd cry of "Negro domination" had silenced reform movements in the past, Democrats in the 1890s had to contend with the highest level of anger on the part of agrarian and working-class people the state had seen since the Civil War. To silence reform now required not just cowardly murders in the dark of night and the blatant stuffing of ballot boxes, as during Reconstruction, but a truly massive propaganda campaign to rally the masses of white men to defend their "manhood" and white women. It required the fantastic image of black men lusting for white women or hovering over the state like vampires and sucking away the lifeblood of the state. It also required the context of a South in which lynching, burning, and mutilating black men had become the favored means of enforcing white power and black deference, justified by the cry of rape. Much like the McCarthyite witch-hunts of the 1950s, the white supremacy campaign had its own kind of magic, which it worked through the media, campaign rallies, lynchings, and white race riots.[22]

Wilmington provided the ideal setting in which to play out white fantasies of "Negro domination." Here African American men indeed held important elective and appointive office. A significant number of Wilmington blacks owned property and had skills that elevated them above the conditions of the average white. Some of them were highly educated and lived in the "better" part of town with white neighbors. Moreover, in this and other predominantly black areas of the state they actively contested white supremacy. Editor Alexander Manly, who ran perhaps the only black daily newspaper in the country, did not hesitate to expose the false image of black men as rapists of white women that Democratic editors promulgated so widely. Black women in Wilmington, as elsewhere in the state, played leading roles in education and community development. While most black men and women worked in menial, low-wage employment, North Carolina also had a successful—too successful from the point of view of whites—class of educated, professional African Americans strongly engaged in politics. With 8,000 whites and 17,000 blacks, Wilmington represented the heart of black political power in the state. Breaking that power, and defeating the upward aspirations of black working- and middle-class people, could not be more logical or necessary from the perspective of the Democratic Party. But it would take considerable doing, since African Americans in North Carolina had a grassroots movement for personal, political, and group advancement as vigorous as any in the South.[23]

Wilmington not only had a two-thirds black majority; it was the state's largest city and most important seaport. Whoever controlled Wilmington controlled the tax rates, property valuations, and investment and improvement policies of a potentially rich metropolis. Many local entrepreneurs, like their counterparts across the state, had used the Democratic Party as a vehicle to power. Since 1875, local businesspeople had benefited from the legislature's gerrymandering of the city's wards, which undercounted African American and working-class white votes and gave wealthy Democrats disproportionate voting power. Through their power to appoint local officials, the state Democrats had placed police and taxing power in the hands of Wilmington's Democratic businessmen, who used such advantages to help create their own fortunes.[24]

The Fusion legislature of the 1890s took power out of their hands. It returned local government to election by the people and made voter registration requirements less restrictive, thus expanding the black electorate. With his appointive powers, Fusion governor Russell named local officeholders who more closely reflected the interests of the whole population of Wilmington and got the legislature to amend the city charter so that Populists and Republicans would gain a greater share of power. The Democrats had never fully succeeded in eliminating a strong African American influence over city affairs. Now, although Wilmington's Fusion government was contested by the Democrats, blacks and whites outside the select circle of the business elites had clearly become more prominent, not only in city and county government posts, but in running the police and judicial system as well.[25]

The white supremacy campaign of 1898 sought to eradicate Fusion's expanded electoral democracy through "class-biased race baiting," as Glenda Gilmore has called it. To their great advantage, North Carolina Democrats controlled an increasingly vast preponderance of newspapers, particularly the mass circulation dailies. According to the state labor department, in 1900 the Democrats owned 145 of the state's newspapers, the Republicans 20, and the Populists 36 (and most of the latter would not last long). It appears that all the newspapers in New Hanover County were Democratic except for Alexander Manly's *Daily Record*, which provided the city's one voice independent of the white elite. The rising media apostles of a businessman's "New South"—*Raleigh News and Observer* editor Josephus Daniels the leader among them—had the propaganda mechanism needed to persuade working-class whites to get in line behind the state's corporations, editors, and party bosses.[26]

These Democratic editors relentlessly sought to drive a racial wedge between black and white Carolinians. They relied heavily on headlines shouting "Negro Control in Wilmington" or, even more ludicrously, "Negro On Train With Big Feet Behind White." They ran daily stories depicting black men as rapists, thieves with chickens under their arms, radicals, thugs, or idiots. Cartoons showed a white man pinned by the large foot of a black man, white girls being sworn as witnesses before a black deputy clerk, a heavyset black man leaning on a cane and smoking a pipe while ordering whites to work on the county roads. "The Vampire That Hangs Over North Carolina," a cartoon showing a bat with a human face and black hands but animal claws grasping the people of the state, conjured up black men as brutes and rapists lusting after white women. Democratic editors across the state used such caricatures to appeal to the racial prejudices of Populist and Republican whites in the western part of the state, far away from majority-black districts of "Negro Republicans." As Gilmore has explained, "The Populist white man who had valued his farm above his race discovered with a shock that he had opened the gates of hell for some distant white woman" by voting against the Democrats.[27]

Democratic media attacks shifted decisively toward this tack once the light-skinned and well-educated Manly published his challenge to Rebecca Felton. In repudiating Felton's suggestion that lynching would be a good antidote to interracial sex, Manly blamed white women and men for the widespread interracial liaisons in the South. The *Wilmington Messenger*, along with the *Wilmington Morning Star*, reprinted the Manly editorial and their distortions of it every day from August to election day, using it to goad white farmers and the poor to "stand by the white race." Concocted newspaper stories from throughout the state purported to show that black men had become insolent and were retrogressing to a stage of barbarism, while fantastic cartoons rubbed raw the sensibilities of white male voters. One cartoon image showed the desired results: masses of white men marching with a "White Supremacy" sign toward the white woman "Goddess of Democracy."[28]

The Democrats' media stereotypes and inflammatory rhetoric about race blotted out nearly all consideration of other matters at stake in the election campaign, and allowed them to avoid discussing the economic

Michael
Honey

goals of white supremacy, which ran counter to the interests of most white people. The *Wilmington Morning Star*, from July through November of 1898, repeated, ad nauseam, warnings that black men "are becoming very assertive and aggressive," issuing calls for "a white man's country," and reprinting over and over a story about the supposed rape of a white woman by a black man. "Every white man," regardless of class, it said, should be ready to take up arms to defend "sanctity of home" and extend their "protection to wives and daughters."[29] When the Populist Party of New Hanover County professed allegiance to white supremacy but in return petitioned the Democratic Party for a program of "reforms that will bring relief to those who labor," they received no response. Instead, the Democratic press continued to insist that "negro domination was made possible . . . through a division of the white men at the ballot box" and to urge every "patriotic white man" to "assert his white manhood" by gathering arms and preparing to defend white homes and families.[30]

The drumbeat of race-baiting shifted the sentiments of white Republicans and Populists far to the right. The argument that Fusion's class alliances between black and white voters meant that "the poor white man is on the same plane as the negro" turned many whites away from economic issues. "We can't blame the negro for wanting to be white, but we do blame the white man for wanting to be a negro," one former Populist wrote, while some Populist and Republican newspapers printed lurid images showing that the Democrats, not Fusionists, had been the ones who had turned white women over to "Negro rule." Cartoons in Republican and Populist papers showed white women lifting picks and shovels to work on public roads, under the supervision of insolent and lazy-looking black men. Undoubtedly, such propaganda was partly responsible for the hundreds of white men who paraded through the streets of Wilmington four days before the state and local elections proclaiming their patriotism and manhood by wearing red shirts and waving flags that said "White Supremacy."[31]

Democrats pressured poorer white farmers and workers to join the white supremacy campaign through the popular media, the Red Shirt parades, and the threat of economic retaliation; but they also mustered an economic argument for white supremacy by claiming Democratic control would remove political instability caused by the black vote, free local capital from excessive taxes, and open the state to outside investments, creating new jobs. Furthermore, they promised their "revolution" would turn over to whites jobs currently held by unworthy blacks.[32]

Arguments in favor of elevating the labor of whites over that of blacks or other racial minorities have always had particular resonance in the United States. Slaveholders in the antebellum period and Social Darwinists during industrialization claimed that white economic dominance and black labor subservience were part of the natural order of things, while white workers, especially during periods of heightened job competition, always tried to preserve the best jobs for themselves.[33] Du Bois pointed out that it did not make sense to believe that the elevation of black workers necessarily meant the degradation of white labor: "My rise does not involve your fall." His point of view, however, ran directly counter to the "zero sum" logic of the capitalist market relations with which white workers were thoroughly familiar. Forcing black artisans out of the labor market and stopping blacks from voting seemed to many poorer whites to be a logical response to the employers' system of divide and conquer.[34]

In Wilmington, supporters of white supremacy favored exclusionary labor policies and disfranchisement, and even seemed to think that slavery and segregated labor markets had been a privilege rather than a burden for blacks. After more than one hundred years of slavery, the *Wilmington Messenger* claimed, "the white laboring men . . . have not been treated fairly. They have been discriminated against and the negro favored."[35] This argument inverted reality, making the worst victims of labor exploitation appear to be the perpetrators of it. Nonetheless, the competing presence of large numbers of skilled black artisans, professionals, and entrepreneurs in Wilmington lent particular salience to the demand that they be replaced by whites. Planters had frequently displaced the labor of skilled white artisans with that of slaves, and Wilmington entrepreneurs continued to prefer cheaper (and usually more skilled) black workers to whites. The city had been populated by a relatively large number of free blacks and artisans under slavery, and succeeding generations of African Americans, largely through their own initiative and effort, gained education and built up businesses that made them the envy of some whites. Migrating to the city in large numbers after the Civil War, they often set the wage rates as brickmasons, carpenters, and mechanics at a time when many unskilled whites could not find work of any kind.[36]

Not Republicans and Populists but Southern Democrats had led the way in pushing down the price of labor and undercutting the political power of workers and farmers. Yet the very Democrats who had nourished the harsh poverty of lower-class whites and blacks succeeded in blaming white poverty on their political opponents. According to Democrats, the degree of black advancement that had occurred in Wilmington resulted not from black striving, but from racial preferences instituted by Fusion. These preferences, they claimed, denied whites their God-given economic entitlements.

Upon close inspection, however, it was evident that black artisans did not have quite the dominant place in Wilmington's economy that many whites believed they did. The city's work force, except for having a somewhat larger number of black entrepreneurs and artisans than that in most places, did not differ greatly from the work force in the rest of the South: white males made up 91 percent of the white-collar workers, 70 percent of the skilled workers, and 57 percent of the semiskilled workers. African American men made up 87 percent of the unskilled workers, and black women worked mainly as domestic laborers and washerwomen. Black progress required more, not fewer, skilled jobs, and despite delusions to the contrary among many whites, blacks had hardly been given preferences. The white supremacy campaign created the impression that blacks lived much better than most whites, but the situation was quite the reverse. Most white males, collectively a minority of the city's population, kept their hands clean and lived off the labor of African Americans, hiring them to do the hard and dirty jobs at low wages. Yet, not surprisingly, unskilled white workers felt blacks should not be hired at all, or at least not while some whites remained unemployed.[37]

Hoping to gain real advantages from the white supremacy campaign, Wilmington whites formed a "white labor union" under the leadership of Irish worker Mike Dowling. We really know very little about white workers in the city, however, so it is hard to gauge their views exactly.[38] We do know they were supported by wealthy benefactor Walter Parsley and cotton mill owner Hugh MacRae, members of the "Secret Nine" businessman's committee that coordinated the revolution to take over the local government.[39] It is safe to say that these and other business owners, not workers, had control over the planning and preparation for the Wilmington revolt. White supremacist organizations called "White Government Unions," however, created an image of all whites joining together in a common cause as they organized ward by ward for the planned takeover. The unions' "right to work" resolutions called upon "all the true Democrats to prove their Democracy by discharging all the negroes in their employment and give the work to worthy white men and women out of work."[40] Democrats at a mass meeting just before the Wilmington massacre struck this theme in their "Declaration of White Independence," which reasserted that black domination over employment idled Wilmington whites and prevented others from immigrating to the city, undermining its prosperity. Democrats claimed white supremacy would change this equation by turning more jobs over to white men and, they also specified, white women. A massive meeting of the White Government Unions of the city on election day embraced this and other objectives of the coming "white man's victory at the ballot box."[41]

The declaration's demand undoubtedly encouraged many of those poorer whites who marched behind Colonel Alfred Moore Waddell and Democratic business leaders in the Wilmington massacre. On 8 November 1898, fraud and massive intimidation gave the Democrats a statewide victory. Two days later, 400 to 500 heavily armed white men invaded the Wilmington black community with guns blazing. With no attempt to conceal their acts, the armed militants sealed off the Brooklyn neighborhood with Gatling guns, set buildings on fire, murdered and beat occupants at random, and rounded up white and black Populist and Republican leaders and exiled them from town. The next day, led by businessmen of the Secret Nine, a mob, more or less at the point of a gun, forced the city's board of aldermen, a Fusion coalition of four blacks and six whites, to resign so that white supremacist Democrats could take their places. The "best men" had retaken control of Wilmington and the state through armed force, intimidation, and racial propaganda.[42] *Collier's Weekly* justified their actions by reporting that Southern blacks, "ignorant as Hottentots," had retrogressed "back into the murderous moods of barbaric Africa" during their participation in Southern governments as voters. Whites had now reclaimed their civilization and democracy.[43]

The presence of poorer whites in the ranks of the rioters and in the White Government Unions created the impression that oppressed white people from the lower orders had to some degree taken the lead in throwing off the yoke of "Negro domination." However, an analysis of the signers of the "Declaration of White Independence" by Hayumi Higuchi suggests a different reality. Higuchi was able to identify the occupations of 351 of the 442 signers through the *Wilmington City Directory*. He discovered that 85 percent of these signers were members of the middle and upper classes—managers, proprietors, wholesalers, retailers, clerks, and foremen. A listing of the White Government Union canvassers of the various wards and divisions of the city on election day, printed in the local press, also suggests that white entrepreneurs, merchants, brokers, clerks, salespeople, lawyers, and other professionals, not white workers, led the Wilmington revolution. And although the popular revolution offered something to both businesspeople and poor and working-class whites, leading citizens Alfred Moore Waddell and Hugh MacRae clearly led the mobs into Brooklyn.[44]

If Higuchi's analysis throws into serious doubt previous notions of poor whites leading the white supremacy revolution, it also shows that whether, or to what extent, they benefited from that revolution is even more in question. Higuchi's analysis shows that white men made up 52 percent of the city's unemployed, and this group more than any other hoped to take over black jobs after the revolution.[45] Some business owners did replace blacks with whites at the urging of Dowling and a committee that canvassed employers urging them to make the substitution. But complaints arose that many poor whites could not count well enough to pile lumber, that it took two whites to do the task once done by one black, and that generally poor whites were not as hard working, tractable, or literate as blacks. Furthermore, whites did not want to take over one of the largest areas of black employment: domestic and service positions, most of them filled by black women. White employees in fact never intended to drive out black workers, and many of them sought to stop black migration out of the area after the massacre. White men in Wilmington could continue to think of themselves as the "Master Builders" of civilization, but black labor, as it always had been, remained the staple of the Southern economic system.[46]

Rather than creating a new day, the white supremacy campaign confirmed the old ways of the South: hard work, bad conditions, low wages and powerlessness for workers, with higher profits for the wealthy. The value of total wages in Wilmington declined slightly between 1890 and 1900, even as the number of wage earners increased by about 8 percent and the value of products went up 18 percent. Subsequently, the booming and "progressive" economy promised for white workers appeared only episodically. Contrary to the predictions of the "best white men," manufacturing in Wilmington did not flower, but alternately expanded and then stagnated.[47]

The white supremacy revolution did deliver on its larger set of promises to businesspeople. "The business men of the State are largely responsible for the victory," boasted the *Charlotte Observer*, and once they seized power the Democrats reconstructed a probusiness government at all levels. They reduced business taxes, dispensed with democratic controls over local elections, and undercut a variety of Fusion programs beneficial to working people.[48] Perhaps more important, they also decisively broke the means by which lower- and middle-class people had joined in political alliance: Democrats ensured that such experimentation would not return by destroying black voting power. Blacks, who were disproportionately represented among day laborers, sharecroppers, tenant farmers, service workers, and artisans, provided the most clearly defined voting bloc that could make alliances for economic improvement with small farmers and poor and working-class whites. As Josephus Daniels pointed out, "White Supremacy cannot be made permanent until the irresponsible negro vote is removed." Democrats as a whole agreed with this view, initiating a state constitutional amendment disfranchising blacks. By 1901, this amendment forced the country's last remaining African American congressman, George White, to leave office. The removal of African Americans as voters did not end social movements in the state, but it did crush hopes for further interracial alliances such as Fusion. Contrary to the promises of white business leaders, black disfranchisement led to other measures that also undercut the votes of lower-class whites.[49]

The "revolution" in North Carolina came at the end of a series of white supremacy movements that swept the South and inaugurated a one-party system that ruled the region for two-thirds of the twentieth century. This one-party system, based on the disfranchisement of blacks and restrictions on poor and working-class white voting, provided the vehicle for the nearly undisputed power of an oligarchy of landlords, commercial leaders, and industrialists. All pretense of genuine democracy disappeared in much of the South, as courthouse rings and political bosses took control of the political system. The power of oligarchy rested fundamentally on suppression of the black vote, without which poor and working-class white voters could hardly be expected to transform class relations in the South. Under this system, workers found it hard to organize politically or on the job, where their ranks were divided by race. Despite ruling-class protestations to the contrary, black disfranchisement was a body blow aimed not just at African Americans, but at working-class white people and small farmers as well. The Democratic Party had promised an all-class "white supremacy," but business supremacy is what poorer whites got.[50]

Most working-class whites, in Wilmington and elsewhere, had glimpsed the potential of biracial class alliances only remotely, for, like most people, they had their hands full feeding, clothing, and educating their own families, difficulties which easily took precedence over broader or more long-term objectives. This short-term view is reflected in the comments of white labor leaders who wrote to the state's Labor Department for its yearly reports after the Wilmington massacre. "I think that the best thing that could be done for the benefit of wage-earners would be to exclude negroes from all the trades," said one. Another wrote that "negro carpenters ruin our wages," forcing whites "to work at the negro price to get anything to do." Another white unionist undoubtedly spoke for many others in proposing his solution to the problem: "Let us educate all white children and this will put them above the negro and avoid race clash. Then the negro associating with his superior will be constantly reminded of his inferiority." He felt that "such association will make the negro honest, humble and industrious, as seen yet in our old slaves to-day. After the white boy is thus educated and his position firmly fixed above the negro, then his sympathies will turn to the negro." In short, a policy of strict segregation and discriminatory funding of schools would elevate the white majority while keeping blacks unskilled and out of higher-paying jobs. The heading of this writer's letter, "Exclude Negroes From Trades—Organize," unfortunately demonstrated the active role of white workers in perpetuating racism and represented the dominant opinion of white trade unionists before, during, and after the Wilmington massacre.[51]

Racism, in the view of W. E. B. Du Bois and Martin Luther King Jr., far from elevating Southern working-class and poor whites played a powerful role in keeping them among the most disadvantaged groups in the United States for much of the twentieth century. Both men felt that understanding race not as a biological phenomenon but as a historical creation rooted in the divisions of labor and wealth in society remained crucial to the possibility of progress in the United States and the world. One hundred years after the Wilmington massacre, low wages, poor living and working conditions, and disunity still plague working people in Wilmington and elsewhere. Many people in power or seeking power continue to obscure the social and economic problems that affect us all by sowing racial division, while turning back the clock on past labor and civil rights gains. The parallels are many between present and past efforts to expand democracy through interracial alliances of working people or to exacerbate racism in order to undo it. Perhaps in this context it is more important than ever to understand white supremacy's delusions and to remember that its legacy is one of defeat for our common humanity.

Notes

Anne Marie Cavanaugh contributed to this essay by researching census statistics, and Steven Estes contributed with thorough research of Wilmington newspapers. My thanks to them and to Otto Olsen, Peter Wood, David Cecelski, and Victoria Bynum, who read drafts of the essay and offered sound editing advice. This article originated in research I did as a graduate student while working on the case of the Wilmington Ten.

1. W. E. B. Du Bois, *Black Reconstruction in America, 1860–1880* (New York: Russell and Russell, 1935), 700–706.

2. David Roediger, in *The Wages of Whiteness: Race and the Making of the American Working Class* (New York: Verso, 1991), explains how white workers in the nineteenth century came to define their interests in racial terms, a tendency that continued long into the twentieth century. For recent historiography on labor and race, see Bruce Nelson, "Class, Race and Democracy in the CIO: The 'New' Labor History Meets the 'Wages of Whiteness,'" *International Review of Social History* 41 (1996): 351–74; Joe William Trotter and Alan Dawley, "Race and Class," *Labor History* 35 no. 4 (Fall 1994): 486–94; Joe William Trotter, "African-American Workers: New Direction in U.S. Labor Historiography," *Labor History* 35, no. 4 (Fall 1994): 495–523; and Herbert Hill, "The Problem of Race in American Labor History," *Reviews in American History* 24, no. 2 (June 1996): 190–208. On the role of white workers in maintaining Southern apartheid, see also Michael K. Honey, *Southern Labor and Black Civil Rights: Organizing Memphis Workers* (Urbana: University of Illinois Press, 1993).

3. Joel Williamson, *A Rage for Order: Black-White Relations in the American South since Emancipation* (New York: Oxford University Press, 1986), 133. See also Williamson, *The Crucible of Race: Black-White Relations in the American South since Emancipation* (Oxford, 1984).

4. Du Bois, *Black Reconstruction*, 15–16, 706–8.

5. Glenda Elizabeth Gilmore, *Gender and Jim Crow: Women and the Politics of White Supremacy in North Carolina, 1850–1900* (Chapel Hill: University of North Carolina Press, 1996), esp. 92, and Williamson, *A Rage for Order*, 70–116.

6. For an overview of this dialectic of "both the interests in democratization and the implacable opposition to it," see Paul D. Escott, *Many Excellent People: Power and Privilege in North Carolina, 1850–1900* (Chapel Hill: University of North Carolina Press, 1985), 31.

7. In 1860, 27.7 percent of the white population owned slaves, but only 2.1 percent of these slaveowners possessed fifty or more. Guion Griffis Johnson, *Ante-Bellum North Carolina: A Social History* (Chapel Hill: University of North Carolina Press, 1937), 56–57.

8. There is an extensive literature on the anti-Confederate resistance in North Carolina. For one overview, see Michael K. Honey, "The War Within the Confederacy: The White Unionists of North Carolina, 1861–65," *Prologue: Journal of the National Archives* 18, no. 2 (August 1986): 75–93.

9. James Lawrence Lancaster demonstrated statistically that the social basis for a lower- and middle-class Republican oppositional movement among whites indeed existed in "The Scalawags of North Carolina, 1850–1868" (Ph.D. diss., Princeton University, 1974).

10. Through the appointive system, "local gentry . . . made the decisions about roads, schools, and tax rates and who adjudicated most ordinary civil and criminal cases." But "Reconstruction had threatened that whole system," according to Escott, *Many Excellent People*, 167.

11. The counterrevolution against Reconstruction, as Paul Escott put it, sought "to break the alliance between poorer whites who wanted more democracy and opportunity and Negroes who were reliable Republican voters," ibid., 165. On the struggle

over Reconstruction and the battle afterward, see Otto H. Olsen, *Carpetbagger's Crusade: the Life of Albion Winegar Tourgée* (Baltimore: Johns Hopkins University Press, 1965); Allen W. Trelease, *White Terror: The Ku Klux Klan Conspiracy and Southern Reconstruction* (New York: Harper and Row, 1971); W. McKee Evans, *Ballots and Fence Rails: Reconstruction in the Lower Cape Fear* (Chapel Hill: University of North Carolina Press, 1966).

12. Helen G. Edmonds, *The Negro and Fusion Politics in North Carolina, 1894–1901* (Chapel Hill: University of North Carolina Press, 1951), 11–14.

13. See Escott, *Many Excellent People*, 169–70, 188–91, 220–40; Hugh Talmage Lefler and Albert Ray Newsome, *North Carolina: The History of a Southern State* (Chapel Hill: University of North Carolina Press, 1954), 479, 483–84. In 1890, North Carolina remained one of only fifteen states that did not have compulsory school attendance, and it had more illiterate whites than any other state; Escott, *Many Excellent People*, 231.

14. Department of Commerce and Labor, Bureau of the Census, *Special Reports: Occupations at the Twelfth Census* (Washington, D.C.: Government Printing Office, 1904), 352–56.

15. *Thirteenth Annual Report of the Bureau of Labor and Printing of the State of North Carolina for the Year 1899* (Raleigh, 1900), 216–97.

16. Wilmington had a relatively small manufacturing base. In 1890, the number of operatives numbered 1,263, and the number of piece workers numbered 95, with the largest single concentration in lumber and other mill products. Department of Commerce and Labor, Bureau of the Census, *Compendium of the Eleventh Census: 1890, Part II* (Washington, D.C.: Government Printing Office, 1894), 185, 1030–31. In 1900, nearly 2,000 persons worked in the factories. *Thirteenth Annual Report of the Bureau of Labor and Printing*, 197, 216–97. For statistics on unions, see *Thirteenth Annual Report of the Bureau of Labor and Printing*, 196–200, and *Fifteenth Annual Report of the Bureau of Labor and Printing of the State of North Carolina for the Year 1901* (Raleigh, 1902), 56–63. See Lefler and Newsome, *North Carolina*, on state legislation, 485.

17. Lefler and Newsome, *North Carolina*, 491–95. In the agricultural economy, blacks were concentrated at the lower end. Farms totaled 1,435 for whites; 861 whites were owners and 97 were part owners, with cash tenants numbering 30 and share tenants numbering 10. For blacks, farms totaled only 178; 92 blacks were owners and 14 were part owners, while 607 were cash tenants and 437 were sharecroppers. *Fifteenth Annual Report of the Bureau of Labor and Printing* (Raleigh, 1902), 116–19.

18. Lefler and Newsome, *North Carolina*, 374.

19. One reason many states outlaw fusion as an electoral strategy today is the success enjoyed by such alliances as that of the Populists and Republicans in the 1890s. On North Carolina, see Lefler and Newsome, *North Carolina*, 513, and Edmonds *The Negro and Fusion Politics*, 24–26.

20. Lefler and Newsome, *North Carolina*, 517; Edmonds, *The Negro and Fusion Politics*, 41, quote on 154, and 138–54. See letters from business leaders in *Twelfth Annual Report of the Bureau of Labor Statistics of North Carolina* (Raleigh, 1898).

21. Edmonds, *The Negro and Fusion Politics*, 222.

22. Jacquelyn Dowd Hall notes that the average number of lynchings, often accompanied by grotesque forms of torture and mutilation, "never fell below two or three a week" between the 1890s and World War I. These lynchings aimed to enforce the sense of black fear and powerlessness needed to enforce white su-

premacy. See Hall, "'The Mind That Burns in Each Body': Women, Rape, and Racial Violence," *The Powers of Desire, The Politics of Sexuality*, ed. Ann Snitow, Christine Stansell, and Sharon Thompson (New York: Monthly Review Press, 1983), 328–49.

23. For a nuanced portrait of the situation for African Americans, see Gilmore, *Gender and Jim Crow*, and Eric Anderson, *Race and Politics in North Carolina, 1872–1901: The Black Second* (Baton Rouge: Louisiana State University Press, 1981). See also Evans, *Ballots and Fence Rails*, and Edmonds, *The Negro and Fusion Politics*. For details on Wilmington, see Jerome McDuffie, "The Wilmington Riots of November 10, 1898" (M.A. thesis, Wake Forest College, 1963), 3, 15–17, and "Politics in Wilmington and New Hanover County, North Carolina, 1865–1900: The Genesis of a Race Riot" (Ph.D. diss., Kent State University, 1979).

24. See McDuffie, "Politics in Wilmington and New Hanover County."

25. McDuffie, "Politics in Wilmington and New Hanover County," esp. 29, 33–38, for the details of how local government influenced who accumulated wealth and how.

26. Quote from Gilmore, *Gender and Jim Crow*, 206. *Fifteenth Annual Report of the Bureau of Labor and Printing*, media statistics, 352. In 1889, Democrats owned 139 papers, Republicans 16, Independents 37, and Populists 4; *Thirteenth Annual Report of the Bureau of Labor and Printing*, 344, 365.

27. Gilmore, *Gender and Jim Crow*, 92; and see Edmonds, *The Negro and Fusion Politics*, 141, 146.

28. The Goddess of Democracy cartoon appeared in the *Raleigh News and Observer*, 16 September 1898, and was brought to the author's attention by Steven Estes.

29. *Wilmington Morning Star*, 9, 18 August 1898, 3; 24 August 1898, 1–2; 27 August 1898, 2.

30. Ibid., 6 September, 2 October, 8 September 1898, 2; 26 October 1898, 1; 27 October 1898, 2.

31. Ibid., 21 October 1898, 1; 3 November 1898. For the cartoons, see figs. 7 and 8 in Andrea Meryl Kirshenbaum, "Race, Gender, and Riot: The Wilmington, North Carolina, White Supremacy Campaign of 1898" (honors paper, Duke University, 1996); "Common Scene on the Public Roads," Supplement to *The Caucasian*, 20 October 1898; *Wilmington Morning Star*, 4 November 1898, 1.

32. *Wilmington Morning Star*, 7 October 1898, 1.

33. On the West Coast, for example, mobs of whites beat and killed Chinese laborers, driving them out of numerous labor markets in the 1870s and 1880s. See Alexander Saxton, *The Indispensable Enemy: Labor and the Anti-Chinese Movement in California* (Berkeley: University of California Press, 1971). Throughout the country, black workers were subject to attacks and various forms of union exclusion by whites trying to force them out of railroad jobs, the crafts, and factory jobs. See, for example, Herbert Hill, "Black Labor and Affirmative Action: An Historical Perspective," in *The Question of Discrimination: Racial Inequality in the U.S. Labor Market*, ed. Steven Shulman and William Darity Jr. (Middletown, Conn.: Wesleyan University Press, 1989); Melvin M. Leiman, *The Political Economy of Racism: A History* (London: Pluto Press, 1993); and Honey, *Southern Labor and Black Civil Rights*.

34. Quote from Du Bois, *Black Reconstruction*, 706.

35. *Wilmington Messenger*, 12 November 1898.

36. See McDuffie, "The Wilmington Riots," 75–77.

37. Hayumi Higuchi, "Black to White Ratio by Occupational Categories" (table),

in "White Supremacy on the Cape Fear: The Wilmington Affair of 1898" (M.A. thesis, University of North Carolina at Chapel Hill, 1980), 145.

38. An interesting and plausible account that considers poor whites and race relations is Philip Gerard's novel, *Cape Fear Rising* (Winston-Salem: John F. Blair, 1997).

39. H. Leon Prather, *We Have Taken a City: Wilmington Racial Massacre and Coup of 1898* (Cranbury, N.J.: Associated University Presses, 1984). For membership of the Secret Nine, see McDuffie, "The Wilmington Riots," 54–57, 87.

40. Quote in McDuffie, "The Wilmington Riots," 75. Gerard, in *Cape Fear Rising*, provides an insightful rendering of the relations between poor whites and their ruling-class benefactors, 119, 179, 286.

41. The declaration stated, "We propose in the future to give the white men a large part of the employment heretofore given to negroes" (McDuffie, "The Wilmington Riots," 176). "White Government" mass meeting, *Wilmington Morning Star*, 8 November 1898, 1.

42. Edmonds, *The Negro and Fusion Politics*, 142–49.

43. *Collier's Weekly*, 26 November 1898, quote from "The Committee of Twenty-Five," by Charles Francis Bourke. A conservative estimate said white rioters killed eleven blacks, though it seems that many more died. No one knows how many were exiled or lost their jobs and businesses to whites. John Hope Franklin, *From Slavery to Freedom*, 3rd ed. (New York: Norton, 1967), 312.

44. Higuchi, "White Supremacy on the Cape Fear," 144, 148. *Wilmington Morning Star*, 8 November 1898, and the *City Directory for Wilmington, North Carolina, 1889* (Wilmington: Messenger Steam Presses, 1889). Because the surviving directory was printed nine years prior to the 1898 election, many of the people listed in the 8 November article do not appear in its pages. Those who do, however, include only a few farmers, mechanics, carpenters, and laborers, versus a wide array of business-people and professionals. My thanks to Steven Estes for painstakingly tracking down this information.

45. Higuchi, "White Supremacy on the Cape Fear," 145.

46. The *Wilmington Messenger* reported that 300 or more blacks fled after the riot, and a year later another paper estimated that 1,000 had left the city; see, Kirshenbaum, "Race, Gender and Riot," 72. George White, the last black congressman from the South for *many decades*, helped lead emigrants out of Wilmington. Quote in *Wilmington Messenger*, 12 November 1898. At the turn of the century, North Carolina blacks still held large numbers of positions on the railroads and as carpenters, masons, and miners, and of course they predominated as laborers, sawmill and tobacco factory workers, nurses, midwives, laundresses, domestic workers, and agricultural laborers. Department of Commerce and Labor, Bureau of the Census, *Special Reports: Occupations at the Twelfth Census*, 352–56.

47. Wilmington had 121 manufacturing establishments in 1890, and 124 in 1900, with 1,358 and 1,469 wage earners, respectively. *Fifteenth Annual Report of the Bureau of Labor and Printing*, 59.

48. Escott, *Many Excellent People*, 258–65, quote on 258.

49. William Alexander Mabry, "'White Supremacy' and the North Carolina Suffrage Amendment," *North Carolina Historical Review* 12, no. 1 (January 1936): quote on 8; and Edmonds, *The Negro and Fusion Politics*, 181–93, 204.

50. See V. O. Key, *Southern Politics in State and Nation* (New York: Alfred A. Knopf, 1949); J. Morgan Kousser, *The Shaping of Southern Politics and the Estab-*

lishment of the One-Party South, 1880–1910 (New Haven: Yale University Press, 1974); and Paul Lewinson, *Race, Class, and Party: A History of Negro Suffrage and White Politics in the South* (New York: Grosset and Dunlap, 1959).

51. *Thirteenth Annual Report of the Bureau of Labor and Printing*, 170, and *Fifteenth Annual Report of the Bureau of Labor and Printing*, 301, 315, 362.

184

Michael
Honey

**Raymond
Gavins**

Fear, Hope, and Struggle

Recasting Black North Carolina
in the Age of Jim Crow

Segregation, or Jim Crow, had its origins in antebellum America and
shaped black-white interactions in the post–Civil War South, where it
reigned from the white supremacy revolt of 1898 until the 1960s. Although a crucial phase of race relations in American society, the age of
Jim Crow has never been studied as widely as the slavery and civil rights
periods. The nature of segregation, its links to slavery and to desegregation, how it was enforced, and how blacks experienced it—building "a
world that white people hardly knew and understood even less"—are
among the matters that I help to investigate as codirector of "Behind the
Veil: Documenting African American Life in the Jim Crow South."

This is a collaborative project of the Center for Documentary Studies at Duke University and historically black colleges and universities, Afro-American Studies programs, and local historic preservation groups.[1]

The purpose of "Behind the Veil" is to recover oral histories, family photographs, personal papers, and other African American sources for enlarging knowledge of the Jim Crow era. We especially seek to interview aged informants who lived through that time, lest the opportunity to preserve their memories is lost. Our aims include publication of a general book, select narratives, and documentary readers exploring the range of African Americans' experiences and identities. Another aim is to develop educational resources for course guides, heritage projects, and museum exhibits on black communities and institutions.

Oral history opens doors into understanding the lived contexts of Jim Crow. During the summers of 1993–95, twenty-five of our graduate students worked at twenty-three community sites across the South. Besides collecting thousands of photographic images and family manuscripts, they interviewed 1,248 individuals representing scores of different occupations and a multitude of class, religious, and educational backgrounds. These visual, print, and audiotape materials are being processed at the John Hope Franklin Research Center for African and African American Documentation in Duke's Special Collections Library and will be available to users by the fall of 1999. Interviews, in the meantime, are yielding rich testimony on everything from blacks' emotions and survival strategies to their work cultures and social movements. Of 196 interviews transcribed to date, 51 are from North Carolina. I use some of the most compelling North Carolina transcripts here to explore the Jim Crow world that emerged in the state after 1898 and the black culture of aspiration that persisted within it.

While the Wilmington riot was a watershed in the career of Jim Crow, both codifying the color line and exacerbating the dangers of crossing it, racial segregation had far deeper roots in the North Carolina past. Before the Civil War, slaveholders needed few regulations to isolate slaves and free people of color, who were kept apart by custom. Slave codes forbade intermarriage, of course, and common jails, as five legislative acts reinforced these taboos between 1795 and 1839. But most proscriptions related to black labor, mobility, and punishment. In a town such as Wilmington, where blacks comprised 46 percent of the population by 1860, whites worried less about master-slave commingling than about the threat of revolt. The state's Free Negro Code of 1830–31, which outlawed "the circulation of seditious publications" and congregating or visiting with slaves, largely amounted to surveillance against insurrection. Authorities were far more careful to guard against sedition than to prevent physical proximity.[2]

After the Civil War, a white backlash against the former slaves began to legalize the customary distance between blacks and whites. Planters intended to defy the emancipation guaranteed by the Thirteenth Amendment and exploit ex-slave workers, who saw free labor as leverage for "forty acres and a mule." The Black Code contained vagrancy and apprenticeship sections, forcing adult blacks back into virtual bondage and apprenticing those under the age of twenty-one. Children of ex-slaves were bound out by the thousands in 1865–66; in Jones and Sampson Counties alone white officials assigned 340 of 510 apprenticed children to their ex-masters. The code also appointed a warden for each race's poor and banned black-white marriage. Still, discrimination was grounded in everyday practice, including brute force, more than it was in law. White employers flogged and even killed freedpeople who dared to assert their new liberties, even in the face of Union garrisons, the Freedmen's Bureau, Northern missionaries, and Republican authority. While the state constitution of 1868 confirmed abolition and legitimated previous black and mixed-race births, it plainly stated that "the children of the white race and the children of the colored race shall be taught in separate public schools." It further mandated an all-white militia.[3]

Caste laws were sporadic during the violent years of Reconstruction and Redemption. Despite the presence of federal and state militias, the Ku Klux Klan terrorized Republican voters and officeholders, black and white. In 1870, when conservative Democrats regained a legislative majority, Klansmen murdered 16 Republicans and whipped at least 121. An act of 1874, echoing the Democratic restoration, proclaimed that no white child could be apprenticed to a black adult. The amended state constitution in 1875 prohibited "all marriages between a white person and a Negro, or between a white person and a person of Negro descent to the third generation," and it reiterated the requirement for dual schools.[4] The legislature soon established industrial and normal colleges for blacks, but it ignored the peonage and terror that drove thousands of them to Kansas and Indiana in 1879–80. It authorized a "department for the colored" at the State School for the Blind and Deaf by 1881, and a college for Indians in 1887. One article stipulated imprisonment for violators of the marital ban, while another provided for Indian-only facilities. Custom, or coercion if necessary, now dictated separate black and white sections on common carriers.[5]

Redeemers escalated the demand for white solidarity. Blacks continued to vote and hold office in much of eastern North Carolina, backing "the Party of Lincoln" despite facing dangerous opposition. For instance, between 1868 and 1889, fourteen black Republicans were elected to seventeen state house and six state senate terms from New Hanover County, home of Wilmington. Between 1874 and 1890, three blacks also won terms in Congress from the Second Congressional District, "a Republican and black stronghold." The "black second" became the Democrats' scarecrow of "Negro Domination," especially when angry white farmers began bolting to the Populist Party.[6]

Legislators in 1892 proposed to segregate railway travel, as eight other Southern states already had done. Republican and Populist assemblymen, perhaps to woo blacks into an embryonic Fusion coalition, opposed the enabling bill. Opposing it before the House were black spokesmen such as president Joseph Charles Price of Livingstone College, an African Methodist Episcopal Zion Church affiliate in Salisbury, North Carolina. "Jim Crow Cars are products of those minds that fear the Negro's power to cope with his white brother," another black spokesman, Professor John O. Crosby of North Carolina Agricultural and Mechanical College at Greensboro, reminded legislators. "The heel of oppression lies heaviest upon the Negro that tries to be a man."[7]

Crosby was prophetic. Oppression increased as black North Carolinians persevered. Their votes enabled Fusion men to gain 74 of the 120 General Assembly seats in 1894 and win the governorship in 1896, while electoral reforms passed by the Fusionist legislature helped blacks to regain numerous local offices. By 1897, in Wilmington, four aldermen, an audit board member, a justice of the peace, the deputy clerk of court, and the coroner were black. Such black strides and Democrats' resolve to destroy Populism fueled what Paul D. Escott has described as "the most massive white supremacy campaign the state had ever seen." In 1898 Furnifold M. Simmons, chairman of the Democratic Executive Committee, warned: "North Carolina is a WHITE MAN'S STATE, and WHITE MEN will rule it, and they will crush the party of negro domination beneath a majority so overwhelming that no other party will ever again dare to establish negro rule here."[8]

Clearly, 1898 marked a turning point in de facto and de jure Jim Crow. The election that year brought into relief not only extreme white racism, but also fallout from the legal disfranchisement of blacks in South Carolina (1895) and the Supreme Court's "separate but equal" decision in *Plessy* v. *Ferguson* (1896). Klansmen, Red Shirts, and White Supremacy Clubs frequently demonstrated at black and Fusion rallies, intimidating the crowds by a show of guns. In 1897–99 seven lynchings were reported in North Carolina, and racial intimidation and terrorism reached into even the most remote crossroads and towns during the fall of 1898. Fraud and ballot box stuffing were decisive where bullying faltered. Democrats reclaimed five of the state's nine congressional seats; Republicans retained three seats, reelecting the nation's only black congressman, George H. White, from the Second District. In state contests Democrats took ninety-four house and forty senate seats to the Republicans' twenty-three (four black) and seven (one black) and Populists' three and three. The coup d'état in Wilmington, a bloody sequel to the Democratic sweep, went well beyond defeating Fusion government. It symbolized the creation of a codified and brutal color line, one that would last through the first half of the twentieth century. Deploring the election's fury, Congressman White contended: "This tendency on the part of some of us to rise and assert our manhood along all lines is, I fear, what has brought about this changed condition."[9]

Disfranchisement and caste in travel inaugurated the new structure of Jim Crow. In 1899 lawmakers adopted voting restrictions based on the Louisiana model of a literacy test, poll tax, and grandfather clause. Scheduled for a referendum in 1900, the suffrage amendment promised a draconian reduction of the black electorate, thereby undermining a multiracial or working-class challenge to Democratic and white dominance. Adult illiteracy then was 40 percent for black males, compared to 20 percent for white males. Registrars did not expect or permit black men to read and explain a section of the state constitution as specified in the amendment. Nor could most blacks afford to pay poll taxes, for they earned only subsistence incomes. Virtually none had grandfathers who voted prior to January 1867, so, as descendants of freedmen, they lost by fiat the protection given to illiterate white men. Complementing the suffrage plan, the General Assembly directed transportation companies to "provide separate but equal accommodations for the white and colored races at passenger stations or waiting-rooms, and also on all trains and steamboats carrying passengers."[10]

The assault on democratic citizenship quickened. At least two acts proscribed racially mixed fraternal orders and mental hospitals; five empowered the utilities commission to enforce Jim Crow in transport. In 1900 black leaders convened in Raleigh and issued "An Address to the White People of North Carolina," protesting the imminent passage of the constitutional amendment that would disfranchise blacks. "It is already urged by an influential portion of the . . . leading men that these amendments are temporary expedients. That the thirteenth, fourteenth, and fifteenth amendments to the constitution of the United States must be repealed," they complained. "Repeal them and slavery again becomes lawful. . . . In view of these facts, it is natural that we should feel the greatest anxiety as to the outcome of efforts now being made not only to restrict our right to vote, but to deny that right altogether."[11]

With the voters' endorsement of the suffrage amendment in 1900, however, black North Carolinians were disfranchised. Migration rumors spread among blacks, but black educator Simon G. Atkins deemed it "unwise for the colored people to contemplate leaving the state in large numbers because of the result of the (August) election. . . . Now is the time for the Negro to show his faith in God and humanity." Black "fear of mob violence and uncontrolled outlawry" would pass, he insisted. "I do not believe that the white people of North Carolina have repudiated the spirit of Christ. . . . I do not believe that race hate can thrive in any considerable part of the state's soil."[12] Time would test this optimism as a source of uplift to the downtrodden.

Civic doors closed and prejudice abounded. For example, the county court surveys of Gilbert T. Stephenson, a judge from Pendleton, reveal flagrant injustices with no hint of regret. The registrar of "County No. 2," reporting 19,000 black and 11,000 white residents, disclosed: "I will say that Negroes do not serve on the jury in this county and have not since we, the white people, got the government in our hands. When the Republican party was in power Negroes were drawn." The respondent from "County No. 5," with 13,000 blacks and 12,600 whites, submitted: "Negroes do not serve on juries in our county, nor are they allowed to vote or take any part in county or municipal affairs."[13]

Legal separation proceeded apace. The state required the board of education to operate all-black school districts and dictated that school librarians "fit up and maintain a separate place for the use of the colored people who may come to the library." It instituted a mental hospital in Goldsboro "for the colored mentally disordered." One statute allowed for relief and pension benefits to "fire companies composed exclusively of colored men." Another instructed the white State Hospital for the Insane at Raleigh "to provide and set apart . . . suitable apartments and wards" for Indians. Furthermore, a "person of negro descent to the third generation, inclusive" was defined as black. Any officer who failed to confine black and white prisoners separately "shall be guilty of a misdemeanor," according to an order on prisons. Three orders similarly charged operators of streetcars and trains.[14]

Racial segregation had become, in the terminology of C. Vann Woodward, "the invariable rule." In 1911 the legislature opened several schools and a college solely "for the purpose of the education of the Cherokee

Indians," extending the triracial direction that Jim Crow had taken in North Carolina. No aspect of life eluded this modern racial divide. For example, housing had been decidedly intermixed by race in most ante-bellum Southern towns, but residential location now bowed to Jim Crow. In 1912 Winston-Salem's aldermen ordained it unlawful for a "'colored person' to occupy any residence on a block where a greater number of residences were occupied by whites."[15] This ordinance became a trendsetter in urban segregation.

Adjusting that model, Clarence H. Poe, editor of the Raleigh-based *Progressive Farmer*, advocated apartheid in farming areas. "Wholesale sandwiching of whites and Negroes in our rural districts" caused needless friction among farmers, he cautioned readers in 1913. For the next two years, Poe crusaded "to divide black and white farm populations into separate enclaves on the basis of landownership." In 1915 the State Farmers' Union and a legislative committee endorsed his proposal, stipulating "that by vote of the qualified voters or of the freeholders of any prescribed district within a county, the lands in that district may be segregated to the ownership, use or occupancy of a particular race." It provoked intense debate, but legislators turned it down on a close vote. Perhaps they agreed with Judge Stephenson, Poe's chief critic, who argued that "the segregation of the races in the country would . . . cause still more of the negroes . . . to move to the city."[16] Meantime, rural customs rarely approved of whites selling land to blacks, one of Jim Crow's many ways to blunt blacks' drive for economic advancement.

The legal and informal contours of Jim Crow covered a wide domain. The restrictions betrayed white fears of black-Indian cooperation, black educational progress and competition for jobs, interracial sex, and blacks political dissent. To wit, the state reordered the segregation of Indians in jails, homes of the aged, and hospitals. It warranted a curriculum of only "practical agriculture and the mechanical arts and such branches of learning as relate thereto" for black colleges. Toilets had to be "lettered and marked in a distinct manner, so as to furnish separate facilities for white males, white females, colored males and colored females." Benevolent societies were obliged to retain exclusive memberships, and black-Indian or white-Indian marriages would be "declared void." Indeed, by the eve of World War I, almost every visible space had been separated. During the war, the state stopped the "organization of colored troops . . . where white troops are available, and while permitted to be organized, colored troops shall be under the command of white officers." Even a breach of the color line among convicts meant a fine or jail sentence for their jailers.[17]

New race laws inevitably piled up, as Woodward has noted, and "they were constantly pushing the Negro farther down." Public services in the wake of twentieth-century urbanization, competitive labor markets, and black demands for justice generated constant pressure to extend Jim Crow. One-party hegemony and white supremacy presumably would defuse the resulting class and race tensions. Politicians, even New Deal Democrats, were forever pledging to keep blacks in their place. In 1943 the former Democratic mayor of a Tar Heel town candidly admitted: "Our attitude is that the white man is superior and the colored are looked on as servants."[18]

A sample of legislative acts from 1917 to 1945 can be useful to suggest the vagaries of Jim Crow. Of sixty-one Jim Crow statutes enacted in that period, three concern black aliens. Education is the subject of nineteen, including a 1935 stipulation that "books shall not be interchangeable between the white and colored schools, but shall continued [sic] to be used by the race first using them." Three deal with schooling for Indians, and three regulate insurance agencies. An act detailing punishment for violations of the toilet restriction applies to all categories of labor. Seventeen measures relate to provisions for the handicapped, and fifteen cover buses and trains. Not until 1947 did the state restrict cemeteries, which had long been separated by tradition.[19]

State permission to segregate the races resonated locally. Cities and towns tended to replicate the Winston-Salem housing pattern. Winston-Salem's black residents had been segregated overwhelmingly into its southeastern corner by the 1920s. Black population clusters, always cordoned off by a main street, railroad track, or similar fixed barrier, shaped the social geography of every city and town. Hayti in Durham and Gilmer in Greensboro typified the urban ghettos. In their segregated communities, veiled from white society, blacks forged a world of aspiration.[20]

Ordinances on accommodations (restaurants, theaters) and common spaces (auditoriums, stadiums) multiplied greatly. Lest there be trespassing, "White Only" and "Colored" signs policed entrances, exits, and seats. Banks, railroads, textile and tobacco factories, and other places of employment regularly exceeded statutory requirements. Black sociologist Charles S. Johnson of Fisk University noted that tobacco plants in Durham, Reidsville, and Winston-Salem assigned "Negro and white workers to separate parts of buildings, or to different workrooms even when performing the same tasks, or to separate sides of the same room, or even to separate rows in the same room." Drugstores in Johnston County doubled as bus stations. Blacks bought tickets and waited outside, ordinarily standing, though passenger benches were unlabeled. Law and practice were inseparable in this instance.[21]

The potential and reality of violence undergirded segregation. Transgressors of the color line inevitably faced white reprisals, and many put their lives at risk. Charlotte minister Walter Cavers recalls his fear of would-be lynchers. After an encounter with his white landlord in 1935, near Selma, Alabama, where three black sharecroppers had just been hanged, he remembers, "I walked off and came home. My mother said to me, I told her what happened, she said well you better move on somewhere else and not let them find you here tonight. Sure enough they came." Cavers fled, catching a freight train to North Carolina. Many black Southerners died in outbreaks of lynching, Klan nightriding, and rioting from 1898 through 1945. Between 1900 and 1931, it is estimated that 566 lynchings occurred in the South, and 97 percent of the victims were blacks. Tar Heel mobs lynched thirty-six persons, all but three black. In 1918 and 1943 North Carolina riots claimed twenty-two black and five white fatalities. Black North Carolinians, and sympathetic whites as well, were intimidated, jailed, maimed, or otherwise punished for violating segregation.[22] Racial civility, for which North Carolina was widely known, prevailed only so long as African Americans abided the legal and extralegal rules of Jim Crow.

Suffice it to say that the white supremacy revolt of 1898 put in place a bifurcated and coercive system. Recalling her youth in Durham ca. 1910–26, activist Pauli Murray declared:

Our seedy run-down school told us that if we had any place at all in the scheme of things it was a separate place, marked off, proscribed and unwanted by white people. We were bottled up and labeled and set aside—sent to the Jim Crow car, the back of the bus, the side door of the theater, the side window of a restaurant.

We came to know that whatever we had was always inferior. We came to understand that no matter how neat and clean, how law abiding, submissive and polite, how studious in school, how church-going and moral, how scrupulous in paying our bills and taxes we were, it made no essential difference in our place.

It seemed as if there were only two kinds of people in the world— They and We—White and Colored. The world revolved on color and variations in color. It pervaded the air I breathed. I learned it in hundreds of ways. I picked it up from grown folks around me. I heard it in the house, on the playground, in the streets, everywhere. The tide of color beat upon me ceaselessly, relentlessly.[23]

That tide had not ebbed in 1940s Durham for author Mary E. Mebane, who explained:

As far as anyone knew, the laws as they then existed would stand forever. They were meant to—and did—create a world that fixed black people at the bottom of society in all aspects of human life. It was a world without options.

Most Americans have never had to live with terror. I had to live with it all my life—the psychological terror of segregation, in which there was a special set of laws governing your movements. You violated them at your peril, for you knew that if you broke one of them, knowingly or not, physical terror was just around the corner, in the form of policemen and jails, and in some cases and places white vigilante mobs formed for the exclusive purpose of keeping blacks in line.[24]

Murray and Mebane echo anger, dignity, endurance, and resistance. They are emblematic of the black men and women who survived Jim Crow and struggled, in the Constitution's words, to "secure the blessings of liberty for ourselves and our posterity." Not until 1935 did a border or Southern state university admit an African American applicant. In 1938 the University of North Carolina denied Pauli Murray admission for graduate study. Two years later at Petersburg, Virginia, she was arrested for sitting in the front seat of an interstate bus. Mary Mebane sat "at the back" of buses, but she admired those who "wouldn't get up" so white folk could be seated. Schooling was often painful for her. "We were paying book rent for books that white children at the brick school had used last year," she writes of second grade. "All of them were second-hand. They felt dirty to me. I wondered about the girl who had had my book last year. She was smug and laughing at me. I had to use her old book. It wasn't right."[25]

Blacks such as Murray and Mebane responded to Jim Crow by pursuing an array of community-building activities to soften segregation's harshest edges and build autonomy and self-respect. Within "autonomous institutions"—including the family, education, religion, cultural expression, labor, business, and politics—blacks built a sense of hope. Consider post-riot Wilmington: by 1930 institutions within the black community included one of five hospitals in the city, two of thirteen homes for the elderly and infirm, two of nine cemeteries, twenty-eight of fifty-two churches, four of fourteen public schools, one of five parochial schools, and nineteen of fifty-five benevolent and fraternal societies.[26] All were part of an essential institutional base, helping blacks to cope and get ahead in the heyday of Jim Crow. Schools, where Murray's and Mebane's statements converge, were crucial. More explicitly than any other institution, black schools fused education with African American goals of freedom and equality.

Motifs of educational achievement, business success, and black leadership entwine richly in the recollections of Dr. York D. Garrett, born in 1894. Praising the Princeville Graded School principal who prepared him for Elizabeth City Normal School and Howard University's School of Pharmacy, Garrett testifies: "He took a particular interest in me and he tutored me for four years. I was the first boy from his tutoring that graduated." Garrett also drew inspiration from his ex-slave grandmother, who told him about their family's survival under slavery and dreams in freedom; from his ex-slave father, who attended a Freedmen's Bureau school, owned a Tarboro grocery, and held a town office during the 1890s; and from the hopeful spirit in the black colleges he attended. An army veteran of World War I, he opened Garrett's Drugstore in Tarboro in 1921. He migrated to Durham in 1932 and operated a drugstore at the Biltmore Hotel from then until 1977, while becoming an influential church, fraternal, and professional leader.[27] Dr. Garrett's account of his life reveals much about how black families motivated children to learn and become independent from Reconstruction through *Brown* v. *Board of Education* (1954).

During the Jim Crow era, Vanessa Siddle Walker has observed, black schools were able "to enhance students' self-worth and increase their aspirations to achieve." Statements by black educators in a 1927 appeal for grade school reform concur with that observation. "There is an intense desire on the part of the colored people in North Carolina to educate their children," the educators attested. "The schools are crowded." These structures, typically one-room and on distant country roads, afforded instruction for black betterment and a refuge from white racism. Pupils had to walk for miles, terms averaged only four months, and dedicated teachers were overworked and underpaid. Instruction combined reading, writing, and arithmetic, plus "sanitation, serving, cooking, basket making, chair caning, mat making . . . simple carpentry . . . [and] how to handle tools." Into this tapestry were woven rural teachers and school buildings financed in part by the Northern-based Jeanes and Rosenwald Funds.[28] Teachers demanded discipline and excellence while supporting their pupils, and they molded an affirmative learning environment despite inequality.

The intellectual atmosphere at black schools was lively, remembers Oliver R. Pope. His career as a teacher-principal spanned the years 1902–49, thirty-seven years in Rocky Mount, North Carolina. "At that time the spelling matches between schools in small towns and districts stimulated rivalry comparable to that of athletic contests today," he remembers. He gave his pupils lessons on character as well as competition.

> I laughed when they laughed, although . . . it was painful. I began to have personal chats with each of them. I pretended not to see many of their pranks. I appealed to their pride. They should be different from children who didn't attend our school. I wanted them to look better, talk better, act better. "Be proud of yourselves," I frequently repeated, "and always remember you're as good as anybody in the whole world—if you think and act that way."[29]

Self-respect and scholastic attainment were core values that mitigated the context of racism controlling black schools. "The old Williston school property on Seventh Street, worth approximately $3,000.00, is the only investment the public school system has made in the way of buildings for the education of the colored people," confessed Wilmington's superintendent in 1917, "and this is so insignificant that we ought to be ashamed to mention it." By this time Wilmington blacks had begun to rebuild their businesses, churches, and schools. They were determined to advance, though the dread of brutal white reprisals did linger in their memory.[30]

William T. Childs, a pupil at Wilmington's Peabody School in the 1920s, describes an ambience of mistrust and silence. "They did not really want to talk too much about the riot of 1898. They did not like to talk too much about that," he says of his parents. "There was . . . a lot of information about it. But they did not like to talk about it." Consequently, he heard little about the white revolt "until I started going to school. And I later learned there was a real traumatic kind of thing and many blacks who lived through that era were quieted. They were not expected to talk too much about it." Childs recollects "an old minstrel man" who witnessed the riot and "used to talk about what happened." Yet his mother and father "were . . . positive people that looked forward rather than back." His father, a train car cook, was "not that formally educated. . . . But he had this thing about reading and learning." Childs was one of three children to finish college.[31]

Black parents and teachers made many sacrifices for educational opportunity. Parents had to double-tax themselves, paying direct taxes that largely funded white schools while contributing extra money, labor, and land to maintain black schools. "Significantly," according to James D. Anderson, "this was the tradition out of which the second crusade for black common schools emerged and by which it was sustained." Founded in 1881 during the first crusade, the North Carolina Negro Teachers' Association had 75 chapters and 2,400 members in 1927. At that year's annual meeting, buoyed by members' school organizing at the grass roots, President Simon Atkins declared: "We love our dear old State because it has never closed the door of hope." Meanwhile, the State Division of Negro Education was creating and standardizing secondary programs. The number rose from 119 in 1921 to 236 in 1950, all with a session of 160 days, four years of classes beyond the seventh grade, an eight-month term, improved physical plants, laboratories, and "libraries of 300 or more approved books." Standard curricula included civics, English, geography, history, Latin, mathematics (regularly algebra or geometry), science, music, and "vocational training."[32]

These black high schools enhanced academic accomplishment. The late Charles A. Ray, professor of language and literature at North Carolina Central University, told me that a Latin course at a Raleigh high school in the 1920s sparked his lifelong study of the classics. Aaron A. McCrae Sr., an alumnus of Williston High School in Wilmington, makes a similar acknowledgment. "Well, I speak fondly of all the people who had a hand in shaping my life to be what it is today. We've come a long way in this community and there are a lot of people who had a hand in shaping our lives," he comments. "My high school graduating class, the class of 1938, had its fifty-fifth reunion the week of the Fourth of July [1993]. And we had some of our teachers present at that time. Mrs. Elizabeth Holmes Salters and Miss Annie P. White and Miss Sarah Ashe were . . . three teachers there but there were many others." A Baptist minister who finished Hampton Institute and served in the air force, McCrae later earned a degree from the University of North Carolina at Wilmington.[33]

Denominational and independent colleges contributed substantially to black North Carolina education as well. They usually offered high school subjects like basic gardening and grammar. But to broaden students' exposure, the leading colleges coupled classical and practical courses. Shaw University in Raleigh had courses in the Bible, French, physics, and psychology, and shops such as blacksmithing. Slater Industrial and State Normal School of Winston-Salem taught geometry, German, and pedagogy alongside agricultural and industrial arts.[34] These colleges also cultivated ambition and self-esteem in their students. They produced the black community's Talented Tenth—its craft, professional, and religious elites. Of the nation's 18,918 black college graduates for 1930, Texas claimed 2,477 and Washington, D.C., had 1,777. The third highest number—1,333—were from North Carolina, the majority graduating from in-state schools.[35]

A handful of colleges led in this effort. Church-sponsored Shaw and Johnson C. Smith University in Charlotte graduated 382 and 412, respectively, for the years 1927–37. As liberal arts majors, the bulk of graduates went into teaching. A profile of 146 of the 461 students who finished Livingstone College in the same decade better clarifies their occupations: education, 66; law, 4; medicine, 23; and the ministry, 53. Most stayed in the professions traditionally available to blacks. State normal and trade school graduates, however, mostly found employment in industries. Agricultural and Technical College (A&T) in Greensboro boasted 408 alumni for the decade ending in 1937; Elizabeth City Normal School, 582; Fayetteville Normal School, 581; and Winston-Salem Teachers' College (formerly Slater), 1,560. Men and women from A&T obtained construction, craft, and other jobs. Several were named county and farm demonstration agents; some started their own businesses. Some chose to teach in specialities like agronomy and home economics. Like Livingstone's preachers and teachers, they would exemplify precepts of character, industry, prosperity, and service.[36]

Among black Tar Heel institutions, Shaw was unique in initially offering programs in law and medicine. The coup de grâce in their demise came from a Carnegie Foundation report conducted by a white evaluator named Abraham Flexner, who effectively maligned the quality of Shaw's Leonard Medical College. In his 1910 report, Flexner concluded that "Flint at New Orleans, Leonard at Raleigh, the Knoxville, Memphis, and Louisville school are ineffectual . . . sending out undisciplined men, whose lack of real training is covered up by the imposing M.D." Close them, he recommended summarily. "Meharry at Nashville and Howard at Washington are worth developing, and . . . effort will wisely concentrate upon them." This blow, amid fledgling attempts to raise its endowment, virtually closed Leonard. Somehow it stayed open until 1918, when "all professional departments were discontinued upon the recommendation of the President of the University."[37] Shaw's seminary eventually reopened, thanks to Baptist dollars, but the end of legal and medical training left a big void.

Measured by its reputation, Leonard deserved a more judicious appraisal of its contribution to African American life. Data from 1882 to 1912 show that 1,811 students enrolled and 399 graduated. Passing certification examinations in North Carolina and other states—a sizable

198

Raymond
Gavins

number with distinction—Leonard physicians assumed the front lines of health care in black communities stretching from New York and Philadelphia through eastern North Carolina to New Orleans and Lake Charles, Louisiana. Inescapably, and in ways Flexner never imagined, they linked the Hippocratic oath and black health care. Norma Jean and Carole Darden, descendants of a Wilson, North Carolina, native and Leonard graduate who practiced in the small town of Opelika, Alabama, describe the important role their uncle played in the community:

> People brought him their sorrows, their joys, and news of gross community injustices. Long outraged at the lack of public medical facilities for black people, he established a private hospital. It was a simple one-story wooden building, but many complicated operations were performed there and many lives saved. Like most country doctors, he had his thumb glued to the pulse of the community and became the town chronicler. He knew who had been born, who had died, and who had moved in or out. Because of his two side jobs as a conscription doctor and the Lee County jail doctor, he even knew who was incarcerated or who was inducted into the Army. Thus, he had first-hand knowledge of the jailing of people for minor infractions of the law, the assaults on defenseless females, and the countless other indignities perpetrated on blacks. During his time, the air was indeed permeated with clouds of sudden and irrational violence.

The blanket castigation of Leonard graduates or black M.D.'s as "ineffectual" and "undisciplined" made a mockery of this man and his generation. The closing of Leonard, which white officialdom in Raleigh ignored, reduced the state's short supply of black doctors to a trickle. A 1930 count turned up only 164 black physicians in North Carolina, a ratio of 1 to every 5,602 black residents.[38]

Students, like their elders, worked with head, heart, and hand for collective improvement. They made fires on cold mornings, repaired outhouses to ensure privacy, scrubbed floors, and washed windows. When books were in short supply, they brought photographs to enrich their lessons. "Gaudy pictures of advertising matter including cigarette girls were replaced with pictures of prominent Negroes and prints of famous buildings—all donated," Oliver Pope reminisces. "I used my limited knowledge of art in explaining the meaning of these. And how eager were my listeners!" Ernest Swain, a Morehouse College graduate and retired principal, finished Brunswick County Training School at Southport in 1933. "Didn't have much equipment . . . didn't have anything to experiment with but what was in the book was taught," he thinks back. Yet this school was special to him because it "always had good teachers. I think I've always had excellent teachers." In fact, his favorite teacher "was from Atlanta and she knew about Morehouse."[39]

Black students evinced a growing self-consciousness and connection to the larger racial struggle. The 1930s, which saw the first lawsuits against segregated higher education and teacher salary discrimination, broadened their outlook. Students and recent graduates were undoubtedly present in 1933 when the fifteen state branches of the National Association for the Advancement of Colored People (NAACP) assembled 2,500 blacks in Raleigh "to voice their protest against the rising tide of white oppression, violence, and discrimination." It was historic. "They made history because they came to give the lie to the oft-quoted libel that Southern Negroes are satisfied with their lot," argued George W. Streator, formerly a professor at Bennett College in Greensboro. "More than a thousand of these people came from outside Raleigh. . . . From 300 towns they came, sometimes a single delegate half afraid of spying white folk and tattling Negroes. They came, and the ruling class in North Carolina was stirred by their coming."[40] That rally articulated black North Carolina's rising expectations, which black schools and colleges nurtured in spite of official neglect and meager funding.

Bertha R. Todd, a former teacher, received this nurturing in Sampson County during the Great Depression. "I had pretty good self-esteem," she reveals. "I never really accepted any idea that those whites in that neighborhood were better than we." Family and school were her anchors. "Yes. We were closely knit. We learned in our high school about Negroes. We played the role of Negroes during Negro history week," she insists. "We'd get on the stage in Garland in that school [where] my father worked so hard for the Julius Rosenwald Fund." She also embraced politics, stating: "We would talk about issues of the day . . . about the schools and regulations and the State Department and all that." Thus did her student cohort form an affirming identity to stem the "tide of color" that Pauli Murray lamented in her memoirs and the "psychological terror of segregation" that Mary Mebane described in her autobiography.[41]

Many other students demonstrated such confidence and intelligence. Retired teacher Mary P. Boddie learned to be proud of her black culture at the Brick School in Enfield, North Carolina. "I went to everything. We took part in everything," she reflects. "I'm pretty sure Marian Anderson came to Brick, and Roland Hayes, and Richard B. Harrison. Isn't that his name, the one that . . . was in the play?" Cultural activities like those at Brick raised students' awareness of what African Americans could really accomplish, encouraging them to believe in their own highest potential. When a white investigator got 1,184 black high schoolers to fill out questionnaires in 1932, he seemed surprised by the results. Fully 98 percent intended to graduate; 95 percent planned to attend college or trade school. He demurred that "only a small part of the total group, probably less than 25 percent, is fitted for success in academic fields of study."[42]

Shaw students, whose agitation for a stronger curriculum and black control forced the university's white president to quit, would have disagreed. Determined to resist the status quo, Ella J. Baker graduated from Shaw in 1926 and moved to New York City. She organized unemployed people during the New Deal era and became a branch organizer for the NAACP. Taking advantage of Shaw's offerings, students like Baker enrolled in courses that deepened their understanding of Afro-American life. History 5 considered the black experience from "the African background of the America Negro . . . to the present day, and his efforts for justice will be studied." English 307 discussed "the contributions of the Negro to American literature." Sociology 303 surveyed "pathological conditions in society," especially alcoholism, insanity, prejudice, prostitution, and poverty. Certain professors were noted for challenging student thinking. Charles Ray, a 1933 graduate, singled out his mentor, English professor Benjamin G. Brawley, who was acting dean, debating coach, department chair, director of the players' guild, editor of the *Home Mission College Review*, and a prolific author. "He was to English what W. E. B. Du Bois was to Social science," writes another student, Wilmoth A. Carter, who graduated in 1937. "His mannerisms, idiosyncrasies, knowledge, and scholarly demands made him a legend at Shaw. . . . No student went to Brawley's class without his work."[43]

An attitude and ideology of protest against Jim Crow evolved at Shaw and other schools. John H. Lucas, who graduated from Shaw in 1940 and later earned advanced degrees at North Carolina College for Negroes and New York University, appreciates having been informed about race in college. "Yes, it came up in class . . . because of the black community's active involvement in seeking equality back then," he calls to mind. Sociology 306 was one class that provided such information, as it introduced "facts and points of view bearing on some of the major problems now confronting American society, with major emphasis on . . . race relations." *Gaines v. Canada* (1938), a Supreme Court decision mandating the admission of a black student to the University of Missouri Law School, as well as the University of North Carolina's rejection of Pauli Murray, stirred continuing activism in campus chapters of the NAACP and the Student National Education Association.[44]

Lucas and his classmates anticipated that black North Carolinians would someday enroll at the University of North Carolina, but he points out that nobody expressed an immediate desire to attend. "Our pride made us loyal to the Shaws, Johnson C. Smiths, and A&T's. . . . It seemed more practical to upgrade them," he adds.[45] Pride in themselves and in black schools would be inseparable from blacks' struggle to enter the mainstream of North Carolina education and society. It is the frame in which we should begin to recast our portrait of blacks who lived and learned through the hard days of Jim Crow.

Courageous and dignified, they fought for "the blessings of liberty." After graduating, Lucas, like many college men, taught school for a while and went into the army. "Although the segregated units created opportunities for Negro officers, there was a general dissatisfaction. . . . We believed the future would be different," he muses. Indeed, throughout World War II, students at Shaw and statewide became impatient with racial injustice. They heard about the "Durham Manifesto," which black leaders drafted at North Carolina College in 1942, proclaiming that Southern blacks were "fundamentally opposed to the principle and practice of compulsory segregation." Students were eager to study "The American Race Problem," to cite a popular elective at Shaw in 1943. They participated in school boycotts and other forms of nonviolent direct action, helping to catalyze the emergent civil rights movement in North Carolina and the South.[46] Their fight on the home front to abolish Jim Crow bequeathed a significant legacy of hope to the next generation.

Notes

1. On the origins and periodization of Jim Crow, see Charles Reagan Wilson, "Jim Crow," in Charles Reagan Wilson and William Ferris, eds., *Encyclopedia of Southern Culture* (Chapel Hill: University of North Carolina Press, 1989), 211–12; Howard N. Rabinowitz, "More than the Woodward Thesis: Assessing the Strange Career of Jim Crow," *Journal of American History* 75 (December 1988): 842–56; and C. Vann Woodward, "Strange Career Critics: Long May They Persevere," *Journal of American History* 75 (December 1988): 857–68. "Behind the Veil" project brochure, 1993 (for quotes). An overview is in "Behind the Veil: Documenting African American Life in the Jim Crow South," *Duke University Libraries* 9 (Spring 1996): 2–6.

2. James Howard Brewer, "Legislation Designed to Control Slavery in Wilmington and Fayetteville," *North Carolina Historical Review* 30 (April 1953): 162–64; Ernest James Clark Jr., "Aspects of the North Carolina Slave Code, 1715–1860," *North Carolina Historical Review* 39 (April 1962): 148, 162–64; John Hope Franklin, *The Free Negro in North Carolina 1790–1860* (1943; reprint, Chapel Hill: University

of North Carolina Press, 1995), 59–74 (quote on 68); *The General Statutes of North Carolina of 1943*, 4 vols. (Charlottesville, Va.: Michie Co., 1943–44), 2:60; Pauli Murray, ed., *States' Laws on Race and Color* (Cincinnati: Woman's Division of the Methodist Church, 1951), 342–43.

3. W. McKee Evans, *Ballots and Fence Rails: Reconstruction on the Lower Cape Fear* (New York: W. W. Norton, 1974), 55, 251 (forty acres quote); Roberta Sue Alexander, *North Carolina Faces the Freedmen: Race Relations during Presidential Reconstruction, 1865–67* (Durham: Duke University Press, 1985), 3, 38–39, 44–46, 116; *General Statutes of 1943*, 2:60; Murray, *States' Laws*, 329 (children quote), 343.

4. Evans, *Ballots and Fence Rails*, 145–48, 255; *General Statutes of 1943*, 1:55, 67; Murray, *States' Laws*, 329 (marriage quote).

5. *General Statutes of 1943*, 3:303, 305; Murray, *States' Laws*, 331–32, 338 (department quote), 340, 342–43; Raymond Gavins, "The Meaning of Freedom: Black North Carolina in the Nadir, 1880–1900," in *Race, Class, and Politics in Southern History: Essays in Honor of Robert F. Durden*, ed. Jeffrey J. Crow, Paul D. Escott, and Charles L. Flynn Jr. (Baton Rouge: Louisiana State University Press, 1989), 178–80.

6. Evans, *Ballots and Fence Rails*, 200 (party quote); Jeffrey J. Crow, Paul D. Escott, and Flora J. Hatley, *A History of African Americans in North Carolina* (Raleigh: North Carolina Department of Cultural Resources, 1992), 209–11; Eric Anderson, *Race and Politics in North Carolina 1872–1901: The Black Second* (Baton Rouge: Louisiana State University Press, 1981), x, 34 (district quotes).

7. Crosby quoted in Elwynn Webster Midgette, "Negro Baptists in North Carolina, 1865–1900" (M.A. thesis, North Carolina College, 1949), 89–90.

8. Crow, Escott, and Hatley, *African Americans in North Carolina*, 113–14; Helen G. Edmonds, *The Negro and Fusion Politics in North Carolina, 1894–1901* (1951; reprint, New York: Russell & Russell, 1973), 160–63; Paul D. Escott, *Many Excellent People: Power and Privilege in North Carolina, 1850–1900* (Chapel Hill: University of North Carolina Press, 1985), 253–55 (Simmons quote, 255).

9. Crow, Escott, and Hatley, *African Americans in North Carolina*, 95 (separate quote); Escott, *Many Excellent People*, 255–59; *Thirty Years of Lynching in the United States 1889–1918* (New York: National Association for the Advancement of Colored People, 1919), 84; Edmonds, *The Negro and Fusion Politics*, 178; Anderson, *Race and Politics in North Carolina*, 252–63 (White quote, 255).

10. Edmonds, *The Negro and Fusion Politics*, 179–81; Richard L. Watson Jr., "Furnifold M. Simmons and the Politics of White Supremacy," in *Race, Class, and Politics in Southern History*, ed. Crow, Escott, and Flynn, 133–35; Murray, *States' Laws*, 344 (transport quote).

11. Address quoted in Gavins, "The Meaning of Freedom," 175–76.

12. S. G. Atkins, "The Situation in North Carolina," *Southern Workman* 30 (April 1901): 197, 199.

13. Survey quotes in Gilbert Thomas Stephenson, *Race Distinctions in American Law* (New York: D. Appleton and Co., 1910), 265–66.

14. *General Statutes of 1943*, 2:634, 3:305–20, 356; *Laws and Resolutions of the State of North Carolina . . . Adjourned Session of 1900* (Raleigh: Edwards & Broughton and E. M. Uzzell, 1900), 58–60; Murray, *States' Laws*, 331, 339, 341–44, 347–48 (quotes on 339, 342, 343); *Public Laws and Resolutions of the State of North Carolina . . . Session of 1911* (Raleigh: E. M. Uzzell, 1911), 355 (quote on Indians).

15. C. Vann Woodward, *American Counterpoint: Slavery and Racism in the North-South Dialogue* (Boston: Little, Brown, 1971), 237; Murray, *States' Laws*, 341 (quote

on Indians); *Public Laws and Resolutions . . . Session of 1911*, 354–55; Jeffrey J. Crow, "An Apartheid for the South: Clarence Poe's Crusade for Rural Segregation," in *Race, Class, and Politics in Southern History*, ed. Crow, Escott, and Flynn, 245 (residence quote).

16. Crow, "An Apartheid for the South," 218, 234, 253 (first three quotes). Also, see *Progressive Farmer* (Raleigh), 15 March, 7, 14 June 1913; Gilbert T. Stephenson, "The Segregation of the White and Negro Races in Rural Communities of North Carolina," *South Atlantic Quarterly* 13 (April 1914): 114 (last quote).

17. *General Statutes of 1943*, 2:339, 882, 3:303–5; Murray, *States' Laws*, 332, 339, 341–42 (quotes).

18. C. Vann Woodward, *The Strange Career of Jim Crow*, 3rd rev. ed. (New York: Oxford University Press), 108. Charles S. Johnson, *Patterns of Negro Segregation* (New York: Harper & Brothers, 1943), 195 (mayor quoted).

19. *General Statutes of 1943*, 2:634, 649, 662; 1949 Cum. Supp. to 2, 230; 3:223, 227, 238, 303–5, 311; 1949 Cum. Supp. to 3, 167; 4:34; Murray, *States' Laws*, 329–33 (textbook quote on 331), 338–48.

20. Johnson, *Patterns of Negro Segregation*, 9–10; Bertha Hampton Miller, "Blacks in Winston-Salem, North Carolina 1895–1920: Community Development in an Era of Benevolent Paternalism" (Ph.D. diss., Duke University, 1981), 125–26; Frank Hollowell White, "The Economic and Social Development of Negroes in North Carolina Since 1900" (Ph.D. diss., New York University, 1960), 36–40, 205–41; T. J. Woofter Jr., *Negro Problems in Cities* (Garden City, N.Y.: Doubleday, Doran & Co., 1928), 66–67, 79.

21. Johnson, *Patterns of Negro Segregation*, 48 (quote), 100.

22. Walter Cavers, interviewed by Karen Ferguson, Charlotte, N.C., 17 June 1993, "Behind the Veil" Collection, John Hope Franklin Research Center for African and African American Documentation, Special Collections Library, Duke University, Durham, N.C. (hereafter, BVC); Raymond Gavins, "North Carolina Black Folklore and Song in the Age of Segregation," *North Carolina Historical Review* 66 (October 1989): 414–15, and n. 8; Miller, "Blacks in Winston-Salem," 210–11.

23. Pauli Murray, *Proud Shoes: The Story of An American Family* (1956; reprint, New York: Harper & Row, 1987), 270.

24. Mary E. Mebane, *Mary* (New York: Viking Press, 1981), 149.

25. Gary B. Nash et al., eds., *The American People: Creating a Nation and a Society* (New York: Harper & Row, 1986), A-3 (Constitution quote); Murray, *Proud Shoes*, 281; Mebane, *Mary*, 152, 155; Gavins, "North Carolina Black Folklore and Song," 414, and n. 7.

26. National Research Conference on the "Behind the Veil" Project, North Carolina Central University, Durham, N.C., 15–17 March 1991 (quote); *Wilmington (North Carolina) City Directory* (Richmond, Va.: Hill Directory Co., 1930), 648–50, 654, 671, 697, 700–701.

27. York D. Garrett, interviewed by Kara Miles, Durham, N.C., 3 June 1993, BVC; cf. "York Garrett III, 100: The Man Who Outlived Bigots," *U.S. News & World Report*, 28 August–4 September 1995, 90, 93.

28. Vanessa Siddle Walker, *Their Highest Potential: An African American School Community in the Segregated South* (Chapel Hill: University of North Carolina Press, 1996), 3 (quote), 141–69; cf. David S. Cecelski, *Along Freedom Road: Hyde County, North Carolina, and the Fate of Black Schools in the South* (Chapel Hill: University of North Carolina Press, 1994), 59–82. Also see James Edward Shepard,

An Appeal Supported by Facts and Reason (Durham, N.C.: Seeman Printery, 1927), 3 (quotes); Hugh Victor Brown, *A History of the Education of Negroes in North Carolina* (Goldsboro, N.C.: Irving Swain Press, 1961), 51 (instruction quote).

29. Oliver R. Pope, *Chalk Dust* (New York: Pageant Press, 1967), 11–12, 13.

30. Superintendent quote in *Historical and Statistical Report, 1916–1917, New Hanover County and Wilmington Public Schools* (Wilmington, N.C.: Wilmington Printing Co., 1917), 20; *Directory of Wilmington, N.C. 1900* (Richmond, Va.: J. L. Hill Printing Co., 1899), 7, 17, 22–26; *Wilmington, N.C. Directory 1909–10* (Richmond, Va.: Hill Directory Co., 1909), 21, 23, 27–28; John Lochlan Godwin, "Wilmington and the North Carolina Way: Race, Culture, and Economy through the Civil Rights Years" (Ph.D. diss., University of South Carolina, 1994), 25–29.

31. William T. Childs, interviewed by Rhonda Mawhood, Wilmington, N.C., 12 July 1993, BVC.

32. James D. Anderson, *The Education of Blacks in the South, 1860–1935* (Chapel Hill: University of North Carolina Press, 1988), 156; *President's address, S. G. Atkins: North Carolina Negro Teachers' Association, Goldsboro, November 23, 1927, Abstract of Address*, N. C. Newbold (n.p., 1927), 9; *Report of the Governor's Commission for the Study of the Problems in the Education of Negroes in North Carolina* (Raleigh: North Carolina Department of Public Instruction, 1935), 7–8, 88, 93; Brown, *Education of Negroes in North Carolina*, 59–65 (instruction quotes on 61, 64).

33. Charles A. Ray, interviewed by Raymond Gavins, Durham, N.C., 4 August 1980, audiotape in author's possession; Aaron A. McCrae Sr., interviewed by Chris Stewart, Wilmington, N.C., 15 July 1993, BVC.

34. Brown, *Education of Negroes in North Carolina*, 66–99; U.S. Bureau of Education, *Negro Education: A Study of the Private and Higher Schools for Colored People in the United States*, Bulletin, 1916, no. 38, 2 vols. (Washington, D.C.: Government Printing Office, 1917), 2:389–90, 405–6, 445–47.

35. Charles S. Johnson, *The Negro College Graduate* (Chapel Hill: University of North Carolina Press, 1938), 23.

36. Ibid., 95–97, 140, 148, 260–61; *Report of the Governor's Commission*, 43; U.S. Bureau of Education, *Negro Education*, 2:414–16.

37. Abraham Flexner, *Medical Education: A Report to the Carnegie Foundation for the Advancement of Teaching* (Boston: Merrymount Press, 1910), 180–81, 280–81; Brown, *Education of Negroes in North Carolina*, 68 (departments quote).

38. Todd L. Savitt, "The Education of Black Physicians at Shaw University, 1882–1918," in *Black Americans in North Carolina and the South*, ed. Jeffrey J. Crow and Flora J. Hatley (Chapel Hill: University of North Carolina Press, 1984), 160–63, 184; Norma Jean and Carole Darden, *Spoonbread and Strawberry Wine: Recipes and Reminiscences of a Family* (Garden City, N.Y.: Anchor Press, 1978), 32; Johnson, *Negro College Graduate*, 140.

39. Pope, *Chalk Dust*, 12; Ernest Swain, interviewed by Rhonda Mawhood, Wilmington, N.C., 16 July 1993, BVC.

40. Raymond Gavins, "The NAACP in North Carolina during the Age of Segregation," in *New Directions in Civil Rights Studies*, ed. Armistead L. Robinson and Patricia Sullivan (Charlottesville: University Press of Virginia, 1991), 108 (rally, Streator quotes).

41. Bertha R. Todd, interviewed by Sonja Ramsey, Wilmington, N.C., 15 July 1993, BVC.

42. Mary Phillips Boddie, interviewed by Karen Ferguson, Enfield, N.C., 25 June

1993, BVC; Hollis Moody Long, *Public Secondary Education for Negroes in North Carolina*, Contributions to Education, no. 529 (New York: Teachers College, Columbia University, 1932), 101–8 (small part quote on 108).

43. Clara Barnes Jenkins, "An Historical Study of Shaw University, 1865–1963" (Ed.D. diss., University of Pittsburgh, 1965), 67; film "Fundi: The Story of Ella Baker"; *Shaw University Bulletin*, September 1929, 39; June 1932, 51; April 1933, 67 (course quotes); Ray interview; Wilmoth A. Carter, *Shaw's Universe: A Monument to Educational Innovation* (Raleigh: Shaw University, 1973), 216–18 (quotes on Brawley). Ray and Carter later earned Ph.D.'s from, respectively, the University of Southern California and the University of Chicago.

44. John H. Lucas, interviewed by Raymond Gavins, Durham, N.C., 18 September 1981, audiotape in author's possession; *Shaw University Bulletin*, April 1935, 63 (quote on Sociology 306); on impact of *Gaines*, see Wade Hamilton Boggs, "State-Supported Higher Education for Blacks in North Carolina, 1877–1945" (Ph.D. diss., Duke University, 1972), 271–72.

45. Lucas interview.

46. *Shaw University Bulletin*, April 1943, 48 (title of elective); Gavins, "The NAACP in North Carolina," 109 (quotes on manifesto). For anti–Jim Crow protests ca. 1930–45, including protests in North Carolina, see August Meier and Elliott Rudwick, "The Origins of Nonviolent Direct Action in Afro-American Protest: A Note on Historical Discontinuities," in Meier and Rudwick, *Along the Color Line: Explorations in the Black Experience* (Urbana: University of Illinois Press, 1976), 307–404.

Raymond
Gavins

John
Haley

Race, Rhetoric, and Revolution

On the cold, damp evening of 10 November 1898, small groups of men searched the swamps and woods on the edge of Wilmington, North Carolina. They hoped to contact the hundreds of terror-stricken blacks who had fled the city when racial violence first erupted earlier that day. Acting upon the authority of the white insurgents who had taken over Wilmington, the search parties urged the black refugees to return to their homes and places of work. Many would eventually return only long enough to pack their bags and leave Wilmington for good. But the changes produced by the white supremacy revolution shocked all those who returned to the city. Dismayed and demoralized by the extent of physical damage to their community, they also discovered that their civil rights and liberties had been radically curtailed. Now blacks could appear in public only with white escorts. Their persons and property would be subject to arbitrary searches, and they would be banished from the city if deemed undesirable by the new government. Black professional, business, religious, and political leaders filled the roads and trains leading out of Wilmington. The safety of those who remained in the city depended upon their adoption of a posture of deference, obedience, and servility to whites.[1] The Reverend J. Allen Kirk, pastor of the Central Baptist Church, fled Wilmington on 13 November and later recalled that the white insurrectionists "intended to remove all the able leaders of the colored race, stating that to do so would leave them better and obedient servants among the Negroes."[2] How Americans, black and white, responded to these events in Wilmington, and how white supremacists consolidated and institutionalized their revolution into a lasting framework of racial "civility" and industrial paternalism are the subjects of this essay.

John
Haley

As blacks trickled back into Wilmington, the white revolutionaries publicly justified their actions to the rest of the world. "There was not a flaw in the legality of our government," the city's new mayor, Alfred M. Waddell, claimed. "It was the result of revolution, but the forms of law were strictly complied with." Waddell, who had led one mob himself, also attempted to shift responsibility for the violence onto the shoulders of "overzealous whites" and "self-appointed vigilantes." Attorney Iredell Meares, one of the revolution's architects, likewise insisted that the city's better-off classes only followed the "spirit of the people." Yet he also proclaimed that the revolution had been necessary "to make the great mass of ignorant negro voters realize the deep-seated purpose of the white man to control in the future." Meares was confident that the new government was legal because it restored order and protected the lives and property of "law-abiding" citizens.[3] In the final analysis, white Americans accepted the new government because it evolved within the context of a statewide conservative revolution organized by the most powerful and affluent people in North Carolina. Even Democrats uneasy with racial violence took pride in "white manhood" and made no apologies for Wilmington. Power, of course, shapes the telling of history, and the white revolutionaries' version of events won the day both immediately after the racial killings in Wilmington and in subsequent generations.

White supremacists in Wilmington had convinced themselves that their actions were legal, and their history, culture, and heritage told them that they were right. White political leaders, intellectuals, and the secular press joined them in this contention. White clergy and the religious press anointed the Wilmington revolution and encouraged white North Carolina to go even further by disfranchising black voters. The *Raleigh News and Observer* reported that the revolution in Wilmington was defended by many of the most important ministers in the state, and it is "well known that no killing of negroes for political purposes would have received an apology or defense from them." Indeed, the Reverend Calvin S. Blackwell of First Baptist Church in Wilmington thought that "the killing of a few negroes was a mere incident. You can't make an omelet without breaking an egg." A. J. McKelway, the editor of the *North Carolina Presbyterian*, felt that "not only did the people need to be informed of the ethical aspect of the occurrences at Wilmington but they need to be defended from the prejudiced utterings" of Northern whites. He urged his paper's readers to understand that Wilmington was a city of "churches, schools, Christian homes and law-abiding citizens." The revolution "was justified by its results," McKelway wrote, and he reminded his readers that political legitimacy was based on the "bullet behind the ballot."[4]

Not all clergymen defended the white supremacists. The editor of the *Times-Mercury* in Hickory, North Carolina—a Republican stronghold—insisted that "God weighs men by what is in their hearts . . . , not the party to which they belong." He felt that the campaign of 1898 "dishonored the Church and damns men's souls." It not only disgraced the state, but it would retard economic development and encourage out-migration. In some of the most prophetic words written in the wake of the white supremacy campaign, the *Times-Mercury* asserted that "the hate and revenge engendered in the eastern part of the state" would require years "before it will disappear from the midst and hearts of the people." Beyond North Carolina, the black poet Paul Laurence Dunbar harshly criticized the clergymen who blessed the violence in Wilmington, calling their hosannas "a disgrace to their calling, a reflection on the intelligence of their hearers, and an insult to the God they profess to serve." The Reverend Francis J. Grimké, pastor of the prestigious Fifteenth Street Presbyterian Church in Washington, D.C., was among many black ministers who castigated the white clergy of Wilmington for apologizing for the "carnival of death" and the "hideous wrongs" done to the city's black citizens. Rev. Grimké argued that those men of the cloth had "brought the religion of Christ into contempt." "If damnation is reserved for anyone, or any class of men," he declared, "it certainly is for men of this stripe—men who dare to stand up in the pulpit, and in the sacred name of the holy religion of Jesus, commend such brutality, such inhuman conduct, such utter lawlessness."[5]

Black political and intellectual leaders also roundly condemned the racial atrocities in North Carolina. Not surprisingly, their voices were best heard outside the South. A few suggested that black Carolinians should leave the South or use retaliatory violence to protect their rights, lives, and property. At a meeting of the National Racial Protective Association in December 1898, T. Thomas Fortune, the editor of the *New York Age*, suggested that one white man should have been killed for every black who lost his life in Wilmington. "If blacks did not have Winchester rifles, they had pitch pine," he argued, "and while the whites were killing, the blacks should have been burning."[6] At a mass meeting of blacks at the Cooper Union in New York City on 18 November 1898, the crowd cheered at any suggestion of retaliatory violence. The *Colored American* and the *Washington Bee* urged black veterans of the Spanish-American War not to be cowards in peace by humbly surrendering their manhood rights. In mass meetings, in pulpits, and in

print media, black leaders censured North Carolina governor Daniel Russell and the McKinley administration for their complacency. The state's lone black U.S. congressman, George H. White, joined the protests, saying that he regretted the many misrepresentations made against blacks "who were faithful as slaves, patriots as citizens, law abiding in the extreme, and who committed no crime other than exercising the franchise."[7] But few blacks expected the racial violence in Wilmington to prick the conscience of white Southerners. Paul Laurence Dunbar thought that powerful whites should openly admit what they obviously felt: "We do not like you; we do not want you in certain places. Therefore, when we please, we will kill you. We are strong people, you are weak. What we chose to do we will do; right or no right."[8]

Outrage at what took place in Wilmington came from every corner of black society. "No language could describe the barbarism of whites in Wilmington," claimed Ernest Lyon, a prominent black minister in Baltimore. Lyon dismissed the claims of the white mob's leaders in regard to the courage of their followers, saying that he was confident that they had shown no courage in shooting down blacks after they had been disarmed and intimidated. Congressman George H. White and District of Columbia recorder of deeds Henry Plummer Cheatham were among many black political leaders who contended that the racial violence was prompted only by greed for office. Another national black leader, Judson T. Lyons, the register of the United States Treasury, asserted that in Cuba the Spanish general "Butcher" Weyler in his "maddest moment was hardly more barbarous" than the white supremacists in Wilmington.[9] In an address to the Interdenominational Association of Colored

Clergymen, a Rev. Morris refuted the arguments used to justify the racial violence. He accused the white supremacists of committing crimes that "threatened the very foundation of republican government." He contended that the United States could not go halfway around the world to establish a government in the Philippines "while the blood of citizens whose ancestors came here before the Mayflower is crying out to God against her from the gutters of Wilmington."[10]

American blacks were also bitterly disillusioned with the national Republican Party for failing to use federal authority to protect black citizens in Wilmington. Even though the Republican governor, Daniel L. Russell, had been elected by a Populist-Republican coalition in which blacks figured centrally, few considered him a friend of blacks. Resolutions passed at a mass meeting in New York censured Russell for failing to prevent racial violence in his state. In a letter to the editor of the *Washington Evening Star*, Thomas L. Jones, a black Republican, expressed the sentiments of many blacks when he wrote that Russell was a "cowardly derelict" who ignored the "most dastardly outrage" ever witnessed in a free country. And black leaders did not accept Russell's failure to request federal assistance as an excuse for inaction by President McKinley, who had neither taken any steps to protect black Southerners nor even uttered a word of protest.[11]

The National Afro-American Council, an organization of prominent blacks that was founded in September 1898 for the purpose of "ameliorating the condition of the colored people of the country," also expressed regret at McKinley's failure to protect black citizens. At its meeting on 29 December 1898, council leaders Ida Wells Barnett and T. Thomas Fortune severely excoriated the McKinley administration, and the council later urged the president to "use his good offices in adjusting the matter affecting the outrages in the Carolinas to the satisfaction of all fair-minded men and to the honor and glory of the Nation." The National Afro-American Council demanded that the president and Congress conduct investigations into the racial violence and bring to justice all persons responsible for election frauds, violence, and the denial of black political rights. The council also favored a reduction in the congressional delegations of those states that had already disfranchised the majority of their black voters. When the executive committee of the National Afro-American Council visited the president on 31 December 1898, it brought many of these issues to his attention.[12]

Neither the president nor Congress responded to the protests of black Americans. McKinley's paramount concern was U.S. imperialism, which had led to a different kind of race problem of his own making.

McKinley needed the goodwill of the Southern white congressional delegation in order to obtain ratification of the Treaty of Paris, which would formally conclude the Spanish-American War, as well as to secure appropriations to pay Spain $20 million in exchange for the Philippines and to administer the United States' new colonies. In addition, he had to convince many influential white Americans that the colonies would not lead the United States to be flooded with additional people of color. When McKinley recommended that the federal government pay for the maintenance of Confederate graves, blacks realized that he needed the political support of Southern whites far more than the goodwill of blacks. The president's annual message to Congress in December 1898 did not even mention racial violence. Indeed, McKinley must have realized that white public sentiment was moving in favor of absolute Anglo-Saxon domination. As the renowned white racist novelist Thomas Dixon Jr. put it, "The Negro must stand alone."[13]

Black political leadership underwent an incredible transformation in the months after the white revolt in Wilmington. Following the city's takeover, Mayor Alfred Waddell assured blacks that "as long as they recognized the fact that past conditions would never again be permitted," whites would look out for their welfare. Men who eagerly, begrudgingly, or bitterly accepted this new reality moved into the forefront of black political leadership. John C. Dancy, the U.S. collector of customs for the Port of Wilmington, echoed Waddell's words—and protected himself—when he counseled his fellow black citizens to be peaceful and submissive in their behavior. The *Wilmington Messenger* reported that Duke Bryan, a black artisan, likewise came forward and "expressed to the new government the gratitude of himself and other blacks."[14]

This new accommodation to white power could be seen among many national black leaders as well. When Professor Hugh M. Browne, a black member of Booker T. Washington's Hampton-Tuskegee clique, visited Wilmington soon after the white revolution, he observed that "it is perfectly natural that the class of citizens, both white and colored, who pay taxes should overthrow [the Fusionists]." He found that there was a warm friendship between blacks and the "very best class of whites in the city." Browne discovered whites "who had some of the bluest blood and largest wealth" still teaching in black Sunday schools and offering friendly advice and material assistance to the parents of the children in attendance. White leaders collected funds to support the black normal school and served as members of the institution's board of trustees. The "best white men" had purchased property in the vicinity of the school, selling it to blacks on easy terms and providing property owners with protection from "the rough element both white and colored." Whites also employed black youth as soon as they became skilled artisans. Browne concluded a report to the *Southern Workman* with the admonition that "blacks could not afford to antagonize the best white people who had nothing but warm friendship toward them."[15]

Other national black leaders went even further. Kelly Miller, a leading black intellectual and professor at Howard University, stood among Booker T. Washington's leading critics. After the Wilmington revolution, however, Miller temporarily accepted Washington's views on blacks and politics, and he published several articles arguing that Anglo-Saxons were the only people in the world capable of self-government. Even in those areas where blacks constituted voting majorities, Miller asserted, they should not compete with whites politically because doing so would only produce an opposition that they could not withstand. "Had the Negroes of Wilmington persisted in the exercise of their abstract right," he insisted, "the death list of that municipality alone would in all probability have exceeded the total casualties of the recent Spanish war." Miller somehow twisted this conviction into a resentment of Southern blacks, who, in his words, had acquired "only a thin veneer of civilization during Reconstruction." As American citizens, blacks had the privilege to vote, but in Miller's eyes they had not wisely used it to advance their states, their race, or their own interests. The black man had consequently "nullified the beneficent intendment of his own franchise." The most rabid white supremacist could not have made a stronger case for disfranchisement.[16]

While the McKinley administration heard black voices like that of Kelly Miller and helped to elevate Booker T. Washington into national leadership, other black voices went unheeded. Increasingly, McKinley was antagonized and troubled by the political demands of nonwhite people both in the United States and abroad. Filipinos decided that they did not want to be dominated by Anglo-Saxons and revolted against American authority. Some black Americans, most notably the Boston attorney Clifford H. Plummer (secretary of the National Negro Protective League) and T. Thomas Fortune, considered waging an armed struggle, either alone or in concert with a foreign nation, to get some relief from oppression. Blacks constantly bombarded McKinley with protests, demanding that he protect their rights before acquiring an overseas empire, and there were faint rumors that Northern blacks would abandon the Republican Party. Many black newspapers condemned U.S. policies in the Philippines, and influential blacks such as Lewis H.

Douglass, the son of Frederick Douglass, and Bishop Henry M. Turner, senior bishop of the African Methodist Episcopal Church, were outspoken anti-imperialists. In 1899, William T. Scott, a black Democrat, founded the National Negro Anti-Expansion, Anti-Imperialist, Anti-Trust and Anti-Lynching League. W. E. B. Du Bois publicly announced his support for William Jennings Bryan, the Democratic nominee for president, because of McKinley's anti-black and pro-imperial policies. Undercutting such black militants, McKinley did everything possible to enhance the stature of Booker T. Washington, who in exchange for the president's support remained a loyal Republican and promoted McKinley's domestic racial policies.[17]

While the racial violence in Wilmington signaled a tragic betrayal to American blacks, its success attracted the attention of white supremacists throughout the South. The *Washington Post* reported that Wilmington's insurrectionists had developed a political method that would "supplant the more ancient process of negro disfranchisement at the ballot box" and would lead to the absolute disfranchisement of blacks. Even before the violence erupted, representatives from other Southern cities were in Wilmington "finding out how the thing was done," and the *Post* accurately predicted that it would be repeated in other sections of the Black Belt South. Governor Russell observed that Wilmington "blazed the way in regard to getting rid of negro officeholders and negro insolence."[18]

While white leaders elsewhere in the South embraced the lessons of Wilmington, many white businessmen and industrialists in North Carolina realized that the lawlessness that marked their own anti-black crusade could not continue without harming the state's economy. They would not abide black political equality, but neither did they want black workers to migrate out of the state. In May 1900, the Durham textile magnate Julian S. Carr reported, "There is now a universal complaint of the scarcity of reliable labor." White economic elites such as Carr recognized the importance of black labor to the emerging industrial economy, and they realized that black out-migration would have a serious adverse impact on the state's business climate. Even in Wilmington, textile owner James Sprunt and other white businessmen who had supported the November 1898 revolt attempted to protect their black labor force. Confident that they had pitted blacks and poor whites against each other sufficiently to preclude their cooperation across racial lines, these business elites began to lay the groundwork for the kind of racial "civility" and industrial paternalism that would distinguish North Carolina in the twentieth century. They began to hint that the masses of blacks were not responsible for what they had called "Negro domination." They had only been led astray, the new argument went, by office-hungry black politicians who were under the influence of white Republicans. While justifying the violence in Wilmington, the editor of the *North Carolina Presbyterian* noted, "When the negro learns to take the advice of Booker T. Washington, the greatest man of his race today, and devote himself to industrial pursuits; when he learns that his white employer is an infinitely better friend of his than the demagogue who wants his vote, a better day will dawn for both races. And it will be both wise and becoming for the leaders among negroes to follow Booker Washington's example."[19]

Likewise, at the opening of the Negro State Fair on 15 November 1898, Josephus Daniels, editor and publisher of the *News and Observer*, reminded blacks of "the genuine friendship which the leaders of white supremacy felt for them and pointed out that it was a campaign not directed at the law-abiding and industrious Negro but at the Negro slave drivers of which Russell was the head." An editorial comment on the fair noted that there were "unbounded opportunities for industrial development" for blacks in North Carolina, and whites were asked to encourage blacks in this direction.

The "unbounded opportunities" that Daniels held out to black workers did not include politics. While confirming their "genuine friendship" for blacks, Democratic leaders began to prepare blacks psychologically for the ultimate step in the white supremacy campaign: disfranchisement of black voters. Daniels's newspaper, the *News and Observer*, noted that racial harmony was the only way to ensure the well-being of both races, but it had to be along economic, not political, lines. Julian S. Carr, a former Confederate colonel, believed that the state's welfare "demands an educational qualification for voting." In the best tradition of paternalism, Carr proclaimed himself a friend of blacks, and he wanted his black friends to know that "thinking men of all parties" had concluded that the wholesale enfranchisement of blacks had been a mistake. Blacks should not take their impending disfranchisement as a sign of hatred, Carr argued, "for we are going to give the colored people, pupil for pupil, exactly the same in dollars and cents as is devoted to the free education of the whites." To Carr, black disfranchisement would produce a more prosperous free enterprise system that would protect property, avoid excessive taxation, "tranquilize labor," and make blacks better workers. Here one can see the groundwork being laid for the racial "civility" that so uniquely marked North Carolina between 1900 and the civil rights movement of the 1960s. Racial civility and industrial paternalism, including white support for black schools and social welfare programs, could thrive in North Carolina only so long as blacks remained powerless, deferential, and segregated from white society. Black Carolinians understood only too well that any unraveling of this political settlement could bring "another Wilmington."[20]

Immediately after the violence in Wilmington, a group of North Carolina black leaders surfaced to agree publicly with Booker T. Washington that politics had only been detrimental to the progress of their race. Prominent in this group were James B. Dudley, a native of Wilmington and the president of the Agricultural and Mechanical College in Greensboro; Simon G. Atkins, president of the Slater Normal and Industrial School in Winston-Salem; the Reverend Samuel N. Vass, secretary of the Colored Baptist Sunday School Institute; Reverend R. H. W. Leake of the African Methodist Episcopal Zion Church; and two members of the General Assembly, Senator Thomas O. Fuller and Representative Isaac Smith. Evoking a mythical image of the Old South, they reminded whites of the faithfulness of slaves during the Civil War and that not all blacks had later supported the Republican Party. Another of these black leaders, Charles M. Eppes of Tarboro, proclaimed that the state needed teachers who were disciples of Booker T. Washington to take charge of the education of blacks. John C. Dancy and other "representative colored men" blamed all the trouble on Alexander Manly, even going so far as to apologize for his editorial defending black men against charges of being sexual predators. These black men hoped to gain the sympathy, protection, and friendship of the state's white elite. They also wanted the support of whites to maintain their educational, charitable, and social welfare institutions.

Some blacks from outside the state, as well as Republicans within, wondered why any black North Carolinian would want to be a friend to white leaders who had consistently deprived blacks of their rights as men and citizens. But the black men who stepped forward at this critical period were not conservatives; they were conservators of what little remained of their people's rights and dignities. Like Hugh Browne, who had expressed the opinion earlier, they believed that "all we can achieve in our day and generation should be placed under our children. . . . We must die that our children may have life, and have it more abundantly." The white supremacy campaign of 1898 had demonstrated that white conservatives were fully capable of backing up even their most vicious propaganda with violence and that they could deprive blacks of life, liberty, and property with impunity. The political terrain had shifted dramatically. Now a "progressive" was a white supremacist who favored black disfranchisement and even minimal public support for black schools; a conservative was a white supremacist who favored black disfranchisement but did not believe public funds should support black schools. No wonder many black leaders were ready to respond to any friendly overtures from whites.[21]

As the disfranchisement campaign of 1899–1900 got underway, black leaders hoped that they had already ceded enough ground. Senator Thomas Fuller, Representative Isaac Smith, the Reverend R. H. W. Leake, and Professor John O. Crosby of Salisbury (former president of North Carolina Agricultural and Mechanical College), men who earlier proclaimed that political privileges were harmful to their race, appeared before the state legislature in January 1899 and asked their "white friends" to reject the suffrage amendment then under consideration. At the same time, a "council of colored men" led by Congressman George H. White and John C. Dancy asked the General Assembly "not to pass any laws, the effect of which would be to blunt their aspirations, reduce their manhood and lessen their usefulness as citizens, but to guarantee to them an equal chance with other men to work out their destiny." The radical racists within the Democratic ranks—and there were more than enough to keep blacks uncertain as to the true intentions of the party— wondered why black leaders thought whites should listen to their appeal. Democrats, they said, had been trying in vain to give political advice to blacks since the Civil War, and their patience was worn out. The architect of the suffrage amendment, Representative George Rountree of New Hanover County, announced that disfranchisement was an act of humanity. He said that whites had always been just to blacks and would continue to support their educational uplift.[22]

The disfranchisement of blacks was the crown jewel of the white supremacy campaigns of 1898–1900. While the *True Reformer*, a weekly publication of the Afro-Union Club published in Littleton, North Carolina, reported that Democrats intended to count every vote "as cast in favor of the amendment," ratification was not guaranteed. A coalition of blacks and whites defeated disfranchisement in Georgia in 1899. The vote on the constitutional amendment in North Carolina would not take place until August 1900, and blacks would still be able to vote. If adopted, the amendment would not go into effect until 1902. That was sufficient time for the United States Supreme Court to declare it unconstitutional or for Congress to take steps to reduce the state's representation under the provisions of the Fourteenth Amendment. Democrats were assisted in their disfranchisement efforts, however, by white supremacists who were calling for a repeal of the Fifteenth Amendment, which gave blacks the right to vote. This was the sentiment of a group of prominent Southern men, mainly high-ranking Confederate veterans, who met at Montgomery, Alabama, in March 1900, to discuss "the Negro problem." In attendance was the Mayor of Wilmington, Alfred M. Waddell, who advised the delegation that the "mind of the country, North and South, especially since the acquisition of Hawaii, Porto Rico and the Philippines, is in a more favorable condition to consider such a proposition than ever before."[23]

The disfranchisement campaign of 1899–1900 used virtually the same propaganda blitz, orators, organizations, and techniques for mobilizing whites that had proven effective in 1898. This time Democrats in North Carolina more effectively placed disfranchisement within a context of U.S. imperialism and pseudo-scientific theories of black racial inferiority. Charles B. Aycock stressed the fact that all residents of the District of Columbia, white and black, had been disfranchised by the United States Congress. Hawaiians could not vote, and in "Cuba, Porto Rico, and the Philippines, the negro not only does not vote, but is shot by our government for even wanting to vote." Much more than in 1898, Democrats also glorified the virtues of poor whites and their instincts for good government. Confederate veterans, especially Julian S. Carr, were pressed into service to testify of the dangers of "Negro rule" during Reconstruction, and of the improvement in the political climate when blacks and Republicans were driven from office in the 1870s. White Supremacy Clubs replaced the White Government Unions of 1898, and white caps, white sashes, and white supremacy badges likewise replaced the red shirts of 1898. The intentions of their wearers had not changed, however.

Although the Democrats cited the black-majority Second Congressional District as being the citadel of black political power, they publicized evidence of "Negro rule" anywhere a Republican organization existed. They also claimed that blacks had driven the best white Republicans out of their own party, leaving only the self-seeking and corrupt. They reminded the remnants of the Populists that their party had repeatedly lost elections in the South because poor whites had never voted with blacks. Democrats also chastised white voters for having George H. White as one of the state's congressmen; they considered his prominence as an indication that black voters had not yet learned the lessons of 1898. Anticipating a repeat of the "tragedy of Wilmington," the *Washington Bee* advised black men not to die with their backs to the wall. Justice demanded that they exert their manhood and "defend their helpless sisters, wives and daughters against unholy slaughter by gangs of bloodthirsty and heartless brutes." If this proved ineffective, the *Bee* asserted, there would be among the black population in the United States 2 million men willing to "get at the throats of white men who have wronged and outraged their citizenship."[24]

North Carolina black leaders such as James B. Dudley, John O. Crosby, and Isaac Smith still remembered the campaign of 1898 too well. Outnumbered and outgunned, they could not speak so loudly as their counterparts in the North. Realizing that Democrats were determined to have their way, they acquiesced in disfranchisement and suggested that other blacks accept the inevitable. Nevertheless, Democrats made public appeals urging blacks to cooperate in their own disfranchisement by either staying away from the polls or voting for the amendment. The *News and Observer* asked "sensible Negroes" to support the amendment, arguing that its passage would eliminate a constant source of race friction and prejudice. The editor claimed that "the Southern white man and the negroes are natural friends, were friends in slavery, desire to be friends now, but cannot be friends with universal negro suffrage." Disfranchisement would also "cut loose the negro from the North and identify the Negro with the South where his interests now are and where his only future lies." Passage of the amendment would open the door of opportunity to blacks, encourage them to become educated property owners, and, the *News and Observer* insisted, remove the stigma of "nigger" from worthy and intelligent blacks by separating them from "the sorry, the vicious, the idle, and the criminal" members of their race. As articulated by the Raleigh newspaper, the argument for disfranchisement went even further. Disfranchisement would remove the color line from politics, the few blacks who still qualified to cast ballots could become independent voters, and they could stand before the world and be recognized as men. Few political acts in Southern history have been defended on more disingenuous grounds.[25] Responding to this argument, Booker T. Washington stunned white supremacists when he publicly restated his contention that suffrage restrictions should be equally applied to both races. "Any subterfuge, any makeshift that gives the ignorant white man a right to express his wants at the ballot box and withholds the same privileges from the Negro is an injustice to both races," Washington was quoted as saying.[26]

The suffrage amendment was adopted on 2 August 1900, and white supremacists interpreted its passage as a permanent memorial to the campaign of 1898. The Populist Party was mortally wounded, the Republican Party had lost its core black constituency and had already shifted to a lily-white course, and the Democratic Party had adopted anti-black electoral measures, including a primary elections system that would keep it in power for seventy years. The war was over, whites had won and—so Democrats said—better feelings between the races would prevail. Having succeeded in identifying themselves completely with white supremacy, Democrats were also sure that no other party would ever emerge in North Carolina—it would inevitably be branded as a party of "race traitors."[27]

White supremacists were so proud of their political success that they commended "the North Carolina Way" to those states that had not disfranchised blacks. When Georgia made a second attempt at disfranchisement in 1906, North Carolina governor Robert B. Glenn, U.S. senators Lee S. Overman and Furnifold Simmons, and former governor Charles B. Aycock—all elected for their leading roles in the white supremacy campaign of 1898—assisted the Peach State's white leaders by sharing their experiences. Senator Overman advised Georgians to be well armed and prepared to use violence similar to that in Wilmington. He extolled black disfranchisement as salutary for whites because it produced a "satisfaction which only comes of permanent peace after deadly warfare." Governor Glenn testified that no respectable white man in North Carolina "either Democrat or Republican" would choose to reverse the results of the white supremacy campaign. "You can say to the people of Georgia that I believe it to have been the brightest day in our history when we adopted the constitutional amendment," Glenn declared, "and if they adopt a similar one, they will never have cause to regret it." Overman advised white Georgians to look at the results of the white supremacy campaign in North Carolina, where only 5 percent of blacks voted. The Georgia audience was impressed, and the white supremacists, led by Hoke Smith, agreed to deal with blacks "as they did in Wilmington" and make the woods "black with their hanging carcasses." Indeed, the Atlanta riot of 1906 and the subsequent disfranchisement of black Georgians closely followed the North Carolina model.[28]

The suffrage amendment of 1900 disfranchised the masses of black voters. In 1896, there were approximately 120,000 black North Carolinians registered to vote, but by 1902 that number had been reduced to approximately 6,100. Those blacks who had regarded the ballot and voting as signs of their manhood rights had been symbolically castrated. George Allen Mebane, an administrator at the Normal and Industrial Institute (later Elizabeth City State University) in Elizabeth City, saw disfranchisement as part of the Southern effort "to legislate the negro out of civilization" and to prove that he is not a man.[29] If they could not pass the qualifications for voting, black males of voting age would always have the same political status as women and children. In many respects, they resembled a colonized people, but their situation was worse because they were natural-born citizens of what was alleged to be the freest republic in the world.

Meanwhile, even black accommodationists wondered anxiously what else their Democratic friends had in store for them. In August 1900, Simon G. Atkins, one of the black leaders anointed by whites, surveyed Democratic rhetoric in the state's major newspapers for clues of what lay ahead. Atkins held few illusions about the Jim Crow world of racial segregation that was emerging in the aftermath of the white supremacy campaigns of 1898 and 1900. But what he reported was that history revealed that North Carolina had always been in favor of giving blacks their rights before the law, and he did not see that they had any reason to expect otherwise in the future. In a statement that in another time and place would have defied credibility, he announced that blacks could expect to receive equal and exact justice before the law and no further legislation to prevent them from voting. He applauded the governor-elect, Charles B. Aycock, for consistently committing himself to the education of blacks. Atkins believed that Aycock's support for black schools was "worthy of the great statesmen, publicists and martyrs who have laid the foundations for human rights and the world's greatest civilizations."[30]

Atkins's flattery was characteristic of the manner in which black leaders would hereafter address their governors in hopes that they would support public funding for the education of blacks. Atkins had also discovered the essence of the rhetoric that white leaders later refined in attempting to explain to audiences both within and outside North Carolina that blacks were receiving equal and just—if segregated—treatment. Blacks and many whites knew better; they realized only too well that the emergence of Jim Crow racial segregation conflicted with many of the most fundamental provisions of the Constitution of the United States. Few would be surprised when North Carolina black schools never received anything close to equal funding and black teachers never received equal pay, both of which had been approximately equal before 1898. And of course they understood that equal justice before the law was a wildly farcical claim not supported by any court in the state.

Yet Atkins also recommended a course of action for black Carolinians that closely resembled the one advocated by Booker T. Washington. According to Atkins, blacks owed it to their communities to be honest, useful, and productive citizens with a genuine love for work, who paid their debts, honored the obligations of contracts, and respected the rights and property of others. Only then would North Carolina be fair in its treatment of the black man "as he rises up to his measure of citizenship and manhood." The hopes for black empowerment that had bloomed so mightily a decade earlier had withered and almost died. Now black leaders such as Atkins were hoping merely for survival. The age of Jim Crow had arrived. White supremacy was a part of the constitutional order of the Old North State.[31]

Notes

1. Alfred Moore Waddell, "The Story of the Wilmington, N.C., Race Riots," *Collier's Weekly*, 26 November 1898; J. Allen Kirk, *A Statement of Facts Concerning the Bloody Riot in Wilmington, N.C., of Interest to Every Citizen of the United States* (n.p., n.d.); Jerome A. McDuffie, "Politics in Wilmington and New Hanover County, North Carolina, 1865–1900: The Genesis of a Race Riot" (Ph.D. diss., Kent State University, 1979), 700–739; James H. Cowan, "The Wilmington Race Riot," Louis T. Moore Collection, New Hanover County Public Library, Wilmington, N.C.; Harry Hayden, *The Story of the Wilmington Rebellion* (n.p., 1936); Harry Hayden, "The Wilmington Light Infantry Memorial," 1954, New Hanover County Public Library, Wilmington, N.C.; Iredell Meares, "The Wilmington Revolution," in *Raleigh News and Observer*, 3 June 1900; George Rountree, "Changes in the Amendment," in *Raleigh News and Observer*, 24 June 1900.

2. Kirk, *A Statement of Facts Concerning the Bloody Riot.*

3. Waddell, "The Story of the Wilmington, N.C. Race Riots"; Meares, "The Wilmington Revolution"; Charles Francis Bourke, "The Committee of Twenty-Five," *Collier's Weekly*, 26 November 1898; Josephus Daniels, *Editor in Politics* (Chapel Hill: University of North Carolina Press, 1941), 308.

4. *Raleigh News and Observer*, 15 November 1898, 3 June 1900; *North Carolina Presbyterian Review*, 17 November 1898; *The Outlook*, 31 December 1898; *People's Paper*, 25 November 1898.

5. Francis Grimké, *The Negro: His Rights and Wrongs, the Forces for him and against him* (Washington, D.C.: n.p. [1898]), 22–23, 92–93.

6. *Washington Bee*, 24 December 1898; *Raleigh News and Observer*, 21 December 1898.

7. *Washington Star*, 1 December 1898; *Colored American*, 3, 10 December 1898; *Washington Bee*, 19 November, 10 December 1898; *New York Times*, 18 November 1898; *Washington Post*, 20 November 1898.

8. *Washington Bee*, 3 December 1898; Paul Laurence Dunbar, "Negro and White Man," in *Chicago Record*, 10 December 1898.

9. *Washington Bee*, 10 December 1898; *Colored American*, 26 November 1898; Judson T. Lyons, "Our Side of the Race Issue," in *Colored American*, 10 December 1898.

10. "The Wilmington Massacre," in Herbert Aptheker, ed., *A Documentary History of the Negro People in the United States* (New York: Citadel Press, 1968), 2:813–15.

11. *Washington Evening Star*, 19 November 1898; *Richmond Planet*, 14 January 1899; *Washington Post*, 20 November 1898.

12. *Richmond Planet*, 7, 14 January 1899; *Raleigh News and Observer*, 1 January 1899.

John
Haley

13. *Washington Post*, 15, 23 November, 25 December 1898; *Asheville Gazette*, 11 December 1898; *Washington Bee*, 24 December 1898; *Concord Times*, 8 December 1898; *Raleigh News and Observer*, 21, 25 December 1898, 1 January 1899.

14. *Raleigh News and Observer*, 3 June 1900; *Concord Times*, 8 December 1898; Daniels, *Editor in Politics*, 308; Hayumi Higuchi, "White Supremacy on the Cape Fear: The Wilmington Affair of 1898" (M.A. thesis, University of North Carolina at Chapel Hill, 1980), 132–33.

15. *Southern Workman* 28 (January 1899): 8–9. For Browne's thoughts on the development of blacks, see "Self Help and Self Activity," *African Methodist Zion Church Quarterly* 4 (April 1894): 255–67. For background on Booker T. Washington and the rise of Browne's political views into the black mainstream, see esp. Booker T. Washington, *Booker T. Washington's Own Story of His Life and Work Including an Authoritative Sixty-four page supplement by Albon L. Holsey* (n.p.: J. L. Nichols, 1901, 1915), 222–54; *New York Times*, 18 November 1898; *Richmond Planet*, 7, 14 January 1899.

16. *Southern Workman* 27 (December 1898): 238–40; *The Outlook*, December 1898, 1059–60; August Meier, *Negro Thought in America 1880–1915* (Ann Arbor: University of Michigan Press, 1963), 215.

17. Aptheker, *Documentary History of the Negro People*, 817–21; Willard B. Gatewood Jr., *Black Americans and the White Man's Burden 1898–1903* (Urbana: University of Illinois Press, 1975), 197–98, 212–13, 222–60; *Raleigh News and Observer*, 7 June 1900.

18. *Washington Post*, 29 October 1898; *Concord Times*, 8 December 1898; Hayden, *Story of the Wilmington Rebellion*, 26.

19. McDuffie, "Politics in Wilmington and New Hanover County," 710, 730–32; *North Carolina Presbyterian*, 17 November 1898; *Raleigh News and Observer*, 20 May 1900.

20. *Raleigh News and Observer*, 18 November 1898; Daniels, *Editor in Politics*, 311–12.

21. *Raleigh News and Observer*, 3, 10, 19 January 1899, 2 January 1900; *Charlotte Observer*, 14 January, 16, 18 February 1899; *Concord Times*, 26 January 1899; *Washington Bee*, 10 December 1898; *Richmond Planet*, 4 March 1899; *Union Republican*, 19 January 1899; *Southern Workman* 27 (December 1898): 239–40; Browne, "Self Help and Self Activity," 265.

22. *Raleigh News and Observer*, 27 December 1898, 10 January, 18, 19 February 1899, 11 January, 17 May 1900; *Charlotte Observer*, 16, 19 February 1899, 15 March 1899; George Rountree, *The Great Speech of George Rountree Esq., Delivered in the House of Representatives of North Carolina on the Subject of the Constitutional Amendment* (n.p., [1899]); *Concord Times*, 26 January 1898.

23. George Allen Mebane, *"The Negro Problem" as Seen and Discussed by Southern White Men in Conference at Montgomery, Alabama, with Criticisms by the Northern Press* (New York: Alliance Pub. Co., 1900); Alfred M. Waddell, *Some Memories of My Life* (Raleigh, Edwards & Broughton, 1908), 244; *True Reformer*, 25 July 1900.

24. *Raleigh News and Observer*, 2 February, 3, 8 June, 25 July 1900; *Washington Bee*, 24 May 1900; *Asheville Gazette*, 11 December 1898.

25. *Raleigh News and Observer*, 2 February, 11 May 1900; *Washington Bee*, 5 May 1900.

26. *Washington Bee*, 2 June 1900.

27. *The North Carolinian*, 9 August 1900; *Biblical Recorder*, 5 November 1902, 4 March 1903.

28. *Views of Distinguished Statesmen of South Carolina and North Carolina on White Supremacy* (n.p., n.d.), 5–8; John Dittmer, *Black Georgia in the Progressive Era, 1900–1920* (Urbana: University of Illinois Press, 1977), 100; *Atlanta Journal*, 24 November 1905.

29. *Raleigh News and Observer*, 28 October, 4 November 1902.

30. *Charlotte Observer*, 14 August 1900.

31. Ibid.

John
Haley

In the present excited condition of the races in certain sections of the South I think it the duty of
all good citizens, black and white, to be cautious and thoughtful and not add fuel to the flames....
All cannot be smooth sailing. We must have the cloud as well as the sunshine. If the colored people
continue securing education, property and character, and cultivating in every manly way the friendship of the people who are their neighbors, no matter what their color, our future is secure.
—Booker T. Washington, 1898

No man, no race will preserve its rights that fears to die to maintain them. Nor will the world regard
him as worthy of freedom who will not give his life if necessary in its defense.
    The greatness of every man and of every race, in its last analysis, is to be measured by indiffer-
ence to death.
—Editorial in *The Herald* (Brunswick, Georgia), 1898

On Santiago's bloody field
Where Spanish hosts were made to yield
The Negro like a phalanx great
Fought hard to save the ship of state
And Wilmington with her disgrace
Stares Santiago in the face
And shows her heartless feelings clear
For those who fought without a fear.
—F. B. Coffin, "Santiago de Wilmington," 1899

**Richard
Yarborough**

Violence, Manhood, and Black Heroism

The Wilmington Riot in Two Turn-of-the-Century
African American Novels

As the twentieth century draws to a close, some commentators on the
state of contemporary race relations in the United States have suggested
similarities between the conservative retrenchment of the 1990s and the
dark days of the post-Reconstruction era, when African American citizens were systematically stripped of the rights that they had only relatively recently been granted. The centennial anniversary of the notorious racial massacre in Wilmington, North Carolina, provides us with a
painful, yet instructive, occasion for retrospective consideration of a
social dilemma that, tragically, a full century later this country has not
yet solved.

Throughout the history of African American letters, moments of political crisis have elicited from black authors diverse literary responses intended to have an impact on the public's view of events. Committed to rewriting the history of the African American experience in the face of widespread distortions and untruths, black authors have sought to exploit the imaginative power and potential mass appeal of popular fiction while simultaneously establishing the documentary reliability of their texts—a difficult agenda indeed.[1] The urge on the part of black writers to effect social change also informs their desire to shape the popular white conception of the African American. In the late nineteenth and early twentieth centuries, the depth and power of white supremacist sentiment made this task nearly impossible. Nonetheless, African American writers from across the political spectrum fought this war over images by asserting not only that blacks were human in the most basic sense but that they had the potential to be exemplary men and women, that they could be, in a word, *heroic*. The Wilmington riot of 1898 produced two noteworthy examples of texts informed by these fictive drives: *The Marrow of Tradition* (1901) by Charles Waddell Chesnutt and *Hanover; or The Persecution of the Lowly: A Story of the Wilmington Massacre* (1900) by David Bryant Fulton (using the pseudonym of Jack Thorne). Published within a year of each other, the novels constitute ambitious attempts to depict Wilmington blacks sympathetically while reporting with historical accuracy the horrifying events that rocked the North Carolina community that each of these authors knew well.

Dubbed by Southern Democrats a "revolution," by some historians a "coup d'état," and by most blacks at the time a "tragedy," the riot that erupted in 1898 in Wilmington, North Carolina, was part of a massive wave of anti-black violence that reflected the extent to which the status of the African American had deteriorated in the post-Reconstruction South. The roots of the Wilmington violence went deep and, like most racial problems in the United States, represent a complex intertwining of cultural, economic, political, and psychosexual tensions. For convenience, we can isolate three related factors that contributed to the unrest.[2]

The first involved a struggle for political supremacy. The late 1890s marked the rise of the Fusionists—an alliance of white Republicans, African Americans, and disaffected white Democrats who had joined the Populist movement. In 1896 the Fusionist ticket put Republican Daniel Russell in the governor's house; and North Carolina Democrats realized that in order to regain control, not only did they have to bring white Populists back into the fold, but they also had to remove blacks as participants in Southern politics. To achieve these ends, Democrats used tactics that ranged from acceding to Populist demands for reform to outright fraud and terrorism. A particularly important weapon was the Southern press, which conducted one of the most extensive, unrelentingly racist propaganda campaigns in this country's history. In the months before the election in November 1898, newspapers not only trumpeted instances of alleged black crime but also disseminated rumors that black servants were preparing to burn their employers' homes and that African Americans planned to take over the state through mass immigration.[3]

The largest city in North Carolina, with roughly 11,300 blacks and 8,700 whites, Wilmington was a crucial prize in this political war. Accordingly, local Democrats took every opportunity to attack a supposed black civic incompetence that was rapidly leading to what they decried as the "Africanization" of the community's political and social order. "Negro Domination" was not, as the black leader Kelly Miller wrote in 1898, "a lexical term, subject to exact definition and meaning, but a racial shibboleth whose potency is wholly independent of its rational import."[4] Such was certainly the case with regard to Wilmington, for the so-called "Negro Domination" of the city consisted of a collector of customs, three aldermen out of ten, two fire companies, one of five members of the board of audit and finance, two lot inspectors, and a number of police officers and magistrates. The mayor, the chief of police, the city attorney, and most of the aldermen were white. In other words, as any moderately unbiased observer could see, blacks hardly controlled the city's political life.

White apprehensions were also aroused by the substantial financial base that blacks had established in Wilmington and the fierce interracial competition for employment among both manual laborers and skilled professionals. One white resident complained, "Negroes were given preference in the matter of employment, for most of the town's artisans were Negroes, and numerous white families in the city faced bitter want because their providers could get but little work as brickmasons, carpenters, mechanics." Although this speaker overstates the extent to which Wilmington actually was "a Mecca for Negroes and a City of Lost Opportunities for the working class whites," the widespread perception that African Americans were forcing whites out of the labor market helped fire anti-black public sentiment to the boiling point.[5]

Finally, there was the notorious Manly editorial. On 12 August 1897, at an agricultural convention held in Tybee, Georgia, a white Southern woman named Rebecca Latimer Felton delivered a speech in which she openly advocated lynching as the appropriate response to what she claimed were numerous rapes committed by black men. At one point she declared,

> When there is not enough religion in the pulpit to organize a crusade against sin; nor justice in the court house to promptly punish crime; nor manhood enough in the nation to put a sheltering arm about innocence and virtue—if it needs lynching to protect woman's dearest possession from the ravening human beasts—then I say lynch; a thousand times a week if necessary.[6]

Angered by this libel upon black character, an ambitious young African American named Alexander L. Manly responded in the 18 August 1898 issue of his newspaper, the *Wilmington Record*. The white outrage that his editorial elicited was due less to the fact that he spoke out against a well-known white woman, the wife of a former congressman in fact, than to the sarcastic barbs that he tossed at the near-sacred myth of pure Southern white womanhood:

> We suggest that the whites guard their women more closely . . . , thus giving no opportunity for the human fiend, be he white or black. . . . Our experience among poor white people in the country teaches us that the women of that race are not any more particular in the matter of clandestine meetings with colored men than are the white men with colored women. Meetings of this kind go on for some time, until the woman's infatuation or the man's boldness bring attention to them and the man is lynched for rape. Every negro lynched is called a "big, burly, black brute," when in fact many of those . . . were sufficiently attractive for white girls of culture and refinement to fall in love with them, as is well known to all.[7]

Tens of thousands read Manly's editorial, for it was reprinted in papers throughout the nation.

For the majority of Southern whites, Manly's indiscretion exemplified the degree to which African Americans had strayed from the necessary restraint originally maintained by slavery and later reimposed at the end of Reconstruction. Moreover, the prominence of the rape issue in this skirmish encouraged white readers to link what they saw as black impudence, presumption, and disrespect, on the one hand, with an allegedly pervasive black male sexual threat, on the other. For example, only days before the November election, the *Wilmington Messenger* published excerpts from Manly's editorial with the headline "A Negro Defamer of the White Women of North Carolina." Immediately following this inflammatory condemnation, and with no clear textual separation, appeared a report of a sexual attack under the heading "Attempted Assault by Black Brutes." The *Messenger's* contention that Manly had spoken from his own personal experiences with "poor white women, wives of white men" underlines how Southern white opinion makers worked to erase any distinction between an alleged sexual violation in word and one in deed.[8] The elopement, widely reported at the time, of a black teenager, coincidentally named Manly McCauley, and the "very comely" twenty-eight-year-old wife of a white North Carolina farmer could only have made Southern white males even more sensitive to the pointed implications of Alexander Manly's statements. (Upon the apprehension of the woman and her "black Lothario," as one journalist called him, McCauley was lynched; his lover was sent home to her father.)[9] Suffice it to say, white Democrats fully exploited Manly's *Record* editorial as well as myriad allegations of black insolence, crime, and sexual misconduct in order to mobilize racist sentiment in North Carolina, especially in the days preceding the election.

Both blacks and whites anticipated trouble in Wilmington, but 8 November came and went with relatively few racial confrontations, at least in part because many African American voters stayed away from the polls. The overwhelming defeat that the Democrats handed the Fusionists further seemed to suggest that conservatives had gotten what they wanted. Whipped into a near-frenzy of anti-black resentment in the months leading up to the election, however, whites in the city refused to wait for the so-called "natural order" to be legally restored. On the morning of Thursday, 10 November, two days after the election, a heavily armed mob led by former congressman and future mayor Alfred M. Waddell broke into and burned Manly's *Record* office. Shortly thereafter, an interracial standoff exploded into violence, and whites went on a rampage, shooting and molesting blacks, destroying property, and expelling prominent Republicans of both races from the city. For weeks, African Americans had been unable to purchase weapons, and during the disturbance they were systematically disarmed. Furthermore, whites generally met physical resistance with immediate and merciless retaliation. As a result, most black residents hid in their homes or fled to nearby swamps and woods, where a number of them died from exposure.

By Sunday, 12 November, the violence had ended; a new city government was in place; and Wilmington was flooded with congratulatory telegrams from white communities throughout the South.[10] However, the Democratic celebrations by no means marked an end to the hardships endured by black Wilmingtonians. The 16 November edition of the *Washington Post* reported that black "refugees" driven from their homes during the turmoil continued to ignore appeals to return, despite the physical toll exacted by their extended stay in the woods outside the city. And according to one African American newspaper, by the end of December nearly 1,400 blacks had left Wilmington altogether. Within a year, local whites were complaining of a scarcity of domestic servants, and the city's most prominent industrialist actually sent a trusted African American employee to Brooklyn, New York, in an attempt to get black former residents to come back to their jobs.[11]

Raised in North Carolina and having worked there, Charles Chesnutt still had friends and relatives in the state in the fall of 1898. A letter to Walter Hines Page indicates the strength of his reaction to the horrible event: "It is an outbreak of pure, malignant and altogether indefensible race prejudice, which makes me feel personally humiliated, and ashamed for the country and the state."[12] Also a North Carolina native, David Fulton spent much of his early life in Wilmington itself and thus could claim close personal ties to the black community that was so devastated by the catastrophe. In addition, after he moved to New York in 1887, Fulton became a leading figure in the "Sons of North Carolina," a group "composed of colored men of North Carolinian birth who are residents of Brooklyn."[13] In the wake of the riot, this organization sponsored a protest rally at which Alexander Manly presented his side of the tragedy; Fulton surely would have met the editor there, if he had not done so previously.[14] Moreover, many of the blacks fleeing Wilmington settled in Brooklyn, where Fulton could have learned firsthand what had transpired in his hometown.[15] A contemporary of Fulton's suggests the tremendous impact that the uprising had on the writer this way: "The latest [sic] powers of his mind and the youthful ambitions of his heart were not fully exercised nor fired to patriotic expressions of indignation until the awful tragedy of the 'race riots,' which occurred some years ago at Wilmington, N.C., in which hundreds of his race were slain and others driven from home and their property destroyed."[16] Galvanized not only by the tragic consequences of the Wilmington riot but also by the skewed depictions of the affair presented in the popular white media, Chesnutt and Fulton sought to intervene in the controversy by creating fictional narratives designed to dramatize the events from the perspective of the African American community. In so doing, each novelist hoped to construct a credible version of just what had occurred in Wilmington and thereby generate a sympathetic response on the part of readers, particularly Northern whites. The goal of this essay is to examine the strategies of characterization adopted by each author and how their extraliterary agendas complicated and, in some cases, actually undermined these strategies.[17]

Brilliantly weaving the story of the riot with a number of subplots, Charles Chesnutt presents in *The Marrow of Tradition* a vivid tapestry that dramatically depicts class, generational, and racial conflict in an interracial Southern community charged with tension. At times melodramatic and perhaps overworked with too fine a filigree of convenient happenstance, the novel is nonetheless a remarkably insightful and even daring recapitulation of forty years of African American life in the South after slavery. In particular, Chesnutt's black characters embody virtually all of the major contending forces in African American society at the turn of the century. The two most important black figures are William Miller and Josh Green.

Another of the educated, handsome, light-skinned black protagonists who often appear in the early African American novel, William Miller is a skilled, impeccably trained physician who moves south with his wife, Janet, and their young child. Raised in relative comfort, William inherits his drive for self-improvement from his father, the ambitious son of an equally ambitious slave stevedore who purchased his own freedom and set up a successful business. Unlike his ancestors, however, Miller chooses to dedicate his life to poor blacks in the South because "his people had needed him, and he had wished to help them."[18]

Miller's optimism regarding race relations reflects not only his own temperament and inexperience but also an idealistic belief in the underlying rationality of humanity and its institutions, a conviction shared by characters in other of Chesnutt's works. In *The House Behind the Cedars*, for example, the light-skinned John Walden can see that he certainly *looks* white; therefore, he has difficulty accepting the fact that society could be so illogical as to define him as black. Likewise, in an obvious paraphrase of Booker T. Washington, William Miller tells himself that "when a colored man should demonstrate to the community in which he lived that he possessed character and power, that community would find a way in which to enlist his services for the public good" (65).[19] Confident both of his own abilities and also of what he takes to be the white community's unspoken endorsement of his actions, Miller sets up a nursing school and a hospital for blacks in Wellington (Chesnutt's fictionalized version of Wilmington). The apparent approbation that Miller receives from local whites is hardly the result of any broad-minded belief in the worth of his project, however. They tolerate him because he is "a very good sort of negro, [who] doesn't meddle with politics, nor tread on any one else's toes" (251–52).

In sharp contrast to Miller stands the aggressive black laborer Josh Green, and the ideological tension between the two men forms the center of Chesnutt's novel. Josh first appears as a stowaway on the train in which Miller is traveling: "As the dusty tramp passed the rear coach, he cast toward it a glance of intense ferocity. Up to that moment the man's face, which Miller recognized under its grimy coating, had been that of an ordinarily good-natured, somewhat reckless, pleasure-loving negro, at present rather the worse for wear. The change that now came over it suggested a concentrated hatred almost uncanny in its murderousness" (59). It is no coincidence that the sight of this embodiment of black rage and vindictiveness interrupts Miller's sanguine reflections upon the race problem. Then, to reinforce further the links between the two men, Chesnutt has them disembark at the same moment: "Simultaneously with Miller's exit from the train, a great black figure crawled off the tracks of the rear car . . . stretching and shaking himself with a free gesture" (62). Unidentified as yet, Green might well embody some dark, inhuman threat, some diabolic specter of black hatred. Earlier, Chesnutt even describes him in animalistic terms: "He threw himself down by the trough, drank long and deep, and plunging his head into the water, shook himself like a wet dog" (59). At this point, one can usefully view him as symbolizing the id—and Miller, the superego—of the African American male psyche.

With the first meeting between the two characters, however, the veil of mystery falls from Green, revealing a man who, unlike the stereotypical black monster, is not motivated by an inherent urge toward savagery but rather by a bitter desire for vengeance after his father's death at the hands of the Ku Klux Klan. Although Miller cannot help acknowledging the moral force of Green's case against whites, he nonetheless warns him of the dangerous consequences of his attitude: "These are bad times for bad negroes. . . . You'd better be peaceable and endure a little injustice, rather than run the risk of a sudden and violent death." Quite aware of his place in American society and of the fate awaiting him, Green responds, "I expec's ter die a vi'lent death in a quarrel wid a w'ite man . . . an' fu'thermo', he's gwine ter die at the same time, er a little befo'" (110).

After Miller then reminds him that the Bible teaches "that we should 'forgive our enemies,'" Josh replies with characteristic bluntness,

It 'pears ter me dat dis fergitfulniss an' fergivniss is mighty one-sided. De w'ite folks don' fergive nothin' de niggers does. . . . De niggers is be'n train' ter fergiveniss; an' fer fear dey might fergit how ter fergive, de w'ite folks gives 'em somethin' new ev'y now an' den, ter practice on. . . . Ef a nigger wants ter git down on his marrow-bones, en' eat dirt, an' call 'em "marster," *he's* a good nigger, dere's room fer *him*. But I ain' no w'ite folks' nigger, I ain'. I don' call no man "marster." I don' wan' nothin' but w'at I wo'k fer, but I wants all er dat. (113–14)

Establishing a pattern that occurs four times in the novel, the debate ends in a stalemate.

The second meeting between Green and Miller takes place after Sandy, a trustworthy black servant, is arrested for a murder he did not commit. Fearing a lynch mob, Green intends to "hunt up de niggers an' git 'em ter stan' tergether an' gyard de jail" (188–89). Convinced that they should instead appeal to local whites for help, Miller successfully restrains Green; but he soon must acknowledge a near total lack of legal alternatives. "The whole thing is profoundly discouraging," he admits sadly. "Try as we may to build up the race in the essentials of good citizenship and win the good opinion of the best people, some black scoundrel comes along, and by a single criminal act . . . neutralizes the effect of a whole year's work." Miller does not know that the real "black scoundrel" here is, in one of Chesnutt's consummate uses of irony, Tom Delamere, a young white aristocrat who disguises himself in blackface when he commits his crimes. He also cannot see that the "good opinion" to which he refers is, in Josh's words, "mighty easy neut'alize'" (190).

The outbreak of the riot brings the third confrontation between these two characters. Miller's reaction to news of the violence is, first, concern for his family and, second, shocked disbelief that such a thing could occur. On his way back to town, he meets an African American lawyer named Watson, who confirms Miller's worst fears and then tries to sell the doctor his property so that he can leave the area. Green approaches the two professional men and asks them to take their places at the front of the group of blacks he is leading:

De w'ite folks are killin' de niggers, an' we ain' gwine ter stan' up an' be shot down like dogs. We're gwine ter defen' ou' lives, an' we ain' gwine ter run away f'm no place where we've got a right ter be'; an' woe be ter de w'ite man w'at lays han's on us! Dere's two niggers in dis town ter eve'y w'ite man, an' ef we've got ter be killt, we'll take some w'ite folks 'long wid us, ez sho' ez dere's a God in heaven,—ez I s'pose dere is, dough He mus' be 'sleep, er busy somewhar e'se ter-day. Will you-all come an' lead us? (281)

Watson replies first: "What is the use? The negroes will not back you up. They haven't the arms, nor the moral courage, nor the leadership." Countering him directly, Josh brings the issue of Watson and Miller's role in the black self-defense effort back to the fore: "We'll git de arms, an' we'll git de courage, ef you'll come an' lead us!" (281). Fearing both for his family and for himself, Watson wilts in despair and advises, "Keep quiet, boys, and trust in God. You won't gain anything by resistance" (282). With a curt "God he'ps dem dat he'ps demselves," Green turns to Miller. Before the doctor speaks, however, Chesnutt intrudes in an attempt to establish that the man's decision is not based upon a lack of courage: "He was no coward, morally or physically. Every manly instinct urged him to go forward and take up the cause of these leaderless people, and, if need be, to defend their lives and their rights with his own,—but to what end?" (282). Miller then argues that resistance is doomed to fail and, hence, worthless:

Suppose we made a determined stand and won a temporary victory. . . . We have no standing in the court of conscience. They would kill us in the fight, or they would hang us afterwards,—one way or another, we should be doomed. I should like to lead you; I should like to arm every colored man in this town, and have them stand firmly in line, not for attack, but for defense; but if I attempted it, and they should stand by me, which is questionable,—for I have met them fleeing from the town,—my life would pay the forfeit. Alive, I may be of some use to you, and you are welcome to my life in that way,—I am giving it freely. Dead, I should be a mere lump of carrion. . . .

My advice is not heroic, but I think it is wise. . . . Our time will come. (282–83)

Realizing the futility of further discussion, Green leads the band of black laborers away, and the chapter ends with his determined words: "Dese gentlemen may have somethin' ter live fer; but ez fer my pa't, I'd ruther be a dead nigger any day dan a live dog!" (284).

The final exchange between Miller and Green occurs as the former searches desperately for his family and the latter is taking a group of blacks to defend their hospital, schools, and churches. Despite having personally witnessed the effects of the white rampage, Miller still refuses to acknowledge that he has horribly misread the situation. He tells Josh, "They'll not burn the schoolhouses, nor the hospital. . . . T]ey'll only kill the colored people who resist them" (295). By this point, however, all possibility of rapprochement between Miller and Green is gone, and they separate one final time.

The roles filled in *The Marrow of Tradition* by the African American servants Mammy Jane, Jerry, and Sandy are linked by the fact that all three characters attempt to align themselves with whites, and all three have to pay for such naivete. Early in the novel, for example, Mammy Jane contends that if the blacks would "not crowd de w'ite folks, dey'd git ernuff ter eat, an' live out deir days in peace an' comfo't" (44). Her murder in the riot underlines the misguided and ultimately fatal nature of her confidence. Even more forcefully than does Paul Laurence Dunbar in his novel *The Sport of the Gods* (1902), Chesnutt examines here the fate awaiting blacks who assume that the interracial accommodations established under the old Southern slave order are still valid.

Determining Chesnutt's ultimate judgment of Miller and Green is a more complex task. W. E. B. Du Bois's description of an ideological dichotomy in African American society in the late nineteenth century might help us, however, in our analysis. In *The Souls of Black Folk*, Du Bois writes: "Thus we have two great and hardly reconcilable streams of thought and ethical strivings; the danger of the one lies in anarchy, that of the other in hypocrisy. The one type of Negro stands almost ready to curse God and die, and the other is too often found a traitor to right and a coward before force; the one is wedded to ideals remote, whimsical, perhaps impossible of realization; the other forgets that life is more than meat and the body more than raiment."[20] In important ways, Green and Miller represent these two opposing "streams."

On one side stands Josh Green, whose portrayal represents perhaps the first detailed fictional look at an aggressive, angry, and outspoken lower-class black male character who is not so brutalized by his experience as to be barely human. In fact, with each exchange with Miller, Josh becomes more appealing as Chesnutt reveals the man's hatred to be righteous anger and his recklessness, a desperate courage. Then, during the riot, as Green directs the defense of the hospital with the "instinct of a born commander," his heroism is undeniable (301). Chesnutt himself seems caught up in the magnificence of Green's courage as he abandons his carefully modulated tone and understated irony, describing the man in mythic, superhuman terms: The "tallest and biggest" of all the blacks, Green looms before the mob like a veritable berserker, a "black giant . . . sweeping down upon them, a smile upon his face, his eyes lit up with a rapt expression which seemed to take him out of mortal ken" (309).[21] Finally, before he is shot down, Green succeeds in killing the Klan leader responsible for his father's murder.

Juxtaposed to Green is William Miller. A strong, determined figure who is selflessly dedicated to his family, his profession, and his people, he is an exemplary representative of Du Bois's "Talented Tenth." Confronted with Josh's willingness to give his life in defense of his rights, however, he must examine his own motivations and, in fact, reconsider his entire conception of black capacity. Before the outbreak of the riot, he thinks to himself,

> The negroes were not a vindictive people. If, swayed by passion or emotion, they sometimes gave way to gusts of rage, these were of brief duration. Absorbed in the contemplation of their doubtful present and their uncertain future, they gave little thought to the past,—it was a dark story, which they would willingly forget. . . . [Green] was a negro who could remember an injury, who could shape his life to a definite purpose, if not a high or holy one. When his race reached the point where they would resent a wrong, there was hope that they might soon attain the stage where they might try, and, if need be, die, to defend a right. (112)

Miller then proceeds to draw a crucial distinction between two different motivations for violence: "To die in defense of the right was heroic. To kill another for revenge was pitifully human and weak" (114). If Miller truly holds this opinion, he should have little trouble supporting the blacks' defense against the white onslaught. Yet when confronted with the inescapable fact that Green and the others are indeed standing up for their rights in the face of a blatantly unjustified attack, Miller shifts the emphasis of his ethical argument onto a question of utility—that is, what *use* would such a certain death serve? This expedient approach satisfies neither Green nor, as Chesnutt points out, Miller himself: "While entirely convinced that he had acted wisely in declining to accompany them, [he] was yet conscious of a distinct feeling of shame and envy that he, too, did not feel impelled to throw away his life in a hopeless struggle" (285). Miller's discovery that his child has been shot and killed apparently deals his optimism a fatal blow. Then when Major Carteret, the white editor who helped instigate the riot, begs Miller to save his own sick child, the young doctor displays real anger for the first time in the book. "There is a just God in heaven!" he declares, "—as you have sown, so may you reap!" (320). Moved by Mrs. Carteret's pleas, however, he finally promises to abide by his wife Janet's wishes in the matter.

Despite Chesnutt's scanty treatment of Janet Miller up to this point, one thing that has been established is her obsession with the refusal of Olivia Carteret, her half-sister, to acknowledge their blood tie. Chesnutt also emphasizes Janet's generosity of spirit: "She was of a forgiving temper; she could never bear malice." In fact, the extent to which she dotes on Olivia, despite the woman's snubs, alarms Janet herself, but she explains away this lack of "a decent self-respect" as "the heritage of her mother's race . . . as part of the taint of slavery" (66). Consequently, it comes as no surprise that after Janet's initial refusal to send her husband to save the Carteret child, Olivia's desperate admission that they are legally sisters and that Janet is entitled to half of their father's estate elicits a more favorable response. Chesnutt carefully notes, however, that Janet sends her husband out of a desire to help *in spite* of injustice, not because of a fulfilled wish for sibling recognition. Furthermore, as William Andrews argues, the Millers' beneficent behavior at this climactic moment of the novel should be read in light of not only the change in Olivia's attitude toward her black relation but also her husband's awakening to the humanity and moral stature of Dr. Miller.[22] If there is hope in the wake of the riot, it resides in the capacity, however belatedly manifested, of some white folks to change. Given the guarded optimism that Chesnutt tries to establish at the end of *Marrow*, it is clear that despite the persuasiveness of his arguments, the justice of his position, and the appeal of his valor, Josh Green and the turbulent energies that he embodies must finally be countered by bourgeois African Americans like Miller and Watson whose commitment to peaceful interracial cooperation and patient assimilation Chesnutt himself shares.

Like Chesnutt, David Fulton felt driven to enhance the power of the facts of the Wilmington riot with the drama, color, and flexibility of fiction. However, in contrast to Chesnutt, who used the historical events as a backdrop for his complex plotting and characterizations, Fulton was motivated by a far more documentary impulse. For example, the narrative line of *Hanover* follows quite closely the actual chain of events that culminated in the explosion of white violence.[23] In addition, whereas William Andrews is quite right when he describes *Marrow* as, "at least in part, a roman a clef," Fulton's cast of characters is even more dependent than Chesnutt's upon actual Wilmington personages.[24] In *Marrow*, for example, we can identify the editor Barber as based on Alexander Manly, the attorney Watson on Armond W. Scott or L. A. Henderson, Major Carteret on Thomas W. Clawson, and Josh Green as perhaps a composite of two blacks who resisted the white rioters and died—Josh Halsey and Dan Wright. In *Hanover*, A. L. Manly and Dan Wright are modeled and named after real people. Moreover, Fulton scantily veils other figures who remain easily identifiable: Mrs. Fells is Rebecca Felton, the Colonel is Colonel Alfred M. Waddell, Officer Bunts is Robert H. Bunting, and Reverend Jose is the Reverend Peyton H. Hoge.

A more significant distinction between Fulton and Chesnutt's dramatizations of the riot is ideological and involves each writer's treatment of violent resistance as a response to the white assault on the African American community in Wilmington. As we have seen, despite the sympathetic portrayal of the militant Josh Green in *Marrow*, it is William Miller who survives as the embodiment of what Chesnutt sees as the most rational and constructive posture for blacks to assume. In contrast, the opening words of *Hanover* manifest Fulton's forthright endorsement of black militancy and open protest: "I will not retract! No! Not a single sentence!"[25] The speaker here is the *Record* editor, Alexander Manly, whose response to Rebecca Felton caused an uproar in the months preceding the riot. While whites think Manly "too *high strung, bold and saucy*" and many blacks feel "a little shaky over his many tilts with editors of the white papers," Fulton approves his actions wholeheartedly: "The Spartan who without a tremor held his hand into the flames until it had burned away was not more a subject of supreme admiration than the little Octoroon editor" (13, 12).

The fulsomeness of Fulton's praise is even more striking when juxtaposed with the corresponding allusions to Manly in Thomas Dixon's *The Leopard's Spots* (1902), one of the most popular and most racist novels of its day, and *The Marrow of Tradition*. In the former, the white Southerner Dixon condemns Manly's editorial for "defaming the virtue of the white women of the community" and sees it as but another example of "Negro insolence." To Dixon, the subsequent white violence is simply the inevitable reflex of a dominant race pushed beyond the limits of its patience.[26] In *Marrow*, when the local *Afro-American Banner* publishes a harsh attack upon whites, Miller considers it "ill-advised"; he thinks, "It could do no good, and was calculated to arouse the animosity of those whose friendship, whose tolerance, at least, was necessary and almost indispensable to the colored people" (277).[27] Unlike Dixon and Chesnutt, Fulton depicts Manly at the outset of *Hanover* as living up to his name, as epitomizing an entirely admirable black male courage.

Both Chesnutt and Fulton recognized the extremely limited degree to which they could count on a white audience to judge their black male characters by conventional standards of manhood. In *Marrow*, for instance, Chesnutt has Miller ruefully observe,

> The qualities which in a white man would win the applause of the world would in a negro be taken as the marks of savagery. So thoroughly diseased was the public opinion in matters of race that the negro who died for the common rights of humanity might look for no meed of admiration or glory. . . . Or, if forced to admire, they [whites] would none the less repress. They would applaud his courage while they stretched his neck, or carried off the fragments of his mangled body as souvenirs, in much the same way that savages preserve the scalps or eat the hearts of their enemies. (295–96)

Fulton makes a similar point in an article written in 1899: "The title of 'desperado,' 'Negro murderer,' is very easily obtained in the South. To strike back in his own defence, even to save his own life, has made the Negro an outlaw in the South and put a price upon his head."[28] Nonetheless, in contrast to Chesnutt's ambivalence toward Josh Green in *Marrow*, Fulton's evaluation of similar characters is consistently enthusiastic. Thus, he lauds Dan Wright, who is brutally butchered after arming himself and confronting the whites alone. Fulton even goes so far as to rank "this immortal hero" with, among others, Daniel Boone, Napoleon, Nathan Hale, Robert Smalls, John Brown, and Nat Turner (85). A related figure is an unnamed black boy who, after being shot by the mob, explains in his last breath, "I tol' um I'd die foe I'd giv' up ma gun." Fulton terms him "the little hero" and notes how even the whites respect his "brave heart" (89).[29]

Despite the divergent ideological paths that these two novelists take in their fictional representations of the riot, Chesnutt and Fulton ironically end up caught in the same conceptual mire in their attempts to dramatize the possibility of black male heroism. At first glance, Chesnutt would seem to have deftly avoided this trap by sympathetically depicting Josh Green while ultimately endorsing the cautious path taken by William Miller. Nonetheless, he finds himself judging his black male characters by mainstream norms of behavior, norms derived from culturally determined assumptions regarding the proper male response to threats. Thus, to Chesnutt, the black townsmen reacted to attack in a largely cowardly fashion: "The negroes of Wellington, with the exception of Josh Green and his party, had not behaved bravely on this critical day in their history; but those who had fought were dead, to the last man" (316). Because Fulton is more committed than Chesnutt to maintaining the value of black courage, he finds such an admission extremely painful to make, even as he rejects outright the implication in Chesnutt's final extenuating clause that such resistance means little. In his celebration of Dan Wright, Fulton confronts this issue directly: "Died Dan Wright as a fool dieth? Was it right for him to stand alone against such fearful odds? Yes, that the chronicler in recording this terrible one-sided fight might be able to mention one act of true bravery; that among so many cowards there was one man" (85). Fulton would doubtless second a statement made in 1899 by Bishop Alexander Waters, the president of the Afro-American Council: "I have come to the conclusion that nothing but manly resistance on the part of the Afro-Americans themselves will stop these atrocities." Or as Ida B. Wells put it in 1892, "Nothing, absolutely nothing, is to be gained by a further sacrifice of manhood and self-respect."[30]

The problem for Fulton, of course, is that so many of the black males in Wilmington simply did not emulate Wright's example. Perhaps the most striking case is that of Alexander Manly himself, whose defiance sets the tone at the beginning of Fulton's novel. In *Marrow*, Chesnutt could quite dispassionately write, "The editor of the Afro-American Banner, whose office had been quietly garrisoned for several nights by armed negroes, became frightened, and disappeared from the town between two suns" (249). In *Hanover*, Fulton has a white character report that "the editor took time by the forelock and made good his escape," a milder rendering of Manly's flight, although still a far cry from the courage this figure displays earlier in the novel (102).[31]

Fulton's dilemma finds fascinating articulation in a meeting of black bourgeois women in *Hanover*. One of the women argues that "colored men must show their manhood, and fight for their rights." In response, Mrs. West, Wilmington's most prominent black woman, asks the question that haunted African American writers who sought to celebrate black male heroism, as traditionally defined, in a context that often precluded constructive resistance: "But how are they to do it? . . . My son tells me that there is not a store in the city that will sell a Negro an ounce of powder. The best thing to do . . . is to stay in our homes, and advise the men to be cool. Rashness on their part would be all the excuse the unprincipalled [sic] whites would want to kill them" (47). In a wrenching personal narrative written after the riot, the real-life African American minister J. Allen Kirk describes the humiliating dilemma to which Fulton's fictional Mrs. West alludes:

> Men stood at their labor wringing their hands and weeping, but they dare not move to the protection of their homes. And then when they

passed through the streets had to hold up their hands and be searched. The little white boys of the city searched them and took from them every means of defence, and if they resisted, they were shot down.

Colored women were examined and their hats taken off and search was made even under their clothing. They went from house to house looking for Negroes that they considered offensive; took arms they had hidden and killed them for the least expression of manhood.[32]

Appreciating the limited options available to most black men in Wilmington, however, does little to simplify Fulton's attempt to cast the behavior of individual African American males in a favorable light. For instance, when he presents in *Hanover* a fictionalized version of this same Reverend Kirk (he calls him "Reverend Selkirk"), how does Fulton expect readers to judge the man's decision to hide in the woods after learning that he has been targeted for death by the town's whites? Only sheer chance, we discover, saves his wife from "revolting indignities" at the hands of the mob (99). Then, after returning and finding his family safe, Selkirk permits his congregation to convince him to go North alone.

Equally vexing for Fulton is the case of Nicholas McDuffy, who also leaves his family behind. This behavior contrasts sharply with Fulton's earlier description of McDuffy's courage—not only as a fireman, but also as a police officer who once risked his life to arrest some rowdy whites. After listing the exploits of this "man without fear," Fulton points out, "I write the above that the reader may know what manner of man this was who was compelled to leave his home, his wife and little ones and flee for his life" (106). The awkward defensiveness of this comment reveals the difficulty that Fulton has in justifying McDuffy's actions.

It would be inaccurate to presume that Chesnutt is insensitive to this issue, if, for no other reason, because he was such an astute observer of the human condition. What is clear, however, is that he ultimately chooses to locate the narrative focus of his novel elsewhere. That is, having established the irreconcilable differences that prevent Green and Miller from arriving at a collaborative strategy for responding to the white onslaught, Chesnutt turns his attention to the relations between blacks and whites in the city, as enacted in the charged exchanges between the Millers and the Carterets in the novel's final pages. As we have seen, however, the distinctive approaches that Chesnutt and Fulton take in their novels occasionally converge in some revealing ways. Here, despite their differing attitudes toward black male militancy, both authors highlight the role of African American women at the climaxes of their narratives.

In Chesnutt's case, after exploring at length the ideological rift between Green and Miller, he ultimately establishes the most morally appealing heroic agency in neither man, but rather in Janet Miller, who can overlook past wrongs and, at the last, proudly make the altruistic, noble, merciful choice. Although this gambit ties up many of the threads of the novel's convoluted plotlines, it also represents Chesnutt's attempt to shift his examination of racial oppression from an explicitly political context to an ostensibly apolitical one. The tactical advantage to be gained thereby was clear to the *New York Times* reviewer who observed that "the book closes leaving the moral victory to them [the blacks]."[33]

In constructing a resolution in *Marrow*, Chesnutt falls back on a well-established African American literary strategy—that of depicting blacks as morally superior to their white oppressors. In practical terms, this approach entails, first, the death of the Miller child. And the fact that Chesnutt presents the killing as the result of an apparently random act relieves William Miller of having to confront a personal embodiment of white violence.[34] Second, Chesnutt depicts the Millers as rising above resentment and anger to help save the Carteret offspring. Here again, Chesnutt preempts the crisis of agency that has dogged William Miller throughout the novel. That is, in arranging for Janet to argue for forgiveness and leniency, Chesnutt can salvage William's male dignity. After all, as a bourgeois Christian woman, Janet can display such softness and generosity without condemnation. William's decision to help the Carterets can thereby be viewed as a demonstration of husbandly love, not as evidence of unmanly self-abnegation in the face of white authority. William's yielding to Janet's wishes in this matter also diffuses his only moment of real rage in the novel, a moment that threatens to deform the bourgeois mask of reason, optimism, and self-control. Chesnutt manifestly cannot afford to let this veneer crack.

Early notebook outlines of *Marrow*'s plot suggest that Chesnutt considered at least two other endings for the novel. In the first, Miller saves Carteret's child and is promised safety in return. Chesnutt writes, "He declines—does not want protection but wants the rights and opportunities of a man." In the second, Janet Miller participates in the dramatic resolution, and there is no mention of "rights and opportunities." This latter sketch differs from the published novel in that at the end, the Millers leave Wellington in despair, traveling in a Jim Crow car.[35] There is also the intriguing possibility that Dr. Miller's portrayal owes something to the case of Thomas C. Miller, a light-skinned, successful black Wilmington businessman who spent the night of the riot in jail after allegedly swearing that he "would wash his hands in some white man's blood."[36] The following morning, he and other African American leaders were escorted to the train station and exiled from the city. If Chesnutt had remained true to his own initial impulses or to the story of Thomas Miller, the bleak, almost nihilistic tone that already dominates the final third of *Marrow* would have colored the book's resolution as well. And if the critic William Dean Howells found the novel as published to be "bitter, bitter," one can only guess what his horrified response to *Marrow* would have been had it had one of these alternative closing scenes.[37]

Although Fulton focuses, as does Chesnutt, on interracial dynamics in Wilmington, the dramatic drive of *Hanover* is primarily centripetal. It forces the reader to attend more consistently than does *Marrow* to the intraracial reverberations of the white violence within the black community and, most movingly, to how what Fulton terms "the demoralization of colored men" affects the black family (129). This crisis is most effectively rendered in the depiction of Bill Sykes, a crippled black carpenter and shopkeeper who can no longer support his family. Reduced to a childlike dependence upon his wife, Henrietta, this once proud man responds to the riot by "hanging on to her skirts like a babe" (129). Although Sykes is an extreme case of the black man's impotence in the face of white violence, his wife draws an explicit parallel between her own situation and that of all black wives in Wilmington: "The burden upon . . . [my] shoulders is indeed heavy; but, then, our men are unable to protect us, anyway, so great are the odds against them" (129). After the riot, Sykes decides to move north not only because of the superior medical care available there but because his family will be less vulnerable to assault; he tells a white Wilmington politician, "I'm not goin' ter stay in er place where a d—n scoundrel can insult ma wife an' I can't pertect her" (131). Unfortunately, like the Hamilton family in Dunbar's *The Sport of the Gods*, Sykes discovers that the North is not the utopia he expects. Both racist labor unions and his infirmity prevent him from finding work, and he must depend upon his wife's industry. When, in a moment of weakness, Sykes gingerly suggests that the family return to Wilmington, Fulton depicts the black woman once again as the source of strength and resolve; Henrietta fiercely declares, "If you wish to go back to that hell, I'll put you on the train and you can go; but I, never! Life is not so easy here, but I can walk the streets as a lady, and my children are free to play and romp without fear of being killed for accidentally or purposely treading upon the toe of a white child. I have been free too long to endure slavery for one moment" (134). In Sykes, Fulton dramatizes what he sees as the black man's tragic inability to fill the role that American society has given to the male head of a family, and the character's physical frailty symbolizes the handicaps that make black men, by conventional definition, "unmanly." (Also notice how Henrietta speaks proper English while Bill speaks in dialect.) As Fulton demonstrates so poignantly in this episode, perhaps the most traumatic effects of the white mob violence in Wilmington could not be gauged by body counts or property losses but rather could be measured in psychological terms.

Standing in contrast to Sykes and reinforcing the pride and steadfastness of Henrietta is Molly Pierrepont, the single most heroic and most complexly depicted character in *Hanover*. In appearance, Molly is a typical nineteenth-century African American fictional heroine: "Though vulgarly called a 'Negress,' her skin was almost as fair as a Saxon's; and because of the mingling of Negro blood—more beautiful in color" (33). The product of a white slaveowner's incestuous relations with his own illegitimate slave daughter, Molly was raised by the aforementioned Mrs. West. With a Hampton degree and substantial musical talent, she seemed destined for a successful, productive future. Unfortunately, she wastes her opportunities and adopts the sheltered life of a kept woman. With the brutal white attack upon the African American community, Molly realizes that she is just as likely a target as any other black, and she rejects her wealthy white lover, who claims that he will guarantee her safety: "*You will stand by your colored girl friend.* Perhaps you think you would, but I doubt it, Ben Hartright. When that time comes that the two races are arrayed against each other, my fair complexion will be of no avail. I am a Nigger, and will be dealt with as such, even by the man who now promises me protection" (38). In this melodramatic yet powerful scene, Molly acknowledges not only her own vulnerability but also the immorality of her present situation, which she finds particularly indefensible when she sees the upright men and women whom the whites have marked for death. She sends Hartright away and declares, "But *here I swear from this hour Molly Pierrepont will live no longer such a life*" (39).

Inspired by her reawakened race loyalty, Molly moves to warn the community of the imminent attack, and she does not hesitate to use force to accomplish her ends. For example, just after witnessing the humiliation of a black man who made "a futile protest against being searched," she physically routs a gang of white boys who try to strip her (81). When they are reinforced by some men, Molly alludes directly to the fact that she, as a black woman, must look to her own protection: "Cowards! . . . Not satisfied at the cutting off of every means of defense from the black men of Wilmington, that you may shoot them down with impunity, you are low enough to take advantage of their helplessness to

244

Richard
Yarborough

insult weak women." At this point, she is so unladylike as to draw a pistol on her assailants, declaring, "I'll be a target for the whole of you before I'm searched; so let the battle begin" (82). Following the riot, Pierrepont's redemption is completed with her religious conversion in New York City.

By focusing upon Molly Pierrepont and the Sykes family in the last four chapters of *Hanover*, Fulton dramatically underlines the extent to which he perceived black women as having stepped in to fill the roles mainstream society defines as typically male. As both Thomas Cripps and William Gleason point out, it is hardly coincidental that Fulton dedicates *Hanover*, one of the most thoroughly militant and feminist novels by an African American male at the time, to Ida B. Wells.[38] The reference to Wells is even more significant when we recall that in mid-1892 she was forced to leave Memphis after her newspaper, *The Free Speech*, published an editorial protesting the lynching of blacks. Like Alexander Manly and, before him, the African American editor J. C. Duke of Montgomery, Alabama, she had aroused the wrath of local whites by suggesting that sexual contact between white women and black men (or "white Delilahs" and "poor blind black Samsons," as she termed them) often occurred by mutual consent.[39]

Concerned as *The Marrow of Tradition* and *Hanover* are with the issue of black heroism and racial victimization, it is appropriate that the shadow of Harriet Beecher Stowe hangs heavily over both novels. For example, Houghton, Mifflin and Company chose to promote *Marrow* by linking it with *Uncle Tom's Cabin*, the extraordinarily successful (and profitable) novel that served to raise to archetypal status the image of the passive, victimized black male. On one occasion, the publishers informed Chesnutt, "There is to be a splendid production of *Uncle Tom's Cabin* in the Boston Theatre for the next two weeks and beside the regular advertising, we are taking a page in their programme connecting your book with *Uncle Tom's Cabin* in such a way as to encourage sales of it, we hope."[40] Chesnutt himself even expressed a desire that *Marrow* "become lodged in the popular mind as the legitimate successor to *Uncle Tom's Cabin* and [Albion Tourgée's novel] *A Fool's Errand.*"

One is struck not that Chesnutt felt obliged to describe *Marrow* in these terms but that he expected this approach to work. The average white reader who approached *Marrow* as a typical plantation tradition tale or as a latter-day *Uncle Tom's Cabin* was in for a serious shock. And Chesnutt was not the only African American intellectual who linked

Marrow with what was probably the most popular political novel of the nineteenth century. In his review of Chesnutt's novel in the *New York Age*, T. Thomas Fortune writes: "It is the strongest work of fiction on the race question published since the appearance of 'Uncle Tom's Cabin,' which it equals in dramatic power and excels in plot situations, technique and literary finish. It would not be surprising if this book should work some such revolution in public sentiment as 'Uncle Tom's Cabin' wrought."[41] Neither Chesnutt nor Fortune is particularly concerned with the ideological similarities between *Marrow* and *Uncle Tom's Cabin*. Rather, what Stowe's book represents is a highwater gauge of the power and influence that a work of fiction focused on race could achieve in the marketplace of ideas in the United States. The dilemma lay in the probability that Stowe's remarkable success and her sentimental representation of black character were inextricably connected.

Stowe's influential novel is a valuable touchstone for Fulton as well. Like Stowe in *Uncle Tom's Cabin*, Fulton depicts almost every woman, white or black, as superior in morality, intelligence, and courage to the male with whom she is associated. In addition, not only does *Hanover*'s subtitle—"The Persecution of the Lowly"—recall that of *Uncle Tom's Cabin*—"Life among the Lowly"—but he has Molly Pierrepont explicitly praise the novel on two occasions. This invoking of Stowe's bestseller might seem incongruous, given Fulton's open endorsement of violence in the face of racist attack. It makes more sense, however, when we note that Molly specifically alludes only to the story of Cassie—that is, to Stowe's dramatization of the sexual exploitation of the black woman, one of Fulton's long-standing concerns (37–38). Uncle Tom himself is never mentioned, and his well-known tactics for coping with oppression certainly never endorsed.

In 1901, the New York black politician Charles Anderson wrote to Chesnutt, praising his achievement in *The Marrow of Tradition*:

> I am very much enamored of the way you handle your materials, without for a moment allowing them to obscure the main purpose of the book—the message. I know many "Doctor Millers" throughout the Southland, but you will forgive me, I know, for confessing hearty admiration for that fellow who rode on the railroad trucks, and who dies, rifle in hand, before the burning hospital. He is certainly one of the many types of which we are in need, as a race. We will never amount to a great deal until we produce a few martyrs, and in my

judgment we can spare a good many A.M.E. ministers to advantage. Thus far in the World's history, the Lord seems to have had but little regard for a people who are at all chary about shedding their own blood, or any other people's blood. He took the Children of Israel out of bondage when they were a lot of whimpering cowards, but he never let them enter the Promised Land until they were brave enough to fight, and stout enough to conquer.[42]

Perhaps to somewhat differing degrees, Chesnutt and Fulton could have endorsed Anderson's sentiments. After all, both writers condemn in their novels a racist white society that destroys African American men who display courage and makes cowards of those who do not wish to die in vain. Unfortunately, what the two men also shared was the limited impact that their books had on the rampant racism of the day.

In Chesnutt's case, his desire to reach a mass white readership may have been doomed from the moment he also committed himself to challenging some of the most deeply entrenched racial attitudes held by that audience. Just after the publication of *Marrow*, Chesnutt wrote to Booker T. Washington about his hopes for the novel:

> I quite agree with you that the medium of fiction offers a golden opportunity to create sympathy throughout the country for our cause. It has been the writings of [Joel Chandler] Harris and [Thomas Nelson] Page and others of that ilk which have furnished my chief incentive to write something upon the other side of this very vital question. I know I am on the weaker side in point of popular sympathy, but I am on the stronger side in point of justice and morality, and if I can but command the skill and the power to compel attention, I think I will win out in the long run, so far as I am personally concerned, and will help the cause, which is vastly more important.[43]

Possessed of more than enough literary skill and certainly "on the stronger side in point of justice and morality," Chesnutt was, in fact, unable to "compel [the] attention" of a white readership that was, for the most part, unable and unwilling to sympathize with African Americans when doing so entailed a discomforting acknowledgment of social responsibility.

In contrast, David Fulton entertained few illusions about the extent to which his political views would permit his attaining popular literary success. In the introduction to his collection entitled *Eagle Clippings*, Fulton proudly relates how a fellow African American once chided him for being "an eccentric on the Race question." With regard to *Hanover* in particular, Fulton recalls, "Many of my friends who listened to the readings, were apprehensive and fearful for my safety, in spite of the fact that I was so far removed from the scene of the awful tragedy which the story relates. Other readers of *Hanover* and other contributions have said with no feigned anxiety, 'Your pen is a very venomous weapon. You are doubtless right; I admire your grit, but you might make it a trifle milder.'"[44] Refusing to moderate his position, Fulton might appear, at first glance, to have selected a more admirable literary path than that taken by Chesnutt. However, if the success of *Hanover* is to be measured in terms of discernible effects on the mainstream discourse around race at the time, Fulton's fictive intervention was as futile as Chesnutt's.

From one standpoint, a close consideration of *The Marrow of Tradition* and *Hanover* may ultimately suggest the limits of political fiction. That is, one can argue that despite Chesnutt's and Fulton's differing literary strategies, both authors attempt to have their texts carry burdens that are simply too heavy for them to bear. However, it might be more fruitful for us to focus not on the absence of obvious results but on the fact that Chesnutt and Fulton dared to enter the literary fray on behalf of African Americans against odds that were as daunting in some ways as those confronting the black community in Wilmington in late 1898. Granted, the protests voiced by Charles Chesnutt and David Fulton may have registered with all too few white readers in their day. Nonetheless, one should overlook neither the possible impact that their narratives and, just as importantly, their bold literary activism might have had on a black audience nor the extent to which the lingering echoes of their work can prove invaluable today as we continue their search for meaningful heroic paradigms with which we might contend for justice.

Notes

I want to express my appreciation to the following individuals, whose responses to this essay have proven invaluable: Frances Smith Foster, Farah Griffin, Jeffrey Rubin-Dorsky, Valerie Smith, Eric Sundquist, Mary Helen Washington, and, of course, the editors of this volume. In addition, my research would have been impossible without the assistance of the staffs at the Wilmington (N.C.) Public Library, the Fisk University Library, the Harvard University Library, the UCLA Library, the Schomburg Research Center, the New York Public Library, the Hampton Institute Library, the North Carolina State Archives in Raleigh, and the Southern Historical Collection of the University of North Carolina Library in Chapel Hill. Finally, I must acknowledge the financial support of the National Endowment for the Humanities, the UCLA Institute of American Cultures, the UCLA College of Letters and Science, and the UCLA Academic Senate Research Committee.

248

Richard
Yarborough

1. See Barbara Foley, "History, Fiction, and the Ground Between: The Uses of the Documentary Mode in Black Literature," *PMLA* 95 (May 1980): 389–403.

2. The single best historical treatment of the Wilmington riot is H. Leon Prather, *We Have Taken a City: Wilmington Racial Massacre and Coup of 1898* (Cranbury, N.J.: Associated University Presses, 1984). Also see Helen G. Edmonds, *The Negro and Fusion Politics in North Carolina* (Chapel Hill: University of North Carolina Press, 1951); Jerome A. McDuffie, "Politics in Wilmington and New Hanover County, North Carolina, 1865–1900: The Genesis of a Race Riot" (Ph.D. diss., Kent State University, 1979); and Herbert Shapiro, *White Violence and Black Response: From Reconstruction to Montgomery* (Amherst: University of Massachusetts Press, 1988).

3. See Edmonds, *The Negro and Fusion Politics*, 165, 148.

4. Kelly Miller, "The Race Problem in the South: A Negro's View," *Outlook*, 31 December 1898, 1061.

5. Harry Hayden, *The Story of the Wilmington Rebellion* (Wilmington, N.C.: n.p., 1936), 2.

6. *Wilmington Weekly Star*, 26 August 1898, 1. Felton was, incidentally, the first woman to become a United States senator. See John E. Talmadge, *Rebecca Latimer Felton: Nine Stormy Decades* (Athens: University of Georgia Press, 1960), and Joel Williamson, *The Crucible of Race: Black-White Relations in the American South since Emancipation* (New York: Oxford University Press, 1984), 124–30.

7. "Race Troubles in the Carolinas," *Literary Digest*, 26 November 1898, 623, 624.

8. *Wilmington Messenger*, 2 November 1898, 6.

9. *Washington Post*, 9 November 1898, 4. One black newspaper rendered the following sarcastic comment regarding the McCauley affair: "The North Carolina white woman who eloped with a Negro during the excitement over the Manly editorial, showed small consideration for the feelings of her indignant brethren, who were vociferously denouncing Mr. Manly as sixteen different kinds of liars" (*Colored American* [Washington, D.C.], 10 December 1898, 4).

10. Rebecca Felton's reaction was predictable: "When the negro Manly attributed the crime to lewd intimacy between negro men and white women of the South, the slanderer should be made to fear a lyncher's rope rather than occupy a place in New York newspapers" (*Washington Post*, 16 November 1898, 8).

11. *Washington Post*, 16 November 1898, 8; *Broad Ax* (Salt Lake City), 31 December 1898, 1.

12. Charles W. Chesnutt to Walter H. Page, 10 November 1898, in Helen Chesnutt, *Charles W. Chesnutt: Pioneer of the Color Line* (Chapel Hill: University of North Carolina Press, 1952), 104.

13. *Brooklyn Daily Eagle*, 5 April 1897, 12.

14. William Andrews notes that Fulton published his first pieces of journalism in the *Wilmington Record*. William L. Andrews, "Jack Thorne [David Bryant Fulton]," in *Dictionary of American Negro Biography*, ed. Rayford W. Logan and Michael R. Winston (New York: Norton, 1982), 589.

15. Ironically, Brooklyn was also the name of a largely black area of Wilmington. (See Prather, *We Have Taken a City*, 21.) That Manly spoke in Brooklyn while African American leader and journalist T. Thomas Fortune thought it unwise to allow him on the stage at a widely publicized protest meeting held two weeks earlier in New York City may indicate the relative militancy of the Brooklyn black commu-

nity. Another example is the extraordinary recommendation on the part of a group of African American ministers in Brooklyn that Southern blacks "arm themselves with guns, knives, pistols and dynamite and sell their lives dearly" (*Brooklyn Daily Eagle*, 15 November 1898, 14). Also see *Brooklyn Daily Eagle*, 2 December 1898, 14, and *New York Evening Post*, 16 November 1898, 1. For more on Fortune's response to the Wilmington tragedy, see Emma Lou Thornbrough, *T. Thomas Fortune: Militant Journalist* (Chicago: University of Chicago Press, 1972), 181–83.

16. W. B. Dodson, "From Porter to Poet," in *Poem: Abraham Lincoln*, by Jack Thorne [David Bryant Fulton] (n.p., n.d.), in Lincolniana 1909, Harvard University Library, Cambridge, Mass.

17. For other examinations of these novels, see J. Noel Heermance, *Charles W. Chesnutt: America's First Great Black Novelist* (Hamden, Conn.: Archon, 1974); Addison Gayle Jr., *The Way of the New World: The Black Novel in America* (Garden City, N.Y.: Anchor/Doubleday, 1975); Arlene A. Elder, *The "Hindered Hand": Cultural Implications of Early African-American Fiction* (Westport, Conn.: Greenwood, 1978); William L. Andrews, *The Literary Career of Charles W. Chesnutt* (Baton Rouge: Louisiana State University Press, 1980); Donald B. Gibson, *The Politics of Literary Expression: A Study of Major Black Writers* (Westport, Conn.: Greenwood, 1981); Dickson D. Bruce Jr., *Black American Writing from the Nadir: The Evolution of a Literary Tradition, 1877–1915* (Baton Rouge: Louisiana State University Press, 1989); William Gleason, "Voices at the Nadir: Charles Chesnutt and David Bryant Fulton," *American Literary Realism* 24 (Spring 1992): 22–41; and Eric J. Sundquist, *To Wake the Nations: Race in the Making of American Literature* (Cambridge: Harvard University Press, 1993).

18. Charles W. Chesnutt, *The Marrow of Tradition* (1901; reprint, Ann Arbor: University of Michigan Press, 1969), 51. Subsequent references to this work will be indicated parenthetically in the text.

19. Compare Miller's contention with this statement by Washington: "I think that the whole future of my race hinges on the question as to whether or not it can make itself of such indispensable value that the people in the town and the state where we reside will feel that our presence is necessary to the happiness and well-being of the community. No man who continues to add something to the material, intellectual, and moral well-being of the place in which he lives is long left without proper reward" (Booker T. Washington, *Up from Slavery* [1901; reprint, New York: Penguin, 1986], 281–82). One significant difference between the two passages is Chesnutt's vague use of the term "power," a word Washington might have avoided in this context.

20. W. E. B. Du Bois, *The Souls of Black Folk* (1903; reprint New York: New American Library, 1969), 222.

21. Eric Sundquist suggests that Josh Green can be usefully viewed as a "figure of folk consciousness" (Sundquist, *To Wake the Nations*, 425).

22. Andrews, *Literary Career of Charles W. Chesnutt*, 194–200.

23. For a discussion of the ways in which Chesnutt altered the facts to fit the needs of his fictional agenda, see Gleason, "Voices at the Nadir."

24. Andrews, *Literary Career of Charles W. Chesnutt*, 180.

25. Jack Thorne [David Bryant Fulton], *Hanover; or The Persecution of the Lowly: A Story of the Wilmington Massacre* (1901; reprint, New York: Arno, 1969), 11. Subsequent references to this work will be indicated parenthetically in the text.

26. Thomas Dixon, *The Leopard's Spots* (New York: Doubleday, Page, 1902), 415.

27. See also *Marrow*, 85.

Richard
Yarborough

28. Jack Thorne [David Bryant Fulton], "The New Orleans Race Riot," in *Eagle Clippings* (n.p., [1907]), 41.

29. In an article on the 1899 race riot in New Orleans, Fulton praises Roland Charles, a black resident who defended himself against the marauding white mob, in similar terms (Thorne, "New Orleans Race Riot," 40–41).

30. *Broad Axe* (Salt Lake City), 9 May 1899, 1; Ida B. Wells, *Southern Horrors* [1892], reprinted in Ida B. Wells-Barnett, *On Lynching* (New York: Arno, 1969), 23.

31. Neither Fulton nor Chesnutt reveals, by the way, that Manly actually escaped Wilmington with the help of a prominent white resident and was able to do so because he was light-skinned enough to pass.

32. J. Allen Kirk, *A Statement of Facts Concerning the Bloody Riot in Wilmington, N.C.* (n.p., n.d.), 10–11.

33. Review of *The Marrow of Tradition*, *New York Times*, 7 December 1901, 939.

34. Bernard Bell notes that in contrast to the Carteret infant, the Miller child remains nameless. Bernard W. Bell, *The Afro-American Novel and Its Tradition* (Amherst: University of Massachusetts Press, 1987), 66.

35. Charles W. Chesnutt, "Plot of Short Story: Race Riot," Charles Waddell Chesnutt Papers, Fisk University Library, Nashville, Tenn.

36. *Asheville Daily Citizen* (North Carolina), 11 November 1898, 1. Also see *Brooklyn Daily Eagle*, 11 November 1898, 2; and Prather, *We Have Taken a City*, 161.

37. William Dean Howells, "A Psychological Counter-Current in Recent Fiction," *North American Review*, December 1901, 882.

38. Thomas Cripps, Introduction, in *Hanover*, vi–vii; Gleason, "Voices at the Nadir," 38.

39. Wells, *Southern Horrors*, 1.

40. Houghton, Mifflin and Company to Charles W. Chesnutt, cited in Helen Chesnutt, *Charles W. Chesnutt*, 175.

41. T. Thomas Fortune, review of *The Marrow of Tradition*, *New York Age*, 21 November 1901.

42. Charles W. Anderson to Charles W. Chesnutt, 11 December 1901, Charles Waddell Chesnutt Papers, Fisk University Library, Nashville, Tenn.

43. Charles W. Chesnutt to Booker T. Washington, 5 November 1901, Charles Waddell Chesnutt Papers, Fisk University Library, Nashville, Tenn. Chesnutt even sent copies of *Marrow* to several members of the House of Representatives.

44. Thorne, *Eagle Clippings*, 3.

Timothy B.
Tyson

Wars for Democracy

African American Militancy and Interracial
Violence in North Carolina during World War II

On 11 July 1943, Governor J. Melville Broughton mounted a podium
beside the Cape Fear River in Wilmington to confront black North
Carolinians about the wartime crisis in race relations. Mob violence in
Detroit three weeks earlier had left thirty-eight people dead. Privately,
Broughton felt it was imperative to take "every step to avoid such con-
tingencies in this state," and publicly he acknowledged in his speech
that many "delicate places as between the races exist in certain places in
North Carolina."[1]

If Governor Broughton was seeking to intimidate black citizens, he
could not have selected a better place to speak than at the mouth of the

Cape Fear, which Democrats in 1898 had threatened to clot with dark bodies. Wilmington had been the shining symbol of Democratic triumph when the "party of the white man" seized power by fraud and by force across the state. Forty-five years later, warning of the same kind of confrontation, the state's leading Democrat singled out for condemnation "radical [black] agitators," impressing upon them the need for a civility grounded in unquestioning acceptance of white domination. Like the Democrats of 1898, Broughton summoned the specter of miscegenation, accusing black activists of "seeking to use the war emergency to advance theories and philosophies which if carried to their ultimate conclusion would result only in a mongrel race." Lest his message be misunderstood, Broughton referred directly to the events of 1898: "Forty-five years ago . . . blood flowed freely in the streets of this city," he reminded his audience. Broughton stood beside the Cape Fear as head of the political party that had orchestrated the slaughter he described: it would have been inconceivable for the black citizens of Wilmington to hear these words as something other than a dire threat.[2]

The white Democrats who overthrew North Carolina's hopeful if halting experiment in biracial democracy in 1898 had indeed relied upon force, not civility. Alfred Waddell, who led the mobs in Wilmington, urged a crowd the day before the election of 1898: "Go to the polls tomorrow, and if you find the negro out voting, tell him to leave the polls, and if he refuses, kill him." Not merely in the Lower Cape Fear, but across the state, armed Democrats kept their opponents away from the polls.[3] Two days later, white mobs raged through Wilmington, leaving black bodies and broken dreams in their wake.

Almost immediately, however, the revolutionaries of white supremacy became the guardians of social order. In North Carolina, the violence of 1898 gave birth to "the spirit of Aycock," as V. O. Key wrote in 1949, which "recognizes a responsibility to [black] citizens who long were unable to participate in their own government."[4] It was the illegitimate and bloody seizure of power in 1898 that gave birth to the state's moderate posture of white supremacy, but it was the resilient and effective nature of that "progressive mystique" that preserved white supremacy. The racial paternalism embodied by Governor Charles Brantley Aycock, one of the leading architects and beneficiaries of the white supremacy campaigns, served to consolidate a social order carved out in murder and violence but preserved by civility and moderation. The racial etiquette that emerged after 1898 featured "patterns of paternalism and accommodation that had to be broken before change could occur."[5] As Governor Broughton's speech in 1943 reminded his African

American listeners, beneath the green ivy of civility stood a stone wall of coercion.

World War II presented fresh political opportunities for African Americans in North Carolina to challenge the social order born at the turn of the century, opportunities that they moved quickly to seize. Even before the United States had entered the war, black North Carolinians began to press for first-class citizenship. From 1941 to 1945, the number of branches of the National Association for the Advancement of Colored People (NAACP) in the state more than doubled, and total membership swelled toward 10,000.[6] Ella Baker, a Shaw University graduate whose radically democratic politics had its roots on her grandfather's farm in Littleton, North Carolina, became the NAACP's national director of branches in 1943 and soon thereafter became midwife to the North Carolina Conference of Branches.[7] Fiery editor Louis E. Austin of Durham's *Carolina Times* published a weekly wartime platform that demanded, among other things, an end to discrimination in the military and in the defense industries, higher wages for domestic workers, the employment of "Negro policemen where Negroes are involved," equal access to the ballot box, and improved housing for black citizens.[8] Black residents in Wilmington jammed city council meetings to insist that the city hire "Negro policemen [who] could be employed in the Negro districts of the city" and to demand that "a place where Negroes might swim at [whites-only] Greenfield Lake be reserved, the place to be supervised by Negroes recommended by Negro citizens."[9] Mayor Bruce Cameron promised concessions but privately complained to Governor Broughton that in Wilmington "the Negroes are ready and willing at all times to go en masse to the court house." The mayor pleaded with Broughton to "tell them as long as you are governor the colored people will have to behave themselves."[10] But official proclamations could not stem the determination of black citizens. "Negroes are organizing all over the state to secure their rights," NAACP official Roy Wilkins wrote after a wartime visit to North Carolina. "They are not frightened."[11]

African American activists in North Carolina first had to fight for "the right to fight." A white physician in Rocky Mount observed that about 80 percent of the black draftees in his community were rejected because "it seemed easier to say IV-F—and send the negro home—and close the case. The army had rather have them in munitions or anything but the army."[12] In Charlotte, a black high school teacher with a master's degree from Columbia University accompanied four of his students to an army recruiting station in 1940 to get enlistment information. Told that the station was for "whites only," he pressed for an explanation. White soldiers beat the teacher severely, breaking his jaw.[13] Fighting for the right to face Hitler, however, was only the first part of the struggle for democracy. "We have to think of the home front whether we want to or not," one black North Carolinian argued. "No clear thinking Negro can long afford to ignore our Hitlers here in America."[14]

The determination of African Americans in North Carolina to confront "our Hitlers here in America" mirrored the attitude of African American activists across the nation. A. Philip Randolph and the Brotherhood of Sleeping Car Porters organized the all-black March On Washington Movement in 1941, which not only foreshadowed the all-black militancy of "Black Power" but also introduced large numbers of African Americans to the Gandhian "disciplined non-violent demonstrations" that Randolph correctly predicted would bring the victories of the postwar black freedom movement.[15] Threatening to bring thousands of black Americans to the nation's capital, Randolph forced President Franklin D. Roosevelt to issue Executive Order 8802, which banned racial discrimination in the defense industries and created the Fair Employment Practices Commission. "One thing is certain," Randolph vowed in 1941, "and that is that if Negroes are going to get anything out of this National Defense, we must fight for it and fight for it with the gloves off."[16]

The international political logic of the war ushered in a global revolution in racial consciousness of which the African American freedom struggle must be seen as a part.[17] "The problem of the Negro in the United States is no longer a purely domestic question but has world significance," Randolph declared in 1943. "We have become the barometer of democracy to the colored peoples of the world."[18] It was Hitler, Roy Wilkins wrote in 1944, who "jammed our white people into their logically untenable position. Forced to oppose him for the sake of the life of the nation, they were jockeyed into declaring against his racial theories—publicly."[19] The Germans air-dropped leaflets in North Africa that depicted police brutality in Detroit; the Japanese highlighted Western white supremacy in propaganda to promote their "Greater East Asia Co-Prosperity Sphere."[20] The distance between democratic rhetoric and American reality—and the fact that race relations in the United States had become a significant pawn in the international struggle—gave wartime black activists new leverage.

African Americans wielded these contradictions like weapons of war. Randolph, at the time the most influential black political figure in America, argued in 1943 that there was "no difference between Hitler of Germany and Talmadge of Georgia or Tojo of Japan and Bilbo of Mississippi."[21] The black press beat the drum for "Double V" campaigns beneath banners urging Americans to "Defeat Mussolini and Hitler By Enforcing The Constitution and Abolishing Jim Crow." Black citizens responded; circulation of African American newspapers increased by 40 percent during the war.[22] Ella Baker set out "to place the NAACP and its program on the lips of all the people . . . the uncouth MASSES included."[23] NAACP membership grew nearly 900 percent during the war, and the number of branches tripled, three-quarters of the new branches in the previously sluggish South.[24] The Congress of Racial Equality pursued nonviolent direct action campaigns in Northern cities that laid the groundwork for the organization's important campaigns of the 1960s.[25]

In North Carolina, University of North Carolina sociologist Howard Odum reported, the arrests of numerous young black men for defying lunch counter segregation reflected a mood of African American insurgency that terrified white North Carolinians, whose fears about the racial consequences of the war bordered on the paranoid. One rampant rumor asserted that "the Negroes were buying up all the icepicks" in the state and "waiting for the first blackout to start an attack."[26] Perhaps because these rumors resonated in the recesses of memory where slave insurrections and the mythical "black brutes" of Reconstruction once dwelled, whites could not see the ludicrous humor in their image of a black guerrilla army wielding icepicks in the dark, overrunning a state whose borders contained tens of thousands of white soldiers with machine guns and armored tanks. Another fearful murmur along the white grapevine asserted that the state police had "raided a Negro church in which was found an arsenal of firearms and ammunition" intended for a black revolution. Less refutable—and thus perhaps even more chilling—was the rumor that black North Carolinians were mail-ordering massive amounts of munitions from the Sears, Roebuck catalogue.[27]

Not all white fears rested upon mere rumor. In 1942, Jonathan Daniels, whom President Roosevelt had selected as his chief adviser on race relations, wrote to the head of the National Urban League to express his alarm at "the rising insistence of Negroes on their rights now" and "the rising tide of white feeling against the Negroes in the South and other sections." Daniels feared both "bloodshed at home" and "material for dangerous anti-American propaganda abroad." Black demands were "logically strong," he conceded: "If we are fighting for democracy and human freedom, it is logical to insist that our pretensions in the world be proved at home."[28] But Daniels was willing to go only so far; he could see the racial crisis only as a problem of silencing black protests. "We thought we had to get a little justice to keep [black citizens] in line," he recalled years later, evoking images of fierce African predators: white liberals like himself, seeking to stop black protests, he said, only wanted to "throw a little meat to the lions."[29] So powerful was the legacy of 1898 that, fifty years afterward, white supremacy still could not be challenged among North Carolina's elite; conservatives differed from liberals largely on the question of whether white supremacy was best defended with raw coercion or with paternalist civility. Liberals like Jonathan Daniels firmly believed in the latter, and they proved to be right.

In part, Jonathan Daniels's apocalyptic sense of the nation's growing racial conflict rested upon a broad bedrock of fact: his post in Washington required him to collect information pertaining to racial tensions across the country. But his anguish flowed also from a source closer to home and closer to heart. After years as editor, Daniels had left the *News and Observer* to the management of his older brother, Frank Daniels, and had accepted the post as adviser to the president. In the summer of 1942, Jonathan Daniels received an angry letter from his brother attacking him for being "in with all the pinkeys and liberals tied up with advancement for the Negro race." "The situation here in Raleigh regarding the feeling of the white people toward the more or less new ideas of negroes," Frank Daniels wrote, "is really alarming." If black Americans continue to "keep on insisting for more privileges," he warned, "a worse condition is going to exist in North Carolina before very long than [in] the period from 1895 to 1902, because white people just aren't going to stand for it." This was a threat that every black and white North Carolinian would have understood, and few better than the Daniels brothers. It required little explanation: Josephus Daniels, father of both men and still the Democratic elder statesman of North Carolina, had played a key role in the white supremacy campaign at the turn of the century, returning the state to what the father celebrated as "permanent good government by the party of the white man." If African Americans continued to press for "equality," Frank Daniels told his brother, "the white people are going to rise in arms and eliminate them from the national picture." Lest there be any confusion about his meaning, the state's most influential publisher warned that the black effort for racial advancement "is going to mean that all of [the blacks] that can read and write are going to be eliminated in the Hitler style."[30]

Words spoken in anger and in private, perhaps, but given this passionate depth of opposition among Southern elites, it is not surprising that white liberals and upper-class black leaders appreciated the benefits of caution even as they moved to address the growing crisis of race. In 1942, Jessie Daniel Ames, the white president of the Association of Southern

Women For The Prevention of Lynching, and Gordon B. Hancock, a conservative black sociologist at Virginia Union College in Richmond, organized the Southern Race Relations Conference. Black college presidents, business leaders, and clergymen met in Durham to confront the ways that the war "had sharpened the issue of Negro-white relations" and reopened "the basic questions of racial segregation and discrimination, Negro minority rights, and democratic freedom." The resulting "Durham manifesto" did not bluntly advocate the outright abolition of segregation, but instead envisioned "in the South a way of life consistent with the principles for which we as a nation are fighting throughout the world."[31] White "moderates" responded favorably, and sixty-six Southerners—thirty-three black, thirty-three white—met secretly in 1944 to found what would become the Southern Regional Council, an interracial organization that would play a significant role in the coming decades of struggle.[32]

Not all wartime resistance to white supremacy in North Carolina was as decorous and sedate as the Durham gathering. As Northern blacks poured into military training camps across the South and as Southern black soldiers took up arms for their country, they inevitably collided with Jim Crow.[33] North Carolina, which had more training camps than any other state, was hardly exempt from such collisions.[34] On 6 August 1941, a furious gunfight near Fort Bragg in Fayetteville left one black soldier and one white military policemen dead; five other soldiers were wounded in a clash over seating arrangements on a bus. Afterward, the provost marshal ordered all black soldiers who were not in their barracks rounded up and herded into the stockade. Angry white guards beat many of the men and the MPs forced more than 500 black soldiers to stand all night with their hands above their heads, even though most had been nowhere near the shooting.[35] Secretary of War Henry Stimson wrote to NAACP leader Roy Wilkins that "in no respect did the incident itself, or its after-effects, acquire any semblance of a conflict of racial sentiments."[36]

Whatever Secretary Stimson might say, few of the military training camps in North Carolina escaped serious racial tensions and many experienced severe interracial violence. At Camp Sutton, near the town of Monroe in the western Piedmont, racial fights were practically a daily affair and larger clashes commonplace. E. Frederic Morrow, later the first African American presidential aide, under President Dwight D. Eisenhower, remembered Monroe as a "racist hellhole." "Every payday," Morrow recalled, "trucks and M.P. vans drove up to our area and dropped off the bloody, beaten hulks of [black] men who had run afoul of the lawmen in Monroe." The violence frequently carried a sexual subtext; white police beat African American soldiers, according to Morrow, because the black men were "thought to be rapists or 'social equality' seekers, and they had to be kept in their place."[37]

Most of the racial violence in Monroe consisted of white police officers beating individual black soldiers. But black soldiers frequently fought back. On 22 September 1943, according to a War Department investigation, when military police tried to arrest a black soldier, "a disturbance occurred at the Negro Service Club at Camp Sutton which threatened to assume riot proportions." A mob of black soldiers fought the MPs, and "shouts were heard from the colored soldiers that 'We may as well die here as over there.'" Authorities considered the affray not "evidence of a planned outbreak but rather further evidence of the volatile character of the general Negro situation."[38]

Editor Roland Beasley of the *Monroe Journal*, a well-known liberal Democrat, claimed that "though the Negro has in this country every right and opportunity that a white man has . . . the agitators are fanning the flames." Despite "white only" signs posted all over town and glaring racial inequalities of wealth and privilege, white editors insisted that "no man can deny that the white majority is seeking honestly and earnestly" to achieve racial justice. The problem, they argued, was that African Americans sought "amalgamation"—the old "social equality" bugaboo. "The races are distinct and that fact may as well be recognized," Beasley declared. "The white race can amalgamate with the black only by committing suicide and any arrangement which tends to encourage amalgamation cannot be encouraged." While the editor remained unwilling to endorse "mob violence, the Ku Klux Klan, or in any way cheating the Negro," racial lines must be preserved inviolate. At bottom, Roland Beasley maintained, the race "problem" was rooted in the biological reality that justified white supremacy: "No one could doubt that upon the whole the white race is superior to the black." Anyone who might "suppose that the two races can mingle socially without restriction" and "have no race riots," Beasley asserted, "is foolish."[39]

If "race-mixing" caused riots, as white editors in Monroe claimed, segregation apparently did little to prevent them, at least not in the wartime South. In late 1943, an intelligence report indicated that "colored soldiers . . . stationed at this post were gathering live ammunition for the purposes of retaliating against taxicab and bus drivers." When military authorities searched several black enlisted men from Camp Sutton, the inspection "resulted in the recovery of substantial amounts of ammunition" and other weapons. Though authorities uncovered this particular insurgency, black resistance to ill treatment and racial discrimination persisted. In a letter to Jonathan Daniels, Federal Bureau of Investigation Director J. Edgar Hoover described a racial clash on 8 February 1944 in which "350 Negro soldiers from Camp Sutton resisted military police as well as civilian authorities," injuring several soldiers and police officers. Hoover blamed the fracas on "friction which has been existing between Negro soldiers and white officers." A few weeks later, the white commanding officer at Camp Sutton was "struck in the back of his head by a Negro private" with a bottle and "had to have stitches in his head." An informer among the black trainees reported that "the Negro enlisted men were planning a concerted program of insubordination."[40]

In the summer of 1944, four black soldiers from Camp Sutton walked into a cafe in nearby Concord and asked to be served. "They were told that colored persons would not be served and they started to leave," a War Department investigator reported. "As they were leaving, a white patron also left and as he started out he shoved one of the Negroes telling him to get out of his way." The black soldier whipped out a knife and stabbed the white man. When the white counterman jumped into the fight, the soldier stabbed the second man as well, killing him. A white lynch mob assembled outside the cafe, but the black soldiers outran them. "The soldiers made their getaway," the report stated, "but had the town's inhabitants caught them undoubtedly they would have been lynched."[41]

One of the closest white observers of wartime racial politics, University of North Carolina sociologist Howard Odum, reported in 1943 on "a surprisingly large number of the ablest and best Negro leaders who had concluded sadly that it might be necessary to 'fight it out,'" and "a growing hatred on the part of many Negroes for the whites."[42] At times, the observation seemed self-evident, particularly in relations between black citizens and law enforcement officials, whom white citizens relied upon to preserve racial etiquette. In Kershaw, North Carolina, for example, a black army sergeant named Smith inquired at the police station about the arrest of one of his men. Apparently, Sergeant Smith's tone or manner somehow violated the code of deference that governed race relations. A white police officer threw Sergeant Smith into a cell, struck him, and then shot him in the leg.[43] "The police can handle these [African American] bad eggs quite handily," one North Carolina editor wrote, "if the uplifters—i.e. social workers and those who think like them—don't barge in. A zoot-suiter should be no great problem."[44]

But the police were not always able to contain black anger over police brutality. In 1943, after white officers first shot an unarmed black man and then bludgeoned him to death on his front porch in Greenville, a tobacco market town a hundred miles north of Wilmington, "a crowd of Negroes—men and women—assembled and threatened the officer," one of the white policemen testified, until he brandished a pistol and promised to "drop them one by one," waving his gun at the protesters.[45] In a separate incident, "several hundred Negroes at Grifton Saturday night attempted to storm the jail," the *Carolina Times* reported, "and prevent police officers from placing a Negro woman, Mrs. Rosa Lee Picott, in jail on a charge of being disorderly and creating a disturbance."[46] The threads that had held white supremacy together in North Carolina since the Wilmington Race Riot of 1898 were beginning to unravel.

A few weeks later in the mill village of Erwin, North Carolina, twenty-two black men wrote a letter informing Governor Broughton of "the disturbment between the white and colored people, of this town." The men told Broughton that "we can't go up the street at night in peace, they are throwing rock at us and threating us with pistols and rifles." The black community would not endure much more abuse, they warned: "If something don't be done in the furture, evidently someone may be killed." Soon thereafter, Governor Broughton received a letter of explanation from Herbert Taylor, a leading white businessman in Erwin. He acknowledged the incidents of white violence but discounted them as "just a case of some young fellows throwing rocks, following some very insolent remarks having been made by some colored men." The trouble was "nothing but the negroes taking advantages of conditions," Taylor protested, and "little by little easing into things the best they can, under their belief that 'they are as good as anybody else.' "[47]

"Social equality," the euphemism of choice for the ancient taboo of sex between black men and white women, provided at least the rhetorical center of gravity in Southern racial politics during the war. White politicians denounced any manifestation of it, and African American leaders denied any interest in it, but sexual anxiety undergirded all discussions of race. Virtually any self-assertion on the part of African Americans seemed to conjure images of "amalgamation" in the minds of white Southerners. Howard Odum, who examined Southern racial politics in his 1943 *Race and Rumors of Race: Challenge to American Crisis*, ranked this taboo "first and foremost" among white racial fears. Racial hierarchy, "although it reflected the cumulative racial and economic heritage of the South," Odum wrote, "was *primarily* one of sex." Odum felt that this underlying reality barred most discussion of reform among black and white Southerners. "If it were not for the sex-caste foundation," he believed, "it might have been possible to make adjustments."[48]

Even in Chapel Hill, supposedly the enlightened seat of Southern liberalism, "the sex-caste foundation" perched atop pure dynamite. According to a War Department intelligence report entitled "Commingling of Whites and Negroes At Chapel Hill, N.C.," the Reverend Charles M. Jones, a liberal Presbyterian minister, "entertained some members of the Navy Band (Negroes) at his church" on 12 July 1944, along with "some co-eds of the University of North Carolina (white, of course)." The local chief of police reported that "the coeds and negroes were seen walking side by side on the streets of Chapel Hill." A state highway patrol officer claimed that Rev. Jones's teenage daughter "had a date with one of the Negro members of the band on the same occasion and they were seen walking together in a lonely section of the campus late at night." Many members of the Presbyterian congregation "refuse[d] to attend the church so long as the present minister remains," according to the report, but the board of trustees voted four to three to retain Rev. Jones. Among the board members who supported the minister were Dr. Frank Porter Graham, president of the university, and Dr. F. F. Bradshaw, dean of students. The chief of police later "talked with Mr. Bradshaw and pointed out to him the seriousness of the situation if Rev. Jones is not dismissed at once."[49]

Black leaders found it necessary to navigate the treacherous political eddies that swirled around the question of "social equality." Many African American speakers, confronted with the intermarriage question, joked to the effect, "Well, I'm married already myself"—but it was not a question that could be easily laughed off. "It stirs Negroes to ironic laughter," Sterling Brown noted, but "on all levels they recognize that the white man's fear of intermarriage is deep-seated."[50] Six of the fourteen African American contributors to Rayford Logan's 1944 landmark collection *What the Negro Wants* address "social equality" at some length. W. E. B. Du Bois's essay spends four pages on the issue, concluding that "there is no scientific reason why there should not be intermarriage between two human beings who happen to be of different race or color." But Gordon B. Hancock was more typical, arguing that "the social and economic advancement of the Negro has not resulted in greater intermarriage but definitely less."[51] James S. Shepard, the conservative black president of North Carolina College for Negroes in Durham, stated in a national radio address in 1944 that "Negroes do not seek social equality and have never sought it."[52] Across town at the *Carolina Times*, Louis Austin stated his own markedly different views with characteristic candor: "Social equality," Austin declared, perhaps thinking of the Wilmington riot, "is the age-old scarecrow that is always brought out of the attic and dusted off to frighten the weak-minded whenever Negroes ask for better jobs, better wages, better schools, and other improvements." Besides, Austin noted dryly, echoing the words of black editor Alexander Manly in Wilmington half a century earlier, "our streets are crowded with Negroes, the color of whose skin bears testimony to the fact that there are individuals in both races who have been engaging in the highest point of social equality."[53]

Louis Austin's militancy matched the spirit of African Americans across wartime North Carolina, thousands of them newly minted soldiers who defied Jim Crow every day. Black soldiers at Camp Butner flouted the segregation laws as a matter of course. White officials from the bus company that operated the Durham-Butner line complained that black soldiers from the camp made it "utterly impossible" to enforce the segregation statutes.[54] Clashes were common even though the legislature had amended the Jim Crow laws in 1939 to give bus drivers "police powers and authority to carry out the provisions of this section."[55] An African American captain at Camp Butner acknowledged that "our men tipped over a couple of buses because they had to wait while whites boarded first."[56] The chair of the State Utilities Board complained to Governor Broughton that "in spite of the [bus drivers'] efforts to control the [African American] passengers, in many instances it is beyond their power to do so."[57] Local white editors argued that racial trouble in North Carolina "was not home grown" but attributable to outsiders who failed to "conduct themselves in an orderly manner and in keeping with the laws and customs of this section."[58] State officials affirmed this view, blaming the troubles on "Northern negro soldiers at Camp Butner and Northern white officers who do not believe in our segregation laws and encourage the negro soldiers to break them."[59]

On 3 April 1943, that spirit of resistance exploded into a riot in the Hayti section of Durham where many black soldiers from Camp Butner spent their free time. An argument about ration books turned into a brawl between an African American soldier and a white liquor store clerk. The clerk brandished a blackjack and the soldier drew a knife. Their violent scuffle spread into the streets, where white police and then hundreds of African American soldiers and local citizens joined the melee. Rioters hurled bricks, rocks, and hunks of cement, injuring a white bus driver and several policemen. Though local police tried to disperse the men with tear gas, the mob slashed tires, smashed windshields, and demolished storefronts until machine gun trucks and military police units from Camp Butner finally restored order.[60] "Durham is one of the worst places we have, due to the large negro population," one state official reported to the governor afterward. "We have already had some open trouble there and I apprehend that we will have more. It is a bad situation."[61]

As the war for democracy raged on around the world, African American soldiers from Camp Butner continued to battle racial oppression in North Carolina. On a Saturday night in June of 1944, a black private named Wilson had accompanied a comrade from Camp Butner into Oxford, North Carolina, a small tobacco market town thirty miles north of Durham. Walking into a downtown cafe, Private Wilson asked for a beer. Told that there was no beer, the young private tried to buy a package of Lucky Strikes. According to the white proprietor, he informed Private Wilson that "we only serve white patrons." As Wilson and his companion stalked out the door, one of them muttered that the proprietor was a "poor white son of a bitch." Chief of Police H. J. Jackson, eating dinner in one of the booths, ran outside and collared Wilson from behind, clubbing him to the sidewalk with his pistol. Wilson's companion fled back to Camp Butner while Chief Jackson dragged the black private to the jailhouse.

Less than an hour later, sixty men from Camp Butner launched what the *Raleigh News and Observer* called "an unsuccessful effort by a squad of Negro soldiers to storm the Oxford jail and release one of their number."[62] Approaching the double front doors, the soldiers sent two representatives to negotiate Private Wilson's release. Chief Jackson met the men on the steps, slapped one, and jabbed the barrel of his pistol into the face of the other. The two men retreated into the crowd. Chief Jackson ordered the black soldiers to disperse, and police fired tear gas grenades into the crowd, but the soldiers decided to rush the jailhouse doors. Swinging the doors wide, Assistant Chief J. L. Cash confronted the oncoming black mob with a large, tripod-mounted .50 caliber machine gun, "expressly purchased for such a purpose," according to the *Oxford Public Ledger*. Only in the face of certain annihilation did the soldiers scatter and flee.[63]

This near-tragedy was, however, only a prelude to the fiery upheavals that rocked Durham five weeks later. By nightfall on 9 July 1944, smoldering embers and what one reporter described as "a vast spread of destruction" were all that remained of a large downtown section of the city. The charred skeletons of horses and cows sizzled in the ruins; frightened livestock bolted through the streets. Automobiles circled far into the night, bumper-to-bumper and packed with the curious. Authorities dispatched 4,000 soldiers and police officers to fight the flames and stop the looters; bone-weary men labored to restrain throngs of onlookers, some homeless, many angry, who milled along the edges of the destruction. Local newspapers noted that such scenes were not uncommon in a world at war. "The heart of the city," one reporter observed, "might as well have been a section of Berlin or some other European Axis-controlled city after a roaring raid by Allied bombers." As one white woman in Durham stated flatly: "Those niggers burned down a whole block of downtown Durham."[64]

The violence began early on Saturday evening, 8 July 1944, when Private Booker T. Spicely stepped onto a Durham city bus driven by Herman L. Council. Council was short and small, thirty-six years old, an ill-educated white man with "a chip on his shoulder," according to a friend. He was in the habit of driving under the influence of alcohol, though Council denied that he had been drinking on this particular day.[65] Tall and broad-shouldered, the twenty-nine-year-old Spicely had until recently served as the assistant business manager of Tuskegee Institute in Alabama. Spicely mounted the steps in uniform, cradling a watermelon that he was carrying for a five-year-old African American boy he had met at the bus stop. Private Spicely, the little boy, the boy's mother, and another African American soldier all took seats at the front just behind the driver.[66]

When two white soldiers approached the bus at a later stop, Council gruffly ordered Spicely and his companions to move to the rear. Carrie Jackson, the mother, took her son's hand and hurried to find seats in the back of the bus. Private Willie Edwards, the other black soldier, likewise complied. But Spicely demanded to know why he had to move; he had paid his fare, he said, and should be permitted to "sit where he damn well pleased." Furious, Council pointed to the North Carolina segregation law posted close at hand and angrily insisted that Spicely move on back. As the white soldiers clambered onto the bus, Spicely stood up and flashed a broad smile, seeking to enlist their support as fellow soldiers. Wasn't he "just as good to stop a bullet" as they were, he implored? Why should he have to give up his seat? "I thought I was fighting this war for democracy," Spicely told the men. The white soldiers "engaged in good natured banter with Spicely," according to one report, "agreeing with him that, since all were in the same uniform, it was ridiculous that he should make room for them."[67] Confused for a moment, the two white soldiers then made a bold and curious gesture: the pair gingerly made their way to seats in the "Negro section" at the back of the bus. What had begun as black insolence now smacked of social overthrow: first a black man in uniform had defied his place in the social order, and now white soldiers followed suit. The humiliated bus driver unleashed a shower of profanity at the servicemen. Spicely was not prepared to match Council's venom, but as the black private turned to join his white comrades in the back of the bus, he muttered, "If you weren't 4-F, you wouldn't be driving this bus."[68]

Amid the atmosphere of national crusade in the United States in 1944, to be called "4-F"—unfit for military service—impugned a man's worth, his patriotism, his very masculinity.[69] To be shamed by a black man who had just defied his authority in front of a busload of passengers was simply too much for Council. "I've got something that will cool you off," he snapped. Perched on the rearmost bench of the bus, Spicely must have sensed that a perilous line had been crossed. As he prepared to leave the bus, Spicely loudly apologized to the driver, trying to re-enter the traditional dance of deference and civility. "If I have said anything that offended you," he reportedly said, "I am sorry." Spicely then departed the bus quickly by the rear doors. But Council snatched a .38 caliber pistol from beneath his seat and lurched down the front steps to the sidewalk. Stalking to within three or four feet of the soldier, Council shot Spicely twice in the chest, killing him almost instantly. It was 7:40 in the evening.[70]

Before night had finished falling, flames began to crackle and sirens began to wail among the tobacco warehouses downtown. "Great clouds of flame and smoke shot hundreds of feet into the air," the *Durham Morning Herald* reported. "Within a matter of seconds," flames engulfed the Big Four Warehouse, whose wide wooden floors were stacked high with furniture. Four large warehouses, several private homes, Dillard's Stables, Brock Motor Company, and the Avalon Cafe were consumed in the blaze. "An estimated 4000 servicemen, firemen, and civilians battled the fire," according to reporters. Without outside help, the Durham fire chief observed, "there is no telling where the fire might have spread." Flames licked hundreds of feet into the night sky; flaming debris fell into residential yards five miles away. Durham's skyline flickered red but fell otherwise dark, as power failures swept the city. The war for democracy had come home.[71]

Riots like the ones in Durham raged across the nation during World War II; according to the Social Science Institute at Fisk University, blacks and whites fought 242 racial clashes in 47 cities in 1943 alone.[72] On 20 June 1943, ten weeks after the first racial battle in Hayti, Detroit exploded in two days of rioting that left 38 people dead, 676 injured, and $2 million worth of property destroyed. The cataclysm in Detroit both concerned and comforted Governor Broughton. A wave of racial violence in North Carolina and across the South had embarrassed and alarmed the governor; Detroit, at least, was above the Mason-Dixon line. "We have been disturbed by the recent Detroit situation which again reveals that racial problems are not sectional," Broughton wired the editor of *Collier's* magazine. "We are apprehensive that the situation has created a state of mind that may be provocative of other riots in other sections of the country," he continued, "and we are taking every step here . . . to avoid such contingencies in this state."[73]

The simmering focus of Governor Broughton's fears was the city of Wilmington, the port and shipbuilding center at the mouth of the Cape Fear River. Just on the outskirts of Wilmington, racial antagonism in the fishing hamlet of Hampstead struck its flashpoint soon after the Detroit riot. The local sheriff reported to state officials that Hampstead had "reached the point where the white people have now refused to let the colored people come to town after dark." Armed white terrorists controlled the streets of the little coastal village. "Sheriff Brown's situation is very unfortunate," a State Bureau of Investigation report stated. "If he says anything in favor of letting the negroes come back to town, it would be interpreted by the whites as meaning that he was taking sides with the colored people." The sheriff had little help restraining the violence, investigators reported to the governor, because some of his own deputies were themselves engaged in racial terrorism against the black community. "Your agent who is familiar with the people in the community wishes to state that *this information should not be taken lightly*. The nearness of this town to Wilmington might start a general race riot in event that trouble were to start in Hampstead."[74]

It was with these things in mind that Governor Broughton decided to make the christening of a new Liberty ship in Wilmington the occasion for a major pronouncement on race relations. The launching was not in itself a singular event; the Wilmington shipyards produced 126 Liberty ships during the war.[75] But this craft would be the first one named after a black man. Flanked by "conservative and reasonable" black leaders C. C. Spaulding of the North Carolina Mutual Life Insurance Company and Dr. James E. Shepard, president of North Carolina College for Negroes, Governor Broughton noted that the first warship launched here in 1941 had been named for "North Carolina's greatest governor, Zebulon B. Vance"—Confederate governor and enduring icon in state politics after the Civil War. This ship, however, would be called the *John Merrick*. The governor reminded his listeners that Merrick, born a slave, had become "the foremost Negro in North Carolina" by the time of his death in 1919. As a hod carrier and bootblack in Raleigh, Merrick put away enough money to open a barber shop in Durham, where he shined the shoes and cut the hair of "outstanding leaders of the white race." Because of Merrick's "unfailing qualities of courtesy and character," he continued, these white men gave the barber "not charity" but "the benefit of wholesome advice which he was wise enough to follow." Thus Merrick was able to open, in the rear part of his barber shop, the first offices of the North Carolina Mutual Life Insurance Company, which had become, by 1943, the largest black-owned business in the world. Merrick's life proved, according to the governor, "the almost unlimited opportunity for the Southern Negro where the virtues of hard work, honesty, and unflinching character prevail."

Broughton painted Merrick's life not merely as a bootstrap homily, however, but as a cautionary tale about the perils of black political activism. Even though "there were radical Negro leaders in his day even as there are today," Broughton asserted, Merrick had advised against "stirring up racial strife" and had urged his fellow black citizens to save their money and to "be courteous to those that courtesy [is] due." The governor charged that "certain inflammatory newspapers and journals" were now "dangerously fanning the flame of racial antagonism." Black editors and activists "who are seeking to use the war emergency to advance theories and philosophies which if followed to their ultimate conclusion would result in a mongrel race" should watch their step. "Forty-five years ago, in the city of Wilmington, where this launching is being held, there occurred the most serious race riot in the history of North Carolina," the governor reminded listeners, referring to the racial pogrom and political coup d'état by white Democrats in 1898. "Blood flowed freely in the streets of this city, feelings ran riot and elemental emotions and bitterness were stirred." Governor Broughton headed the party that had come to power by the bloodshed he now described; the black citizens of Wilmington could only interpret these words as an ominous ultimatum. But having made himself forcefully clear, Governor Broughton concluded his address with a gesture of the civility that in the years since 1898 had become known as "the spirit of Aycock." North Carolina had "come a long way since that event," the governor added. The Tarheel State could now be proud of its great strides in the field of race relations, which "have been accomplished by harmonious cooperation and mutual respect."[76]

At that very moment, only two blocks from the shipyard where Governor Broughton was delivering his oration, a black woman named Mamie Williamson refused to get off a city bus. The driver sought to have her arrested for violation of the segregation ordinance, but Williamson maintained that she had a legal right to her present seat. According to the police report written by Officers Wolfe and Leitch, Williamson asserted "that she had not done anything but that if the driver would give her money back she would get off and get another bus." The two policemen, aided by the white bus driver, dragged Williamson off the bus. "She was fighting and kicking," Mayor Bruce Cameron reported, "and when she attempted to bite Mr. Wolfe on the hand he slapped her." Officer Leitch then slapped Mamie Williamson also, apparently without the desired effect. "She continued to fight, kicking and biting," according to the police report, "and had to be slapped again." The two men knocked out several of Mamie Williamson's teeth during the struggle. The officers had "used only such force as was necessary to subdue the prisoner and keep her in custody," Chief of Police C. H. Casteen reported to the mayor. "I do not feel that the officers in this case did anything except what they should have done under the circumstances." In a letter to Governor Broughton, Mayor Cameron downplayed the incident: "This is just another case of [those] which we have been having for several months."[77] If Mamie Williamson had somehow obtained a newspaper in jail and read the accounts of Governor Broughton's speech—her own story, like most of the wartime violence in North Carolina, did not appear in the white press—one wonders what she would have thought about the "racial harmony and progress" that the governor celebrated from the platform.

If Broughton's lofty pronouncements of racial conciliation seemed odd amid all the violence, that paradox reflected perfectly the framework of civility that had governed racial politics in North Carolina since 1898. There was a mutually accepted framework for race relations— agreed upon at the turn of the century by white North Carolinians with guns and black North Carolinians without options. So long as African Americans made no overt challenge to white domination, "the spirit of Aycock" prevailed and the violence that had built the reigning social order need not recur; it was peace, but a peace firmly rooted in the triumph of white supremacy. When World War II provided realistic chances for African American citizens to resist white domination, they did so in large numbers, sometimes organized by the local NAACP chapter, more often as groups of friends or defiant individuals who refused to dance for Jim Crow any longer. Black citizens who violated the framework of civility risked the violence that had undergirded it all along, frequently the violence of white police, sometimes the violence of white mobs or individual enforcers along the color line. But even bloodshed could not contain black insurgency much longer; World War II marked a genuine watershed in racial politics in North Carolina and across the nation. When the black veterans that historian John Dittmer has called "the shock troops of the modern civil rights movement" returned to North Carolina, white supremacy would come under two decades of sustained assault.[78] But World War II marked the decisive moment, when African Americans broke away from the decades of patient black institution-building that preceded the war and pointed toward the decades of black political activism that followed it. In 1944, one defiant black soldier from Winston-Salem could already reply to Governor Broughton with great confidence about the shape of the postwar world. "There will have to be a change in the old form of Democracy that has been handed down to my group I mean the colored people," O. E. Clanton wrote to the governor. "If I could bear arms and shed blood for this Great Democracy my people should share in the spoils."[79] The wars for democracy in North Carolina did not end with World War II, but the "old form of Democracy" would never be the same.

Notes

Two students in my 1993 and 1994 seminars at Duke University, Jo Hunt and Tanisha Bostick, uncovered evidential gold mines that completely altered my understanding of the period of World War II in North Carolina, and I am grateful to them for sharing their findings.

1. J. Melville Broughton, "Address by Governor J. Melville Broughton at the launching of the Liberty Ship *John Merrick* at Wilmington, N.C., Sunday, July 11, 1943, 5:15 P.M.," box 82, Race Relations folder, Governor J. Melville Broughton Papers, North Carolina State Archives, North Carolina Division of Archives and History, Raleigh (hereafter, RRF, BP).

2. Ibid.

3. Glenda Elizabeth Gilmore, *Gender and Jim Crow: Women and the Politics of White Supremacy in North Carolina, 1896–1920* (Chapel Hill: University of North Carolina Press, 1996), 110–11 and 271 n. 92.

4. V. O. Key, *Southern Politics in State and Nation* (New York: Knopf, 1949), 209–10.

5. William H. Chafe, *Civilities and Civil Rights: Greensboro, North Carolina, and the Black Struggle for Freedom* (New York: Oxford University Press, 1980), 3.

6. Jeffrey J. Crow, Paul D. Escott, and Flora J. Hatley, *A History of African Americans in North Carolina* (Raleigh: North Carolina Department of Cultural Resources, 1992), 151.

7. Raymond Gavins, "The NAACP in North Carolina during the Age of Segregation," in *New Directions in Civil Rights Studies*, ed. Armistead L. Robinson and Patricia Sullivan (Charlottesville: University Press of Virginia, 1991), 109.

8. Clipping of the masthead from the *Carolina Times*, n.d., box 82, RRF, BP.

9. *Wilmington Morning Star*, 15 July 1943, 5.

10. Bruce Cameron to J. Melville Broughton, 11 August 1943, box 82, RRF, BP.

11. William H. Chafe, *The Unfinished Journey: America since World War II* (New York: Oxford University Press, 1995), 22.

12. Dr. C. T. Smith to Nell Battle Lewis, 26 November 1944, Nell Battle Lewis Papers, North Carolina Department of Archives and History, Raleigh.

13. Roy Wilkins, "It's Our Country, Too," *Saturday Evening Post*, 14 December 1940, 61.

14. Charles S. Johnson et al., *A Preliminary Report on the Survey of Racial Tension Areas* (Nashville: Julius Rosenwald Fund, 1942), 119.

15. Neil Wynn, *The Afro-American and the Second World War* (New York: Holmes and Meier, 1976), 47. For an excellent account of the wartime transmission of nonviolent direct action to large audiences of African Americans by the March on Washington Movement, see Sudarshan Kapur, *Raising Up a Prophet: The African-American Encounter with Gandhi* (Boston: Beacon Press, 1992), 101–23.

16. A. Philip Randolph, "Call To Negro Americans," 1 July 1941, Office File 93, Franklin Delano Roosevelt Papers, Franklin Delano Roosevelt Library, Hyde Park, New York.

17. John Dower, *War Without Mercy* (New York: Pantheon, 1976).

18. *Philadelphia Tribune*, 10 July 1943, 7.

19. Roy Wilkins, "The Negro Wants Full Equality," in *What the Negro Wants*, ed. Rayford W. Logan (Chapel Hill: University of North Carolina Press, 1944), 115.

20. Walter White, *A Man Called White* (New York: Viking, 1948), 260; Dower, *War Without Mercy*.

21. A. Philip Randolph, "A Reply to My Critics: Randolph Blasts Courier as 'Bitter Voice of Defeatism,'" *Chicago Defender*, 12 June 1943, 13.

22. Harvard Sitkoff, "Racial Militancy and Interracial Violence in the Second World War," *Journal of American History* 58, no. 3 (December 1971): 662.

23. Charles Payne, *I Got the Light of Freedom: The Organizing Tradition and the Mississippi Freedom Struggle* (Berkeley: University of California Press, 1995), 88–89.

24. Harvard Sitkoff, "African American Militancy in the World War II South: Another Perspective," in *Remaking Dixie: The Impact of World War II on the American South*, ed. Neil McMillen (Jackson: University of Mississippi Press, 1997), 77.

25. Sitkoff, "Racial Militancy and Interracial Violence," 662.

26. Howard Odum, *Race and Rumors of Race: Challenge to American·Crisis* (Chapel Hill: University of North Carolina Press, 1943), 93, 97.

27. Ibid., 100, 103.

28. Jonathan Daniels to Lester B. Granger, 14 August 1942, Jonathan Daniels Papers, Southern Historical Collection, Wilson Library, University of North Carolina at Chapel Hill (hereafter, JDP).

29. Patricia Sullivan, *Days of Hope: Race and Democracy in the New Deal Era* (Chapel Hill: University of North Carolina Press, 1996), 162.

30. Frank Daniels to Jonathan Daniels, 25 August 1942, JDP. The quote from Josephus Daniels is from J. Morgan Kousser, *The Shaping of Southern Politics: Suffrage Restriction and the Establishment of the One-Party South, 1880–1910* (New Haven: Yale University Press, 1974), 76.

31. "A Basis For Interracial Cooperation and Development in the South: A Statement by Southern Negroes," Southern Race Relations Conference, Durham, N.C., box 82, RRF, BP. The delegates included thirty-seven academics—twenty-two of them college presidents—eight labor representatives, four ministers, and five newspaper editors. Interestingly, the NAACP did not have a delegate.

32. John Egerton, *Speak Now Against the Day: The Generation Before the Civil Rights Movement in the South* (New York: Knopf, 1994), 305–12.

33. See James Albert Burran, "Racial Violence in the South during World War II" (Ph.D. diss., University of Tennessee, 1977).

34. Lindley S. Butler and Alan D. Watson, *The North Carolina Experience: An Interpretive and Documentary History* (Chapel Hill: University of North Carolina Press, 1984), 388.

35. This account is drawn from Burran, "Racial Violence in the South," 46–51. See also Ulysses S. Lee, *The Employment of Negro Troops* (Washington: Center for Military History, 1990), 351; Lou Potter et al., *Liberators: Fighting on Two Fronts in World War II* (New York: Harcourt Brace Jovanovich, 1992), 69–71; Herbert Shapiro, *White Violence and Black Response: From Reconstruction to Montgomery* (Amherst: University of Massachusetts Press, 1988), 306; Sitkoff, "Racial Militancy and Interracial Violence," 668.

36. Henry Stimson to Roy Wilkins, 10 November 1941, NAACP Papers, Library of Congress, Washington, D.C.

37. E. Frederic Morrow, *Forty Years a Guinea Pig: A Black Man's View from the Top* (New York: Pilgrim, 1980), 37–38.

38. "Camp Sutton, N.C. Racial Tensions," JDP, 1–2.

39. *Monroe Journal*, 3 August 1943, 2.

40. "Camp Sutton, N.C. Racial Tensions," JDP, 1–2.

41. Ibid., 2.

42. Odum, *Race and Rumors of Race*, 6–7.

43. Johnson et al. *A Preliminary Report on the Survey of Racial Tension Areas*, 98.

44. *News-Journal and Durham Messenger*, 15 July 1943, 5. Zoot suits, with their baggy trousers, loud colors, and swinging watch chains, became a potent wartime symbol of racial identity and political dissidence. "By March 1942, because fabric rationing regulations instituted by the War Department forbade the wearing of zoot suits," Robin D. G. Kelley writes, "wearing the suit (which had to be purchased through informal networks) was seen by white servicemen as a pernicious act of anti-Americanism—a view compounded by the fact that most zoot suiters were able-bodied men who refused to enlist or found ways to dodge the draft." See "The Riddle of the Zoot: Malcolm Little and Black Cultural Politics during World War II," in Robin D. G. Kelley, *Race Rebels: Culture, Politics and the Black Working Class* (New York: Free Press, 1994), 161–81.

45. *Carolina Times*, 3 July 1943, 1.

46. Ibid., 1 May 1943, 1.

47. Petition to J. Melville Broughton, 27 July 1943; Herbert B. Taylor to J. Melville Broughton, n.d.; both in box 82, RRF, BP.

48. Odum, *Race and Rumors of Race*. While the quotes in the text are from pp. 30–31 and 54–55, Odum's survey finds the idea of interracial sexuality at the center of racial conflict across the region; for more examples of "sex-caste" tension in North Carolina, see also pp. 27–28, 54–57, 61–62, 64–65, 117. The *Raleigh News and Observer*, 5 June 1945, 4, reported that a black man was sentenced to two years on the chain gang for "assault on a female" and "forcible trespass" for making "improper advances" to a white woman over the telephone. The man was accused of trying to persuade a white women to go on a date with him.

49. War Department memo, "Subject: Commingling of Whites and Negroes at Chapel Hill, N.C.," 19 August 1944, Franklin Delano Roosevelt Library, Hyde Park, N.Y. I am grateful to Christina Greene for sharing these and other documents.

50. Sterling Brown, "Count Us In," in Logan, *What the Negro Wants*, 329.

51. Logan, *What the Negro Wants*, 66–69, 233. Logan himself argues on p. 28 that "mixed schools, mixed employment, even social mingling in the more liberal parts of the United States have resulted in very few mixed marriages." F. D. Patterson states on p. 260 that "the argument that the common use of restaurants and public facilities by Negroes and whites will lead inevitably to race admixture has much evidence to the contrary." Langston Hughes, on p. 306, exclaims: "Why [white Southerners] think simple civil rights would force a Southerner's daughter to marry a Negro in spite of herself, I have never been able to understand." Sterling Brown on p. 326 states flatly that "Negroes have long recognized [the sexual question] as the hub of the argument opposing change in their status" but assures white readers that "intermarriage is hardly a goal that Negroes are contending for openly or yearning for secretly."

52. James E. Shepard, "Race Relationships In North Carolina," 17 February 1944, box 82, RRF, BP. In an interesting response to the broadcast, sociologist E. Franklin Frazier of Howard University wrote to Shepard and accused him of supporting "the ignorant and barbarous elements of the South" by "engaging in the old game of southern Negro leaders who have pretended that the Negro feels and believes that he is different from other people and is, therefore, unfit to associate with whites. . . . I believe in *Social Equality*." See E. Franklin Frazier to James E. Shepard, 19 February 1944, box 82, RRF, BP.

53. Crow, Escott, and Hatley, *A History of African Americans in North Carolina*, 147.

54. Stanley Winborne to J. Melville Broughton, 17 June 1943, box 82, RRF, BP.

55. Chapter 147, section 3537, *Laws of the State of North Carolina*, North Carolina Collection, Wilson Library, University of North Carolina at Chapel Hill.

56. Mary Penick Motley, *The Invisible Soldier: The Experience of the Black Soldier, World War Two* (Detroit: Wayne State University Press, 1975), 320–21.

57. Stanley Winborne to J. Melville Broughton, 17 June 1943, box 82, RRF, BP.

58. *Oxford Public Ledger*, 2 May, 5 May 1944, in Hays Collection, vol. 22, 139, Richard B. Thornton Public Library, Oxford, N.C.

59. Stanley Winborne to J. Melville Broughton, 17 June 1943, box 82, RRF, BP.

60. Jean B. Anderson, *Durham County: A History of Durham County, North Carolina* (Durham, N.C.: Duke University Press, 1990), p. 254; *Durham Morning Herald*, 4 April 1943, 1; *Carolina Times*, 10 April 1943, 1–2.

61. Stanley Winborne to J. Melville Broughton, 17 June 1943, box 82, RRF, BP.

62. *News and Observer*, 3 May 1944, 3.

63. Hays Collection, vol. 22, 139, Richard B. Thornton Library, Oxford, N.C.; *News and Observer*, 3 May 1944, 1. See also *Heritage and Homesteads: History and Agriculture in Granville County, North Carolina* (Oxford, N.C.: Granville County Historical Society, 1988), 121. Walter White of the NAACP reported that "a number of Southern cities and towns and a few in the North had invested huge sums in machine guns, grenades, tear gas, armored trucks, and other riot-quelling equipment." See White, *A Man Called White*, 308.

64. *Durham Morning Herald*, 10 July 1944, 1; the last quote is from Jo Hunt, "Beans and Potatoes: Booker T. Spicely and the Bus Driver's Daughter" (unpublished paper, Duke University, 1993, in possession of the author), 4. See also Tanisha Bostick, "One Act of Defiance: Booker T. Spicely's Story" (unpublished paper, Duke University, 1993, in possession of the author).

65. *Durham Morning Herald*, 11 July 1944; according to city records, Council had

been convicted of drunken driving three times. The quote is from Hunt, "Beans and Potatoes," 4.

66. Carrie Jackson testimony, quoted in *Durham Morning Herald*, 12 July 1944, 4.

67. Murray, ed., *The Negro Handbook, 1946–47*, quoted in Herbert Aptheker, ed., *A Documentary History of the Negro People in the United States* (New York: Citadel Press, 1968), 4:538.

68. War Department report, "Subject: Racial Incident, Shooting of Negro Soldier, Durham, N.C. on 8 July 1944 at about 1940," Headquarters Fourth Service Command, 12 July 1944, Franklin Delano Roosevelt Library, Hyde Park, N.Y.; *Durham Morning Herald*, 11 July 1944, 1; testimony by Private Willie Edwards, Catherine Tembers, Corporal Rudolph Hass, Herman Council, and "Miss Fuller," quoted in *Durham Morning Herald*, 10, 11, 12 July 1944. See also *Pittsburgh Courier*, 22 July 1944, 1.

69. See, for example, Allan Bérubé, *Coming Out Under Fire: History of Gay Men and Women in World War Two* (New York: Free Press, 1990), 4.

70. C. Jerry Gates to Thurgood Marshall, "Re: *State v. Herman Lee Council* (for murder of Booker T. Spicely)," 11 August 1944, NAACP Papers, Reel 14, No. 9.

71. *Durham Morning Herald*, 11 July 1944, 1, 18 September 1944, 1; *News-Journal and Durham Messenger*, 13 July 1944, 1.

72. Dominic J. Capeci Jr. and Martha Wilkerson, *Layered Violence: The Detroit Rioters of 1943* (Jackson: University Press of Mississippi, 1991), 87, 90. An excellent short account of the Detroit riot of 1943 can be found in Shapiro, *White Violence and Black Response*, 311–30, 337.

73. J. Melville Broughton to Walter Davenport, 30 June 1943, box 82, RRF, BP.

74. J. F. Bradshaw to SBI Director, State Bureau of Investigation Intra-Bureau Correspondence, 24 August 1943, box 82, RRF, BP. The emphasis is in the original.

75. Hugh Talmage Lefler and Albert Ray Newsome, *North Carolina: The History of a Southern State* (Chapel Hill: University of North Carolina Press, 1973), 624.

76. "Address by Governor J. Melville Broughton at the launching of the Liberty Ship *John Merrick*."

77. Complaint report, Wilmington Police Department, 11 July 1943, 5:10 P.M.; C. H. Casteen to Bruce B. Cameron, 11 August 1943; Bruce B. Cameron to J. Melville Broughton, 11 August 1943; all in box 82, RRF, BP.

78. John Dittmer, *Local People: The Struggle for Civil Rights in Mississippi* (Urbana: University of Illinois Press, 1994), 9.

79. O. E. Clanton to J. Melville Broughton, September 1944, box 82, RRF, BP.

William H.
Chafe

Epilogue from Greensboro, North Carolina

Race and the Possibilities of American Democracy

From the beginning of the American story, race has occupied center stage in the evolving drama of how this community of citizens, sometimes aspiring to be "a city upon a hill," might come close to practicing the civic arts of political democracy. The very notion of "freedom" in the American colonies grew out of and depended upon the reality of slavery, as historian Edmund Morgan has pointed out. Virginia, the home of Washington, Madison, and Jefferson, could envision relative equality of rights among *white men* only because poor yeoman farmers and wealthy plantation masters shared the common bond of white manhood; set alongside the absolute otherness of being black and a slave, or even being a white woman, this white manhood, in a different way, defined citizenship and freedom. White men could thus set aside their differences of class and power and act as though they were free and equal—because their democracy was built on a foundation of racial oppression.

This covenant of paradox constitutes the "original sin" at the heart of America's quest for democracy. It is because the sin is so fundamental—and so morally embarrassing—that throughout our history we have gone to such lengths to obscure it. Jefferson toyed with the idea of facing the truth in early drafts of the Declaration of Independence, but concluded that he could not invoke the rhetoric of natural rights, "inalienable" to "all men," if at one and the same time he acknowledged the existence of slavery. The Founding Fathers continued the deceit, this time using the oblique classification of chattel slaves as "⅗ of a man" for purposes of calculating the constituent base for the new nation's House of Representatives, while once again failing—except for a nod to the inhumanity of the slave trade—to recognize the fundamental contradiction of aspiring to freedom while practicing slavery.

Even the inevitable crusade to escape this original sin more often than not sought rhetorical cover in language designed to evade the real issue. "Free Soil, Free Labor, Free Men" went the slogan heralding the new Republican Party. But rarely did politicians confront the anomaly of racial slavery. Abraham Lincoln, as gifted a writer and orator as ever graced the White House, chose words that circumvented the issue—"a house divided against itself," the rolling King James elegance of evoking "malice toward none, charity toward all"—but no engagement of the terrifying reality beyond the walls of that cloven house.

Interestingly enough, one of the few ways that a white man could acknowledge, at least verbally, the existence of the original sin of race was by imagining—or fantasizing about—the sexual attraction that might exist between black men and white women, arguably the two commodities in the lives of white men about which they might share the same degree of fear and guilt. Psychologists, of course, point to the degree of projection involved, especially in the case of white upper-class men who regularly imposed themselves sexually on women slaves or servants, even as they elevated "white womanhood" to confining heights of supposed purity. "The more trails the white man made to back-yard cabins," Lillian Smith has written, "the higher he raised his white wife on her pedestal when he returned to the big house. The higher the pedestal, the less he enjoyed her whom he had put there, for statues after all are only nice things to look at." The inevitable fears that black men might finally seek revenge—and that white women might even welcome such an initiative—fueled paranoid rumors and pornographic visions of black revolt and black rape, still powerful enough in the white imagination to undergird George Bush's infamous Willie Horton ads in the 1988 presidential campaign.

But beyond that psychological truism there lay a deeper reality—that only through demonizing the oppressed could justification be found for relying on the physical brutality necessary to keep white supremacy in place. If black men were beasts, then it could hardly be wrong to exploit them, to restrain them, even to kill them. Portraying black men as predators provided a language of terror that was essential in order to obscure democracy's original sin.

It thus appears that two basic responses characterized white America's handling of the compelling centrality of race in American history. The first was denial or avoidance, using the forms of democracy to undercut its possibilities and deploying the rhetoric of democracy to disguise the racial oppression at its foundations. The second response was to demonize the victim, using caricatures of black savages and black rapists to rationalize physical terror, should denial or avoidance fail to finesse the contradictions. In effect, the two responses represented mutually reinforcing strategies. Although dramatically different in appearance—burning a black man at the stake clearly conveyed a message quite distinct from denying him the ballot—the object of each exercise was the same.

The essays in this volume testify powerfully to the persistence of America's original sin in North Carolina politics, as well as to the alternating ways in which whites with political and economic power have reinforced the status quo. They speak quite clearly, moreover, to the larger possibilities of American democracy more generally. As all the authors make clear, the use of white terrorism in Wilmington in 1898 represented not an aberration, but rather a decisive and violent intervention to prevent a still deeper confrontation with the betrayal of democracy embodied in the denial of citizenship to the descendants of slaves. No matter how often later generations of white politicians in North Carolina boasted of the state as a progressive example to the South— much like the nation boasted of itself as a beacon of liberty to the world—their rhetoric politely preserved the same social order that the white vigilantes built through the violence of 1898. The two forms of social control that emerged not only coexisted; as Steven Kantrowitz's essay illustrates, each depended upon the other, violence the fist beneath the glove of civility, the instrument of evasion that, in most instances, made unnecessary the invocation of terror. But violence and civility both supported the common end of evading the reality of black citizenship.

The history of North Carolina in the twentieth century has represented a persistent acting out of the racial dynamics depicted here in the story of Wilmington. North Carolina historians celebrate the administration of Governor Charles B. Aycock, dubbing him "the education governor," using his "progressive" leadership to exemplify why political scientist V. O. Key could in 1949 call North Carolina an "inspiring exception to Southern racism"—all the while forgetting, or ignoring, the degree to which Aycock helped to design and inflame the campaign of white supremacy capped by the slaughter in Wilmington and thus to institutionalize the disfranchisement of African Americans in 1900. To this day, leading North Carolina politicians invoke "the spirit of Aycock," hailing him as the leading saint of North Carolina's political past, never acknowledging his role in the white supremacy revolution in Wilmington and across the state.

The Aycock legacy has enabled political and cultural leaders in North Carolina to convey a message to the outside world that I have called, elsewhere, North Carolina's "progressive mystique." The mystique involves a set of ground rules that support the notion of North Carolina as a more civilized, enlightened, and tolerant place than the rest of the old Confederacy. The first rule is one of courtesy to the expression of different ideas—an apparent openness to varied points of view. The second rule is that of consensus—a political community should proceed on a course of action only when everyone signs on. The third rule is that of paternalism—those who are better off must look after those who are less privileged, understanding that this is a responsibility to be shouldered with personal grace and reciprocal deference. What all of this amounts to is a culture of civility, a world characterized by politeness, respect, and an acknowledgment of civic obligation—but firmly based in everyone's accepting his or her "place" and not rocking the boat.

The message of the progressive mystique has advanced North Carolina's image in the nation and promoted its interests as an attractive place to locate a business, a vacation home, or a residence. Witness the extraordinary success of the University of North Carolina at Chapel Hill as a superior public institution of higher learning. Witness, too, the phenomenal flourishing of the Research Triangle Park, North Carolina's answer to the Silicon Valley of California and Route 128 in Massachusetts. Now the home of two of America's top ten banks—NationsBank and Wachovia—and one of its premier private universities—Duke—

North Carolina has attracted the talent, sophistication, and economic resources that journalists and social observers associate with innovative, progressive political economies.

Nevertheless, this same progressive mystique has served as an exquisite instrument of social control, defining the terrain of political discussion in such a way that African Americans, factory workers, and field hands have found it virtually impossible to break through the veil of civility and insist on change. Black citizens continue to be politically isolated, wages in North Carolina continue to stagnate as some of the lowest in the nation, and most of the state's economic growth continues to cluster in metropolitan counties increasingly populated by newcomers. It is not that a homegrown will has not been present. As David S. Cecelski's essay on Abraham Galloway demonstrates, African Americans have been persistent and imaginative in devising ways to demand recognition of their humanity. Yet all too often, the ground rules of the progressive mystique have confined black aspirations even more effectively than the more brutal measures whites elsewhere adopted. Civility has operated to stifle protest or to channel it into ineffectual expressions. White political and economic leaders have given the impression of listening to black concerns; they have even made paternalistic gestures recognizing the existence of problems that should, in the long run but not now, be addressed. But rarely if ever did white leaders permit the infantry of black freedom fighters to penetrate the multiple layers of defense constructed by the progressive mystique. The forces used to repel the insurgents might vary from legal arguments, court decisions, and economic intimidation, on the one hand, to buying off black leaders with patronage and paternalism, on the other. But the mystique held the line.

When the line was truly threatened, however, the ultimate weapons of violence and demonization could always be deployed. For the progressive mystique existed hand in hand with a less attractive but ultimately decisive willingness to use caricature, mass hysteria, fear, and violence to maintain the racial status quo. Timothy B. Tyson's essay on World War II in North Carolina suggests some of the ways that white authorities used violence to contain black expressions of self-determination. As ever, Glenda E. Gilmore and LeeAnn Whites demonstrate in their essays, the most reliable and effective means to justify coercion was to raise the pornographic specter of "miscegenation"—of robust and powerful black men seeking to ravage delicate white womanhood.

Nor was it always necessary to use violence per se in such responses. Merely to evoke the image of "miscegenation" could often suffice to ring the alarm bells that would mobilize a solid phalanx of white resistance to change. Thus, when Frank Porter Graham ran for reelection to the U.S. Senate in 1950 (he had been appointed in 1949 to fill out an unexpired term), some white Democratic leaders, fearful of Graham's support for workers and black citizens, determined to demonize the former University of North Carolina president. Graham himself was too congenial to depict as a raving radical. Instead, supporters of Graham's rival, Willis Smith, suggested that he bore communist sympathies, that he appointed a young black man to West Point over a white competitor, and that he favored "mongrelization" of the races through "social equality." In a literature campaign that reflected the substantial influence of a young and aspiring Jesse Helms, Senator Graham was shown dancing with a black woman. In fact, the head of a black woman had been superimposed on his white dancing partner—his wife, Marion—but the truth never caught up with the fiction. White supremacists cropped other photos to show Graham side by side with black civil rights leaders. The viciousness of the Smith campaign was not of the same order as the brutality inflicted by Aycock's allies at the turn of the century, but it served the same coercive purpose.

How, then, is democracy to be made possible in North Carolina or in America, when the original sin of white supremacy and racial oppression so vigorously eludes confrontation? There have been moments, it seems, when the multiple defenses of the progressive mystique have been breached. One of those came in the aftermath of the sit-in movement of 1960 in Greensboro, North Carolina. The sit-ins themselves represented an ingenious way of confronting the progressive mystique on its own terms. Parents and students had sought repeatedly to find redress for their grievances from the school board and local authorities in light of the *Brown v. Board of Education* decree in 1954. In classic fashion, the Greensboro school board had responded with a gesture— token desegregation of one school—and a policy of resistance toward any further steps. The young black college students who went to Woolworth's on 1 February 1960 to sit down and demand service knew that the moment to assert their own humanity in the simplest terms had arrived. Buying toiletries and paper supplies from other counters in the store, they then took their receipts and asked for identical service at the lunch counter. Wearing white shirts and ties, opening their books to study, the four asked politely for a cup of coffee. Using the civility that represented the progressive mystique to their advantage, they challenged the social and political system to hear a new language of revolt.

Because the manners of the sit-in demonstrators were so refined, because they spoke their message with such calm and quiet eloquence, their antagonists had little room to maneuver and their allies sprang to their aid. So compelling was their tactical brilliance that within two months, sit-ins had occurred in fifty-four other cities in nine different states. The Greensboro "coffee party" played a role in the civil rights revolution comparable to the role of the Boston Tea Party in 1773. And both of them still speak to the best in America's conflicted political heritage. Although not all cities in the South proved as amenable to change as Greensboro, the movement had discovered a form of self-expression that simultaneously demanded change, acknowledged civility, and conformed to some of the most deeply held mores of the larger society.

Still, however brilliant, the Greensboro sit-ins penetrated no further than the outermost defenses of the progressive mystique. Repeatedly in the years after 1960, additional demands for equality in public accommodations, employment, and education encountered polite dismissal or the traditional promise to "look into the question" at some more favorable time. It soon became clear that, once again, a more direct form of expression was necessary. Hence in 1963, along the same lines as the massive demonstrations led by Martin Luther King Jr. and the Southern Christian Leadership Conference in Birmingham, blacks in Greensboro took to the streets. Nearly 2,000 were arrested and incarcerated in an old polio hospital. This time, the demonstrators were not only students but parents and older residents as well, members of the professional class as well as workers. Led by wily strategists represented in public by the young Jesse Jackson, the Greensboro movement used intergenerational solidarity, a willingness to risk arrest, and the threat of total embarrassment to the city's reputation to force new concessions. Under pressures that showed no sign of relenting, the city fathers once more chose to compromise rather than resist.

Yet again, however, once the point of crisis had passed, the defensive lines of the progressive mystique regrouped. Unnecessary delay, endless negotiation, and convoluted plans to provide "freedom of choice" to school children—in fact, a brilliant means of blocking integration—once again dominated discussions of race in Greensboro. Little if anything was accomplished. Under extreme pressure, the status quo had bent only enough to keep from breaking, and the inner citadels of racial inequality remained untouched.

It was in such a context that a new black militancy developed, a militancy that echoed the tradition embodied by Abraham Galloway one hundred years earlier. In Greensboro, the new armies of black self-assertion were led by Nelson Johnson, a veteran who refused to accept second-class citizenship any longer. (Elsewhere, the Nelson Johnsons took the names of a Larry Little in Winston-Salem, a Ben Chavis in Oxford and Wilmington, a Hollis Watkins in Greenwood, Mississippi.) Johnson understood a primary lesson of the years that preceded his leadership: to play according to the rules of the progressive mystique automatically meant to lose the right to self-determination. The rules had been rigged to support and strengthen the status quo. Hence one had to break them and insist on one's own rules in order to penetrate the inner defenses to the core where authentic negotiations could occur. For Johnson, that meant organizing rent strikes among tenants in housing projects, mobilizing high school students to reject paternalism and insist on electing their own student leaders, and refusing to comply with the prevailing etiquette of politeness and civility when dealing with people in power.

In the end, of course, Johnson and his allies proved less successful than they might have wished. The rights of poor people in Greensboro did not materially improve, nor were cafeteria workers able to unionize. But what did emerge was a new measure of fear—and respect—on the part of the white leaders who controlled Greensboro. To be sure, these same leaders called out the National Guard and sent armored personnel carriers into North Carolina Agricultural and Technical College—one of the city's historically black colleges—when that campus was occupied by angry black students. And a student was killed, in all likelihood by a police bullet. But in the aftermath of that violence, in the clear knowledge that Johnson and his allies were not about to retreat, city leaders finally embraced and actively pursued a course of substantial change in the city's educational system and overall racial climate. The chamber of commerce joined hands with parent groups and black leaders to design and implement a bold plan of school desegregation. "Cell groups" sponsored by the chamber asked local citizens to gather and confront their own feelings about issues of race. And for a brief moment, there seemed to be a possibility of democratic dialogue based on mutual respect, candor, and some form of common vision.

Clearly, the moment of breakthrough—if it can be called that—did not last. Nor did it spread from Greensboro the way the sit-ins had. Arguably, these changes represented simply the most subtle and sophisticated forms of social control the supporters of the progressive mystique could craft. Certainly Nelson Johnson felt that this was the case and later went on to help organize the Communist Workers Party (CWP).

Moreover, if one looked at the history of Greensboro during the rest of the 1970s and 1980s, it is possible to argue that the oldest forms of terror and demonization remained at work. Nelson Johnson and those who joined him in the CWP were brutally cut down in a hail of Ku Klux Klan and Nazi bullets at a "Death to the Klan" rally in 1979. Five CWP members were killed in an attack that occurred when the Greensboro police were mysteriously missing. And although much of the killing occurred while television cameras were running, the white supremacists who shot down much of the CWP leadership were acquitted.

Still, there are important ingredients in the Greensboro developments of the late 1960s and early 1970s that may impart lessons for those who hope to find an optimistic answer to the possibilities of democracy in the United States.

First, African Americans in Greensboro, in the spirit of Abraham Galloway, insisted on defining their own terms and on conveying, in their own words and from their own base of support, exactly what they sought in the way of recognition and citizenship. Black citizens challenged the facade of civility, demanding that white leaders negotiate in a framework of realistic engagement that transcended the traditions of paternalism.

Second, because the old patterns were broken, to some extent, it became possible to address issues that had festered for decades without official attention. It may be that the school desegregation plan in Greensboro did about as much harm as good, destroying the integrity of black institutions such as Dudley High School, for example; yet the changes represented a breakthrough in dealing with issues that could no longer be addressed by incremental, moderate measures.

Third, and most important, there existed for a brief period an honest dialogue that compelled individuals on both sides of the color line to take each other seriously, with neither preordained stereotypes nor facades of false etiquette impeding the communication. Clearly, the possibilities of democracy hinge upon a measure of mutual respect and public recognition across lines of gender, class, and race, which in turn require a degree of empowerment and self-determination that places all participants on common ground. There is no democracy where citizenship is doled out moderately from one party to another.

Ever since Americans first dreamed of a democratic commonwealth, the possibility of such an open and mutually respectful dialogue has been blocked by the original sin of racial hierarchy. If there is a lesson to be learned from these essays, from Greensboro, from our common history, it is that white supremacy can neither be obliterated by denial nor forever reinforced by caricatures and violence. It can only be exorcised by constant struggle, by honest confrontation, and ultimately by creating a new political language that affirms rather than diminishes the common humanity of all Americans.

William H.
Chafe

Acknowledgments

This book has been an unusually collaborative effort even for an anthology. We are especially grateful to the ten other scholars whose essays are featured in *Democracy Betrayed*. They not only wrote fine essays that make us proud to be associated with them, but also played an active role in every stage of this book's rather hurried birth. They have recommended authors, shared ideas, turned up new research sources, and done very careful readings of essays other than their own, both ours and other contributors'. Without the encouragement and insights of Glenda Gilmore and Steve Kantrowitz, in particular, this book would not have been possible. From the first forkful of chicken and dumplings, meeting Glenda Gilmore has been like finding a long-lost sister. Steve Kantrowitz not only named and renamed the book several times; he sustained us with his literary skills and warm friendship. William H. Chafe has been a priceless mentor and friend; he read the entire manuscript and has been a ready source of advice and inspiration. Whenever our spirits lagged, the intensity of Laura Edwards's and Raymond Gavins's faith in the book and its importance helped us to rediscover the strength of our own convictions.

Several scholars who did not write essays for *Democracy Betrayed* were also a crucial help to us. We especially want to thank Lu Ann Jones, Peter H. Wood, Katherine Mellen, John Herd Thompson, Nellie McKay, Craig Werner, and Paige Raibmon for their steady encouragement and thoughtful criticism. In addition, we could not possibly have pulled this book together without Jeffrey Crow, who took time from his many labors as director of the North Carolina Division of Archives and History to help us at every difficult juncture. And we will never find adequate words to thank David Perry, editor-in-chief of the University of North Carolina Press. He conceived of this book, nurtured it faithfully, protected it from the worst impulses of its editors, and lent it his own sharp historical and literary gifts. Centennials do not grant extensions, and neither did David Perry, but he and others at the University of North Carolina Press—among them, David VanHook, Alison Waldenberg, and Ron Maner—provided the extra support necessary to complete this book on time.

Many other friends and colleagues read parts or all of the manuscript, which has benefited immeasurably from their wisdom. We would like to thank Eric Anderson, David Carter, Kirsten Delegard, Christina Greene, Bob Hall, Jacquelyn Dowd Hall, Gerald Horne, John Howard, Melody Ivins, Beverly Jones, William Jefferson Jones, Robert Korstad, Rhonda Lee, Danielle McGuire, Doris Morgan, Sam Morgan, Richard Ralston, Richard Reid, James Schiffer, John David Smith, Boo Tyson, Vernon C. Tyson, Vern Tyson, William L. Van Deburg, Michael Ward, Lane Windham, and Barry Yeoman.

As always, our families have been our greatest source of strength and inspiration. Laura Hanson and Perri Morgan, brilliant women with large blind spots which it is our privilege to occupy, have endured with remarkable patience the sense that their husbands were married to each other rather than to their wives. They both provided decisive intellectual assistance at crucial points in preparing this book. Finally, we came to edit this book and persisted in it because we are committed to making a better world for our children—Vera, Guy, Hope, and Sam—and to them it is dedicated.

Contributors

David S. Cecelski is an independent scholar and writer from eastern North Carolina. He is the author of *Along Freedom Road: Hyde County, North Carolina, and the Fate of Black Schools in the South.* Currently he is a research associate with the Southern Oral History Program at the University of North Carolina at Chapel Hill, as well as a teaching fellow at Duke University's Center for Documentary Studies.

William H. Chafe is dean of the College of Arts and Sciences and professor of history at Duke University. He is the author of many works on United States history, including *Civilities and Civil Rights: Greensboro, North Carolina, and the Black Struggle for Freedom* and, most recently, *Never Stop Running: Allard Lowenstein and the Struggle to Save American Liberalism.*

Laura F. Edwards is assistant professor of history at the University of California at Los Angeles. She earned her Ph.D. in history at the University of North Carolina at Chapel Hill. She is the author of *Gendered Strife and Confusion: The Political Culture of Reconstruction.*

Raymond Gavins is professor of history at Duke University. His publications include *The Perils and Prospects of Southern Black Leadership: Gordon Blaine Hancock, 1884–1970.*

Glenda E. Gilmore is the author of *Gender and Jim Crow: Women and the Politics of White Supremacy, 1896–1920.* She earned her Ph.D. at the University of North Carolina at Chapel Hill and has a B.A. from Wake Forest University. She is assistant professor of history at Yale University in New Haven, Connecticut.

John Haley is professor of history at the University of North Carolina at Wilmington. He is the author of *Charles N. Hunter and Race Relations in North Carolina.*

Michael Honey teaches U.S. history at the University of Washington, Tacoma. He has published extensively on labor, Southern, and civil rights history, including *Southern Labor and Black Civil Rights: Organizing Memphis Workers.* He was a civil liberties organizer in the South from 1970 to 1976 and worked to free the Wilmington Ten.

Stephen Kantrowitz teaches Civil War era and Southern history at the University of Wisconsin–Madison. He is completing a book about Ben Tillman and the reconstruction of white supremacy.

H. Leon Prather Sr. is a retired professor of history from Tennessee State University who currently resides in Nashville. He is the author of *Resurgent Politics and Educational Progressivism in the New South: North Carolina, 1890–1913* and *We Have Taken a City: Wilmington Racial Massacre and Coup of 1898.* He was recently a recipient of the Distinguished Scholar Award from the American Historical Association.

Timothy B. Tyson is assistant professor in the Department of Afro-American Studies at the University of Wisconsin–Madison. He has written for a wide array of publications, including *Southern Exposure, The Crisis, In These Times,* and the *Journal of American History.* Currently he is completing *Radio Free Dixie: Robert F. Williams and the Roots of Black Power.*

LeeAnn Whites is associate professor of history at the University of Missouri at Columbia. She is the author of many works on the Civil War and Reconstruction South, including *The Civil War as a Crisis in Gender: Augusta, Georgia, 1860–1890.*

Richard Yarborough is associate professor of English and director of the UCLA Center for African American Studies in Los Angeles, California. He was most recently one of the editors of the *Norton Anthology of African American Literature* and is the author of the forthcoming *Ideology and Black Characterization in the Early Afro-American Novel.*

Contributors

Index

19, 158, 211; ignites white supremacy campaign, 4, 6, 21, 25, 26, 36, 106, 132, 159, 170, 171, 212, 229, 254; legislation of, 19, 169, 188; loss of white support for, 107, 173, 177; organization of, 18, 19, 169, 171, 188, 226

Gaines v. Canada, 201
Galloway, Abraham H., 6, 7, 43-65, 281, 283, 285
Galloway, Celie, 58, 67 (n. 9)
Gandhi, Mohandas K., 256
Garrett, York D., 195
Garrison, William Lloyd, 100
Gay, Green, 123
General Assembly (N.C.), 4, 18, 30, 38, 62-63, 188-89, 216-17
Georgia State Agricultural Society, 148, 153-54
Gilchrist, William, 20
Glenn, Robert B., 21, 220
Goins, John, 30
Graham, Frank Porter, 262, 263
Grandfather clause, 189
Grannis, Elizabeth, 160
Green, Josh (*The Marrow of Tradition*), 116-17, 127-28, 134, 231-42 passim
Greenfield Lake, 255
Greensboro, N.C., 9, 282, 285
Gregory, Sam, 33
Grimké, Francis J., 209
Guthrie, William A., 26

Haitian revolution, 97, 101
Halsey, Josh, 116, 238
Hamilton, J. G. de Roulhac, 35, 114-15
Hampstead, N.C., 268
Hampton Institute, 24, 197
Hancock, Gordon B., 259, 263
Hankins, William, 67 (n. 11)
Hanover; or The Persecution of the Lowly: A Story of the Wilmington Massacre (Fulton), 226, 237, 241, 243, 245, 248
Harpers Ferry, Va., 101
Harris, Essic, 103
Harris, Joel Chandler, 247
Harrison, Richard B., 200
Harvey, Joseph, 103

Hayden, Harry, 20
Hayes, Roland, 200
Hayti, 192, 264
Helms, Jesse, 282
Henderson, L. A., 30, 237
Hickory Times-Mercury, 209
Hitler, Adolf, 10, 256
Hoge, Payton H., 5, 238
Holden, William, 56, 103
Holloway, John, 30
Home Guard, 51
Home Mission College Review, 201
Home protection, 27, 75, 78, 80, 82, 173; and sexual politics, 21, 74, 76, 82
Hood, James W., 57
Hoover, J. Edgar, 261
Horton, Willie, 279
House Behind the Cedars, The (Chesnutt), 231
Howard University, 79, 195, 198, 213
Howe, John H., 30
Howell, Clark, 160
Hughes, Langston, xii

Illiteracy, 189
Imperialism, 164, 211, 213, 218
Incubus, 7, 74, 77, 80, 81, 89, 90
Independence Day, 54
Industrialization, x, 131, 168, 174, 215
Interdenominational Association of Colored Clergymen, 210-11
Intermarriage. *See* Miscegenation
Intimidation, 39, 58, 106, 130, 194, 216, 220, 254, 281

Jackson, Carrie, 266
Jackson, Jesse, 283
Jacobs, David, 30, 31, 35
James, T. C., 33
Jarvis, Thomas J., 21
Jeanes Fund, 195
Jefferson, Thomas, 278
Jim Crow. *See* Segregation
John Merrick (Liberty ship), 268
Johnson, Nelson, 284-85
Johnson, W. A., 20
Johnson C. Smith University, 198, 202
Jones, Charles M., 263
Jones, Thomas, 211

mystique, 280, 281, 282, 285; and
racial stereotypes, 57, 60, 89, 120,
158, 172, 176, 279, 281, 286; and
Secret Nine, 20, 23, 29, 31, 36, 37,
77, 84, 85, 176, 175; and sexual politics, 76, 82, 79, 80, 82, 89, 163–65;
and Furnifold Simmons, 12 (n. 8),
20, 21; and Alfred Waddell, 4, 5, 25,
26, 29, 30, 35, 95, 96, 84, 85, 86, 176,
218, 208; and white working class,
89, 163–64, 174, 175, 178–80, 218, 227
White Supremacy Clubs, 22, 188, 218
White womanhood, protection of:
  as electoral appeal by Democratic
  Party, 7, 21, 22, 62, 79, 170, 172; as
  justification for racial violence,
  25–27, 74–78, 89, 143, 149, 152, 159,
  228, 278, 281
White working class, 23, 76, 168, 169,
  176; history of conflict, 18, 165–68;
  and racial violence, 31–32, 130–31,
  177, 176; and sexual politics, 75, 78;
  and white supremacy, 89, 163, 164,
  174, 175, 178–80, 218, 227
Wild, Edward A., 49, 50, 54
Wilkerson, Scott, 124
Wilkins, Roy, 256, 259
Williams, Anthony, 143–44
Williams, Rene, 144, 160
Williamson, Mamie, 269–70
Williston High School, 197
Wilmington, N.C.: demographics of,
  3, 16, 18, 38, 58, 227, 175
Wilmington Business Directory, 17
Wilmington Centennial Foundation,
  xv

Wilmington City Directory, 176
Wilmington Daily Journal, 62
Wilmington Daily Record, 18, 77, 85,
  95, 171, 238. *See also* African Ameri-
  can newspapers
Wilmington Evening Star, 211
Wilmington Journal, 65
Wilmington Light Infantry, 33, 35, 85
Wilmington Messenger, 20–36 passim,
  74, 78, 80, 83, 84, 106, 128, 133, 172,
  174, 212, 228
Wilmington Morning Star, 172, 173
Wilmington Post, 115, 214, 230
Wilmington Star, 24
Wilmington Ten, xiv
Wilson, Woodrow, 21
Winston, Francis D., 21, 81, 83
Winston-Salem Teachers' College,
  198
Woman's Christian Temperance
  Union, 147, 148, 155, 156, 159
World War II: and African American
  resistance, 262, 264–65, 268, 271;
  African American soldiers in, 257,
  259–61, 264–65, 268, 271; armed
  resistance during, 257, 259, 260–61,
  263, 265, 268, 271; racial violence
  during, 254–71 passim
Worth, Charles, W., 36
Wright, Dan, 34, 36, 116, 238, 239, 240
Wright, Silas, 36

Yancey, William L., 22
Young Men's Christian Association, 60

Zoot suits, 261, 273 (n. 44)